SHAME!

(An Other Guide for the Perplexed)

John W. McGinley

(on behalf of Johanna Elton and the Other Friends of Jude)

UNIVERSITY PRESS OF AMERICA

Lanham • New York • London

University Press of America®, Inc.
4720 Boston Way
Lanham, Maryland 20706

3 Henrietta Street
London WC2E 8LU England

Printed in the United States of America
British Cataloging in Publication Information Available

Library of Congress Cataloging-in-Publication Data

McGinley, John W.
Shame! : an other guide for the perplexed / by John W. McGinley.
p. cm.
1. Psychoanalysis and feminism. 2. Psychoanalysis and philosophy.
3. Shame. I. Title.
BF175.5.F45M34 1993 150.19'5—dc20 93–18431 CIP

ISBN 0–8191–9093–4 (cloth : alk. paper)
ISBN 0–8191–9094–2 (pbk. : alk. paper)

™ The paper used in this publication meets the minimum requirements of American National Standard for Information Sciences—Permanence of Paper for Printed Library Materials, ANSI Z39.48–1984.

This book is dedicated, in friendship, to

Len Gougeon

A friend in need is a friend in deed

Sometimes the person I am in the dream isn't me. Who it is I don't know.

Joyce Carol Oates

(from "Heat" contained in Heat and Other Stories; Plume; New York, 1992. Page 144.)

1.
This book procedes syn-aptically. So to speak.

In the dialectic which sometimes obtains between a writer and her publisher it was deemed advisable to delete some of the synapses. This is OK. Furthermore the reader is advised to realize that the relative choppiness of this book is not due to these deletions. Indeed it is arguable that the choppiness of this book would have been considerably increased if these deletions had not been made.

The alert reader will find in these pages something akin to a Kantianesque investigation into the conditions for the possibility of experience. Such an investigation asks the pre-and-post empirical question, "what must be the case" given that synapsis/synapse-imbued """experience""" does in fact take on certain contours. When such an investigation is syn-aptic -- as this one is -- a sustained idiosyncricity is the only assurance that the results will <u>not</u> be merely idiosyncratic.

First time readers are pre-alerted to the fact that throughout most of its composition this book, *Shame!*, was matrilineally entitled *Thinking Psycho-analytically*. For a short period late in its composition *Shame!* was patrilineally entitled *Misogyny*. *Shame!* is the offspring of these and it is of *Shame!* that you will have your interest. The reader will discover that this version of *Shame!* -- which is the only published version -- attests to a divisional structuring (i.e., "Preface", "Part I", "Part II", "Notes" "Glossary", "Supplement", etc., etc.) of *Thinking Psycho-analytically/Misogyny* which divisional structuring, however, is not retained in this version of *Shame!*. Finally, it is useful to know that for the instantiations of this book which came forth as *Misogyny* the pen-name "Johanna Elton" was used.

It is most remarkable that a dimension of this most revealing """concept""" -- {{{ i.e., "syn-apsis/syn-apse" is to Johanna Elton as "differance" is to Derrida and as "eksaiphnes" is to Plato }}} -- of modern biological/psychological science should be developed by a science (neuro-physiology) which is least likely to understand the "logic" of contact/connection and which is also least likely to understand the "Freudianism" which it -- i.e., neuro-physiology -- thinks that it is replacing and superseding.

This entire book is about the Freudianism which neuro-physiology thinks it is replacing and superseding

Concerning the logic of contact/connection the reader is referred to <u>Parmenides</u> 148D, 6 to 149D,9 <<Loeb lining>>. The passage under discussion is imbued with Plato's logic of the "between" and with emphasis on how a "between" (i.e., a "third") does and does not obtain (i.e., "abtain"?) "between" two terms. ((Please understand that Plato's analysis is <u>dialectical</u> which for Plato always entails the <u>break</u> from -- (a procedure which is quite radically different from either Aristotelian "abstraction" or Hegelian "sublation") -- aisthesis. The passage, then, is radically misunderstood if it is read through the "physicalizing" prism of Aristotle's treatment of similiar matters in <u>Physics V</u>-3, 226b,9 to 227b, 2.)) The silent appearance and non-appearance -- at once -- of "difference as eksaiphnes" permeates lines 149A, 5-149D, 9 <<Loeb lining>> and requires -- for the passage to be completely understood -- this book's (i.e. *Thinking Psycho-Analytically*'s) analysis of the all-important passage of hypothesis # 2 of <u>Parmenides</u>, namely 147A, 4-147A, 10.

Verification-and-resiliation of these Platonic matters is dispersed all throughout this book. But you must read carefully or you shall miss it when and as it happens. Likewise for these matters of neuro-physiology.

"Syn-apsis/syn-apse" is the surrogate of "mis-ogyny."

2.
Misogyny -- as well as *Thinking Psycho-analytically* -- is not a work of scholarship although it depends quite heavily upon the scholarship of others. It is difficult to say what "genre" of writing *Misogyny* belongs to. Is it a genre unto itself? Do I dare to eat a peach?

3.
What I don't know about the authors and works cited in this book could fill many volumes. Many libraries. Most recently my hit-and-miss approach to authors/writers who seem to have also spoken around the "topic" I am trying to speak about has put me into contact with Sarah Kofman. The one book was written in 1974 and translated in 1991. The other was written in 1980 and translated in 1985. Knowledge of their existence came my way, so to speak, and then they became available to me. Hit-and-miss.

The reference is to <u>Freud and Fiction</u> by Sarah Kofman; translated by Sarah Wykes; Northeastern University Press, Boston, 1991. Hereafter: <u>F&F</u>.

The reference is to <u>The Enigma of Woman: Woman in Freud's Writings</u> by Sarah Kofman; translated by Catherine Porter; Cornell University Press, 1985. Hereafter: <u>Enigma</u>.

4.
I have no idea what Sarah ----- *{{{{{De Vere: Should he call her "Sarah"? Amy: Of course he should ask her. That would only be proper. On the other hand it is not at all clear that <u>Misogyny</u> falls within the range of propriety. I really don't know.}}}}}* ----- has done since 1980. And I have damn little idea of what she has done at all.

5.
One thing, however, is her most interesting "chapter" on Freud's usage of Empedocles supplemented by her extensive knowledge and efficient review of this strange "pre-Aristotelian." In this regard, what Kofman has done for "Freud and Empedocles" I have done for "Freud and Plato" in *Thinking Psycho-analytically*.

Confer Kofman's account of Freud and Empedocles in *Freud and Empedocles* contained in <u>F&F</u>, pages 21-52. On Kofman's usage of "pre-Aristotelian" Confer <u>F&F</u>, *Aristotle and the 'presocratics'*, pages 9-19.

6.
Another thing is her amazing ability -- especially for the woman writer who, in these days of hyper-sensitivity to questions of chauvinism and misogyny in the text of Freud, runs the constant risk of being charged of "sleeping with the enemy" -- to remain open to the full range of psycho-analytic teachings as put forth by Papa Freud himself.

In some Feminist circles -- particularly in the United States -- it has become customary to pre-sume that the chauvinistic/misogynistic bias of the Freudian text renders <u>all</u> of Freud's psycho-analytic insights into female psychological make-up irrelevant. Sometimes the <u>presumption</u> of the irrelevance and wrong-headedness of Freud in these matters in these circles has become so extreme that it unintentionally parodies itself. Readers of *Thinking Psycho-analytically* will recognize that the phallo-centric/phallo-cratic presumptions of the Freudian text are also very much discussed relative to the question of the psychological make-up of both males and females, although the discussion in *Thinking Psycho-analytically* does not emanate from the prevailing presumptions relative to the Freudian text of most American feminists.

Of course -- and in contrast -- this theme of "sleeping with the enemy" has also been quite thoughtfully discussed in numerous books of the past decade. One such thoughtful discussion comes in the form of Gynesis by Alice A. Jardine which is a review/account of French psycho-analytic and deconstructionistic writers who engage "the feminine" in their writings. (Gynesis: Configurations of Woman and Modernity; Cornell University Press, 1985. Hereafter: Gynesis.) Particulary useful, in my opinion, are her reviews/accounts of male French writers (Derrida and DeLeuze) who harbor both subtle and significant unconscious chauvisnistic bias even as they expose with great sophistication the phallo-cratic/phallo-centric bias of Freud and of philosophers of the Tradition. (Confer especially *The Hysterical Text's Organs: Angles on Jacques Derrida* and *Becoming a Body without Organs: Gilles DeLeuze and His Brothers* pages 178-223.)

Although with an agendum significantly different from that of Jardine *Thinking Psycho-analytically* also pursues this theme of the inherent weakness of Derrida relative to the questions of things feminine and the question of things Freudian.

7.

The writing of this book goes back to late December of 1984 (around the time of solstice) and its developmental history is measured by events in Madonna's public career. It first appeared as Shelley's Song in 1985 and brings back memories of "Like a Virgin." Several incarnations later it became Old Lainge's Eye-becoming-Plato and Difference-becoming-Dream-Weaver. Old Lainge's Eye was written about two months after I had gotten out of the hospital (viz., Friends Psychiatric hospital in Philly). If my memory serves me correctly "Like a Prayer" came out in the Fall of '88 contemporaneous with the writing of Old Lainge's Eye. The song haunted me from the very first. Indeed it was a while before I realized that it was Madonna who sang it. You should also realize that my Madonna experience in those years was without the benefit of videos. It was my ear and not my eye which first related to Madonna. Like a prayer. In the Spring/ Summer of 1990 I was transforming my book into a major work on "the 'wo-man' principle" and was inspired repeatedly by her song "Hanky Panky." That Fall -- late that Fall or does my memory deceive me? -- I became mesmerized by the haunting lyrics of "Justify my love." Again, I did not realize right away that it was Madonna who was singing. But by virtue of the attendant publicity surrounding the song and video I made sure to watch her when she made her Nightline appearance and in that fashion finally got to see Madonna on video. I was even more mesmerized.

Often enough, in *Thinking Psycho-analytically*, I used the incarnation motif as a way of describing how my writings since late 1984 -- all of which were separately printed and bound -- evolved, the later from the prior. But perhaps the metaphor of "evolved" is itself more accurate especially considering the multi-faceted way in which the earlier appears, disappears, and sometimes (and partly) re-appears in and as the later sometimes modified radically sometimes modified slightly and sometimes unmodified as well as how what did re-appear came to subsequently disappear and how, finally, what was new in each "species" was integrated into what had priorly appeared earlier in this evolutionary process.

8.

I don't think I got to see Truth or Dare until the late Fall of 1991. Her "tour" version of "Like a Virgin" (contained in the movie) knocked me out. And I started reading more about Madonna. Especially about New York City based "explorations" of well-hung guys. One gets the impression that Madonna knows more about penises and their various workings and usages than most guys ever get to know about their very own penises. The more I read about Madonna the more I realized -- (I really started having this fantasy when I first heard "Hanky Panky") -- that I would willingly become her sex slave although, it must be acknowledged, no-one would ever accuse me of being well-hung according to the Madonnaesque standard.

9.
It was also in the Fall of 1991 that I started writting a series of renewed incarnations of this book which finally became my cherished *Thinking Psycho-analytically* and which took its final form in February of 1992.

10.
Now (relatively early Spring of '92) I am transforming *Thinking Psycho-analytically* into the *Misogyny* which you are now reading. At the same time Madonna is negotiating with Warner Communications about the publication of her erotic/pornographic/pornosophic "coffee table" book.

11.
I hope Madonna does not compromise.

12.
Madonna is generally not understood, perhaps especially by those who celebrate her. (The paradox of this being said by one who is here in the process of celebrating the Goddess is not lost on me. However, my over-taxed brain has now become too old and tired to say something clever about this situation. One is certain that Frere Jacques would not be so lax on such a matter.)

13.
Madonna is an extremist on things sexual. Madonna is a vector on things sexual which points far beyond the hyper-sophisticated and hyper-clever reams of articles and papers which are now being produced in Academia about Madonna. There is no current form of "feminism" (i.e., as the term is now commonly used) which can contain what Madonna is about. Madonna is not politically correct. Yet Madonna leads the way to the liberation of women and, in the wake of woman's liberation, the liberation of men.

14.
In the words of this book, Madonna takes us through misogyny and in the process brings misogyny both back to and ahead towards the origin and destiny of misogyny: "mis-ogyny." Only a few will understand how this neo-logism works in this book which you are reading. Don't compromise, Madonna!!!!!

"Mis-ogyny" is, of course the entire subject matter of *Thinking Psycho-analytically*. You must read and read carefully, my dear reader. My pleasure comes, so to speak, only with the arrival of your understanding. Please don't leave me this way.

15.
Do you seek the golden connecting thread for *Thinking Psycho-analytically* and now *Misogyny*? Shame. Erotic shame as the most secret name of the good. And more than anything else, Madonna understands shame. She understands erotic shame AS the good. Write on!, Madonna!

{{{{{If this book were more academic -- (of either the traditional or post-modern variety) -- one would pause and make some clarifications.

One would point out that in *Misogyny* (i.e., in *Shame!*) "shame" functions as something like a "pros hen" equivocation with erotic shame being shown to be the primary meaning of shame and it being shown that, ultimately, all other meanings of shame are deriviative from erotic shame.

One would point out that the derivative meanings of shame would have considerable positive and negative significance -- (and, furthermore, a significance not without paradox) -- relative to the working out of a shame-based account of the polis -- (i.e., that space where religion, morality and "the political" hold sway through each other) -- and of "arete." In such an analysis it could also be pointed out that while societal "conventions" condition the ways in which the individual enters into patterns of erotic shame, nonetheless, in the history of the species it is precisely patterns of erotic shame which brought about those very societal "conventions" in the first place which then in turn condition the way in which individuals enter into patterns of erotic shame.

Because *Misogyny*'s (i.e., *Shame!*'s) interest in the vector called "Plato" is immense, then one would trot out a whole concatenation of Early and Middle dialogues (along with the appropriate passages from the very late Philebus and Laws) in which Plato's usage of "shame" is critical. One would then point out that Plato's sustained deflection from the positive significance of erotic shame cripples his whole ability to engage shame (and the full dimensions of eros as well), particularly with regard to questions concerning the polis -- (again, that space where religion, morality and "the political" hold sway through each other) -- and "arete."

In this review of Plato one would playfully luxuriate in the see-ing/seen/un-seen dimensions of one of the Greek words for shame and -- with a breathless (even if etymologically inaccurate) Cratylean gesture -- fool around with the phonetics of our friend "obscene." In all of this the reader would be constantly alerted to the fact that it is precisely Misogyny's (i.e., Shame!'s) unique appropriation of the light/un-seen/good theme from Republic VI which positions *Misogyny* (i.e., *Shame!*) to listen to these seen/un-seen resiliations of "shame."

<<<*On* Misogyny's (i.e., Shame!*'s) unique appropriation of "the good" in Republic VI you must be both patient and perservering.* Misogyny/Shame! *will deliver. Generously. For now just take up this teasing hint from Plato himself at 507A of Book VI:*

> Have a care, however, lest I deceive you unintentionally with a false reckoning of the interest [offspring].>>>

But this is not an academic book. So none of this will be done.}}}}}

16.
The jig is up.

17.

Male patterns of domiance begin to self-disintegrate. They begin to parody themsleves without intending to parody themselves. It is not yet generally recognized, but Patriarchy is already over

No doubt, of course, that -- in various and sometimes paradoxical ways -- as Patriarchy comes to self-dissolve, there will emerge multiple regressive reaction formations which will actually come to promote extreme forms of Patriarchal convention. This will especially be the case in regions of the world in which religious fundamentalism now obtains. But Patriarchy -- even in these regions -- is on the way out. These regressive reaction formations -- ugly and violent as they may be in actual practice -- are but surface and passing phenemona relative to a wave which no longer will be stopped.

18.

In the first place it dawns on more and more men that genital sexuality is no longer necessary for reproduction. The penetration motif -- which was so central to the male's perception of himself as a sexual being -- no longer was necessary. It had become superfluous. It could still have its uses, particularly relative to the multiple ways in which males could now become the playtoys of females. But it no longer played any essential role relative to the maintenance of the species.

In the second place it dawns on more and more men that the male proclivity towards violence no longer has any positive social value. To be sure, during the millenia when war was part of the inevitable baggage of our species, this proclivity towards violence could still be celebrated and integrated into the various "narratives" by which peoples and cultures understood themselves. The warrior as hero. But with the changing technology of weaponry the "heroic" dimesions of this proclivity towards violence begin to dissolve. The male proclivity twoards violence comes to be seen only as a burden. Like the appendix, which no longer performs a function and which, when inflamed, can become deleterious to the organism as a whole.

In the third place it dawns on more and more men that upper body strength has lost its social utility and value. Techological advances render obsolete the value associated with physical labor. Upper body strength also becomes something of a playful past-time ultimately in the service of women's enjoyment/usage of male bodies.

The male proclivity towards violence is the psycho-physiological heritage resulting from that long period (i.e., many, many thousands of years) of incubation involving the self-selective interfacing between biological evolution and the beginnings of psycho-social evolution in the pre-history of our species. It is true but trivial to point to the presence of testosterone in such a high quantity in the male of our species. The explanation, in part, for the presence of such high levels of testosterone in the male of our species must itself be a function resulting from the sexual dynamic which is the spin-off from upright posture as speculated upon by Freud in that long footnote at the beginning of Chapter Four in Civilization and its Discontents. Although it is not mentioned in so many words by Freud in that important footnote this sexual dynamic must have involved the beginnings of castration fear as a corollary to the emergent "mis-ogyny" resulting from this development (i.e., upright posture) in biological evolution. An eventual effect of castration fear in the male of these proto-human species leads -- self-selectively over many thousands of years -- to a genetic heritage such that the male of the species homo sapiens sapiens comes to be endowed with (and eventualy cursed by) these high levels of testosterone.

19.

It dawns on more and more men that there was never anything "intrinsically", so to speak, advantageous about male anatomy. There was, for many thousands and thousands of years a biological necessity about male anatomy and for thousands of years some social utility to male anatomical and psychological dispositions in the psycho-social evolution of our species. But that age was now over.

It dawns on more and more men and more and more women that the real action and "intrinsic" advantage was, is, and always will be with female anatomy and female psychological dispositions. Being-a-woman, it finally turned out, was the only intrinsic excitement left on this third planet from the sun for the members of the clothed species. Power and the rule of law soon flowed to the female of the species by default, as it were, as males more and more began to understand the overall dimensions of the situation. Scientists began to realize that it was most signficant that "XX" was, effectively, the default value of the human "XX-XY" version of sexual differentiation which version -- it could reasonably be argued -- was but an instantiation of the whole constellation of sexual differentiation in which "female" was the default value. In other words, female is both origin and destiny of sexual differentiation. Parthenogensis giving rise to sexual differentiation only to return to a more complicated system of parthenogneis in the species which, by virtue of the intricate outcomes of sexual differentiation, maximized ontogenic variation and adaptability. The hidden genius was there all all along.

Even so, the phallus -- now bereft of its reproductive function -- does not disappear. The now-arriving age of matriarchal androgyny is not one in which sexual differentiation disappears. Quite to the contrary. As used in this book, "matriarchal androgyny" refers to the new order in libidinal economy in which human sexual differentiation is alive and quite robust but in which the function of sexual differentiation is radically altered. This emerging condition is referred to as the "hegemony of difference."

20.
It was all predicted by Papa Freud at the end of Civilization and its Discontents. Listen:

> ----- *And now it is to be expected that the other of the two 'Heavenly Powers', eternal Eros, will make an effort to assert himself in the struggle with his equally immortal adversary.*

Translation: A new order of libidinal economy is now on the verge of emerging, globally, for the clothed species on the third planet from the sun. Yet it must also be admitted that the actual "content" of this new order of libidinal economy would have caused the relatively naive Freud to have turned scarlet with embarrassment. Sigmund, no less than anyone in the Tradition, had no inkling of erotic shame as the good.

Civilization and its Discontents. Translated and edited by James Strachey. Norton; 1961; New York. Page 104. [Hereafter: *Civ.*]

21.
First a growing fascination -- among both males and females -- in all things female and feminine.

Secondly, a growing desire on the part of males to be in the service -- particularly in libidinal matters -- of females. A growing disposition of males to become voluntarily slavish relative to their female partners.

Thirdly, a growing desire on the part of males to achieve the psychological condition of actually being a woman. ((((It is taken as axiomatic that "gay" behaviors among men will exponentially increase in the emerging new libidinal order. But these "gay" behaviors -- as well as lesbian behaviors -- will be radically misunderstood if they are understood as exclusively "gay" or exclusively "lesbian" and as "alternatives" to the prevailing "heterosexual matrix". (*) On the contrary, what is at issue in this emerging new libidinal order is such a fundamental retructuring of "the heterosexual matrix" that the traditional meanings of "gay" and "lesbian" will lose their significance.))))

*. This is a term coined and used by Judith Butler in her extremely thoughtful book, Gender Trouble: Feminism and the Subversion of Identity. (Routledge, New York, 1990. Hereafter Trouble.) She defines her usage of the term in note # 6 on page 151. In *Thinking Psycho-analytically* I have also used this most fertile phrase although at times -- as was already indicated in my text -- in ways which are not perfectly congruent with Butler's usage of it.

Butler's book was very influential on the emergence of *Thinking Psycho-analytically.*

*****

The current usage of the terms "lesbian", "gay", "straight" and even of "bi-sexual" only shows that the discourse of those who are "politically correct" is often just as imprecise and shallow as the discourse of those whose thinking is shot through with various shades of conscious and pre-conscious homophobia.

The fact of the matter is that no-one at all is merely and exclusively "gay", or "lesbian" or "straight." And the correlative fact of the matter is that "bi-sexual" is far too imprecise to catch the nuances contained in these questions of sexuality, gender, and gender identity. Matters of sexuality, gender, and gender identity are a function of a three-variable matrix.

In the first place there is one's sex or gender. This is an anatomical given and usually allows for little or no ambiguity relatve to the classification of one as a "male" or "female." {{{{{Clearly this three-variable matrix under discussion will become a different three-variable matrix if and when the technology of reproduction should come to include some kind of significant variation on the workings of biological evolution which, thus far, has pretty much ordained the logic of the "either/or" on these matters.}}}}}

In the second place there is the question of gender identity in terms of which one identifies oneself as "masculine" or "feminine." Gender identity is achieved -- and never completely as a once-and-forever kind of status -- as we pass through the vicissitudes of life, particularly as we pass through the Oedipal variables in childhood. Thus gender identity is acquired and is NOT a given of anatomy.

All throughout *Thinking Psycho-analytically* the Feminist contention that the meanings of "masculine" and "feminine" are culturally determined -- and thus are not determined by nature or biological destiny -- is taken as axiomatically true and in need of no further discussion. On the other hand *Thinking Psycho-analytically* also recognizes that the individual achievement of gender identity through the vicissitudes of life does involve something like a pre-conscious "stance" towards anatomical realities and in particular a pre-conscious "stance" towards the question of penetration. ((Please understand that *Thinking Psycho-analytically* allows -- indeed insists -- that, for example, the so-called "feminine" stance towards questions of penetration can and does come to be acquired by, and become dominant in, some who are anatomically male. Indeed both what is called "masculine" and what is called "feminine" stances towards penetration come to be achieved in both anatomical males and anatomical females even though it is also true that one of the stances usually comes to be suppressed largely due to the child's need to position herself in accordance with the prevailing categories of social convention. In addition, *Thinking-Psycho-analytically* insists that the overly used paradigm of "active/passive" is of little value in determining what constitutes a pre-conscious "stance" towards questions of penetration.))

In the third place there is the question of "object choice" or what is also referred to as "sexual preference." Using anatomical givens as a frame of reference it is customary to speak of "homosexual" and "heterosexual" object choices. This convention is suitable so long as it is remembered that -- again as an example -- an anatomical male who has acquired what is called a "feminine" gender identity may end up with a "heterosexual" object choice <u>without</u> being "straight" -- as <u>that</u> term is customarily used -- in either his actual sexual behaviors and/or fantasies.

The permutations and combinations of this three-variable matrix are not infinite but they are without finality.

To what extent *Thinking Psycho-analytically* is either-and-or-both-and-or-neither (and all at once) "pre-Freudian" or "post-Freudian" on these matters is a question answered in subsequent parts of this book.

*****

"The vicissitudes of life." They begin at conception and end at death. Throughout the entire process there is a wondorous and continuous play of adaptation of genetic coding to and with its environment. This play of adaptation is poorly understood through the various biological and psychological debates concerning "nature" and "nurture." At times -- particularly prior to birth and around the time of birth -- this play of adaptation is largely a function of the "innate" genetic coding involved. At times -- particularly some time after the birth period -- this play of adaptation in its unavoidable interaction with the environment is such that the outcomes of genetic coding for the individual are significantly affected by the environmental interaction. (((And there are "stages" of life -- one thinks of early childhood development; of early adolescence; perhaps even the stage of what is often called "a midlife crisis" -- in which the outcomes of genetic coding are most significantly affected by the environmental interaction. And furthermore, the <u>human</u> version of "XX"/"XY" in the constellation of sexual differentiation is precisely the phylogenic version which allows for a <u>variety</u> of ontogenically produced outcomes relative to sexual orientation.))) <u>In any case</u>, it is the brain and nervous system which becomes, in effect, both the instantiation of this play of adaptation and <u>the living fossilized record</u> of this play of adaptation.

It is only when the above becomes understood that the growing fascination with brain autopsies relative to questions of sexual identity and sexual preference will become scientifically meaningful. ((((Clearly there will have to be refinements in the very procedures of brain autopsy before this kind of experimentation will yield these meaningful results. One looks ahead to the "fingerprinting" of individual brains in contrast to the gross guesswork which is characteristic of present day methods of brain autopsies.)))

Neuro-Physiology has yet to fully appreciate that genetic coding is never genetic coding pure and simple, but rather genetic coding in the continuous process of adapting to the environment. In the development of the individual there is some truth to the old saw that ontogeny mimics phylogeny. But from the broader vista of evolution it must always be remembered that it was adaptation -- through the chance-goverened play of what is called "natural selection" -- to the environment which first brought about this or that genetic coding. In the individual developments of our respective brains and nervous systems -- and, correlatively, the "outcomes" relative to gender identity and sexual preference -- it is not surprising that <u>all</u> aspects of this complex interaction between ontogeny and phylogeny come into play in a most intricate and paradoxical manner.

*****

However, it needs to be noted that *Thinking Psycho-analytically* -- and now *Misogyny* as well -- speaks of the primacy of lesbian modes of sexuality.

22.
Misogyny. "Mis-ogyny". Right now, only a few are in a position to understand. Yet if we do not come to terms with "mis-ogyny" all is lost. All.

23.
His real name was Tiresias.

24.
How many will find the need to call this book "sick" or "the product of a pathological mind" in order not to confront what this book is about? And how many will miss the very point of this book by reading with and projecting unconsciously into *Misogyny* the very categories of interpretation which even the most """"""sophisticated"""""" readers tend to bring to this kind of topic and which categories *Misogyny* is written so as to dis-mantle? Oh well.

25.
Misogyny (i.e., *Shame!*) generates the very frame of reference in terms of which it can be understood. In the process *Misogyny* dis-mantles and dis-credits various frames of reference which even today still keep thinking from the proper vocation of thinking. But inevitably *Misogyny* will be perceived, judged, and dismissed (sometimes with contempt, sometimes with condescension) from those very frames of reference which *Misogyny* so painstakingly attempted to dis-mantle and dis-credit. *Misogyny* will be misundertsood.

26.
Misogyny (i.e., *Shame!*) will be misunderstood by most Feminists even though it is the book which, when understood, can lead to the liberation of women and, in the wake of that, the liberation of men.

27.
Misogyny (i.e., *Shame!*) will be misunderstood by most Psycho-analytically oriented thinkers even though *Misogyny* "re-covers" for Psycho-analytic thinking the teaching without which Psycho-analytic thinking is destined to disappear (without dis-appearing).

28.
Misogyny (i.e., *Shame!*) will be misunderstood by the self-appointed guardians of Jewish mysticism even though *Misogyny* "re-covers" and pursues the hitherto hidden animating vector of all Jewish mysticism.

29.
The glory of *Misogyny* (i.e., *Shame!*) is that it will be radically misunderstood by that tribe -- living on both sides of the Channel -- whose members have appropriated the label "Philosophy" for themselves. It would be a disgrace for any serious written work not to be radically misunderstood by that tribe of charlatans.

30.
And then there are the findings of Patrick Donegal.

Dear reader: You will have to be a very perservering reader to find out about Patrick. Good luck!

31.
Things are really quite simple.

32.
Pure oscillating need. That's the whole ball of wax. All energy reduces down to "pure oscillating need." *Eros*. *Thanatos*. These are but theoretical constructs. Useful for Freud's purposes. But not primary. Pure oscillating need.

33.
Please do not misperceive me. Please don't get me associated with that ever-so-sophisitcated crowd for whom "deconstructing" real or pereceived "dualities" is more important than having sex. There is a root duality in the make-up of things. But "Eros"/"Thanatos" is not it.

34.
Pure oscillating need. Let it also be called "Angst". All instinctual/drive energy is anxiety. In the course of biological and then psycho-social evolution some patterns by which "Angst" (i.e., at bottom, pure oscillating need) expresses itself emerge. These patterns come to be phylogenically "wired in" -- (to use an overused and inexact metaphor on these matters) -- and thus are capable of being labeled in such a way that, nominally and phenomenologically, one might distinguish between and among various manifestations of such energy displayed in these "patterns" and even differentiate such displayed energies from a circumscribed meaning of "Anxiety." Thus the phylogenically wired in patterns which are in the service of reproduction -- particularly with regard to the human species -- might be labeled "libido". Then Freud -- both before and after his revision of "Anxiety" theory in 1926 -- can talk about the various ways "Anxiety" and "libido" affect and effect each other. Fair enough if one is only doing Psycho-analysis. But at root, all instinctual/drive energy reduces down to "Angst". That is to say that all instinctual/drive energy reduces down to pure oscillating need.

It was not until 1926 that Freud reached his final point of equilbrium relative to his analysis of "anxiety" in a book which, in English translation, was called (I believe) The Problem of Anxiety. But Freud's most economical and efficient statements about his revised theory of anxiety comes up in the first part of lecture xxxii of his New Introductory lectures on Psychoanalysis. (Confer here pages 72-84 of the Norton 1965 edition of the book; translated and edited, of course, by James Strachey. [Hereafter *New*])

35.
IF you caught the subtlety in # 34 above then be prepared to find, here in # 35, the subtlety within the subtlety. If you did not catch what was being said in # 34 you are free to pass on to # 36, right now.

Since evolution's (I conflate biological and psycho-social evolution intentionally since both operate self-selectively, so to speak, although in this # 35 it is only biological evolution which is at issue) process of self-selection operates through chance (tukhe) it follows that there is something very -- and, so to speak, intrinsically -- strange in the very make-up of things. For these chance-goverened workings have come to privilege something like "cavity" in the way in which reproductive patterns come to be phylogenically wired into biological evolution and have done so long before "cavity" became privileged in human psycho-social development. For those who have the eyes to hear and the ears to see this means that the privilege of cavity in biological evolution constitutes, so to speak, the very "pre-history" of "mis-ogyny." For those who have the eyes to hear and the ears to see this means that God -- Shekhinah -- is a woman. For those who have the eyes to hear and the ears to see this means that "truth" really is a woman. The privilege of cavity. This is the "real" allegory of the cave.

My idiosyncratic usage of "Shekhinah" permeates the whole of *Thinking Psycho-analytically* and there is no efficient way of saying how that term functions in the book. Nonetheless, the persevering reader will come to discover how "Shekhinah" functions in the book so long as that reader makes no prior assumptions -- based on either an expert or inexpert appropriation of "Kaballah" -- concerning what "Shekhinah" allegedly "must" mean.

The "metaphysical" connection between Shekhinah and chance (tukhe) permeates all of *Thinking Psycho-analytically*. It must be understood -- if one is to make any headway with *Thinking-Psycho-analytically* -- that the ontological presumption of the entire book is that very "tortured teleology" (i.e., the teleology which is not one) which results from the way (according to the logic of *Thinking Psycho-analytically*) in which chance and Shekhinah are the same.

*****

This privilege of cavity elicits/e-vokes even more attention:

Olfactory stimulation in mammals other than human explains the dynamic of sexual arousal. But that relief from sexual arousal involves insertion into a certain "cavity" is not itself a behavior explainable by pointing to the role of the olfactory relative to sexual intercourse in mammals other than human. So the question then becomes: what neuro-physiological dynamic predisposes to insertion when arousal is set in motion by and through olfactory stimulation? What is the phylogenic wiring, achieved, presumably, in multiple ways over self-selective evolutionary time, which comes to link reproductive eroticism and the privilege of cavity?

In these matters one could do far worse than to return to Sartre's ruminations on "the hole" towards the end of Being and Nothingness. (Confer "III. Quality as a Revelation of Being" in the Doing and Having section; pages 612-615 of the Barnes translation. <Philosophical Library, New York>.)

Yes, of course it is acknowledged, in advance, that these days it is relatively "unsophisticated" -- especially in these "post-Tel-Quel" times of hyper-sophistication -- to admit to finding the Sartrean text to be thought e-voking.

Yes, of course it is acknowledged, in advance, that the Sartrean text -- much like Freudian text in this regard -- has layers and layers of unconscious chauvinism/misogyny/phallo-cratism reflecting a most uncritical influence of prevailing social convention concerning women. Yes, of course it is acknowledged, in advance, that the Sartrean text is not "politically correct."

Yes, of course it is acknowledged, in advance, that the Sartrean encounter with the Freudian text begs most of the important questions.

Finally, yes, it is acknowledged, in advance, that Sartre's ruminations on "the hole" deal mostly with the human condition and that it is only by extrapolation that one finds his ruminations to be significant in understanding the dynamic of "holeliness" in pre-human evolution.

Yes, let all of the above be acknowledged. In advance. Even so, go to those ruminations on "the hole." There -- despite himself, so to speak -- you will find not only a misogynist but a "mis-ogynist" as well. The privilege of cavity is the "pre-history" of "mis-ogyny". This can only mean that even before the emergence, in evoutionary history, of those enormous consequences (*) of upright posture there had already obtained, in evolutionary time, a "biological", so to speak, fascination with "the hole." Already the "privilege of cavity" obtained prior to the emergence of upright posture and the correlative changover from the primacy of olfactory stimulation to sight stimulation for sexual arousal. Read these ruminations of Sartre! Extrapolate from them back to the ever so strange working of Shekhinah in, through, AND AS the unfolding of biological evolution. The sophistication of the Tel Quel crowd notwithstanding, never be too proud to learn -- at least by way of extrapolation -- from the Sartrean text.

*. The reader is here referred, on the one hand, to the long footnote towards the beginning of Chapter Four of Civilization and its Discontents and, on the other hand, to other speculative guesses dispersed all throughout this book.

36.
This "preface" and *Thinking Psycho-analytically* all of which is now gathered together under the heading of *Misogyny*. I've already given you the connecting thread: erotic shame AS the good. Do you wish some information on the "pre-history" of erotic shame? Do you wish to enter fully into the logic of *Misogyny*?

With the second or third reading one discovers that *Thinking Psycho-analytically* (and, now, *Misogyny*) involves itself in that nexus in which biological evolution interfaces with the beginnings of (pre-)human psycho-social evolution so as to ultimately produce the human "XX-XY" version of sexual differentiation. Although Freud does not enter into any speculations about the human "XX-XY" version of sexual differentiation it is, nonetheless Freud who opened up this terrain concerning this nexus between biological evoultion and the beginnings of (pre-)human psycho-social evolution. One thinks most especially about those long footnotes which sustain the argumentation in Chapter Four of Civilization and its Discontents. But really -- if you read slowly enough -- you will find that Freud engages in these kind of ruminations all throughout his lifelong text.

And there is one more piece of the puzzle. A piece not given to us by Papa Freud nor even given to us in the trans-Freudian (i.e., both beyond and before) ruminations of *Thinking-Psycho-analytically*.

37.
Female orgasm. What else could it be?

What other mammal -- indeed what other animal -- gives evidence that the female of the species experiences orgasm? It can be supposed that in many mammal species at least the male of the species experiences something like an ejaculatory type of orgasm in his reproductive activity. Indeed, domesticated male animals and male animals in captivity seem to engage in acts of masturbatory arousal as well. Likewise the female of such species undergoes some hormonal arousal such that her genitalia are receptive to male penetration when she is in a condition of estrus. But -- so it seems to me -- it seems to be stretching the point to say that the females of other mammal species experience anything remotely like human female patterns of orgasm.

(((To be sure someone has or will have found some female primate whose pre-human clitty can be induced to spasms under laboratory conditions and/or spot some female primate rubbing her clitty area against the upper thigh of another -- possibly (especially?) even female -- primate. But get real. All of this falls far short of human female patterns of orgasm. For those who have the eyes to hear and the ears to see.)))

38.
In this regard the self-selection process which came to produce the human version of the clitoris is even more noteworthy that the self-selection process which came to produce the primate with the exaggerated phallus. The "key" is the clitoris. The <u>kind</u> of clitoris developed by the female of the human species and its subtle connection with (what, over self-selective time, would come to be) the most subtle and discriminating parts of the brain. The "missing link."

39.
The sounds of female patterns of orgasm and the emergence of "voice."

One is speaking of many, many, thousands of years for all of this to come about. Many, <u>many</u> thousands of years of self-selection refinement. The grunts. The moans. The intense effort -- responding to even more intense need -- for her to get herself 'there' (i.e., to that magical dream-like space; i.e., to 'khora'). The high pitched delirium as she enters into those emerging <u>dyadic</u> strategies for staying on the edge. The fascination and appeal this would come to have for males. Prior to birth control the reproductive advantage went to the more manic.

Even back then: *Women prolong; men, on the average, only postpone. There is a difference*. The action and excitement of our species is with the female.

(((Indeed this voice-inducing delirium of the emerging female patterns of orgasm most likely dribbled over into the <u>kind</u> of brain capacity for consciousness characteristic of Homo sapiens sapiens. For those who have the eyes to hear and the ears to see.)))

Many, <u>many</u> thousands of years of self-selection refinement. A <u>differentiated</u> phonetic competancy comes to be "wired" , (so to speak), into the emerging human "XX-XY" version of sexual differentiation. Acuity with regard to sound and voice. The dawn of Speech. It is through the female that the "XX-XY" version of genetic coding characteristic of Homo sapiens sapiens comes, over self-selective time, to be instantiated. The dawn of "voice."

For those who have the eyes to hear and the ears to see.

{{{And with such voice/sound discrimination comes an exponential increase in the possibilities for deception unique to Homo sapiens sapiens. Always and everywhere the primacy of deception.}}}

Correlatively, it is probable that the quantum leap in brain organization characteristic of emerging Homo sapiens sapiens -- in addition to the clitoris factor -- was supplemented, in the pre-history of our species, by the widespread practice of delirium-inducing anal eroticism. Widespread. Perhaps initially male to female. But eventually male to male, female to male, and female to female. Presumably the intense and widespread prohibition concerning anal eroticism was itself a kind of cultural reaction formation to the real and perceived dangers of this presumably widespread practice. (Among the real dangers is the fact that libidinal energy can exhaust itself in the practice of anal eroticism without producing offspring. It is likely that the transition from the biological privilege of genital sexuality to the cultural privileging of genital sexuality traverses through this great digression in the pre-history of our species involving widespread anal eroticism.) In any case the impetus for the widespread human explorations into the delirium of anal eroticism emerges from those dyadically-clitoris-centered and delirium-inducing developments in the human female's version of reproductive sexuality. *{{{{{B: Could one add on here the speculation that biology was effectively forced for the first time to do the bidding of social convention in this regard by bringing about -- through a self-selection engineered unconsciously through social convention -- of male voice change at puberty? D: Would your meaning be that the deepening of the male voice made them less attractive as sexual partners thus sending this libidinal energy back to the female and, correlatively, back to the service of reproduction? B: Yes. That is my meaning. D: You may have something there.}}}}}*

{{{{{{{This upsurge into the anal is both the psycho-social analog for and psycho-social instantiation of the "Godhead-as-excess;-Godhead-as-'de-trop' " as examined later on in this book. **Imago Dei.** *For those who have the eyes to hear and the ears to see. }}}}}}}*

In all of these unproven speculations one is quite conscious of the debt owed to Papa Freud in his painstaking way of showing the many currents and counter-currents between the anal and phallic/genital stages of psycho-sexual development. Perhaps even more significant are the ruminations of Papa Freud concerning that nexus between biological evolution and the beginnings of the psycho-social evolution characteristic of our species. Again -- even as one goes both beyond and before Freud on these matters -- one always returns with appreciation to those two long and remarkable footnotes towards the beginning and at the end of Chapter Four of Civilization and its Discontents.

40.

Leave it as an open question, however, whether any of the ruminations contained in # 37, 38, and 39 are to be construed as "Derridean", "anti-Derridean", or neither and/or both; at once. On the other hand, let it be noted that Frere Jacques, having flirted with *thinking psycho-analytically*, shied away from this, the very vocation of thinking.

(caesura).

*----- Qui dira le secret de cette tendre, de cette amere "douceur de vivre" dans cette monde tout plein d'absence? Seul le pourrait celui qui, parvenu au coeur de la detresse, verrait encore le Sacre dans l'envers du Sacre, la grace au coeur de la disgrace et les Dieux au paroxysme de l'***Entgotterung.** *Cet homme, c'est le poete: son chant est le chant de la salutation poetique universelle, et sa parole sacredotal la* **consecration** *de toute chose en son etre.*

Citation from Henri Birault's *De l'Etre, Du Divin, et Des Dieux chez Heidegger* contained in *L'Existence de Dieu*; Casterman, 1963. Page 60.

<[{("The third." Does it ever show up at all in "the Tradition"? Yes, of course it does in Plato. But Plato is not in the Tradition.

In Kant.

(((Oh, that tribe of Vicians claim to find it in Vico. But listen to them as they speak of Vico and you will hear Kant. Furthermore you will hear a Kant emanating from the systematics of the third critique rather from than the cries, hints, and whispers of Kant in the first edition of his first critique. Enough.)))

A little bit in the best of Schelling. But mostly in Kant.

With Kant -- I speak of those postulations (and even there I speak, really, only of freedom) -- there is something like the break from aisthesis. Later on -- beginning with the third critique, and then with the part of Schelling who gives birth to Hegel, and finally with Hegel himself -- this break from aisthesis gets lost in favor of various ways of returning to Aristotle's *nothing is in the mind/soul unless it is first in sensation*. These various ways of returning to the Stagirite's non-break from aisthesis culminate in the self-indulgent delirium of Hegelian "Aufhebung." But with the first edition of the first critique there is a Kantianesque break from aisthesis.

One is speaking, in this regard, of his hints, cries, and whispers -- (((contained in the first edition of the first critique. These hints, cries and whispers -- as noted -- lose their force when, in the third critique, they are systematically married to those very contours emanating from the Tradition which suppress any fruitful meditation on "the third."))) -- concerning "the imagination." There is a spark in Kant. There is some appreciation in Kant of the "between" obtaining *between* noesis and aisthesis which "between" can obtain only by virtue of the break from aisthesis. Even so, even the Kant of the first edition of the first critque remains, at bottom, so unambiguously tied to the contours of the Tradition that it was probably inevitable that that wonderful tension -- (allowing for both to be what they come to be even as it depends on both) -- of and between the noumenal and the phenomenal should collapse and find itself disappearng (without dis-appearing) in the Tradition's last attempt at Nous (i.e., "Geist") idolatry which last attempt came to be called German Idealism.>]})

The final caesura
(1/21/93)

johanna speaking the lure of insanity it's just so attractive oh God! Jude! where are you just when will the rest be silence????? freud and the platonic break from aisthesis i know i know it's like mixing apples and oranges so to speak and to grovel in cliche they are so non-symmetrical so non-isomorphic in what they do freud only for instance doesn't even pose the question of concept-ing giving birth (cute there was never a play on words which wasn't good enough for me and jude we are whores when it comes to puns we have no shame we are shameless which come to think of it is the very quintessence of being shameful but this "conceiving" business happens to be the literal truth for plato) even so it must be asked where do they meet three things come to mind

the timelessness of the id the timelessness of the unconscious listen from new, page 66:

> There is nothing in the id that corresponds to the idea of time; there is no recognition of the passage of time, and -- a thing that is most remarkable and awaits consideration in philosophical thought -- no alteration in its mental process is produced by the passage of time.

first this timeless resting place for the repressed until it is time so to speak!!!!! for the repressed to return timelesseness right in the psyche itself has anyone thought this through this is the mystical the one fragmented beauty """""in""""" the psyche itself what """""we""""" go to as we break from aisthesis that in terms of which we dream

did he get this from spielrein but afraid to acknowledge the source lest he appear to be paying indirect homage to the betrayer who knows and one would have to note the difference between jung and spielrein when they before Freud toyed around with what was timeless in the unconscious even so if the mystical """""in""""" the psyche is spoken of one is tempted sorely tempted to take a foray into that "collective unconscious" of the betrayer when the mystical is at issue "collective unconscious" seems to say it better than freud's "archaic heritage" and the connection with beauty as the very aim of eros rather than as the sublimated expression of eros comes across better in the "collective unconscious" of the betrayer rather than in the "archaic heritage" of siggy so the temptation is there

but jung can never be the vehicle by which either plato or freud can be approached spielrein who for so long lingered on in her masochistic attachement for jung understood with plato and freud it's like comparing apples and oranges with freud and jung it's like comparing apples and maggots the flight from libido (effectively, the flight from difference) jung is among those so often castigated in this book you are reading dear cherished reader who give the mystical a bad name jung too is among those who live the

(continued on page 110)

41.

a). Even so, the greatest homage which one can offer to Freud and the Freudian text is to worship the God worshipped by Freud. This God is a Goddess. This God is <u>the</u> Goddess. This Goddess is God. Her name is """"""""""""truth"""""""""""".

Forever it is impossible to go "beyond" the Freudian text. But one is still obliged to go "before" Freud; to become even more sub-terranean than Freud himself; to out-spelunk, so to speak, The Great Spelunker.

Is this parricide? No. Not at all. The Parricide which is and must be in question is of another order. Rather, let us take up the task of an older brother, so to speak, who first discovered the magical cave. In a dream-like move which is only apparently the reverse of Plato (and, in another sense, which is only apparently the instantiation of Plato) let us struggle to enter the cave. For the first time, really. For just as the starry night appears only when the sun disappears, so too we shall find The Moral Law only by going underground.

{{{{{ Confer the "dream" imagery at 517B of <u>Republic</u> VII which dream "imagery" is the diacritic marker put in by Aristocles to get the reader to understand the cave allegory in conjunction with those other critical "dream" passages: the end of <u>Cratylus</u> (439C-D); the letter/syllable dream towards the end of <u>Theaetetus</u> (201E-202E; -- *(note, please, that the rest of the dialogue turns on an analysis of this "dream")* --); the dream terminology when he speaks of the forms in Book V of <u>Republic</u> (476C-D); the dream reference to "the good" at the end of the allegory of the cave in <u>Rebublic VII</u> (517B); the brief reference *suddenly, as in a dream* in hypothesis # 7 of <u>Parmenides</u> (164D); and, most importantly, the famous "khora"/receptacle passages from <u>Timaeus</u> (52B). *[The logic and intertwining of these diverse "dream" motifs is more carefully spelled out in my unpublished manuscript, <u>Madonna</u>.]* }}}}}

b). All throughout <u>Shekhinah</u> I have, simultaneously, used Freud's Eros/Thanatos duality (one hopes) in the very way it is presented by Freud and also -- again, simultaneously -- transformed (i.e., "deepened", it is hoped) the meaning of Eros and Thanatos in such a way that "Eros" and "Thanatos" no longer appear to be saying what Freud, in his text, says about Eros and Thanatos. This admittedly paradoxical procedure is significantly different from what Derrida et alia (although Derrida, for the most part, stands head and shoulders above the "et alia" of that crowd) do to the Freud text in places like the second half of <u>The Post-Card</u> where -- to particularize on <u>The Post Card</u> -- the agendum (as was the case, analogically, in "Plato's Pharmacy") is to render the Freudian text a speaker of "differance." In the process it almost ceases to matter what Freud intended or even presented. In contrast, the paradoxical procedure of <u>Shekhinah</u> was to "re-cover" Freud's fundamental and incredibly fertile insight into a root duality in and of the make-up of things and then -- bringing to bear the "method" which I refer to as "regressive kathalysis" -- to regress that insight back into an originary equation (of two variables) whose <u>integration</u>-- ((an integration, it is to be noted, determined by the need to make this root duality speak -- in that relevant quadrant of the fictional graph -- to the findings of Psycho-analysis)) -- comes to be "Eros" and "Thanatos" in Freud's usage. This procedure -- while the cousin of a "deconstructive" approach and which procedure is often inspired by Derrida himself -- aims to remain faithful to the vocation of the text under discussion and is guided by the task of "reconstructing" in accordance with the truest vocation of the text what the author did/could not construct for herself. If you want, "regressive kathalysis" -- which can function as an apt name for this procedure -- makes the claim that some previously ususpected texts speak something like "differance" -- (which, by the way, is ultimately better spelled with an "e" rather than with an "a") -- not so much despite themselves but rather and especially because of themselves.

Shekhinah is an unpublished manuscript of mine which in some ways functions as the Mother to *Thinking Psycho-analytically*. It is acknowledged in advance that "Shekhinah" is just but one of several possible transliterations of the Hebrew word under discussion which word refers to the female aspect of God or God-in-creation in Jewish Kaballah. (And, likewise, "Kaballah" is just but one of several possible transliterations of the Hebrew word for "Tradition" under discussion.)

42.
Sigismund: I know of whom you speak. In the living years I mostly stayed away from his thought. Besides, in the living years I would never have begun to appreciate his metaphysical subtlety. You speak of Nietzsche and his explicit rejection of of the "entropic" possibility in # 1066 of The Will to Power.

Aphorism # 1066 of The Will to Power. As contained in The Will to Power; edited by Walter Kaufmann; Vintage, New York, 1967. Pages 548-549. Hereafter: WP.

Eurydice: Yes. Of course. Nietzsche is one of the grand ones. Of all time. But even he is not in your league. Nor in Plato's. Do you begin to see the flaw in "the little pastor"?

Sigismund: It dawns on me that # 1066 is the explicit and uncompromising denial of equilibrium. Indeed that whole section of The Will to Power is precisely to show that the very logic of The Eternal Recurrence of the Same is the denial of equilibrium. Thus it must be the case that Nietzsche's thinking bypasses what you are calling "the draw -- the attraction -- OF equilibrium."

Eurydice: You are a quick learner. You were basically right to stay away from the Nietzschean text. It kept you from being enmeshed in the charm of Nietzsche's basically monotheistic metaphysics. You most likely would have not taken those decisive steps towards duality had you been drawn into the subtle monotheism of the will to power. As you know, enchantment with Nietzsche has destroyed some of the most subtle minds who ever walked on "Earth."

Sigismund: You mean Adler's fascination with Nietzsche and then Jung's somewhat different fascination with Nietzsche?

Eurydice: No! No! No! They are minor thinkers, not worthy of our attention. Indeed it is debatable whether they should even be called thinkers. No, not them.

Sigismund: Then of whom do you speak?

Eurydice: I speak of one of the finest minds of the "twentieth" century, although he published nothing until you were dead for quite some time. This thinker -- he too was Jewish, I might add, -- was quite creative with your writings. And this thinker was very influential in forming the mind-set of our friend, the writer of Shekhinah. This thinker is, arguably, the second greatest thinker of the twentieth century (as they call it up there on "Earth"), second only to you. He was certainly, as far as the vocation of thinking is concerned, a superior thinker to Nietzsche. Yet this thinker was radically hampered in his thinking by being overly charmed by the monotheistic metaphysics of "the will to power."

Sigismund: Who is this marvelous person? And can you tell me about his Achilles heel?

Eurydice: His name is Jacques Derrida. We will speak of him, as a digression. It will help to clarify matters. But let us pause again for a rest and to get our bearings. So to speak. We shall meet again tomorrow.

43.
Sigismund: Then, by all means, let us get started.

Eurydice: Derrida, in the second half-of The Post-Card does an excellent job of showing just how deliciously and multi-valently ambiguous you were as you addressed the question of the "beyond" of "beyond-the-pleasure-principle" in your text Beyond the Pleasure Principle. Among other things -- if we may now use language which Derrida and others have developed in texts other than The Post Card -- he shows that your usage of "Pleasure" is "anasemic" and "polysemic", so to speak.

Sigismund: I'm listening. These people do seem to have an appetite for jargon. But I'm listening.

Eurydice: Derrida becomes practically white-hot in his writings in what might be called Chapter Four, so to speak, of his analysis of your Beyond the Pleasure Principle in the second half of The Post Card. Believe me, Sigismund, no-one has danced with the text of Beyond the Pleasure Principle more assiduously than Frere Jacques. If he makes love with only one-tenth of the care and nuance with which he probes your text he would, most assuredly, be counted among the greatest lovers of all time. Yet perhaps to no avail.

Reference to "Seven: Postscript"; as contained in The Post Card: From Socrates to Freud and Beyond; translated with an Introduction and Additional notes by Alan Bass; University of Chicago, Chicago, 1987. Pages 387-409. Hereafter: PC.

Sigismund: Hmmmmmmm. I find all of this very interesting and also a bit exciting. Certainly, during the living years, no-one read my texts with the care they merited. Yet this Frere Jacques fellow ----- he certainly did not stop, I hope, with Beyond the Pleasure Principle. After all I did not bring these things concerning pleasure and its "beyond" to any equilibrium until 1924 in "The Economic Problem in Masochism." Certainly this Frere Jacques fellow -- if indeed he was all that assiduous -- would not have limited himself in these matters to Beyond the Pleasure Principle.

"The Economic Problem in Masochism"; Volume II of The Collected Papers of Sigmund Freud. Edited and translated by Joan Riviere; Basic Books, New York, 1950. Pages 255-268. Hereafter: *Economic.*

Eurydice: He cites that 1924 article but he does not really use it. Also, in his defense, it should be noted that his "analysis" of Beyond the Pleasure Principle is in the service of the Derridean agendum (involving multiple deconstructive projects including his assault on the Lacanian account of things Freudian which follows, in The Post Card, his analysis of Beyond the Pleasure Principle) and is not meant to be a "scholarly" account of the pleasure principle in the writings of Freud. Also, I must remind you, Sigismund, we are here today precisely because the deepening of your position which you achieved in the 1924 "The Economic

Problem in Masochism" article relative to Beyond the Pleasure Principle was not really sufficient. That is why we are here today. So let me suggest the following, in the service of an overall economy of effort on these matters.

Confer especially "Le Facteur de la Verite"; PC, pages 411-496; and, to a lesser extent, "Du Tout"; PC, pages 497-521.

Sigismund: What is that?

Eurydice: Let us take an aspect of Derrida's most flawed account of Beyond the Pleasure Principle and use it as a catalyst to vault us not only into "The Economic Problem in Masochism"; not only "beyond" "The Economic Problem in Masochism"; but also and far more importantly before "The Economic Problem in Masochism."

Sigismund: And I have come to know how your mind works. Your "before" has little or nothing to do with chronology in the ordinary sense of time. Your "before", in this case, is a "before" which pre-supposes having gone through "The Economic Problem in Masochism" to say nothing of having gone through Beyond the Pleasure Principle.

Eurydice: You are understanding me better and better. Soon you will be ready for Aristocles.

Sigismund: I look forward to the day. So let us get on with our present task.

Eurydice: The Derridean move could have been made at any point in his analysis of Beyond the Pleasure Principle. The theme of Derrida's analysis is the very elusiveness of "pleasure" as it is used in Beyond the Pleasure Principle and the multiple number of ways in which your usage of "pleasure" actually includes what is and/or appears to be "pain." So far, nothing all that revelatory. But on page 404 he makes the move which he, Derrida, had intended all along.

Sigismund: What is that?

Eurydice: Through a clever and not un-thoughtful resiliation of some of your phrases, particularly with regard to the meaning and genesis of sadism as well as with regard to your famous "fort-da" remarks relating to "mastery", he manages to bring Nietzsche center stage just at the point when he has made your analysis of "pleasure" collapse in upon itself.

Sigismund: I'm getting strange vibrations from all of this. Does Frere Jacques -- in this fascination with Nietzsche -- represent yet another "flight from libido"? First there was the ever so crude case of Adler. Then there was the somewhat more subtle but still basically crude case of Jung.

Eurydice: There is nothing at all crude about Frere Jacques. He is infinitely more subtle than Jung -- to say nothing of Adler -- on Jung's very best of days. And "Eros" is very very prominent in the writings of Frere Jacques. Yet even so, your "vibrations" are basically accurate. There is something of a "flight from libido" in the writings of Frere Jacques. For Frere Jacques -- who was the best of the lot --, as well as for his male confreres in that French crowd, a jazzed up reading of the text of Nietzsche becomes a "defense" of sorts against having to really deal with the text of Freud. Their condescending sophistication relative to the text of Freud along with that Shibboleth which they invented for themselves -- I mean "phallo-centrism" -- combined to protect them from fully encountering the text of Freud.

Sigismund: How very, very sad. But let us get on with our task. You were saying that Derrida brings Nietzsche center-stage on page 404 of The Post Card.

Eurydice: Yes. What he does is not all that amazing. He transforms your "pleasure/pain" ruminations into a dynamic of power. He cites a text of Nietzsche which reminds us -- as Speusippus already understood and as which only the most shallow reading of your text would lead one to believe otherwise -- that pain is not the simplistic opposite of pleasure, but rather something other than pleasure.

Sigismund: Please pause, one moment. I get nervous with this allusion to Speusippus. I never knew anything about Speusippus during the living years. But now -- with the benefit of this education down here -- I realize that it most likely that one speaks of the Speusippian connection in these matters only by extracting his teaching from Philebus. Yet I have heard it rumored that Frere Jacques -- precisely in The Post Card and precisely with regard to my analysis of "pleasure" in Beyond the Pleasure Principle -- himself bounces off of Philebus.

Eurydice: Frere Jacques deserves much credit for resurrecting Philebus and bringing it on-stage as far as mainstream philosophical discourse is concerned. And Frere Jacques has some very creative and resiliative usages of Philebus in The Post Card and all throughout his writings up until 1987. Yet -- up until 1987 -- Frere Jacques' reading and presentation of Philebus suffers on two counts.

[One will recall here that in this conversation -- and in this book as a whole -- one is limiting oneself to the writings of Frere Jacques only up through his publication in 1987 of Psyche. Likewise, 1987 functions as a *terminus ad quem* relative to the writings of Kristeva. This *terminus ad quem* is such that the writings referred to include her Black Sun book on melancholy published in French in 1987 with the English translation appearing in 1989.]

(((In contrast to a rather careful reading of Derrida and Kristeva (up to the 1987 terminus ad quem along with the 1989 translations of their French publications of 1987) there has been only a guerrilla-like incursion into an American author who will also be at issue in Part II of these ruminations. I speak of Judith Butler and her 1990 work, Gender Trouble. *(Gender Trouble: Feminism and the Subversion of Identity; Routledge, New York, 1990. Hereafter: Gender.)*

With Kristeva and Derrida I have come -- perhaps rashly -- to the conclusion that the differing and respective vectors of their work does not and will not go in the direction of what these ruminations are attempting to accomplish. With Butler I am less certain. One senses a writer of surprises in Butler. Even so, I choose not the wait around for the forthcoming work of Butler. This is written on November 5, 1991.)))

Sigismund: Yes?

Eurydice: In the first place he does not disentangle (neither in The Post Card where such disentanglement would be most relevant nor, to the best of my knowledge, anywhere else in his writings through Psyche) the Speusippian teaching on Pleasure/Pain (reviewed but not endorsed by "Socrates" in Philebus) from Plato's account.

Concerning the Spesusippian-but-not-Platonic doctrine of pleasure confer A.E. Taylor's remarks contained in Plato: "Philebus" and "Epinomis". (Thomas Nelson and Sons, London, 1956. Especially pages 25-26. Hereafter: Plato) The lines from Philebus which refer to the Speusippian (as opposed to the Platonic) teaching on pleasure are: 44B-51E. One may also confer Chapters

One and Three of Book X of Aristotle's Nichomachean Ethics for a further indication of this distinction between the Speusippian and Platonic accounts of pleasure. Finally, most of the citations from Philebus have been taken from the Hackforth translation. Confer Hackforth's translation contained in Plato's Examination of Pleasure; a translation of "Philebus", with Introduction and Commentary. (Cambridge University Press, 1958. Hereafter: Pleasure)

Sigismund: And in the second place?

Eurydice: This is far more important. The Philebus (i.e., the second dialogue of the third tetralogy), functioning as the introduction to Symposium (the third dialogue of the third tetralogy), is the key for understanding Plato's teaching on "the good". It is the key for understanding Plato's remarks on the "offspring/interest" of the good contained in Book VI of Republic. All of this is completely absent from Frere Jacques' resiliations -- even when they are most creative -- of Philebus. In "Comment ne pas Parler" he started to manifest some glimmer of understanding concerning these matters. But even there -- his best work on Plato -- he's like a lost child.

Confer the Chapter of Diogenes Laertius on Plato where he cites Thrasylus that Plato himself was responsible for the tetralogical arrangement of the dialogues. In the listing of the dialogues contained in each tetralogy, Diogenes gives the Ancient sub-titles of each dialogue. (Diogenes Laertius; The Lives of Eminent Philosophers; in two volumes, Volume I. translated by R D Hicks; Harvard University Press, 1972. Pages 327-331. Hereafter: Lives)

This book follows the suggestion of Diogenes concerning the tetralogical arrangment of the dialogues. In this sense, Philebus, the second dialogue of the third tetralogy, functions as a kind of introduction to Symposium, the third dialogue of the third tetralogy. It will be noted that the ancient subtitle of Symposium is "concerning the good." Plato's remarks, towards the end of Philebus, contextualize the Symposium for those who are alert to the esoteric in Plato. The following passage from Philebus is important:

> *Socrates: And haven't we in a sense found a way toward the good?*
> *Protarchus: How?*
> *Socrates: If you were looking for somebody and began by ascertaining correctly where he lived, I imagine that would be a big step toward discovering the man you looked for.*
> *Protarchus: Of course.* [61A-B; according to Hackforth.]

The Symposium takes place at the home of "the good" (i.e., at the house of "Agathon").

That a "later" dialogue, Philebus, (indeed, a very "late" dialogue) can function as an introduction to a dialogue said to be from Plato's "middle" period of intellectual development will surprise only those who have not done much original writing.

Generally speaking this book takes Platonic references to "the third" to be, in effect, diacritic notices that one is speaking about "the good." Thus the "third kind" mentioned at Timaeus 49A turns out to be the all-important "khora". So to "light" is referred to a "a third thing" which allows the see-er to be the see-er and the seen to be the seen in the discussion of the "offspring/interest" (tokos at 506E-507A) of "the good" in Republic VI at 507D. {{Please understand that this book always takes "light" as being different from and other from the sun which -- one will see who attends carefully to the text -- means that Plato, through Socrates, is quite serious and most literal about deceiving unintentionally with a flase reckoning of the "interest"/"offspring" (tokou) at 507A. }} Finally, this book contends, it is not at all accidental that the Symposium -- whose ancient sub-title is "concerning the good" -- should appear as the third dialogue of the third tetralogy.

Jacques Derrida, in "Comment ne pas Parler" (appearing in Psyche; Inventions d l'autre put out by

Galilee in 1987; pages 535-595), draws the reader's attention to the significance of "the third" in the Platonic text. However the Derridean meditation on the Platonic "third" and the meditation on the Platonic "third" which obtains in this book are neither parallel nor congruent.

Confer Republic VI and its discussion of the "interest"/"offspring" (tokos) of "the good" at 506E-507A.

Confer "Comment ne pas Parler" appearing in Psyche, 1987. Hereafter: *Comment.* Derrida is especially attentive to the "khora" teaching on pages 563-587 of this article.

Sigismund: Can one get any help on these matters?

Eurydice: Oh yes. From the writer of Shekhinah. But that must wait for another time. For now the most economical thing to do is to ignore Frere Jacques' intimations about Philebus as they are contained in The Post Card since, sad to say, they remain, on principle, irrelevant.

Sigismund: Then let us return to his way of bringing Nietzsche center stage [404-409] after he, Frere Jacques, arranges to have my analysis of "pleasure" collapse in upon itself.

Eurydice: Oh yes. There is not much more, in fact. After citing what he takes to be that insightful teaching of Nietzsche -- (i.e., to the effect that pain is not merely the opposite of pleasure, but rather something other) -- he starts trading on that Deleuzian/Derridean understanding of the "will to power."

Sigismund: What do you mean by that?

Eurydice: Oh that jazzed up understanding of Nietzsche by which the will to power -- as the very "stuff" of ""reality"" -- is always and continually the movement of self-referential differentiation.

Confer Nietzsche and Philosophy by Gilles DeLeuze. (Translated by Hugh Tomlims; Columbia University Press, New York, 1983 Hereafter: NaP). Derrida refers sympathetically to the treatment of Nietzsche put forth by DeLeuze in Derrida's essay "Differance" as contained in Margins of Philosophy. (Translated with additional notes by Alan Bass; Chicago University Press, 1982. Page 17. Hereafter: Margins.) Also informative on these matters concerning the "deconstructionistic" reading of Nietzsche is Derrida's own Spurs: Nietzsche's Styles. (Translated by Barbara Harlow; Chicago University Press, 1979. Hereafter Spurs.)

Sigismund: Is this a false reading of Nietzsche?

Eurydice: Not really. Its only fault, as we shall see, is that it tends to make one -- i.e., Deleuze and Derrida themselves as cases in point -- overly comfortable with Nietzsche and the Nietzschean perspective for the task of encountering/resiliating "difference"/"differance". But that shortcoming of these Frenchmen can be held in abeyance for now. To repeat, the Deleuzian/Derridean reading of Nietzsche's "will to power" is not necessarily unfaithful to the Nietzschean text.

Sigismund: So then what happens?

Eurydice: Then Derrida gets real solemn about this Nietzsche and quotes a sentence from one of Nietzsche' posthumous aphorisms about the complexities of pleasure and pain. He quotes it in the German saying [[--- drums rolling, please; high drama; even I, the great mocking/playful Jacques Derrida can get deadly serious and oh! so!

reverential!!! ---]]: --- *this sentence which I no longer wish to translate ---*

Pages 408-409 of PC.

Sigismund: So, in effect, Frere Jacques takes the garland -- symbolic of having understood "pleasure/pain" -- away from Freud and crowns Nietzsche. {{{ And in the process pays back the debt which Frere Jacques thinks is owed to Nietzsche by Sigmund. {{{{{Bappy: And really, is this not a warm-up for the analogous settling of accounts with the "other" Jacques which becomes the subject matter of the last two "chapters" contained in the second half of The Post Card? Dewchee: Yes. Of course.}}}}} }}}

Eurydice: That is correct.

Sigismund: So what is to be made of this situation?

Eurydice: Two things.

In the first place, the fatal flaw of Derridean deconstructionism is revealed.

Sigismund: How so?

Eurydice: The inability of this whole lot of Derrideans -- including Derrida himself -- to understand that there is an irreducible duality or dualism about things and that the very thing with which they are concerned (i.e., "differance" or any of the other hundred-thousand words/concepts which are not words/concepts which they use synonymously to "differance") is a function of this duality/dualism. They are all so hyper-sophisticated to what they call the "onto-theological" underpinnings of "duality" in the Tradition -- as they appropriate it -- that they blind themselves to the very possibility of seeing what duality is all about. They have thrown the baby (i.e., that duality without which "there is" no "differance") with the polluted bath water (i.e., the hundred-thousand "dualistic" "pairings" presented by the Tradition in its flight from difference). They got so good -- so cleverly sophisticated -- at "deconstructing" these "dualistic" pairings that they drifted, unconsciously, into the very heart of thoughtlessness. They, of all people, end up in a "flight from """differance""" ". How strange!

Sigismund: With the benefit of all the education which I have acquired in these "years" down here, I have an understanding of what you are referring to. As our friend -- the writer of Shekhinah -- has so often pointed out, Frere Jacques and his confreres suffer from an unconscious reliance on Aristotle's Act/Potency paradigm. ((This reliance obtains even when they are "deconstructing" the Stagirite himself.)) This reliance becomes a most serious deficit since it keeps them -- their relative sophistication concerning the Platonic text notwithstanding -- from even getting in touch with the "difference" theme in Plato.

44.
Eurydice: That is correct. And you are correct to credit the writer of Shekhinah on these matters, although we cannot here further pursue this business of the unconscious Aristotelianism which pervades both the Tradition and, paradox noted, the "deconstructors" of the Tradition. I hope you also realize that it is precisely your stubborn commitment to a root duality about things which brought you to our attention all those years ago. To be sure, you are here precisely because your appropriation of your own insight into the duality of things needs some finessing. But even in the living years you stood head and shoulders above both

Frere Jacques and Nietzsche.

Sigismund: But never above Aristocles?

Eurydice: Stop being so jealous. You spoke of things he never spoke of. I need you both. You both bring me to orgasm. In different ways, and that is OK.

Sigismund: I take it then, that what we have said so far means that Nietzsche -- at bottom and even with the benefit of that jazzed up reading of the Nietzschean text accomplished by Deleuze and Frere Jacques -- is a monotheist: a monotheist of the "will to power."

Eurydice: That is essentially correct.

Sigismund: What was the second point which you wanted to make about Derrida's bringing Nietzsche center stage on pages 404-409 of The Post Card?

Eurydice: Thank-you for reminding me. The second point brings us back to "Eros" and "Thanatos" and back to our real undertaking.

Sigismund: Which is getting """before""" "The Economic Problem in Masochism" once we have gotten to and through "The Economic Problem in Masochism."

Eurydice: That is correct. The second point:

On page 408 Frere Jacques says:

> *If one follows this series of statements, the beyond of the pleasure principle would be the affirmation of life rather than the aspiration to the return to the inorganic.*

To be sure, when Frere Jacques speaks these words he is in the midst of that Deleuzian/Derridean reading of and commitment to the framework of Nietzsche with all the liabilities -- (but particularly its monotheism) -- which such a commitment entails. Also, following your own practice (whose sloppiness has priorly been recognized), these words take "life" as the opposite of "Death" (i.e., the "aspiration" to return to the inorganic) rather than understanding "life" as the compromise formation of and between two "forces." Even so, do not these words of Frere Jacques make you think about the terms of your own dualism?

Sigismund: In the living years I did wonder about this and I believe there are some formulations of mine which might allow for the interpretation that for Freud it is "Eros" (and its representatives) which are "beyond" the pleasure principle rather than "Death". Indeed, in and through that journey which took me to and through Beyond the Pleasure Principle and then to and through "The Economic Problem in Masochism" I came to realize how "the pleasure principle" and what I came to call "the Nirvana principle" were so very analogous to each other. I came to realize that in a sense all of those apparently "unpleasant" manifestations of the "Death-drive" were releases of tension in one form or another and thus were, in a sense, actually (and paradoxically) forms of pleasure even if experienced in some sense as pain since they followed the relase-from-tension paradigm of "the pleasure principle." It was for this reason that I, in "The Economic Problem of Masochism", dethroned "the pleasure principle" in favor of "the Nirvana principle" allowing that "the pleasure principle" comes into being as a modification of "the Nirvana principle" brought about by the influence on "the Nirvana principle" of and by the "libido/Eros"-drive which (in my sloppy usage) I sometimes called the "Life"-drive since the other of the "Nirvana/Death"-drive, in ordinary language, would be called "life."

Confer *Economic*, pages 256-257.

Often enough -- and especially in Beyond the Pleasure Principle -- Freud uses "life" and "life-drives" as roughly synonomous with Eros. Yet when Freud is careful it is quite clear that he counts "life" as the compromise formation of and between the Death-drive and the Eros drive. The following citations are representative.

From Civilization and its Discontents: "I drew the conclusion that, besides the instinct to preserve living substance and to join it into ever larger units, there must exist another, contrary instinct seeking to dissolve those units and to bring them back to their primaeval, inorganic state. That is to say, as well as Eros there was and instinct of death. The phenomenon of life could be explained from the concurrent or mutually opposing action of these two instincts." *(Translated and edited by James Strachey; W. W. Norton and Co., New York, 1961. Page 73. Hereafter: Civ.)*

From New Introductory Lectures on Psycho-analysis: "If it is true that -- at some immeasurably remote time and in a manner we cannot conceive -- life once proceeded out of inorganic matter, then, according to our presumption, an instinct must have arisen which sought to do away with life once more and to re-establish the inorganic state. If we recognize in this instinct the self-destructiveness of our hypothesis, we may regard the self-destructiveness as an expression of a 'death instinct' which cannot fail to be present in every vital process. And now the instincts that we believe in divide themselves into groups -- the erotic instincts, which seek to combine more and more living substance into ever greater unities, and the death instincts, which oppose this effort and lead what is living back into an inorganic state. From the concurrent and opposing action of these two proceed the phenomena of life which are brought to an end by death." *(Translated and edited by James Strachey; W. W. Norton and co., New York, 1965. Page 95. Hereafter: New.)*

The best and most sustained statement by Freud concerning life as the compromise formation of and between "Eros" and "Thanatos" comes in Chapter Two (*The Theory of the Instincts*) of his 1938 An Outline of Psycho-analysis. What is sustained there throughout the Chapter is said quite economically on page 6: "This concurrent and mutually opposing action of the two basic instincts gives rise to the whole variegation of the phenomena of life." *(Translated by James Strachey; W. W. Norton and co., New York, 1949. Pages 5-8. Hereafter: Outline.)*

Finally, it needs to be noted that Freud's 1924 article (i.e., "The Economic Problem in Masochism") alters the "beyond" problematic of Beyond the Pleasure Principle." The argumentation of the 1924 article makes it clear that the pleasure principle is also a compromise formation between the Death/"Nirvana"-drive and the Eros-drive. (Cf. the argumentation of *Economic*, pages 256-257.) For the alert reader it becomes evident that the constellation obtaining between the two basic drives and the pleasure principle has become much more clear in Freud's mind from the time of the 1919/1920 Beyond the Pleasure Principle. Even so, Freud continued to "wonder" about the relationship between the two "drives" *{"instincts" in the Strachey translation}* and the pleasure principle. Listen to this formulation from his "Outline" book of 1938:

> *The consideration that the pleasure principle demands a reduction, at bottom the extinction perhaps, of instinctual needs (that is, "Nirvana") leads to the still unassessed relations between the pleasure principle and the two primal forces, Eros and the death instinct.* (Outline, page 55)

Eurydice: Keep going. I am listening. It is better that you adumbrate these things.

Sigismund: All of this can only mean, I now realize, that "the pleasure principle" (inclusive therein of the multiple ways in which the actual operation of "the pleasure principle" <u>includes</u> the experiencing of multiple kinds of pain), after 1924, is itself something of a compromise formation of and between "Eros" and "Nirvana/Death." To be sure, the "pleasure principle" mimics "Nirvana/Death" more obviously than it mimics "Eros". In this sense "Eros" and its representatives (which are, uncritically, associated by me in one way and by Frere Jacques in another way, with "Life") are more properly "beyond" "the pleasure principle" than the representatives of the "Nirvana/Death"-drive. In one sense Frere Jacques is vindicated (relative to the cited comment he makes on page 408 of <u>The Post Card</u>), even by my standard. Yet, if "the pleasure principle" is a compromise formation of and between "Eros" and "Nirvana/Death", and if "the pleasure principle" -- while mimicing the "movement" of the "Nirvana/Death"-drive -- is not identical with the "Nirvana/Death"-drive, then there is "another" ""beyond"" of "the pleasure principle."

Eurydice: This "other" "beyond" would be the "Nirvana/Death" drive in its pure form, so to speak.

Sigismund: Yes. And, in "The Economic Problem in Masochism" I referred to this purity of the "Death-drive" as a "primal sadism". This "primal sadism" is ""prior"" to the "ordinary" sadism which shows up in psycho-sexual development and which eventually becomes part of both """normal""" and """deviant""" sexual behavior. This "primal sadism" is a kind of "ur-masochism", so to speak, <u>within</u> the organism, and when joined by libido becomes the "erotogenic masochism" which itself precedes the "ordinary" manifestations of masochism which ordinary manifestations of masochism, following social convention, I called "feminine."

"Primal Sadism" as Death Drive in *Economic*, page 261.

Freud does refer to the "ordinary" manifestations of masochism as "feminine." In doing this he is not only blindly following the dictates of patriarchal social convention but he is also trading upon Psycho-analytic findings. (Confer especially, <u>New</u>, page 102.) However, it is precisely this point -- to what extent does Freud's "unconscious" following of chauvinistic/misogynistic social custom affect his alleged Psycho-analytic "findings" concerning women -- which brings so much confusion and misprecision to discussions of the Freudian text.

It is now almost a commonplace to presume a priori that almost all of Freud's Psycho-analytic "findings" concerning women are merely a function of his "unconscious" following of chauvinistic/misogynistic social custom. And in many particulars this charge is accurate. Yet there is reason for caution in these matters.

In the first place, it is Freud himself who makes the quite Feminist point that it is social custom which pre-ordains females to certain roles and behaviors. (Again, page 102 of <u>New</u> makes this point clearly enough.) In this sense it is often <u>Freud himself</u> who distinguishes between the male-oriented dictates of social custom and the findings of Psycho-analytic theory.

In the second place the chauvinistic bias -- which is manifestly evident in all of Freud's writings -- of the Freudian text has, with the passage of time, taken on the aura of an almost self-mocking quaintness. Perceptive readers learn to pass through this veneer and engage the Freudian text at a more decisive and serious level relative to his "findings" on female psychology. Indeed, such an engagement of the Freudian text has been the major purpose of this book.

Finally, it needs to be noted that, according to the multiple contentions of this book, it is Freud's radically incomplete account of <u>male</u> sexuality which is his most serious flaw. Here Freud's enmeshment in social custom had its most serious drawbacks. Freud constantly attributes to "orthodox" (i.e., "genital") male behavior a completeness and sufficiency which -- if the multiple contentions of this book are correct -- truly misrepresent the dynamic of male sexual desire. Yet even here one's orientation still inevitably remains tied to that one central and unavoidable tenet of Psycho-analysis, namely the male and female versions of the castration complex.

Eurydice: We will not pursue here the blame your text incurs by all too often following "social convention" in your accounts of the soi-dissant "masculine" and the soi-dissant "feminine" even though it is precisely your own theories which show that "social convention" is not at all a dependable guide for understanding the soi-dissant "masculine" and the soi-dissant "feminine."

> {{{Bappy: In addition, "male" sadism is really a mask for and defense against a kind of "feminine" desire on the part of males for passive/"masochistic" treatment. Often, they visit upon their "beloved" the very behavior which they wish to be visited upon themselves.
>
> Dewchee: Oh yes. But you know they cannot stop here and review the work done in Shekhinah and, still less, the work done in Madonna.}}}

Madonna is yet another unpublished manuscript which the present book draws upon. Madonna was the mother, so to speak, of Shekhinah which was in turn the mother, so to speak of *Thinking Psycho-analytically.* This makes Madonna the maternal grandmother of *Thinking Psycho-analytically.*

Even "up there" intelligent readers of your text -- including Feminists and non-Feminists alike -- are no longer hindered from jumping over your chauvinistic "obiter dicta" so as to find, finally, and fully appreciate your root insights on these matters. And "down here", of course, you spent forty "years" getting those patterns of chauvinism and misogyny catharted from your psyche.

Sigismund: Thank-you for sparing me the need to re-affirm those things. And I understand that this tension in my text between social custom and Psycho-Analytic theory relative to questions of chauvinism/misogyny will be more carefully dealt with in the second part of the book which is now being put together. Getting back to my train of thought:

There are, after all, two kinds of "beyonds" relative to "the pleasure principle". That is the only fair inference which one can make after one has gone through "The Economic Problem in Masochism." Yet I still don't feel all that good about these matters in my gut. It's as though there is still something else which needs to be said.

Eurydice: That is because you have gone to and through "The Economic Problem in Masochism" but you have not arrived "before" "The Economic Problem in Masochism." And for this project you are at a disadvantage.

Sigismund: How so?

Eurydice: You lack the proper training.

Sigismund: Can you explain yourself?

Eurydice: By shying away from Philosophy for all those years you gained much. You avoided the shallowness which is endemic to practically the whole History of Philosophy. By and large it was to your advantage not to be part of the History of Philosophy even though you are a philosopher of the first order. Yet by avoiding the History of Philosophy you kept yourself from stumbling onto the one training exercise which would have helped you in these matters of getting "before" "The Economic Problem in Masochism". Since most in the history of Philosophy have avoided this training exercise you too -- had you entered the field of Philosophy -- may very well have bypassed this training exercise which is (along with a couple of correlative conversations) the only positive occurrence in the whole canon-blessed Tradition. Indeed, had you ended up entering this terrain as an extension of your brief brush-up with Franz Brentano, you would -- any sophistications notwithstanding -- drifted into yet another clever instantiation of the Tradition incorporating into your appropriation of the Tradition an unconscious-of-itself paradigm of an Aristotelian "Act/Potency" motif. Indeed even thinkers like Derrida and Heidegger -- who claim to be making the Tradition problematical to itself in its entirety -- still unconsciously and paradoxically do nothing but instantiate the Tradition since they are themselves unconsciously married to Aristotle's "Act/Potency" motif even when "deconstructing" the Stagirite himself. Thus you might have ended up being a cousin of Husserl. Or, by another route, you would have been a cousin of Derrida/Heidegger. Either way you would not have become "Freud." You basically did us all a favor by bypassing the History of Philosophy. Your mind was too fertile for such rubbish.

Sigismund: Please!! You are still not telling me to what you refer when you speak of "this training exercise."

Eurydice: Even the vast majority of those schooled in the History of Philosophy avoid this training exercise like the plague. They remain vague and confused about it. So, as has just been mentioned, even if you had entered into, in a thematic manner, the parameters of the History of Philosophy there is no guarantee that you would have availed yourself of this training exercise. Frere Jacques -- up through the writings of 1987 -- shows no evidence of really having passed through this exercise in a rigorous manner. Nor does Martin Heidegger, the Nazi. And they were subtle thinkers of the first order. Many who have touched this training exercise and who have walked around its interior -- one thinks of that tribe of Neo-Platonists and also of Hegel -- had no idea at all about the intricasies of this training exercise. So, who knows? Since you most likely would not have availed yourself of the only benefit involved in attaching oneself to the History of Philosophy and since by avoiding a deep encounter with the History of Philosophy you avoided the endemic shallowness which pervades the History of Philosophy and its expositors, it is probably better that you ended up writing the way you actually did write, relatively unencumbered by the most infantile of infantile behaviors: Philosophy.

Sigismund: Are you going to tell me what in Hades you are talking about or not?

Eurydice: May I remind you that it is a bit redundant -- in this conversation -- to speak of "Hades"? Be that as it may, I will tell you. I speak of Plato's <u>Parmenides</u>.

Sigismund: Yes. I have heard of it. "Down here", that is.

Eurydice: Yes. The intricasies of handling a duality with the finesse and subtlety appropriate to the vocation of thinking are well worked out in that training exercise. Sooner or later it will be necessary to prune your "Eros"/"Thanatos" duality with and through the rigors of those eight hypotheses. Then and only then will you succeed in getting "before" "The Economic Problem in Masochism."

All references in this book to Plato's dialogue <u>Parmenides</u> take the main argumentation of that dialogue as falling into eight hypotheses. In doing this I follow the outline generated by F.M.

Cornford. *(Plato and Parmenides; Parmenides' "Way of Truth" and Plato's "Parmenides"; Library of Liberal Arts of Bobbs-Merrill, New York. Hereafter Parmenides.)* I follow Cornford on this although my reasons for doing so are based on an idosyncratic reading of 135D-136D which I devleoped in my privately printed (1976) Commentary on "Parmenides".

Admittedly, the structuring of the Parmenides into eight hypotheses makes problematic the "insert" hypothesis which I have referred to as "2a". This "insert" hypothesis begins: *To take up the argument yet a third time* --- (Parmenides 155E; Emphasis mine, JWM)

There are both Neo-Platonic and Hegelian ways of appropriating this "third" hypothesis which sometimes has led commentators to suggest that there are nine hypotheses, although such would not be predictable from a reading of 135D-136D. For reasons too digressive to enumerate here, this book completely dismisses both the Neo-Platonic and Hegelian accounts of Parmenides.

Yet the "thirdness" of this "third argument" is quite striking. I believe it was intended by Plato to stand out like a sore thumb. And Plato -- it is contended -- always used "the third" to indicate diacrtically that something esoteric concerning "the good" was being revealed. It is the contention of the '76 commentary that the "eksaiphnes" teaching of this "insert hypothesis" is Plato's most secret name for "difference" and that "difference" in turn is the key for understanding "the good."

Sigismund: Tell me this: is the Parmenides only a training exercise or do you have something else up your sleeve?

Eurydice: That's for me to know and for you to find out. But please remember: I sleep with Aristocles, as well as with you. It is perhaps through this "training exercise" that you shall meet him. But for now, let us back up. So to speak. Let us review some of the difficulties associated with the "Eros"/"Thanatos" duality even when that duality has been appreciated through the lens of an appropriately nuanced reading of "The Economic Problem in Masochism." It would be better if you list and briefly elaborate upon these difficulties.

Sigismund: Fair enough. But perhaps we could take a small break. I feel the need to get my bearings.

Eurydice: As you like it.

45.
Eurydice: Yes. But your hesitancy is well founded. After all it must be admitted that the monism -- indeed the monotheism -- of Nietzsche's "will to power" was tremendously fertile and that all of us owe to Frederick a debt of gratitude for making it so clear that the Emperor -- called 'The Tradition' -- was wearing no clothes. Indeed it was the genius of Nietzsche to understand that monistic/monotheistic thinking is incompatible with anything like equilibrium. Thus his monotheism of Change/Becoming. And Nietzsche everywhere is fully cognizant of the impossibility of conjoining equilibrium and monism/monotheism. Even when the "chance" of equilibrium wears the clothes of secular mechanistic science it is rejected by Nietzsche out of hand as incompatible with the uncompromising demands of thinking to which we are called by virtue of the Nietzschean text. Yet of the "equilibrium" made possible by a dualism Nietzsche had no inkling. Nor do Deleuze, Derrida, and that crowd. Even so the very "differance" which animates the thinking of that allegedly sophisticated crowd is itself -- and unbeknownst to Derrideans and "deconstructionists" -- a function of a root duality in the "make-up" of things.

Confer Nietzsche's remarks directed to William Thompson and mechanistic theory in aphorism # 1066; WP, pages 548-549.

Sigismund: Yet even so my duality of "Eros" and "Thanatos" stands in need of modification?

Eurydice: Yes and no. The terms of your duality are servicable as a theoretical construct by which the findings of Psycho-analysis can be presented. In this sense "Eros" and "Thanatos" constitute an "integration" (in the mathematical sense) of a two-variable equation. Or perhaps it would be more apt to say that in one quadrant of the graph the variables of the originary equation take on "values" compatible with your usage of "Eros" and "Thanatos" as "first principles". Yet, in the final analysis: Yes. For the sake of """""""""""truth""""""""""", "Eros" and "Thanatos", as used by you, are not servicable without significant modification.

Sigismund: Why is that?

Eurydice: In the first place -- (and to return to the point from which we digressed when we started speaking of Nietzsche and Derrida) -- you treated your "first principles" as both belonging, so to speak, in the same "genus". You treated both variables as "forces" or "energies." {{{Indeed, if you did not you were not a dualist at all since under the assumption of a merely "entropic" understanding of the "Death" drive you would have been yourself a monist with "Eros" as your only "energy" and, correlative to such a stance, the "Death"-drive being but the running out or running down of "Eros." If such is the proper understanding of "Eros"/"Thanatos" you are of even less value to us than either Nietzsche or Frere Jacques.}}} But as we mentioned above, the "terms" of the duality (in terms of which "there is" anything at all,) are not necessarily symmetrical to each other at all. On other words it is possible that there be only one "energy" or "force" (as opposed to your postulation of two "energies"/"forces") provided that there be some other even if it is not construed as an "energy" or "force." This, I trust, will become evident.

This unity-in-duality and duality-in-unity theme is only being inaugurated here. The discerning reader will hold this issue in suspension -- i.e., without adjudication as to its meaning -- until *Shame!* has a chance to interface a reading of the band "Schelling/Kaballah/Plato/Nietzsche" with the more "metaphysical" aspects of mania. Be patient, even as you are persevering.

Sigismund: I trust so as well. Shall we get on with it?

Eurydice: There is something else which you need to know about "duality" although I do not present it as a critique of what you wrote during the living years. Even so, it needs mentioning.

Sigismund: Please proceed. I am all receptacle.

Eurydice: The "terms" of the duality never did or do ""exist"" in themselves and by themselves, so to speak. There is always mixture. The condition of mixture always obtains, never started to obtain (although it never ceases to begin), and never ceases to obtain (although it is always ending). To be sure, many religious and/or philosophical "dualisms" present the "terms" of their duality as though they somehow did "exist" in themselves and by themselves and then, somehow, come together. But such naivete has nothing to do with the duality whose "terms" we wish to decipher.

Sigismund: How is this deciphering to be accomplished?

Eurydice: I am glad you asked that. Since "there is" only mixture, it is from the mixture -- i.e., from the experience of the mixture -- that one must "extract", so to speak, and "postulate", so to speak, the very "terms" in terms of which "there is" mixture at all. This takes great mathein. It takes great pathein as well. In this respect your "Eros" and "Thanatos" reflect great pathein and mathein. We have learned much from you. But our "voice" reveals to us two considerations which will lead us towards a modification of "Eros" and "Thanatos" as the first principles in the "make-up" of things.

Sigismund: What are those two considerations?

Eurydice: It seems that "the draw -- the attraction -- OF equilibrium" requires a better accounting of its pervasiveness than is afforded by your schema.

Sigismund: OK. That is one consideration. What is the other?

Eurydice: It seems that the connection between sexuality and violence likewise requires a better accounting than is afforded by your "Eros"/"Thanatos" schema. Yet even in saying this, I acknowledge that of all mortals who have ever lived -- even including Aristocles himself -- you have contributed more towards an understanding of this connection than anyone. Even so, one must go "before" you. So to speak.

Sigismund: Can you make yourself clearer?

Eurydice: It all comes together through the subject which even you shied away from.

Sigismund: Orgasm?

Eurydice: Yes. Patterns of female orgasm. The dictum of Tiresias. The male attitude towards all of this. All of this constitutes the factor <u>in</u> the mixture in terms of which the "terms" of the mixture show themselves.

46.
Eurydice: Thank-you for reading the citation. You read my mind perfectly. Shall we now get to the "example" which our conversation begins to mimic and in terms of which the "terms" of our duality will, eventually, be revealed?

Sigismund: It seems that our conversation is all digression and it is not always evident that "there is" that from which there is digression.

Eurydice: Calm down, my friend. Digression is of the essence. So to speak. It is the best and most creative usage of aggressive energy. But how about our "example"/"paradigm"?

Sigismund: Let's get to it.

Eurydice: Orgasm.

Sigismund: Orgasm???

Eurydice: Yes, Orgasm. I mentioned this before our little rest period.

Sigismund: Do you have in mind the male patterns or the female patterns of orgasm?

Eurydice: Ultimately both, since in the on-coming age of matriarchal androgyny male patterns of orgasm will approach the female patterns. As a limit, so to speak. And even now, the "example" is exemplified by both kinds of patterns. Even so, one might more especially keep in mind the female patterns of orgasm.

Sigismund: And what is your point?

Eurydice: The pre-orgasmic state. Staying on the edge, sometimes for an incredibly long period of time. Right on the edge.

Sigismund: That brings to mind the refrain which our friend practically turned into a mantra when he wrote Shekhinah: *Women prolong; men, for the most part, merely postpone. There is a difference.*

Eurydice: Those were inspired words. I know. Yet all the staying on the edge in the world is for nought unless "there is" as well the actual spasmotic release of the orgasm proper. Without the release there is but frustration. Yet again -- provided there is the release of the orgasm proper -- in many ways the best part of the "orgasm" is that incredible staying-on-the-edge which some people can prolong for such a long period of time.

Sigismund: I did not write about these things much at all during the living years. But I have learned much -- much -- from you down here on these matters. That weird, strange "feeling". "Un-heimlich", so to speak; and delirious. Ah! I get your point! We are now on the edge in this conversation of ours! This is the best part!

Eurydice: Provided, of course, that we do finally get our release.

Sigismund: This hope for release sends me back to the dream by which this digression in our conversation is occurring. In my dream -- which was mostly about Nietzsche -- the "draw -- the attraction -- OF equilibrium" kept making an incursion into my reverie about Nietzsche.

Eurydice: It does not surprise me in the least that you would have the weirdest dreams of all. Please elaborate. Tell me about your dream and any associations you have relative to your dream.

Sigismund: It was that business of the will to power. How uncompromising Nietzsche was. Goal-less-ness; Value-less-ness as the condition for the possibility of being a creator of values. First of all, # 55 on that most radical form of nihilism which entails the Eternal Recurrence; then # 1062, 1064, and, most especially, 1066.

On this topic aphorisms # 55 (especially pages 35-36), # 1062, # 1064, and, of course, # 1066 are unambiguous.

Eurydice: Nietzsche was white-hot in # 1066.

Sigismund: I understood his point perfectly. The will to power as the eternal recurrence and the eternal recurrence as the will to power. How they entail and require each other. The point was perfectly clear.

Eurydice: And?

Sigismund: How rigorously -- one only has to read # 1062, 1064, and, again, most especially 1066 -- he forbade any possibility of equilibrium; he forbade any possibility of stasis. Even the secular, "scientific" hypothesis -- (i.e., the "entropy" hypothesis as put forth by Thompson and as reported in # 1066) --, which would entail no commitment to "God", or value, or "goal" in the sense of intelligent teleology, was forbidden by Nietzsche. He was uncompromising. NO STASIS. He was true to his God of Change and Becoming. He was true to his God of "the will to power." Even his grand thought of the Eternal Recurrence was put in the service of insuring on principle, so to speak, that no "objective" value/goal could emerge. Given the grand postulate of his system -- i.e., the Eternal Recurrence -- everything else (*) is consistently disallowed by this thinker. Nietzsche's postulated "non-truth", (**) so to speak, insures Change-without-goal.

*. {{{including the possibility of eternal novelty, the intriguing alternative to his system which, as it is adumbrated by Nietzsche in # 1062, often is accompanied by a ""theological"" motivation but which does not -- Nietzsche notwithstanding -- necessarily entail such a ""theological"" motivation (Confer aphorism # 1062, pages 546-547.) }}}

**. {{{{{ ----- and one does -- it can be noted totally on the side for the benefit of any Deleuzians out there who think Nietzsche interpretation begins and ends with Gilles -- fully appreciate all of the intricasies of # 853 concerning the priority of deception/lie over ""truth"" ----- (Confer WP, pages 451-453.) }}}}}

Eurydice: It seems your dream has been fair to Nietzsche. What was so troubling about your dream?

Sigismund: Nagging doubt intervened. I thought of the Pythagoreans. I thought of the Stoics. I thought of Buddhism.

Eurydice: You refer, of course, the the ancient and more-or-less continuous pedigree of the "Eternal Recurrence" motif. Indeed, the structure of much of mythology instantiates this motif.

Sigismund: Of course I understand the difference in flavor and motivation between other paradigms of the Eternal Recurrence and Nietzsche's somewhat "mechanistic" paradigm of the Eternal Recurrence.

Confer aphorism # 1061 in WP, page 546.

Eurydice: You are a sharp and careful reader. I would expect that you especially would be attuned to nuantical differences. Yet I ought to remind you that Nietzsche himself maintains his own appropriation of the Eternal Recurrence to be the cousin of Buddhism, the difference hinging upon the distinction between the consistent (for Nietzsche) stance of "the perfect passive nihilist" (i.e., the Buddhist) and the consistent (for Nietzsche) stance of "the perfect active nihilist" (i.e., the tragic-Dionysian type). Also -- if you check # 55 -- Nietzsche himself noted the analogs between a Spinozistic "pantheism" and his own "nihilistic" appropriation of the Eternal Recurrence.

Confer aphorism # 55 (WP, pages 35-36 especially) and, by implication, aphorism # 1065 (WP, pages 547-548).

Sigismund: And that is just the point. Not only in those "other" appropriations of the Eternal Recurrence *but in Nietzsche's own appropriation of the Eternal Recurrence as well* I see something of what we are calling "the draw -- the attraction -- OF equilibrium."

Eurydice: I'm beginning to see what troubles you. That some analog of "the draw -- the attraction -- OF equilibrium " should make an appearance {{{however appropriately or inappropriately being yet another question}}} in those "other" Eternal Recurrence motifs is not all that surprising. After all the theme of "stasis-in-and-through-Change" is a dime-a-dozen in a hundred thousand mythological, religious, and philosophical accounts of the "make-up" of things. But its appearance -- or should we say, the appearance of its appearance -- in the Nietzschean text is disconcerting since its very appearance at all appears to defy the most fertile dimensions of Nietzsche's critique of the Tradition.

{{{And of course it is fitting and practically inevitable that the great originator -- for the "Tradition" -- of these monistic/monotheistic "stasis-in-and-through-Change" paradigms should have been the most subtle by conflating God/Nous with "energeia"/"entelecheia". But we can't pause now to re-capitulate how Shekhinah delineates the Stagirite's inauguration of the "flight from difference" -- i.e., effectively, the "flight from libido" -- which characterizes the Tradition. However we can pause here to at least alert the reader that Part III and Part IV of this book ((which are no longer Parts III and IV but rather "subsequent" parts of the book)) will deal to the Stagirite's "flight from difference" and the effect which this largely un-noticed flight has had on the Tradition's ability to read the Platonic text.}}}

Sigismund: Yes. Even though it appears that Nietzsche was precisely putting his version of the Eternal Recurrence into the service of an absolute denial of any stasis and even though he repeatedly denies even the remotest possibility of equilibrium ----- so in spite of all of this -----, I still can't shake the intuitive feeling that he too incorporates into his thought "the draw -- the attraction OF equilibrium." It is, so to speak, un-becoming of Nietzsche.

Eurydice: Perhaps now -- precisely because of your precise understanding of the radicality of Nietzsche's commitment and painful fidelity to the God of Change/Becoming -- you will begin to appreciate just how strong and inevitable is this "draw -- attraction -- OF equilibrium." {{{{However long and exquisitely one might stay on the edge, it is as nothing without the release of orgasm proper. Indeed the possibility of release is the very condition for the possibility of that wildly differential state of staying on the edge.}}} Of all men born of women only one person was more radical than Nietzsche in his committment to the God of Change/Becoming. But do not inquire of this person just yet. Alluding to him would entail the digression which leads, so to speak, to orgasm proper and it is not yet time for that.

Sigismund: Then are you saying that this this "draw -- this attraction -- OF equilibrium" is not an illusion and that, in the final analysis, it is present in Nietzsche's thought, despite himself, so to speak?

Eurydice: Yes and no. We are all well advised to stay with the spirit of Nietzsche and uncompromisingly reject the the appearance of the "idol" called "stasis" when it makes its appearance in any monistic/monotheistic account of things. Stasis-in-monism/monotheism is the very death of thought. Its most obvious alternative, "kinesis"-, so to speak, -in-a-monistic/monotheistic-frame-of-reference, also leads to the death of thinking although in the process the "kinesis" alternative becomes a vector to the "space" in which thinking can find itself.

Sigismund: By this "space" you speak of some forms of "dualism", do you not?

Eurydice: Your caution is well taken. Most soi-dissant dualisms (all of which are so ever quickly dismissed by the "sophisticated" crowd) are not really dualisms at all but rather little quirks in a system which is ultimately monistic/monotheistic.

Sigismund: You refer to things like Descartes' "mind-body" ""dualism"" and the "sensible"/"super-sensible" ""dualisms"" of Plotinus and of Christian Medieval Philosophy.

{{{Of course only those who have still not yet read Shekhinah would look upon the "real"/"really-real" schema of Aristocles as instantiating a sensible/super-sensible ""dualism"". It must also be kept in mind that with Plato/Aristocles there is a real break from aisthesis. Aristotle's account of these things notwithstanding, a Platonic form is anything but a duplication on the level of some soi-dissant "super-sensible" of the sensible.}}}

Eurydice: Yes. Exactly. To limit ourselves to only the most obvious and babyish of examples.

Sigismund: Whereas the kind of dualism which opens up the path for thinking is a dualism, as a first approximation, of "first principles."

Eurydice: Yes, provided that these dualisms of "first principles" avoid the thought-throttling but all-too-human tendency to come forth as "Good"/"Evil" dualisms.

Sigismund: Yes. As we have often noted, such "Good"/"Evil" schemas often end up being or becoming consciously or unconsciously misogynistic and, paradoxically, impede entrance into "mis-ogyny" in the sense which our friend, the writer of Shekhinah, developed in his book of happy memory.

Eurydice: Precisely. And let it be noted that the obvious-but-correctible chauvinism/misogyny of your writings did not keep your Psycho-analytic theories from entering into the "space" of "mis-ogyny". Also, your first principles -- I speak of "Eros" and "Thanatos" -- were precisely not reducible to a "Good"/"Evil" dualism.

Once again the intersection and distinction of misogyny and "mis-ogyny" is at issue. It is the subject matter of the entire book. Be patient -- and persevering! --, dear reader.

Sigismund: Yet even so my friends "Eros" and "Thanatos" require some amending before before we allow ourselves the right to rest easy, even in a relative sense. Do we have any allies in this endeavor?

Eurydice: Yes. Plato. {{{{Keeping in mind, however, that Platon-**ism** is the invention of Aristotle and that Nietzsche's critique of "Platonism" says practically nothing at all about Plato.}}} And also Kaballah. Kaballah, that is, if we let Kaballah speak, resiliatingly, contrary to itself, so to speak. But these things must wait for a bit. Do you not see something present at hand, so to speak, which requires our attention more immediately?

Sigismund: I suspect you refer to the "Nirvana principle" appellation of my "Death-drive." In the present context it seems not to ring true.

Eurydice: You seem endowed with the gift of thought-transference!! You understand my meaning precisely.

Sigismund: On the one hand the appellation "Nirvana principle" for the "Death drive" -- which as you know originated with Barbara Low but to which I acquiesced, at least in "The Economic Problem of Masochism", -- is appropriate since it is a way of pointing out that my thinking is affected by "the draw -- the attraction -- OF equilibrium". On the other hand, now that we have, by virtue of my dream, paid the homage which needs to be accorded to Nietzsche, the appellation "Nirvana principle" for my "Death-drive" resonates with some of those thoughtless appearances -- ever so properly critiqued by Nietzsche -- of "the draw -- the attraction -- of equilibrium" which constitute the death of thinking. On balance, "Death-drive" says it better.

Confer *Economic* pages 256-257.

Eurydice: The name-giver will be happy with this decision. And I have spoken with Barbara. She is happy with this amendment if it makes you happy. Shall we break again in preparation for the final lap since we had, apparently, not priorly arrived at the final lap yet despite what said at that time?

Sigismund: I have been on the edge for some time now. Longer than usual. And I appreciate the attention which you accord to me. Likewise, if I don't come soon I may have a heart attack. Even so I must postpone -- (perhaps I should just prolong and let whatever happens happen) -- the "break", so to speak, in our conversation which break will lead the conversation to its denouement.

Eurydice: Why must you delay our caesura, my cute friend?

Sigismund: Just a while ago you said that Nietzsche was only the second most radical thinker in his commitment and painful fidelity to the God of Change/Becoming. My curiosity will not give me rest. Who is first?

Eurydice: You must keep it a secret. This is not for dissemination up there on "Earth". It is for the initiated few.

Sigismund: You may trust me. Of whom do you speak?

Eurydice: Cratylus.

Sigismund: Cratylus?

Eurydice: Yes. Crazy Cratylus. Not much is known about him on "Earth". But down here he is a Giant among Giants.

Sigismund: Is he a God?

Eurydice: No. But he is much honored.

Sigismund: If he is indeed more radical than Nietzsche himself on these matters, then a double contrasting pattern emerges.

Eurydice: Tell me about it.

Sigismund: That "difference"/differance" crowd of the "twentieth" (as they say it) century -- I speak of Deleuze and Derrida et alia -- is animated by Nietzsche.

Eurydice: From start to finish. Even to the point of engaging in subtle instantiations of the "flight from libido" as we pointed out above.

Sigismund: They think they have gone to the limit of radicality when, in fact, -- precisely by their """"""sophistication"""""" concerning the hundred-thousand dualities from the "Tradition" which they "deconstruct" with such verve and finesse -- they have not even arrived at the home of radicality. Yet "difference"/"differance" can only reside at the home of radicality.

Eurydice: You are correct. Continue with your contrasting pattern.

Sigismund: But -- in contrast -- if your first teacher -- at a young and impressionable age-- were the Giant even among the best of the Giants then you might just have a shot at eventually coming to see what the stakes are. You might just have a shot -- over the course of a lifetime -- of building the only kind of home in which "difference" can make its "dis-appearing" appearance as opposed to coming out still-born, so to speak, from the very womb of soi-dissant """sophistication""". The way one walks away from Cratylus makes all the difference in the world. To walk away from Cratylus and yet not deny Cratylus. The moment of "difference" and episteme; at once. Difference and episteme as the same, which "same" is sustained by ever-elusive-and-never-present-but-always-"there" -- i.e., the very quintessence (the fifth, for God's sake!!!!!) of oscillation !!! -- eksaiphnes. Only a few will ever understand. Listen to the highpoint, so to speak, of the meditation:

> *If there is no way in which the one and those other than the one are different then one cannot say that any other than the one (namely the many of any given form) participates in a form. For if there is no difference between the one and other than the one then "methekhein" would simply mean to be one and these many which allegedly participate in a form would not be many at all, but rather only be the one. Furthermore, if there is no way in which the one and those other than the one (viz., its "not-ones") are different then these other then the one cannot have number. This is so because any of these alleged numerical units, which to be units would have to be other than the one, would no longer be other than the one since there would be no other to speak of. Nor, finally, are these other than the one parts of the one even though the one was earlier described as whole of parts. For without difference, to participate in a one does not mean to participate in a one at all since without difference to participate in a one means to be that one. And in that case parts cease to be parts.*

This is my paraphrase -- contained in that unpublished '76 commentary on Parmenides -- of a critical text in the "Sameness/Difference" passage of hypothesis # 2. (147A, 4-147A, 10 <Loeb lining>)

In that '76 commentary it is presumed that "difference" is Plato's appellation for "the contrary-to-the-one" (which, in hypothesis # 5 is called "the-one-which-is-not) and, correlatively, that "eksaiphnes" -- which makes it appearance in hypothesis # 2a -- is Plato's most esoteric name for "difference." The claim is made that Plato has recourse to this "notion" of "eksaiphnes" -- even when it is not mentioned by name -- when he is unpacking the dyanamic of "difference", especially in hypothesis # 2 and most especially in the "sameness"/"difference" passages of hypothesis # 2. Thus the '76 commentary maintains that it is the un-appearing "presence" of the timeless "eksaiphnes" in "sameness" which allows "sameness" to be the ground of a form and its participant. Finally, it is to be noted that the fertile "timeless-'in-itself'-but nevertheles-time-generative-ness" of "eksaiphnes" is the very substrate (so to speak) in terms of which "there is" time at all and is to be radically distinguished from the total absence of any dimension of time (even of something like an "eternal now") which is the condition of the one in hypothesis # 1 which hypothesis examines the one "by itself" separate from mixture with its contrary.

Eurydice: Bravo. "Down here" you have indeed learned much. You are citing the paraphrase given by the friend of the writer of Shekhinah. As I recall, the paraphrase was given as part of this friend's attempt to show that, according to "Parmenides", difference must animate all of "sameness" in order for there to be discourse/episteme at all and that this animation of "sameness" by difference is through the ever-elusive, never-present, never absent, "eksaiphnes." And, because of the joint work of the writer of Shekhinah and his friend, we are privileged to know that such ever-elusive, always-absent, always present, oscillating "happening" in the make-up of things called "eksaiphnes" occurs by virtue of the mixture of and between the "terms" of that root duality in the make-up of things revealed to us by Aristocles through "Parmenides."

Sigismund. You are speaking my lesson for me.

As you know, practically all of the copies of that '76 commentary were thrown away by our friend. But enough was saved in the text of Shekhinah. However let us not digress too far from our present point. How one walks away from crazy Cratylus makes all the difference in the world.

Eurydice: You are now just on the very edge of completing the contrast. Please continue, my cute one.

Sigismund: Whereas, -- to complete this contrast -- the "sophisticated" crowd has only the surrogate of a Cratylus -- i.e., Nietzsche -- and they end up walking with rather than away from this surrogate. And by walking with this surrogate this crowd unconsciously ends up walking with that thought-destroying monism/monotheism characteristic of this surrogate.

Eurydice: Now you are ready. But remember. When and as you come you must keep your beautiful eyes open all the while and stare into my demonic eyes. I want to see the pupils flow over your beautiful hazel-green irises.

Sigismund: I don't know if I can bear it my Goddess!!! The shame of it all!

Eurydice: It is for the good. The shameless shame of the Shekhinah is possible only through the most shameless. Your pleasure -- which is to please me -- requires courage. But I know you are equal to the task. You are to return tomorrow at the same time. If another dream interferes with our denouement, then so be it. Dream delivers us unto dream and there is no end to allusion.

47.

that peace which the world cannot give   that peace   what the "one" would have about it if per impossibile   it could ever be experienced AS SUCH in the world (i.e., the mixture)   yet the world (i.e., the mixture) really is all that is the case   Lyotard is not retarded to have spent some time with Wittgenstein   thus   *that peace which the world cannot give*   tantum ergo sacramentum   cernui   laus et jubilatio!!!!!!!!!!   QED   and yes Deleuze et alia reading Nietzsche   and me reading Deleuze right before going into the hospital   did they think one had not read AND APPRECIATED say, 853   just for example   ?????????   the will to power as the will to deception   art being worth more than truth   did they think I didn't know AND Appreciate that   ALREADY!!!!!!!

?????????   for God's sake it's already in the Heidegger reading of Nietzsche   that French crowd   they are so dismissive of the Heideggerian reading of Nietzsche   but certainly Heidegger was no stranger to that "art is worth more than truth" stuff and to that will to power as the will to deception business   granted   Heidegger was an asshole   and in thinking he was stodgy to a fault   stodgy   i.e., not jazzy like Deleuze et alia   but most of what Deleuze et alia claim to be finding in the Nietzsche text is already found by Heidegger in his stodgy non-jazzy fashion   and some of what Deleuze et alia putatively find in the Nietzschean text is projected by them into that text   they had to jazz up Nietzsche in order to make Nietzsche an ally   one must appreciate Nietzsche's subtlety as a prerequisite to accusing him of his monotheism of the will to power   that peace which the world cannot give   Nietzsche's monotheism not only keeps him from """differance""" kinds of subtleties   the claims on the part of Deleuze and Derrida et alia concerning the Nietzschean text notwithstanding   it also keeps him from even the glimpse of beauty   the beauty of the one fragmented and dispersed throughout all as it is   without ever beginning to "is" for God's sake!!!!!!!! throughout all   by all means read Nietzsche for God's sake   is there anyone on this planet   inclduing Deleuze and the sophisiticated ones   who is more close to Nietzsche in spirit than I???????   is there??????????   yes read Nietzsche   and then have the grace to walk away   and then he trots out   as though it were the crowning point of the whole ball of wax   that whole business of 1052   about Dionysus versus the Crucified   didn't they understand that   even before encountering Derrida in 87 that I had taken care of that whole number????????   One begins with 1052   one begins   it only starts to get interesting when 1052 is taken as axiomatic   don't they see   Nietzsche does not even begin to get into things Jewish   still less into things Platonic   they all think they are so fucking sophisticated   and now finally   is it yet understood???????   even the most simplistic dualism is a ten thousand times more sophisticated than the most subtle monotheism one is not even in the arena without a dualism   but they were too sophisiticated to hear that peace which the world cannot give   Nietzsche forswears it and pays the price willingly they, on the other, hand don't even have a clue   not even a clue   and even in reading this they will remain clueless they are so in love with their jazzed up sophistication

48.
Non: OK. But why exactly are we pausing?

Sic: For two reasons. One minor and one major.

Non: The minor?

Sic: She brings an element of realism to the reading of the Nietzschean text. She unmasks the infantilism which animates Nietzsche's celebration of "the Dionysian." She shows that it only a little baby infant -- and precisely NOT "the feminine" -- which lurks behind Nietzsche's celebration of things Dionysian.

The reference here is to Luce Irigaray. Irigaray is the author of Amante marine, de Friedrich Nietzsche and also of Corps-a-corps avec la mere; Pleine lune, Paris, 1982.

Non: In that way she serves as a corrective to the Deleuzian/Derridean obsequiousness before the text of Nietzsche in their infantile delusion which was that the text of Nietzsche -- (which in fact is unconsciously and predictably -- to the very edge of boredom!!! -- misogynistic without at all being "mis-ogynistic") constitutes an exploration, in a significant manner, of things feminine. The Deleuzian/Derridean idolatrization of the Nietzschean text is one of the sad chapters in "deconstruction." And Luce deserves unambiguous acknowledgment for being the corrective to the Deleuzian/Derridean appropriation of the text of Nietzsche.

Non: OK. Enough said. What was the major reason for this Irigarayan pause?

49.
a). The Pleasure Principle is the modification of the Nirvana Principle due to the influence of another "principle" on the Nirvana Principle. This other principle Freud sometimes calls "Eros." This other principle Freud sometimes calls "libido." This other principle Freud sometimes calls -- and this time inconsistently -- "Life" or the "Life-drives."

Confer *Economic*, pages 255-257.

b). Bappy: Why "in this case" inconsistently? Are not the other appellations -- "libido" here, "Eros" there -- inconsistent as well?

Dewchee: Ultimately and, "metaphysically" (so to speak), yes. Very much so. But the appellation "Life" (or "Life-drives") is immediately inconsistent with what the later Freud says about "Eros" and "Thanatos."

Bappy: I'll take it as axiomatic that you understand that Freud -- in his written text -- does not use "Thanatos." He uses "death drive." I also will take it as axiomatic that even if you, me, or Johanna, bowing to a convention of English usage, should ever use the word "instinct" instead of "drive" none of us are at all implying -- by such a usage -- that a "drive", in the Freudian sense, is to be conflated with "instinct" in the ordinary biological sense even though "drive", in the Freudian sense, is also not unrelated to "instinct" in the ordinary biological sense. (In other words, we will not re-invent the wheel trotted out by Lacan and a hundred-thousand Lacanians and modified Lacanians of both the Feminist and non-Feminist varieties.)

Dewchee: Why do you take us back to kindergarten on these minor clarifications?

Bappy: We may be gaining new listeners.

Dewchee: That is most unlikely.

Bappy: In any case, why do you say that the appellation "Life" (or "Life-drives") is so grossly inconsistent, as opposed to the other appellations which are, so to speak, only (only!!!!!?????) "metaphysically" inconsistent?

Dewchee: In a hundred thousand places in the text of this "later" Freud, Freud makes it abundantly clear that Life is, so to speak, the compromise formation of and between the two principles of Eros and Thanatos. Life, in other words, requires Thanatos -- (basically understood by Freud as a kind of positive energy although that this is Freud's understanding of Thanatos will be at issue later in this very Holy Trinity text) -- just as much as it, Life, require Eros -- (also understood by Freud as a kind of positive energy). To be sure, the ordinary practice of language is to understand "Life" and "Death" as opposites. Thus it is understandable that, if one (i.e., Freud) speaks of a "principle" which is "other" than the Death/Nirvana principle, that same one might very well all too quickly refer to this "other" principle as "Life" and that, correlatively, if that same thinker (i.e., Freud) used the language of "drives", that that thinker might, correlatively, speak of a "Life-drive" or "life-drives" when referring to the principle "other" than the Death/Nirvana drive. Still, such an appellation is technically inconsistent with the actual dynamic --according to the Freudian analysis in which "life" is treated, so to speak, as a compromise formation of and between the two drives -- by which "there is" life at all.

Holy Trinity is a kind of father to *Thinking Psycho-analytically.* Clearly some portions of Holy Trinity have been integrated into the text of *Thinking Psycho-analytically.*

{{{{{Indeed this was even Plato's understanding of the two, as is indicated by the argumentation of Phaedo. It is noteworthy, that in Phaedo "Death" has status as a form/kind and stands, as such, with "Life" as a form/kind. For Plato, in Phaedo (circa 103A-107A) , "Death" is not the same as the mere absence of "Life."}}}}}

Bappy: Thank-you, Dewchee.

c). The schema of the Nirvana principle (i.e., the Death-drive) and the Eros principle is quite servicable for Freud's purposes and by using this schema he does a remarkable job of giving the taxonomy of masochism -- (i.e., erotogenic, "feminine", and moral) -- in this article (i.e. "The Economic Principle in Masochism") and giving as well an account of how, dynamically, the three types of masochism obtain in conjunction with each other.

50.

... ...
... ...

The call explains itself. Intense remorse, guilt, fear, cowardice. Indeed the shabby surprise of what actually did happen gave it the aura of rape anyway. (And that, in turn, could function as the mask on the mirror by which the betrayal could be denied as a betrayal.) All in all, a real crazy emotional jumble/// The crazy guy was right after all. There was nothing to forgive. Peace.

... ...
... ...

51.
Lou, more than Freud, understood the aura of the anal. Her reflections on anal eroticism and narcissism are more fundamental than Freud's. It is Lou -- despite her continued conceptual dependency on Freud -- who enables one to understand that self-identity is formed in the very heart of darkness. Indeed, had Lou rather than Sigmund been playing the role of magister ludi there would have emerged in Psycho-analysis a far more integrated account of how both "guilt/super-ego" and the multiple workings of narcissistic libido emerge from and return to anal eroticism. The "super" (ueber) of the "super-ego" would then be understood as anally grounded in a kind of pre-and-"unter"-ego made possible through the ivresse of anal eroticism, an ivresse first occaisioned through sphincter control of feces.

In any case, Lou did not allow herself to play "magister ludi." And even when, in her letters to Freud, she hints at playing the teacher to Sigmund, such boldness is quickly stifled by Sigmund. This is, of course, the irony of the Psycho-analytic Church set up by Freud. Those who did challenge the Master --Adler, Jung, and even the belated moves by Rank all come to mind -- were not worthy of walking in the Master's footsteps, let alone striking out on thier own. The one whose mind might have been equal to the task remained subservient, always wanting to please Daddy and willing to settle for such a role.

But let us not idolatrize Lou. Her greatest conceptual weakness was a directional one: trying to go home again, when, in fact, one cannot go home again. The telos of anal eroticism and the corresponding ivresse of proto-narcissism is for the sake of differentiation, not return. Nonetheless, he who would go back to the font of creativity will find Lou waiting for him. Listen to Lou.

One might refer to New, page 90, concerning Freud's appropriation of "Lou."

*****

+++++

{{{Anal eroticism with an interesting partner and a vibrator is safer than anal eroticism with an interesting partner and a penis.

And probably better.}}}

esoterica

<[{(**freedom.** in various pre-incarnations of Shame! -- (and the residues of these are present in Shame! given the manner in which Shame was composed) -- "freedom" was often used as synonymous with and a further specification of "differance/difference" which, in turn, was understood as the meaning of Plato's "fifth" which is to say "pure oscillating need." In contrast, **the free** -- both in Shame as well as in Shame!'s pre-incarnations -- is understood as the utterly unconditioned and is synonymous with "the one" (i.e., "the will which does not will, not even itself"). "Freedom" and "choice" in the mixture is made possible by virtue of the mixture. "Choice" begins to disappear when a one in the mixture approaches -- as impossible to reach limit -- "the free" just as "knowledge" -- which occurs only in the mixture -- begins to disappear when a one in the mixture approaches -- as impossible to reach limit -- the condition of "pure oscillating need."

Circularly "the fifth" becomes "the first" in this book's imaginative usage of the four-but-really-five classes of Philebus. Causally, however, "the one" is the fourth while the principle contray-to-the-one (i.e., the "one-which-is-not" of hypothesis # 5) -- ((and it ought never be forgotten that "principles" are also "elements" in and of that of which they are "principles")) -- is the "fifth" with the first class being the "raw material", so to speak, for the causality of the "fifth" while "the second" is the "raw material", so to speak, for "the causality of "the fourth." The perceptive reader, accordingly, now realizes that while "there are", so to speak, two Godheads, "there are" four classes in which there can be discerned the one (Godhead) apart from the other (Godhead). But in "reality" -- i.e., the third class; i.e., the class of mixture; i.e., the class of ousia; i.e., the class of "the good"; -- the two Godheads are but one. Unity in duality and duality in unity. Amen.)}]>

(((The Celtic soul returns. Imagine. Killed by the pens of his students!!! But the soul returns. This time with a vengeance.)))

(caesura)

Tonight, clouds willing, look at the moon. It should be full by the time you read this. Know that I think of you especially as the moon approaches its fullness. Like a climax. Of course I expect that your future infidelities to me (which, now, are not infidelities) will occur during these times. But know also that I think of you in ways other than with jealousy during these times especially. Our special time. Now come with me to a place where dreams inflict their logic on """""reality""""".

difference in size -- albeit there is some -- is not the fascinating thing definition is everything some so utterly lack definition that it is hard to distinguish baby clitty from the surrounding ill-defined lumps of flesh in which it is ensconced others are well defined it clearly is the tip of a little penis just as the embryologists inform us yours was in the middle definition but more like a pearl *half-hidden and yet beautiful half-hidden and yet beautiful half-hidden and yet beautiful* the war is over you are as free as the wind sweet freedom whispered in my ear someone saved my life tonight freedom's just another word for nothing left to lose (you wouldn't remember -- or appreciate? -- Janis Joplin) and most of all Philadelphia freedom took me knee-high to a man ----- ----- freedom the Godhead of God and the source of evil both at once another time Dawn did me good she started off lightly built up she was giving it all her might towards the end and with concentration on just one spot while I was face down my hands were tied tied behind my back when I put my ass up my chin was right on the pillow I put my ass up, hungrily, as you used to say, and defiantly daring her, with my defiant ass motions, to belt me even harder I really got into it really into it what I think I now want is to be so completely tied that I really would be <u>powerless</u> and at the mercy of my belter/whipper everything at her discretion over the borderline way way beyond the initial shock and pain to a place *{{khora}}* where each additional <u>Crack</u> brought joy I'm with you Johnny K then to be so trained that the same could happen without my being tied I would be freely cooperating in and endorsing my own beating yes, I said beating then to kneel in front of her and do whatever she commanded eating shit if that was her desire the masochistic turn in my sexuality and your leaving me for later for now just the details for, surely, in things of this nature, God is in the details or God is not at all to <u>find</u> God in all things that is the secret Luscious was the girl in Philly black she used a rope whip Philly of the Thanksgiving trip I wasn't tied she hit me so hard that I had to jump we both burst out laughing at the overall ludicrousness of the situation wanting desperately to be hit and beaten and wanting desperately not to be hit and beaten she was good and then beautiful Laura doing the dripping candle wax bit all over the front of my body including every square centimeter -- tip-opening, front, tender back -- of my hardened dick that's when a sad song says so much OK, bitch would it be better if I beat it out of you? remember those fantasies -- which scared the hell out of both of us -- about wickedly, repeatedly, and viciously punching the stomach of some slut? eros did get a little too dark then like when I slapped your face while making love so instead of getting beat up just listen to Bob Dylan the yup-yups of the eighties think that music in the sixties was born with the Beatles by no stretch of the imagination how does it <u>FEEL</u> how does it <u>FEEEL</u> to be on your own like a rolling stone go get that record and listen not just the words listen the rage I always identified with his rage the usual comfort of the past being the past was denied to me because of your lie even after you left and it became time to put the past behind me it was impossible was always there like banquo's ghost there is still rage but it ebbs and it has been ebbing for some time now and yes, some day I will know that there is nothing to forgive just as you will know, some day, that there is nothing to forgive for the way I treated you during those two and one-half years persevere we come near the end this masochism of mine I must work it through I need distance from you in order to get a handle on it it was there already the Spring semester of 86 remember the ass probing and finger fuckings you would administer to my "hungry" ass with the Elton John tape on so as not to disturb our nosey fellow tenant upstairs do you remember the hard spankings you administered while doing this to my hungry cheeks? how about the verbal humiliations of those sessions but then, around Easter-time, it ceased ----- ----- there was also some evident masochism in the way, morning after glorious morning, I would subject my nipples to your lovely-but-intense way of squeezing, twisting, stretching and pulling them while you told some variation of the big-breasted slut who was getting abused to incredible dimensions I was always that slut those morning sessions are among the happiest memories I have of us together but the dike broke after you left me I had been conditioned and prepared for what is going on now by listening for some two years to your crazed manic semi-ironic voice as it described being on the edge of orgasm and then that Doppler-like cry/shout/wail as you went over the edge Oh, O!, look at me now!!!! your eyes would be wide open dark pupils expanding over your green-blue irises and seeing nothing I'm going!!!!!!!! e e e eeeeeeeEEEEEEEEEEEEHHHHHHHHHHHhhhhhhhh h h h it seemed so much better than my orgasms orgasm envy!!!!---------- so this masochism of mine first and foremost it is the male in me bowing down and adoring the unbridled nature of female sexuality you gave me the wisdom of Tiresias I thank you for giving me knowledge of this before you were Eurydice you were Eve I thank you for this knowledge and yes it was masochism -- and you know it -- which brought you your best and most haunting orgasms so I -- who had <u>become</u> E -- eroticized pain pain as a sexual stimulant you and I, my love, know this more than any other couple we are special but there's more Qui sait? one was speaking of masochism, n'est-ce pas Derrida does a nice number on the "pas" of "ne---pas" the subtleties of male masochism more fundamental than the connection between female sexuality and masochism already unpacked by the Freudian text the ever-wanting-never-having veneer which maya-like maia!!-like appears to define the female <u>does in-deed</u> very subtlely define the male! a thirst for which there is no satisfaction Mick Jagger was there already in his own way a new chapter in psycho-analytic theory but a very very old chapter in life Oh God!!!!!! I can actually <u>feel</u> it now the permutations of humiliation more! please more the Jesus connection *{{{my God! is nothing sacred? that's just the point! nothing <u>is</u> sacred the crack! it's always slipping slipping into the crack <u>CRACK!</u> <u>CRACK!</u> <u>CRACK!!</u> please more nothing is sacred and everything is sacred do you yet understand are you running with me Jesus???? <u>CRACK!!!!</u> <u>CRACK!!!!</u> <u>CRACK!!!!</u> <u>CRACK!!!!</u> without surcease Sweet Jesus I'm <u>Coming!</u> coming home to you }}* never forget that Yehoshua was a man with balls and a dick I betcha it was an A- even without grade inflation probably had a nice tush and, of course, an asshole the passion play it was the narrative of his passion which held the early community of his followers -- all Jewish and not even the hint of a new religion -- together in Jerusalem this was powerful stuff some twenty or thirty years ago the most powerful liturgy in the Church centered around the stations of the Cross along with Holy Thursday and Good Friday <u>Good</u> Friday always the happy Fall always the necessity (working through freedom) of the broken vessels for another time Jesus suffers and Mary -- the Mother; miraculously a virgin (and therefore not having betrayed Yehoshua) -- vicariously suffers for the Church a virgin but what about for Yehoshua himself? did someone whisper that it was a Roman soldier? our little Jesus (named after Joshua the soldier/hero of the Jews) had quite a psychic burden to deal with and who was that other Mary who intersected so often in his life? did someone mention that she was a whore? *--- and many women were there, watching from a distance, the same women who had followed Jesus from Galilee and looked after him. ---* seems we need to know a lot more about this Yehoshua from Galilee a lot more crowning with thorns hmmmm <u>nailing</u> to the cross hmmmmmmm hmmmmmmmmm the scourging at the pillar these were Romans, my friend capable of at least as much cruelty as the cruelest of Nazis you don't think that the Romans were into teaching the population a lesson by leaving a polite covering for the tush and the dick, do you? the scourging at the pillar they probably did get a few shots on his dick powerful stuff resonates deeper than female masochism is male masochism a new chapter in Freudian analysis the scourging at the pillar HMMMMMMMMMMMMMMMM! then as well as now one needed an offsetting principle lest the passion of the passion play go too far the resurrection of the body Paul and his hokum about victory over death but the subterranean message stayed with Christianity throughout its history hmmmmm! Manic tears of joy John Lennon's Christmas song tears of joy are more difficult to handle than tears of melancholy manic Bing's white Christmas I cede to Jack I claim as my own the blue Christmas of Elvis to the baby I give Lennon's Christmas song *{{{{{ did Elvis really sleep with his mother did the mob take out Monroe with a suppository of barbituates for those who have the eyes to hear and the ears to see only a few know how to discriminate the """""truth""""" from the trash ho-hum and while we're at it maybe the more nuanced and true way of putting it is this that the news of Dion's assassination reached him while i.e., during i.e, not after he was writing Timaeus that from about 48-49 right on through the end of the dialogue and right on through the opening of Critias was done in a strange manic surge which often precedes a bout of deep depression food for thought }}}}}* the song of hope the war is over if you want it we're running the last lap now but I'd rather be lapping your moist, --- dripping wet!!! --- clit right now your legs straddling my face my tongue a slave to your whim your tongue telling me just how good it is right there on the edge Oh GOD!!!! how you could keep it on the edge for so long so fucking long and so fucking good then that (now) haunting and ever so needful cry trailing off with a doppler-like effect and affect Oh God did I envy your way of orgasm indeed, more and more, as you know, I tried to imitate you fuck the dick as an instrument of penetration so babyish and power-oriented I came to treat it *{I came to treat it!!!!! Listen!}* more and more as a big clit to be manually stimulated (stimulation, more and more by the way, sustained and increased by pain) learning to stay on the edge longer that's where I go crazy it's delirious there pure oscillating need and darkly "weird" the root of all mania then coming still I have the intimation that the spurting coming of the male -- while visually exciting -- is not quite the same as the presumably exquisite and terribly needful spasm of the clitty please, E, let me lick you out I'll do anything for you anything lick out your ass as well but please, please, let me lick your wet twat for as long as you like for ever turn the radio up, I go crazy a summer full moon a blue moon maybe they play that song at aerobics as well some day I'll tell you of all my associations with Hey Jude my favorite of all time in any case listen to the manic way in which the song ends I figure that John Lennon was about two years away from AA when he took the hit in his heart all those years ago he was lucky enough not to see what the eighties would do to the sixties sour grapes, of course Elvis was too melancholic to get help more die of heartbreak I guess that's why they call it the blues rolling like thunder under the covers *---I simply loved you more than I loved life itself* the sin many lovers are wont to commit I did with you never again let there be love once more!!!!!! but in love choose life in the mean time some expiation and purgation is appropriate are you clever enough to hear me, sweet one? you know and I know it doesn't matter look into a child's wide eyes some day look, as you must each day, into the baby's beautiful eyes don't get me wrong I have huge respect for dick, clit, twat, ass questions the New Year's Eve version of dick and orifice (along with your active kissing that night) put me into the hospital in Philly the meaning of all meaning is cunt power we are prisoners of Eros for sure you and I a bit more than others but clits and dicks and marvelous orgasms are just the tools of eros they trick us into doing the work of eros Freud knew life is so much more infinitely fertile and interesting than the thrust of Kevin's dick and the position of E's obscenely open asshole all is forgiven there is nothing to forgive please help me, E I love you know this for all of us, for you, for me and for God Choose life! for God's sake choose life! choose life!

...

... ... Near the moment of my climax the crazy number "e" exploded into my mind and completely displaced my anticipation of coming. It was orgasm without orgasm. Pleasure without pleasure. For an instant (eksaiphnes) it was love without death. Release was all bonus and incidental. A hint. My meaning will become -- come-to-be -- clear.

...

*****

+++++

obiter dicta

The apogee of the Stagirite. --- *a this in a this* --- ((Confer De Anima III-4 at 429b between 10 and 15.)) The formal principle of individuation animating the material principle of individuation. Just because some medieval Aristotlelians will stumble over this and not quite get it right does not mean at all that Aristotle himself stumbled.

It's all over the text of the Metaphysics if you know how to understand what Aristotle is saying about sensible ousia and his idiosyncratic meaning of "form" when it comes to sensible ousia. ((E.g., the last meaning of ousia, given in V-8; The joining of hupokeimenon and form -- (i.e., what will turn out to be an idiosyncratic meaning of "form") -- as a third and "most perplexing" meaning of sensible ousia which is implied at the end of VII-3; the formal principle of sensible ousia as "something other" and as principle rather than element of sensible ousia in VII-17; the adjudication of knowledge questions concerning senible ousia at the end of XIII-10.)). It's all over the place.

Just how idiosyncratic? It is only in De Anima (III-5) that we find out. Aristotle's grand invention. *Nous Poietikas* That which causes what is potentially intelligible to be actually known. This is the apogee of the Stagirite. The final inference drawn from Aristotle's great alternative to Plato. With Plato there is the break from aisthesis and all which follows therefrom. With Aristotle there is no break from aisthesis. There is abstraction, but no break from aisthesis.

Of course this invention of Aristotle brings with it the raw material from which "the fetish" will emerge with all of the horrible consequences thereof.

And what about Plato's move? The break from aisthesis. That is what this book is all about. Stay tuned.

52.
Note on Kristeva's *Life and Death of Speech.*

Confer *Life and Death of Speech* contained in Black Sun; Depression and Melancholia. (Translated by Leon Roudiez; Columbia University Press, New York, 1989. Pages 31-68. Hereafter: Black.)

a). For Kristeva the "normal" subject deals with loss through the process which Freud called "negation" (Verneinung) of the loss. The melancholic subject remains more true to the loss as a loss through a "denial/disavowal" (Verleugnung) of the "negation." To be sure Kristeva tends to underline the symptomotology of such a condition as pathology before she goes on to make her various and sundry analyses concerning the connection between the melancholic disposition and literary/artistic creation. In contrast, this book which you are now reading glosses over the pathological symptomotolgy of "melancholia" in order to concentrate on the melancholic disposition (which disposition ought not at all be conflated with simply "being serious") as the disposition which is pre-requisite to living a life in "good faith." Even so both Kristeva and the writer of this book which you are now reading recognize in the melancholic disposition a fidelity to loss as loss.

Confer Black, page 43.

b). For Kristeva "loss" is basically a pre-Oeidpal loss of "Mommy" although she -- Kristeva -- is more sensitive than most to the connection between this "loss" and the "loss" occaisioned by the Oedipal discovery -- by both little girls and little boys -- that "Mommy" is castrated.

c). Kristeva and the writer of this book which you are now reading are both in agreement that melancholy entails a remaining faithful to "loss" although in this book -- which in this respect is more Freudian than Kristevanesque -- one is quite insistent that the "loss" occaisioned by the Oedipal castration complex -- ((there being, of course, male and female versions of the castration complex following upon the discovery of the counter-facutal "fact" that Mommy is castrated)) -- is the primary "loss" which retroactively colors and permeates the pre-Oedipal "loss" of "Mommy" and, correlatively, retroactively renders the pre-Oedipal loss deeply ambiguous. However, in Kristeva's terminological logistics, this remaining faithful to "loss" on the part of the melancholic subject is called a "disavowal of 'negation'" whereas in the terminological logistics of the book you are presently reading the failure to remain faithful to "loss" is called, perjoratively, "disavowal." The perceptive reader, however, will have thought past terminological appearances and such a perceptive reader will have understood that -- appearances of terminology notwithstanding -- both *Life and Death of Speech* as well as *Thinking Psycho-Analytically* are in agreement in recognizing the fidelity to "loss" characteristic of melancholy.

Confer New, pages 114-115. Also, Outline, pages 46-51.

d). Kristeva, particularly in this *Life and Death of Speech*, still finds herself caught up in that Lacanian heritage whereby her most fertile ability to *think psycho-analytically* is constantly self-subverted by understanding psychic states primarily as linguistic/signifying states or as that which allow for as well as interfere with a linguistic/signifying state. *Thinking Psycho-analytically* -- while often inspired by Kristeva and, less often, by Lacan -- engages a psychic state such as "melancholia" with a rather different agendum than the linguistic/signifying agendum of Lacan which Lacanian agendum is not always absent from the works of Kristeva (even the ones which were produced after Powers of Horror). Thus, and accordingly, this fidelity to loss on the part of the melancholic subject recognized through different terminological strategies in both *Life and Death of Speech* and *Thinking Psychoanalytically*, ends up servicing significanlty differing agenda.

53.
To be noted: the inability of this whole lot of Derrideans -- including Derrida himself -- to understand that there is an irreducible duality or dualism in the very make-up of things and their correlative inability to understand that the very "thing" with which they are concerned -- (i.e., "differance" or any of the other hundred-thousand words/concepts which are not words/concepts which they so charmingly use synonomously with "differance") -- is a function of this duality/dualism. They are all so hyper-sophisticated relative to what they call the "onto-theo-logical" underpinnings of duality in the "Tradition" --(i.e., "Tradition" as they appropriate it) -- that they blind themselves to the very possibility of ever seeing what duality is all about. They have thrown the baby -- (i.e., that duality without which "there is" no "differance") -- with the polluted bath water -- (i.e., the hundred-thousand dualistic pairings which emerge from "onto-theo-logy" in its flight from difference). They got so good -- so cleverly sophisticated -- at "deconstructing"" these dualistic pairings that they drifted, unconsciously, into the very heart of thoughtlessness. They, of all people, end up in a "flight from """differance""" ". How strange!!!

54.
It can be noted briefly here that the Derridean text, for all of its subtlety, generally follows the Tradition in a failure to understand what this book refers to as "ontological dualism."

55.
It seems that Frere Jacques' courting of the Platonic text will have always suffered from a fatal flaw: Martin Heidegger. In every conceivable way Frere Jacques is more nuanced, thorough, subtle and substantial than Marty both in his overall "re-covery" of the "Tradition" and especially in his "re-covery" of the Platonic text. Indeed, Frere Jacques is exceptionally nuanced, thorough, subtle and substantial in his "re-covery" of the Heideggerian text as has been recently demonstrated yet again with his 1987 Geist book on Heidegger and also as well in the last few pages of "Comment ne pas Parler" in which he is exquisitely nuanced in saying what it would mean to speak of a "Heideggerian Theology." Even so. Derrida -- here following Marty -- cannot free himself from the Heideggerian perception that the fateful "turn" in Western Metaphysics occurs with Plato. Derrida -- again following Marty -- exhibits no evidence of having understood that "the Tradition" is inaugurated with Aristotle and that Plato -- far from being the pivotal nodal point by which the "Tradition" is inaugurated -- stands outside the "Tradition" and remains untouched by any analysis -- "deconstructive" or otherwise -- of the "Tradition" in so far as such an analysis counts the Platonic text as inaugurating "The Tradition." To be sure, by 1987 in "Comment ne pas Parler" Derrida takes Marty to task for apparently not even having seen the connection between Plato's "khorismos" teaching and the "khora" teaching from Timaeus. This is an advance on the part of Frere Jacques. Yet the very existence of "Comment ne pas Parler" is predicated on the assumption that the Neo-Platonic [sic!!!] musings of a Pseudo-Dionysius are even in the same kind of genus as the Timaeic meditation on "khora". Thus even in "Comment ne pas Parler" Frere Jacques evidences no appreciation of how -- as a first approximation -- *very radically different* is the kind

of thing which Plato is doing from anything in the "Tradition" ("Neo-Platonism" [sic!!!] most definitely therein included).

Confer Of Spirit: Heidegger and the Question (translated by Geoffrey Bennington and Rachel Bowlby; Universit of Chicago, 1989; hereafter: Spirit) and also confer Derrida's multiple references to Heidegger in *Comment*, especially the last eleven pages in which Derrida so very carefully and thoughtfully unpacks what it would mean to speak of anything like a Heideggerian "Theology."

Confer the argumentation in *Comment*, page 585.

56.
It is Derrida, of course, who notices what Heidegger did not even notice: that for Nietzsche "truth" becomes a woman. Let it pass, for now, whether Derrida's remarks on the Nietzschean passages which he cites are far too generous to the still misogynistic-but-still-not-yet-"mis-ogynistic" flavor of the Nietzschean text. It is enough to note that Frere Jacques is attuned to the womanly "nature" of """"""truth"""""". ((And let his -- Derrida's -- quarrel with the "other" Jacques on the womanly "nature" of """"""truth"""""" be reserved for another sitting.)) But even Frere Jacques does not marry """"""truth"""""".

Nietzsche and the account of "truth" as a woman is, effectively, the concern of Derrida in Spurs Nietzsche's Styles. (Translated by Barbara Harlow; University of Chicago Press, 1979. Hereafter: Spurs.) One might especially confer pages 47-123.

Despite this attempt on the part of Derrida to hyperbolize Nietzsche's scattered remarks about the womanly character of "truth" into a major Nietzschean theme, it still remains the case that Nietzsche remains misogynistic without achieving any significant insight into what this book calls "mis-ogyny". Derrida commenting on Nietzsche on this topic tells us far more about Derrida than it does about Nietzsche.

In this matter concerning the womanly character of "truth" the reader is advised to withold judgment until reading those entries which, in a previous incarnation of the book, constituted Part IV. It will be some time yet.

*****

In this book "mis-ogyny" functions as something of a neo-logism and refers jointly to the two versions, male and female, of the castration complex. It is argued that "mis-ogyny" in this sense is the animating nodal point which makes the human species so noteworthy. It is taken for granted that misogyny -- in the clinically pathological sense and in its wider current usage as well -- is deriviative from "mis-ogyny." Yet it is also argued that misogyny -- in its clinically pathological sense and in its wider current usage as well -- is not the only possible outcome of "mis-ogyny" in the sense of that neo-logism as it is used in this book. Quite to the contrary.

57.
She -- Kristeva -- exhibits no understanding at all of the eclipse of Platonic dualism -- a dualism of first principles -- by Aristotelian monotheism which created the stage in which the puerile teaching of "agage" could come to be so persuasive as it got instantiated overtly and covertly in Western metaphysics.

The reference here is to Kristeva's Chapter on "agape", *God is Love*, contained in Tales of Love. Translated by Leon Roudiez; Columbia University Press, 1987. Pages 137-150. [Hereafter: Tales.]

58.
Sigismund: But how do we get it right relative to shame?

Eurydice: First of all with honesty. Particularly with regard to our sexuality. Most of this work has been accomplished through Shekhinah and the Madonna version of the book which preceded Shekhinah.

Secondly, by avoiding the temptation to short-circuit this honesty -- (i.e. this means that me must submit without reservation to the Goddess of Truth) -- by thoughtlessly seeking a cowardly security in paradigms of """morality""" (whether based on ""religion"" or not) which have clearly failed in their function -- i.e., their function being the control of violence and aggression. Indeed, adherence to these "accepted" paradigms of """morality""" is now aggravating the situation, as is evident for those who can really hear and see what is going on in that century which they refer to as the "twentieth."

59.
Bappy: Isn't he doing a bit of "short-circuiting" himself, here?

Dewchee: Yes. We ought to help him out. As Freud already understood "up there" "religions" are mass delusions which partially did perform their function but certainly no longer can perform their function. Indeed organized "religions" now make matters worse.

Bappy: So what is one to do? Just forget about "God"?

Dewchee: Of course not, Silly. Nor could one do so even if one tried to.

Bappy: So what is to be done? What happens to mass delusion and its energy -- as well as the power of these various mass delusions to "bind" energy -- when mass delusion is exposed not only as a delusion but, more importantly, a delusion which no longer even performs the function for which it was invented (unconsciously in the psycho-social evolution of our species)?

Dewchee: Good question. And, at all costs, we must steer our course between Scylla and Charybdis.

Bappy: What do you mean, Dewchee?

Dewchee: On the one hand, we must not -- as Freud did "up there" -- throw the baby out with the polluted bath water. We are called to pay homage to the sacred. We are called to pay homage to Shekhinah. On the other hand we must avoid drowning in the polluted bath water which will happen if we follow the path of Jung and a hundred-thousand others thoughtless jerks in getting too comfortable with the "organized mass delusions" which have obtained hitherto.

Bappy: How shall we do this? How shall we steer our course between Scylla and Charybdis?

Dewchee: With Andreia.

Bappy: What does that mean?

Dewchee: Servicing Shekhinah does and will require the "explorers" to find ways more fundamental than "religion" to stay true to <u>that</u> psychosis without which "there is" no truth.

Bappy: I sense what you are saying. You speak of that counter-factual deception which is getting called, in this book of "sentences", "mis-ogyny." You speak of that nexus which is the ur-spring of "desire" in the Lacanian sense.

Dewchee: That is correct. I speak, to be more precise, about fidelity to that root deception without deflecting from it or disavowing it.

Bappy: And yet I see a problem.

Dewchee: Indeed, there are many. But speak your mind.

Bappy: Now that one is aware of this root counter-factual "fact" <u>AS</u> counter-factual what will become of the counter-factual "fact"?

Dewchee: For the child the counter-factual "fact" is just a fact and it will always be the case that the child is father to the man. Yet it is true that the evolution of consciousness has brought about that strange and paradoxical condition in which the root counter-facutal "fact" comes to be understood -- by the suave and sophisticated of the species -- <u>AS</u> counter-factual. But what follows from this is not at all the ever so rational program of corrective education now envisioned by the suave and sophisticated.

Bappy: Then what <u>does</u> follow from this emerging and ever more universal condition by which the counter-factual "fact" is recognized <u>AS</u> counter-factual?

Dewchee: *Dream delivers us unto dream and there is no end to allusion.*

Bappy: As ususal you taken quantum leaps just when I am least prepared for them. Can you make yourself clearer?

Dewchee: Not now. But you are advised to read on and dream on. For now let it simply be said that we enter into a time of "history" -- we have been in it already for some time now -- when our dreams (which have always included demonic nightmares) will be recognized as "more real" than "reality." It is a strange time which will require courage.

Bappy: Hmmmmmmm. This business about psychosis is really strange. It's as though religion was just a preparation; a kind of practice training for the "brain" of the species.

Dewchee: You are beginning to understand. Let us remember the phrase of our old friend.

Bappy: I think I remember that to which you allude.

Dewchee: Then speak it.

Bappy: *The other: creating as well as discovery.*

Dewchee: Very good, Bappy. Now you may rest.

Bappy: Just brush my cheek before you leave me.

60.
Bappy: It's beginning to come back to me.

Dewchee: If so, you are beginning to remember that death is God's hint about humiliation. Humiliation is inevitable. What counts is how we integrate humiliation into our lives for the sake of the good.

Bappy: You mean we -- both males and females -- must seek to eroticize it. We must seek out the condition of pure oscillating need and integrate it into our sexual strategies. All of this for the sake of the good. This is your meaning, is it not?

Dewchee: Yes. Precisely. And if you are beginning to remember all of this you are also beginning to remember the most important thing of all.

Bappy: Yes I do remember. The vision of the alternative is what gave us those terrible nightmares when we woke up retching with the dry heaves: Auschwitz as a global destiny. It makes me so afraid!!!!

Dewchee: But fear -- yes fear of our God Shekhinah -- is the beginning of wisdom. We must be courageous.

Bappy: What is the crystallizing key to your scenario of eroticization for the good?

Dewchee: You will remember this as well. Shame. Embracing the shameless shame of the Shekhinah and becoming the shame of the Shekhinah. Mutually imposed and mutually shared. Shame -- when it comes through eroticism -- is both the most secret and most glorious name of the good.

Bappy: I do begin to remember. One more thing. Why is this alternative -- the tilt towards sex and eroticization which is in the service of the good -- also called melancholic? Is there no joy there?

Dewchee: Of course there is joy there. Jouissance. The very greatest and most ecstatic of joy. But in the very temple of delight melancholia reigns and must reign.

Bappy: Why? And wouldn't that imply that melancholia is the good?

Dewchee: It is. And it must be. Beauty must die for the sake of the good. The draw -- the attraction -- OF equilibrium requires death. This is sad and this is good. Yet because of death there is renewal.

Bappy. Renewal. Dionysian or Christo-centric?

Dewchee: Neither. Both models suffer from an implied monism/monotheism. Rather, what I speak of is the renewal of ur-other/othering through its other. This renewal is "the hegemony of difference" which no longer is a hegemony of power.

61.
Bappy: And now, what is the alternative to this erotic scenario of the good?

Dewchee: Evil. Reminding ourselves, all the while and as we have so often noted, that "good" and "evil" are not first principles of the mixture but rather come to be IN the mixture.

Bappy: I hope there is no need to remind our readers of that well-established point of so many previous conversations. But tell me this: just what is this "evil" you speak of?

Dewchee: Auschwitz now become a global destiny.

Bappy: And how might that come about?

Dewchee: All too simply and all too banally. Technology and the receding of work/labor as the vehicle by which to slurp up our "instinct"/drive energy has created a terrible and most dangerous vacuum. If we do not courageously embrace the erotic alternative we shall simply drift into Auschwitz as a global destiny. We will either change our libidinal economy -- as suggested, by implication, by Freud at the very end of Civilization and its Discontents -- or drift into the retching alternative of Auschwitz as a global destiny. The frightening thing is how banal this drift can be. It is already going on -- (note, for example, the increase in violence, torture, and brutality which spreads throughout the globe not only in wartime but in "peace"-time as well) -- which each year takes hold in our communal life, often with the overt sanction of governments.

Confer the ending of Civ, page 104:

> *And now it is to be expected that the other of the two 'Heavenly Powers', eternal Eros, will make an effort to assert himself in the struggle with his equally important adversary.*

Bappy: Is this due to the still pervasive patterns of male dominance which even now infest all our social institutions?

Dewchee: Yes. Partly. But the pervasiveness of male dominance is aided and abetted by something even more subtle.

Bappy: What is that?

Dewchee: An unwillingness to really examine our libidinal economy, now that technology no longer allows for the slurping up of our instinct/drive energy through labor/work. This unwillingness takes the form here -- and on the "right", so to speak -- of thoughtless refuge in the old (and no longer feasible) patterns of guilt and libidinal regulation which find support in and through the religions of mankind. There -- and on the "left", so to speak, including some forms of Feminism -- this new version of "flight from libido" takes the form of an oh-so-secular (but secretly still religious and unconsciously in the pattern of male dominance) regulation of social arrangements in the service of the idol of propriety. This unwillingness allows shame -- which is the key -- to drift into those deep crevices of the psyche where it marinates in the wrong fashion and comes forth in the joint forms of institutionalized patterns of violence and of individual patterns of violent crime. In the face of all of this unwillingness to really examine our libidinal economy, young people drift into frightening patterns of promiscuous sex and random violence in which -- if one can read the signs of the times -- violence prevails over eroticism since violence, ultimately, is easier than eroticism.

Bappy: This is so frightening. The banal victory goes to violence by virtue of inertia.

Dewchee: Yes exactly. The unbounded demonic -- which is cousin to yet opposite from the "eu-daimon" of mutual eroticism -- makes its appearance in our time with the dissemination of technology. The checking of the unbounded demonic -- the failure to do which would be the failure of God as well as our failure -- does not at all entail the flight from or denial of the demonic. The demonic must be incorporated -- quite literally -- and pressed into the service of the good. The good cannot be at all unless it is demonic. But the unbounded demonic can obtain without the good coming to be. The unbounded demonic renders the draw -- the attraction -- of equilibrium for naught in an orgy of exhaustion which is truly entropic. It results in the very death of death itself closing off the possibility for renewal and creation. Avoiding this alternative of unbounded horror will require both courage and the ability to wean ourselves from simplistic accounts of "good" and "evil." (*) It will not be easy. Indeed, all of this is the very essence, so to speak, of "dis-ease" -- i.e., the analog of "mis-ogyny" so that "disease" -- i.e., the analog of misogyny -- (which would, in its unbounded form, result in the very death of death) will not prevail.

*. {{{These simplistic accounts include Nietzsche's mode of avoidance which goes by the name " ""beyond"" good and evil". His avoidance simply begs the question of what the "good" "would" be by, allegedly, moving "beyond" what cannot be "beyonded", so to speak.}}}

Bappy: It was said long ago: *khalapa ta kala*. I love your stories so much. I am tired now. I must go to sleep. Just brush my cheek before you leave me. I love you, Dewchee.

Dewchee: And I love you, Bappy. Sleep tight. Don't let the bed bugs bite.

62.
When those marvelously random workings of natural selection {{Shekhinah, please note, not only works through chance/tukhe but is chance/tukhe. Does your conceptual imagination have the ability to understand the teleology which is not one?}} produced the human {{{{{and let us never forget that HUM-an and HUM-iliation -- there being no meaningful humility which does not entail humiliation -- are linked inevitably and forever beyond our power to control}}}}} "XX"/"XY" version of sexual differentiation, more was at issue than reproduction. {{{Of course the rubric "XX"/"XY" is a rubric which -- in time -- will be shown to have contained more subtlety than is now presently understood.}} Indeed, it took the technologization of reproduction before the hidden genius of "XX" and "XY" (human version) could show itself. The "XY" variation of "XX" has a function which precedes and transcends at once its reproductive function. The "XY" variation in the "matrix" "XX" -- this variation being engineered by, in, and through "XX" -- deepens the "XX" experience of itself. Only now does one begin to appreciate the hidden genius of this teleology which is not one: The lesbian appropriation of the de-centered and "post-phallo-cratic" phallus. The libidinal permutations of this lesbian appropriation of the "post-phallo-cratric" phallus are without finality. Further, these libidinal permutations can both deepen the lesbian bond and also allow men to enter into a lesbianesque play of and between the female as object choice and the female as that with which one identifies. Through this truly revolutionary process of becoming thoroughly sexualized male libidinal economy can come to transform the male proclivity towards violence into erotic and "post-phallo-cratic" expression.

{{{{{Even today it is still not generally understood that chance (tukhe) and design are not antinomies.}}}}}

63.
Non: So will males just disappear? After all, "XX", is, so to speak, the "default-value" of the whole system and "XY" is the variation which, although necessary for some time now, has evolved into a no-longer-necessary variation which, in addition, has become an aberration which is harmful to the well-being of the whole.

Sic: How interesting! To be sure there will still have to be some fine-tuning of the technology of reproduction before such a proposal could be implemented. And in any case the aberrancy of males will be purged in the future matriarchal patterns of society-(re)formation as females come to control the rule of Law. But the answer is no. On "metaphysical" grounds in a manner of speaking although those "metaphysical" grounds are actually played out in psycho-social evolution. The play of the human version of sexual differentiation has whys and wherefores other than reproduction. Indeed, the play only now begins. The whys and wherefores of Shekhinah constitute a matrix without finality.

Non: Can you give any hints?

Sic: Two things come quickly to mind.

Non: Yes?

Sic: The very primacy of lesbian sexuality requires the continuing presence of and interference from the phallus, even if now radically de-centered and taking on these "post-phallo-cratic" functions.

In this book it is argued that lesbian sexuality is best suited for the fulfillment of "desire" as "desire" is used in this book.

Non: Why is that?

Sic: The animating force of lesbian sexuality -- as with all forms of human sexuality -- is that crazy, psychotic, and counter-factual perception in the part of little boys <u>and</u> little girls (which is mostly rendered unconscious and remains mostly unconscious/preconscious) -- that Mommy is castrated. It is this species specific perception which constitutes the "between" in terms of which "there is" "culture" and "nature" at all. Of course it is predictable that a hundred-thousand ideologically oriented Feminists will -- irony noted -- substantiate the point by vehemently denying it and/or satirizing what they deem to be the presumed "phallo-cratic" orientation of such a statement. They belong to a generation of Feminists who do not yet realize that "Patriarchy" is <u>already</u> ancient history. They are fighting the wrong war.

{{{To be sure, the very point of <u>Shekhinah</u> was that the dying of Patriarchy brings with it the possibility of a reactive violence which would -- should such occur -- turn the Holocaust into the ultimate prophetic sign of signs. But "denial" -- I speak here of "denial" of the reality of that whole castration motif in the male <u>and</u> female perceptions of female genitalia -- has never been a life-sustaining strategy. ((It is conceivable, then, that the dying of Patriarchy might bring with it the self-destruction of the species in an orgy of masculine violence. The transition to matriarchy will occur with Odysseus-like cunning or it will not occur at all. Either way, Patriarchy is ancient history.)) }}}

Non: Well, no-one in this book has ever been cautious relative to the "reception" it may have in some circles. Let us ignore the hundred-thousand, then. They will be replaced by a generation of Feminists who no longer look over their shoulders worried that they will be accused of "sleeping with the enemy", so to speak. Is it your point, then, that the very thriving of lesbian sexuality requires the continuing presence of and interference from "the phallus" in order to obtain? That would constitute a curious and rather tortured "teleology" in these matters if I dare to use such a thoroughly discredited word.

Sic: Let the dirty word -- teleology -- be spoken and let the reader go to Shekhinah to understand how tortured teleology (i.e., the teleology which is not one) works.

Non: You mentioned a second hint on these matters.

Sic: Yes. Again, one must refer to the hidden genius of the human "XX"/"XY" variation in the constellation of sexual differentiation (using, of course, this biological rubric as a kind of convenience and realizing that this rubric will have been shown, in time, to have contained subtleties not yet scientifically understood). And, again, one must repeat that this hidden genius could not fully show itself until the reproductive function of the "XY" variation of "XX" had been superseded by technology.

Non: Please inform us of this hidden genius.

Sic: It has shown itself already. The genius of the human "XX"/"XY" version within the larger constellation of sexual differentiation -- ((And, as often noted, the more specific "genetic" coding which constitutes the hitherto specifically human instantiation of this version will most likely be found to have had revealing and surprising subtleties about it.)) -- is to have produced a species which is phylogenically equipped to produce members subject to the most radical ontogenic variation (which coalesces into multiple and ever-shifting patterns of what is called "psycho-social" evolution) and still survive as a species even as its susceptibility to ontogenic variation, via the technological offshoot of its psycho-social evolution, affects the parameters of its own phylogeny. This incredible susceptibility for ontogenic variation is the very glory and continuing promise of our species. It must be presumed that this incredible susceptibility for ontogenic variation -- within the species -- will achieve forms hitherto unsuspected as the reproductive function of "XY" is sublated by technology. The human "XX"/"XY" version of the larger constellation of sexual differentiation is now positioned to instantiate the most wondrous -- alchemical, so to speak -- transformations. We have really only just begun.

Non: Then Eros really does live as Shekhinah.

Sic: Yes.

64.
More significantly, the revelation/dissemination of the content of the unconscious brings about a real change in both libidinal and aggressive economy.

65.
Sublimation comes to be, then, a continual "play" which repeatedly and consciously re-energizes itself as a process by going back to that complex and bi-sexual nexus of multiple repressions to which it -- the process of sublimation -- owes its origin.

66.
"Mis-ogyny"-having-become-conscious plays itself out quite differently from "mis-ogyny"-as-that-which-requires-continual-repression.

67.
"Mis-ogyny"-having-become-conscious becomes that transformation called "Androgyny."

"Androgyny", as the term is used in this book of "sentences", names that future re-alignment, for our species, of libidinal economy which re-alignment will be basically matriarchal in character and in which sexual differentiation remains quite robust -- psychologically and physiologically -- although having a "different" function. "Androgyny", in some popular usages of the term (which popular usuages are not operative in this book of "sentences"), can also mean the condition in which sexual difference fades away or disappears. It is to be noted in passing that Irigaray in distancing herself from "androgyny" uses, in fact, this popular (i.e., difference-fleeing) notion of "androgyny."

Prior to the forming of *Thinking Psycho-analytically* there were several productions of manuscripts entitled <u>Sentences</u> up thorugh <u>Sentences-IV</u>. These "sentence" manuscripts can be considered as elder siblings to *Thinking Psycho-analytically*. *Thinking Psycho-analytically* is very much directly affected by her elder siblings.

68.
To be noted: misogyny, in the clinically pathological sense which is so often on people's minds these days, requires, as its pre-condition, the repression -- by males and females alike -- of "mis-ogyny." "Mis-ogyny"-having-become-conscious-of-itself is the condition by which misogyny, in the clinically pathological sense, comes to disappear.

69.
But even -- indeed especially -- with Androgyny the play of difference remains. The not-being-present (which <u>is</u> the unconscious) becomes and is transformed into the continual project of <u>not</u>-being what one is and, at once, becoming what one is not as the very condition of being at all. Hypothesis # 5 becomes the very destiny of what it means to be human. *{{{This would mean -- unbeknownst to Sartre -- that it is not at all a matter of being Sartrean (i.e., in the sense of* pour soi *structure)* <u>or</u> Freudian (i.e., in the sense of his topographical alignment of the psyche) but rather of being and becoming both. And neither as well. {{{{{Hmmmmmmmmmm! A lesson here for those oh-so-suave-and-sophisticated-Derridean types who take an ever-<u>so</u>-sophisticated-and-dismissive stance to the Sartrean text. For in the final analysis, <u>there is</u> something, so to speak, *pour-soi-esque* about achieving one's proper daimon. Hmmmmmmmmmmmm!!!}}}}} *}}}* Indeed achieving this always restless, never finished, daimon is our appointed way of servicing God Herself: fidelity to Difference.

"Hypothesis # 5" refers to <u>Parmenides</u>, 160B-163B. In another kind of study it could be shown that this hypothesis is Plato's technical discussion of the principle contrary-to-the-one. (This was pretty much done in my 1976 <u>Commentary on "Parmenides"</u> in two parts.) In this book which you are now reading it is presumed that the strange "one-which-<u>is</u>-not" of hypothesis # 5 represents a kind of dyadic oscillating in its purest form lacking any self-same identity over time. The suggestion being made here is that the ontological structure of this strange "one-which-is-not" is remarkably similar, structurally, to what Sartre says about *pour-soi* in Being and Nothingness. That our individual "daimon" should come to mimic in an essential way the very structure of the ontological principle most associated with "the good" ((according to the logic of this book and its idiosyncratic appropriation of the Platonic text)) is, after all, not all that strange.

The reader is further helped in these matters if she realizes that "the one" IN the mixture effectively becomes the principle of beauty. Beauty which must die. (Dead by fragmentation and fragemnted by the oscillating, ensnaring other.)

Diotima tells us that Eros is "Daimon." Getting one's daimon right is eu-daimoneia. ((Nor is doing so easy. *khalapa ta kala*)) Aristotle had the word, but no clue.

Symposium, 202E.

70.
There is only one libido and its its first flush is active. That is the challenge and opportunity of a lifetime. Self-transformation. Nurturing the playing field of the active to become the scene -- the khora -- of the active surrender in which one is a fully compliant participant. This is the greatest pathein.

Confer, again, the aready cited passage from New, page 116.

With females, anatomical structure and phallo-cratic "social custom" conspire to force the transformation in such a way that the "transformation" often ends up being but the hideous mutilation of possibility. In our time the phallo-cratic presuppositions of "social custom" are being systematically dismantled and will, in fact, disappear in about a century bringing about the re-instatement of full possibility for females. Then the advantages of female anatomical structure will be fully appreciated.

Males have a more difficult journey. In the final analysis, the vicissitudes of biology have not at all been kind to males. But at least the dismantling of phallo-cratic presupposition will destroy those dungeons of self-deception which have been the self-imposed lot of males from time immemorial. A new freedom awaits men. More difficult than the freedom which is dawning for females. Yet, *khalapa ta kala*. The mystery and joy -- and mania -- of the active surrender. The very antithesis of "a-pathein": *laus et jubilatio*

71.
Non: So?

Sic: So what?

Non: Sew buttons on ice cream!!! Come on. Get serious. What did you get out of it?

Sic: Well, he continues to resist any connection between "khora" and the feminine. He does an interesting self-defensive dance on that one. Then at the end he said: *(Introduction a un travail en cours. Fragment)*

In *Comment* Derrida refers to an article (published on the same day as the Psyche version of

Comment), "Chora", contained in Poikilia: Etudes offertes a Jean-Pierre Vernant. (EHESS, Paris, 1987; Pages 265-296. Hereafter: *Chora*). The penthetical comment cited here is from the end of the text on page 293.

Non: That's it!!!??? That's all you got from it. That much you already knew from "Comment ne pas Parler."

Sic: Basically. Please understand me. There was much of what I would call "obiter dicta" about the article. But not anything on "khora" which went beyond "Comment ne pas Parler."

Non: What do you mean when you refer to the "obiter dicta" about the article?

Sic: My sense of it is that Frere Jacques wants to -- (----- who knows; perhaps these things have already been published -----) -- to use his "khora" meditation as a stepping stone, so to speak, to some kind of "political" treatment of things Platonic. He was getting very """"""Straussian"""""" (if you know what I mean) in his treatment of "Socrates." And again, please don't get me wrong. If anyone can thoughtfully do the "political" thing relative to the Platonic text it is Frere Jacques. Certainly he will have produced -- if indeed this is what he is up to -- something which is orders of magnitude more thoughtful and more subtle than the kind of stuff produced by those """"""Straussian"""""" types.

Non: What would be wrong with that? After all, it would be true to the very flavor of the Platonic text. Indeed I have noticed that you and the writer of these "sentences" tend to bypass the "political" in Plato.

Sic: You are most perceptive. So now let me tell you what I have kept secret all this time.

Non: What is that?

Sic: It is Plato's own obsession which "the political" (i.e., with its corresponding meditation on "arete") which causes Plato and the Platonic text to deflect from the proper vocation of the Platonic text.

Non: Is this not a bit presumptuous of you? At the very least won't it be said that you and the writer of these "sentences" are "inventing" rather than "discovering" """"""Plato""""""?

Sic: I can't control what might be said. But this much I do know.

Non: What is that?

Sic: The proper vocation of the Platonic text must be serviced and serviced fully before "the political" (i.e. with its corresponding meditation on "arete") can have its expression let alone its time of fruition. Plato fails in this endeavor. He had Des - cart (es) before the horse, so to speak. Frere Jacques, [who is post-cart (es)] in some respects, does a little better than Plato himself in servicing the proper vocation of the Platonic text. Yet he too stumbles.

Non: This we have discussed. When it is all said and done Frere Jacques stays circumscribed by the legacy of Heidegger relative to the "re-covery" of the Platonic text.

Sic: Yes. And he has another failing. Having flirted with the possibility of *thinking psycho-analytically* he shied away from it. This was his deepest failing. One can survive the legacy of Heidegger relative to the text of Plato. But one will never begin to service the proper vocation of the Platonic text if one shies away from thinking psycho-analytically.

Jacques Derrida. Magister Ludi. Did Frere Jacques -- even moreso than Jacques Lacan -- become himself ensnared in the "phallogocentric" *kettle logic*? *(Confer Spurs, page, 67; PC, pages 482-483;)* Was Frere Jacques, unbeknownst to himself, referring to himself just as much as to Lacan when he says (in Spurs, page 59):

> *The feminine distance abstracts truth from itself in a suspension of the relation with castration. This relation is suspended much as one might tauten or stretch a canvas, or a relation, which nevertheless remains -- suspended -- in indecision. In the "epoche". It is with castration that this relation is suspended, not with the truth of castration -- in which woman does not believe anyway -- and not with the truth inasmuch as it might be castration. Nor is it the relation with truth-castration that is suspended, for that is precisely a man's affair. That is the masculine concern, the concern of the male who has never come of age, who is never sufficiently sceptical or dissimulating. In such an affair, in his credulouslness and naivety (which is always sexual, pretending even at times to masterful expertise), castrates himself and from the secretion of his act fashions the snare of truth-castration.*

????? This is a most interesting question.

One could cite many examples. Derrida's stance towards Freud, Psycho-analysis, and Lacan. Particularly when these three speak the language of castration. Always the same stance: mocking and parodic. But Frere Jacques should have listened to his own words (Spurs, page 101):

> *No, somewhere parody always supposes a naivety withdrawing into an unconscious, a vertiginous non-mastery.*

Of those who ended up, in the final analysis not *thinking psycho-analytically* Derrida is -- far and away -- the thinker of the twentieth century most familiar with the relevant texts concerning the "castration complex." In forging the charge of "phallogocentrism"/"phallo-centrism" against Psycho-analysis Derrida was, in fact, -- it is the contention of this book -- deflecting from the "truth" of "mis-ogyny". In deflecting from the "truth" of "mis-ogyny" Derrida bypasses the significance -- theological and otherwise -- of the "womanly" nature of "truth."

Non: And with that observation we circle back to "khora." But why are you so depressed? What a stupid question. We both know.

Sic: I know.

Non: Then take the advice which you always knew to have been the case: You are not a Derrida scholar. You are not a person doing a commentary on Derrida. Derrida's writings happen to be among the things which *tua res agitur*. Just accept that as what has come to be part of your daimon. You are not free not to read Derrida nor are you free to avoid Derrida. But don't confuse yourself with being a scholar of and/or one doing commenatatary on the writings of Derrida. You know, in your heart of hearts that your agendum and Derrida's agendum are quite different one from the other although they necessarily intersect. Accept it. You don't even have any readers to worry about. But if you ever do, the intelligent ones will understand and there's nothing you can do about the less intelligent ones. And if -- in this "work in progress" by Derrida (which, for all you know, may already have been published) or anywhere else -- he makes (or had made) the "khora"-

"light" points which you have made about Plato, so what? You will both have been like Newton and Leibniz relative to the discovery of "the calculus". Besides, you know in your heart of hearts that Derrida's appropriation of things Platonic will never uncover/recover that "dualism of first principles" which animates the Platonic text precisely because of the "deconstructionistic" way in which the Platonic text becomes problematical to Frere Jacques. So chill out, my friend.

Sic: I am chilling. Out.

72.
{{{{{Amy: So we are back. Yet again.

De Vere: It's like a never-ending story.

Amy: And what is it for this time?

De Vere: Nothing much. Just his side musings.

Amy: About what?

De Vere: Derrida. Kristeva. Lacan. Tel Quel. The hints in The Post Card as though something personal had gone sour. The change in Kristeva's writings at the end of the seventies and the beginning of the eighties. Derrida's apparent turn-away from things psycho-analytic around the same time. Then Kristeva's turn to the novel format in Les Samourais just this past year. So many details, of a personal nature, which he -- the writer of our "sentences" -- has no clue about. He feels like he's on the outside looking in.

Amy: And he is, of course! He simply is not one of the cognescendi.

De Vere: He realizes that. He knows that there will have to be two or three biographies about all of these connections and cross-connections before these things settle and one can get to the matter at hand for which Derrida et alia were but acolytes. Even so, he always feels like a stranger. On the outside looking in. Like the kid who wanted to play in the majors but whose closest encounter was when Lou Piniella deigned to give him an autograph after he -- now in his thirties -- had waited for a half-hour outside of the players' entrance at Yankee Stadium. -----

Amy: Such trite melancholy! Yuk! I haven't got time for the pain.

De Vere: ----- I guess it's like at the Academy. Just what was Aristotle's status at the Academy? Was he privvy to the esoteric in Plato or was he excluded from the inner circle and left to make inferences about it? What was the Academy like especially after Plato went into his Depression after learning the news of Dion's assassination in 354/353? What kind of factionalism emerged? Speusippus. Xenocrates. Eudoxus. Diogenes tells us that Xenocrates and Plato were lovers. Yet Xenocrates leaves the Academy along with Aristotle in 347 as Speusippus takes over. Then again Xenocrates succeeds Speusippus in 339. The connections and cross-connections. And again, our friend is on the outside looking in.

Amy: And Heidegger joined the Nazi party in 1933. I told you, I haven't got time for the pain. These things work themselves out. Tell our friend that there are no guarentees. But his dialogue -- even if no-one other then himself gets to appreciate it -- with Derrida and Kristeva does not depend upon what went on with the Tel Quel crowd circa 1968 nor upon what may or may not have happened -- on a kind of personal level -- as Kristeva and Derrida, separately and quite differently, took the measure of the Lacanian text as the middle/late seventies oozed into the early eighties.

De Vere: I think you're right. As usual. And I think our friend understands this as well. Farewell, my sweet.

Amy: Fare thee well.}}}}}

73.
By "thinking psycho-analytically" I do not mean at all taking the insights of Psycho-analysis and using them as a grid of interpretation for the reading of texts both literary and philosophical.

74.
Nor do I mean integrating Freudian variables into something like a "deconstructive" and/or "feminist" stance towards texts and thinkers of "the Tradition."

75.
In both cases one still has an "external", so to speak, relationship to Psycho-analysis and thus both cases still radically fall short of what I am calling "thinking Psycho-analytically."

76.
Thinking Psycho-analytically would mean being SO unambiguously permeated by the very ambience of Psycho-analytic "reality" that every philosophical distinction and/or ideological agendum comes to self-dissolve into, at once, both its "Psycho-analytic" components and, so to speak, its "Psycho-analytic" "Ge-stell."

77.
This permeating kind of thinking does not at all imply a slavish attachment to pronouncements of Papa Freud.

78.
Yet anyone who *thinks Psycho-analytically* never ceases to make love with the text of Freud.

79.
Why do you keep ignoring me?

80.
Imperfect and ever-shifting patterns of identification. With Mommy. With Daddy. With siblings. With lovers; male and female; aim-inhibited as well as overtly sexual. With children. With various kinds of societal surrogates for all of the

above. *melancholia interruptus* The passion; the cutting sadness; the manic joy; the glory of our species. AMDG.

81.
"There" where "truth" is difference, "truth" is truth by, in, through, with, and, as well, against deception. Where there is no deception there is no life. {{{Nietzsche was but half-way there}}} Choose life.

82.
Getting it "right" relative to deception: all the difference between dreams and nightmares.

83.
--- *nevertheless you shall learn these things as well, that it needs must be that appearing be in appearing way; permeating ALL completely* ---

The Poem of Parmenides, Fragment 8, as contained in Parmendies of Elea; Fragments; A Text and Translation with an Introduction by David Collop; University of Toronto Press, Toronto, 1984. Page 52. Translation modified. [Hereafter: Parmenides.]

84.
Once again, let's make the point clear.

85.
It is in all respects embarrassing to be reading or to have read the text of Lacan.

86.
The cultishness of the situation. All the marks of having achieved a slavish set of followers before he -- Lacan -- could handle the adulation. The slef-congratulatory, self-indulgent way of presenting himself. The sloppiness and shallowness of his way of encountering Heidegger, Aristotle, Plato and other figures from the history of Philosophy. Surely if there was a case in which the emperor was wearing no clothes it was the case of Jacques Lacan.

87.
Even so.

88.
Lacan is one of the very few -- Kristeva and Freud himself come to mind as well -- who *thought psycho-anlaytically*.

89.
So let us take into consideration his contrast between pleasure and "desire." {{{And in so doing we shall pass over for now what Freud himself did not pass over: that mysterious nexus in which biological evolution -- upright posture et alia -- sets in motion the conditions for our species-specific "mis-ogyny" which is the secret for

understanding the kind (i.e., "desire" oriented) of psycho-social evolution which characterizes our species.}}}

90.
Lacan understood the pleasure principle. He understood the dynamic by which homeostasis is always aimed for.

91.
What is beyond the pleasure principle? Hmmmmmmm. Let us not repeat here what has been said on so many other occassions. Let us simply grant that "desire" in this Lacanian sense does initially counteract the pleasure principle. It gets associated with arousal and excitation. It gets associated with "eros".

One may, of course, consult Holy Trinity on this matter.

92.
I would want to add that it gets associated with angst. Anxiety also initially entails arousal and excitation. With the thoughtful analysis of anxiety one more easily and obviously understands how "eros" wires itself in phylogenically such that the whole complex -- phylogenically produced over evolutionary time -- of hard wiring (so to speak) which which goes by the name "the instinct of self preservation" is the work of "eros."

93.
Freud understood this, at least at the end of his life.

Confer Outline, page 5. There you will find Freud giving this interesting parenthetical remark:

> *The contrast between the instincts of self-preservation and the preservation of the species, as well as the contrast between ego-love and object-love, fall within Eros.*

94.
In humans the special and unique occasion for arousal/excitation is that whole nexus of associations contained in the male and female versions of the castration complex. Freud and Lacan both understood this. (It is this nexus which is operative in the Lacanian sense of "desire.")

95.
In both males and females the complementary versions of the castration complex retroactively affect what gets analyzed as anal and oral sexual behaviors. Freud and Lacan both understood this although most of the people who get excited about the "pre-Oedipal" dimensions of development tend to miss this retroactive working over of the anal and the oral by the complementary versions of the castration complex.

96.
How, then, does "desire" function? Complexly. Having started our spelunking with Lacan one must now pass both beyond and before this Jacques who can never

be a Frere Jacques.

97.
The anxiety ocassioned in the boy/man upon recognition of the "other's" castration has multiple outcomes. *{{{And, speaking of "outcomes", let it be stipulated from the outset that in "reality" one is in fact speaking of various and ever-shifting combinations and permutations of these various "outcomes" both in the life of fantasy and in actual practice as well. But for purposes of initial presentation it is more efficient to speak of these "outcomes" as though they obtained in isolation one from the other.}}}*

98.
One famous outcome -- noted by Freud and then talked to death by both Lacan and Kristeva -- is the outcome of <u>disavowal</u> and the corresponding fetishism resulting from this <u>disavowal</u>. In the terminology of this book of "sentences", this is the cowardly psychosis.

Confer <u>Outline</u>, pages 58-61 with its discussion of "the splitting of the ego" and fetishism.

99.
The other outcomes -- all involving various kinds of <u>repression</u> (as <u>opposed</u> to disavowal) of the recognition of castration in the "other" -- have been worked over so much by Freud and the others that it is almost boring to run through them again. Salient among these are: i)., exaggerated penis narcissism resulting in the kind of homosexual orientation in which one desires to play the "male" role in a male/male homosexual relationship; and ii), "normal" (i.e., relatively aggressive and control-oriented) "heterosexuality" in males. These two outcomes are first cousins to each other and both of them share the same kind of misogyny.

100.
Yet another outcome is <u>identification</u> with the castrated "other." If such a tendency towards identification with the castrated other is accompanied by a strong penis narcissism (and its corresponding misogyny) the outcome leads to a kind of male/male homosexuality in which one desires to play the "female" role.

101.
A more rarefied form of "identification" with the castrated "other" takes place when the boy/man first acquires a firm attachment (involving some degree of misogyny) to the female as "object choice" and then -- through the long journey of tortured teleology entailing the "adult onset" re-configuration of the the oedipal contours -- has this "heterosexual" orientation mature into the lesbianesque play involving the female as both "object choice" and that <u>with which</u> one identifies. Such "adult onset" re-configuration undergone by some males is set in motion through experiences of "orgasm envy" along with a corresponding surmounting of the "fear of feminization" which fear is the usual product of a boy's oedipal experience. These are the disciples of Tiresias.

102.
<u>Being</u> the castrated oscillating love object -- impossibly <u>with</u> a penis -- <u>For</u> the castrated oscillating love object. This is the ultimate telos of male "desire."

Being the castrated oscillating love object -- impossibly with a penis -- For the castrated oscillating love object. This is the ultimate telos of male "desire."

103.
On the other hand, the anxiety/arousal of the girl/woman upon her discovery of being the castrated other has complexities about it which are quite different from the boy/man's recognition of the "other" as being castrated.

104.
Although "penis-envy" is real, "penis-envy" was never -- Freud himself notwithstanding -- the best or even the most basic way to understand the complex nexus involved in female "desire."

105.
There is -- first and foremost -- a kind of scopic eroticism in females. A desire -- subject to much repression and/or suppression -- to be seen and recognized in one's own castration. This is the shame element in female sexuality. It is the stepping stone to that "shame" which -- according to this book of "sentences" -- is the most secret name of "the good". (As corollary it follows that males must take on -- at least psychically -- the condition of being castrated in order to position themselves for the achievement/instantiation of "the good" -- i.e., "the good" qua shame -- in their lives.)

On this one might confer, paradigmatically, Freud's remarks on pages 116-117 of New. This book which you are now reading goes considerably both beyond and before Freud in its attention to the nexus involving "shame" and female genitalia and female patterns of orgasm. Shame -- here understood as erotic shame -- is nothing less than "the desired". Nothing less than "the good."

106.
Female "desire" becomes counter-productively convoluted and short-circuited if it settles for being "love object" and "phallic place-holder" for the male. Yet much of Psycho-analytic theory and phallo-cratic cultural norms conspire to hold this as the "normal" outcome of female desire. (Understanding this insidious phallo-cratic dynamic has been one of the great achievements of politically oriented Feminism.)

107.
Female "desire" also becomes counter-productively convoluted and short-circuited if it acquiesces to the tempation to disavow the counter-factual """"""fact"""""" (i.e., what this book of "sentences" is calling the "psychosis of the brave") of being castrated. Such a move precludes that positive entrance into the experience of "shame" which is the very telos of all sexuality, male as well as female. (Falling into such a disavowal has been one of the great failures of much of politically oriented Feminism.)

108.
Females who can free themselves from the phallo-cratic dictates of cultural expectations can more easily and fully enter into that charming dialectic of female

as oscillating "object choice" and female as that with which one identifies. This is so because females pass through the oedipal contours free of that "fear of feminization" which keeps most males from their sexual telos.

109.
In all of this the primacy of lesbian sexuality is recognized and affirmed. Both heterosexuality and male/male homosexuality are modes of behavior which keep participants from the proper "telos" of sexuality.

110.
Yet even lesbian modes of sexuality achieve the proper "telos" of sexuality only thorugh the """"""reality"""""" of castration shame (and its correlative psycho-physiological possibility for oscillating delirium). This means that -- ontogenically for individuals and phylogenically for the species -- the penis/phallus orientation is/was the pre-requisite even for the fullness of lesbian modes of sexuality. (In actual practice the details of how the "non-phallo-cratic-phallus" makes its appearance for males and females alike -- both psychologically and physically -- in lesbianesque love-making are reserved for another kind of study.)

111.
Now back to the pleasure principle.

112.
The inevitable return to a state of homeostasis.

113.
What actually happens as "desire" plays itself out?

114.
Sooner or later, orgasm. Perhaps the melancholic/ejaculatory version of male orgasm in which, on the average, "desire" tends to have been short-changed. Perhaps the dyadic non-ejaculatory "jouissance" version of female orgasm in which and through which "desire" gets more of a play. In either case one finds that even "desire" -- which initially runs counter to the pleasure principle -- services the pleasure principle by way of a return to homeostasis.

115.
It was Plato himself who played around with this primacy of "pleasure" as "pleasure" inter-faces with Eros. One must learn, in these matters, how to read the Philebus as an introduction to Symposium. One must learn, in these matters, how and why "pleasure" in the listing of goods is twice teasingly singled out as "the fifth." One must learn that Alcibiades is allegoric of "pleasure" just as Socrates is allegoric of "eros"/("desire") in that amazing dialogue and how there is a struggle between the two -- Alcibiades and Socrates -- relative to """"Agathon"""". And yet -- is there not something comic about all of this? -- the final triad is not Socrates-Agathon-Alcibiades but rather Agathon-Aristophanes-Socrates. How interesting!!!

Philebus, 66C and 67A. Also: {{{{{One turns to the unrefuted dictum of mysterious Philebus "himself" (at 12A) as he says -- contra both Socrates and Protarchus -- : *What I think, and shall continue to think, is that pleasure is victorious whatever happens.* --- }}}}}

{{{{{{{{{*Aristotle's treatment of pleasure:* Nichomachean Ethics *Book X, Chapters One through Five (with special attention on Chapter Four).* The quiet and for the most part unobstrusive Act/Potency underpinning of Nichomachean Ethics becomes quite explicit in Aristotle's review of pleasure in these Chapters. Particularly in Chapter Four. Clearly any treatment of "pleasure" which is based on such a "flight from difference" -- which is endemic to the very Act/Potency paradigm itself -- will have missed on principle the "dis-appearing" manner in which "pleasure" is and is not the good for the Plato of Philebus. On the other hand these five Chapters of Aristotle offer enough indications that the burning question at the Academy during Plato's last years was this question concerning the status of "pleasure" relative to the good. Particularly intriguing is Aristotle's report in Chapter One that Speusippus and Plato came from significantly different perspectives when they each allowed "pleasure" to be presented in a negative light. Plato's "noble lie" relative to "pleasure."}}}}}}}}}

116.
Mommy is castrated. Mommy is castrated. This is the delusion which energizes our species. The counter-factual "fact", so to speak, whose power and influence over the psychic life of males and females alike is without parallel. This delusion is the deception which is more true than "the truth." {{Thus it is deception and not "the truth" which will set us free. For those who have the eyes to hear and the ears to see.}} This delusion is the ur-spring of "mis-ogyny"

117.
"Mis-ogyny" is this sense, while it is the ultimate source of 'misogyny' in the clinically pathological sense, does not necessarily entail pathological misogyny and indeed the proper offspring of "mis-ogyny" is anyting but misogyny. Not everyone will understand.

118.
Nietzsche did and did not understand.

119.
Of course, Nietzsche understood that "truth" is a species of error. One immediately recalls his bold statement from # 493 of The Will to Power. More to the point one immediately resonates with his celebration of the fertile-and-deceptive play of """Art""" relative to the sterility of mere truth as it -- this celebration of deception -- lyrically comes forth in # 853 of that marvelous posthumously published "book."

Confer aphorism # 493 of WP (page 272):

> *Truth is the kind of error without which a certain species of life could not live. The value for life is ultimately decisive.*

Confer aphorism # 853 of WP, pages 451-453.

120.
But Nietzsche never even comes close to understanding the "ur-spring" of

deception's power. As this book has repeatedly shown, the Nietzschean text is predictably -- to the very point of boredom!!!! -- misogynistic without at all being "mis-ogynistic".

121.
Derrida, and Deleuze more especially, trip over themselves in announcing to the world how well they understand the subtleties of # 853. But in and through their tendency to idolatrize the text of Nietzsche they too remain -- but not to the point of boredom -- misogynistic without achieving "mis-ogyny."

Confer especially Spurs, pages 41-123. {{These matters are more fully developed in my book, Holy Trinity.}}

122.
Freud. Lacan. Kristeva. Whatever their shortcomings may be, these three have been in touch with "mis-ogyny". Despite their numerous shortcomings, all three -- but most especially Kristeva -- achieved the beginnings of what this book calls *thinking Psycho-analytically. {{{For those who have the eyes to hear and the ears to see: please note that being "phallo-centric" in one's orientation does not, eo ipso, keep a writer from being in touch with "mis-ogyny". Indeed, too much attention to this "Shibboleth of the soi-disant sophisticated" -- (this Shibboleth being* phallo-centrism*) -- is a guarentee that one will stay out of touch with "mis-ogyny". Even so, it must be admitted that Lacan's phallo-centrism is far more insidious and counter-productive to achieving the vocation of thinking than is Freud's phallo-centrism.}}}*

Are you still with me, reader? Stay around a bit longer to see why Lacan's phallo-centrism is far more insidious and counter productive than is the phallo-centrism of Freud. The issue only incidentally deals with Feminism. The reall issue has to do, as noted, with the proper vocation of thinking.

123.
Mommy is castrated. Mommy is castrated. The animating delusion of our species. The counter-factual fact. So to speak. The "truth" which is "worth more" than "the truth." **--- We are such stuff/As dreams are made of; ---**

124.
The epiphenomenon (which turned out to be the whole ball of wax).

125.
Towards the end of his life Freud spoke of a special twist in this "mis-ogynistic" nodal point of all Pscho-analytic theory (and, a fortiori, life itself) in those texts dealing with "fetishism" and "the splitting of the ego." A psychotic disavowal rather than a repression. Fair enough.

Confer Outline, pages 58-61.

126.
Fair enough. And fair enough as well that Lacan should draw our attention to the

significance of these often passed-over texts of the later Freud.

127.
But this other Jacques -- {{{who, please note, despite the fertility of some of his meditations, never became a "Frere Jacques"}}} -- entered with his typical suave and sophistication into these most interesting waters but had no clue as to what he had entered. And young Julia followed suit.

128.
Yes. The meditation on psychosis is essential. But it must be properly "located". And it must be understood that there are, in a sense, <u>two</u> kinds of psychosis involved. What is at issue here is the <u>kind</u> of psychosis by which we remain in fidelity to that "place" ("khora") -- the site in terms of which -- where dreams are made. To their credit Lacan, and, Julia of the spirits, draw proper attention to the psychosis of disavowal. Their attention to this disavowal <u>qua disavowal</u> keeps them from getting caught up in the kind of symbolic nexus which is animated by submission to such a disavowal. Nonetheless they bypass completely the significance of the <u>kind</u> of psychosis -- (i.e., the psychosis of good faith; the psychosis of the brave) -- which obtains when Mommy"s castration (albeit repressed) is <u>not</u> disavowed. <u>This</u> is the fidelity to the counter factual fact.

{{It is inevitable -- indeed even charming -- that the disavowal should occur at all. But that it should be sustained is cowardly.}}

{{{{
Non: Are you certain that we should be breaking in right here? It seems out of place.

Sic: I am certain. Johanna was going too fast here. She realizes that now and so we have to be sent in for some claification.

Non: Well let's get to it. Indeed it seems strange that the <u>disavowal</u> of the counter-factual fact (that Mommy is castrated) should be at all compared to a psychosis. After all, Mommy, in fact, is <u>not</u> castrated.

Sic: But in the child's (male or female, it doesn't matter although this experience is a deep desenchantment <u>and</u> fear-engendering trauma for the little boy while it is only a deep disenchantment for the little girl) <u>experience</u> such a <u>disavowal</u> is a break from and denial of the <u>experienced</u>-fact. And if the disavowal -- (which, as Freud recognized, is quite different from acknowledging Mommy's castration <u>and then</u> repressing it) -- is sustained it becomes, effectively, the psychosis of bad faith. The cowardly psychosis.

Non: But surely, later on in life, one comes to understand that Mommy in fact is <u>not</u> castrated.

Sic: That is true. But nothing supersedes the child's original experience on these matters. It is the <u>counter-factual</u> fact which makes all the difference in the world. The primacy of deception. Fetishizing the whole business -- which occurs when the denial/disavowal is sustained -- is to short-circuit the <u>return</u> to Mommy -- (even and especially as castrated) -- which is so esssential if we are to come to be attuned to the way in which "Mommy" (i.e., "the fifth") is sustained in the mixture. Even so the original turn away from Mommy's castration is <u>also</u> essential (and in the service of the vocation of thought) so long as it is not sustained.

Non: Already I am confused by your allusions. My presumption is that Johanna or some of her surrogates will have talked adequately about some of these allusions farther on on the book. But continue. What do you mean by your last statement?

Sic: The turn away from Mommy puts us in touch with the "other" (i.e., "the one") relative to "the Mother" (i.e., "the fifth"). This "other" (i.e., "the one") is what is truly mystical in the mixture (even though in the mixture its only destiny is to be fragmented) and we must be in contact with it even -- and especially -- when we return to Mommy in our fidelity to the counter-factual fact if our return is to bear fruit of 'offspringing.' And there is something else yet.

Non: What is that?

Sic: As we turn away from (castrated -- **the horror!** *--) Mommy we displace the impulse for union/wholeness/integration away from Mommy towards the "other" (i.e., the "other" relative to Mother). Our disenchatment sends us "au dela". The romantic motif. ("Somewhere my love"---).*

Non: And what is wrong with that?

Sic: In one sense, nothing at all. For this turn away -- combined with the contact with the mystical made possible by the turn away -- allows us to dream the impossible dream. We bring this back with us when we return to Mommy (which is to accept the horror) as we achieve -- as children and as adults -- fidelity to the counter-factual fact. It must be let in first, even if it is almost immediately repressed. Far better than never letting it in at all. We die unless we make **the horror** *our own. Eventually, repression can and does fruitfully ease. That is, if repression occurs at all since without forsaking the disavowal we have no chance at all to remain faithful -- even in the mode of repression -- to the counter-factual fact. This -- recognizing, owning, and making our own* **the horror** *(of what is, of course the counter-factual fact which animates our species in a special way) -- is the task of a lifetime. As children and as adults we engage the tendency to deny/disavow* **the horror** *as we -- (each one of us) -- through that long series of conscious and pre-conscious "choices" creates one's own "daimon" which -- with the passage of time and through the chance-goverend vicissitudes of life -- becomes our destiny.* Character is fate! *Indeed. Our "Moira" is self-chosen (throughout a lifetime and through chance-goverened viscissitudes). The antinomy dissolves.*

Non: Why can't we seek to sustain the impossible dream in and with "the other" (i.e., relative to the Mother)? Why the necessity to return to Mommy which return involves integrating **the horror** *into our appropriation of Mommy? In a word, why can't the roamntic impulse -- which does in fact put us in touch with what is mystical in the mixture according to your formulation -- be sustained?*

Sic: Because what is mystical in the mixture is -- necessarily -- fragmented in the mixture. There is no wholeness there. There is no refuge there. There is no-place to tarry. Contact is made with its fragmented presence in the mixture when we turn away from Mommy. But there is nothing to hold us there. There is no-place. We must return. Beauty yes. The piercing desire for it. Getting in touch with it such as is possible. But beauty-which-must-die. In this sense Johnny Keats was a more complete Platonist than Plato himself. Tortured teleology.

<[{(It is noteworthy that the turn away from Mommy in that romantic lust for the "au dela" (i.e., for the "beyond"; for untarnished and unfragmented beauty; for the "somewhere-my-love") usually

brings for males some degree of covert or overt homoeroticism -- (one thinks, most especially, of Plato) -- and for females some exaggeration of the heterosexual love-object. For males caught up in the turn away from Mommy and the correlative romantic thrust towards the "other" relative to Mommy -- but whose homophobia is too great to allow for the expression of any homoeroticism -- the lust for the untarnished beauty of the "au dela" is projected, unrealistically, unto the heterosexual love object. One thinks, in this regard, of how Beatrice had to function in the romantic mind of Dante. The one who traversed these waters with some finesse and subtlety was Shelley with his bi-sexual orientation at around the time he composed "Fragments Connected with Epispsychidion".>]})

Non: I think I understand and then right away I am thrown back into confusion. But tell me. What is wrong with what you call the bad faith fetishizing which is the result of sustaining the disavowal? I have often heard Johanna and her helpers talk of the androgynous ideal. Is this not actually achieved in the fetish?

Sic: No! No! No!. On the contrary. Thw worst possible short-circuiting of this whole business is instantiated by the fetishizing. The impossible dream -- as impossible dream -- is ruined by the fetishizing. The real and only advantage of the male -- i.e., as instantiation of the androgynous ideal -- is taken away in the fetishizing. It is, so to speak, the worst kind of pre-mature ejaculation in which the climax occurs before copulation is even initiated. It is sterility itself and inhibits the coming to pass of the "offspring/interest." In all respects the fetishizing leads to disaster. ((And please note: the fetishizing takes on so many forms, some of which are quite subtle -- and not without paradox -- in their own right.))

Non: I get so confused.

Sic: Just be patient. Johanna has arranged to unpack these things here and there thorughout the book. Especially in the "long caesura" and in the section of the book which used to be called the "mania" supplement. You will recognize them when you get to them. Then we can all come back to this very conversation and it will -- quite literally -- make sense.

Non: Thank-you, Sic. Adieu for now.

Sic: Likewise to you.
}}}}}

129.
The fetishistic disavowal is the psychosis of bad-faith/self-deception. The psychosis of the coward.

{{{ Non: Would I be correct, then, in inferring that much of contemporary Feminism is caught up, unconsciously, in the nets of sustaining such a disavowal? Sic: Yes, provided that, in making such an inference, you realize as well that the literal fetish -- the big toe; high heels; etc.; etc.; -- is replaced, symbolically, in much of contemporary Feminism by a fixation on a series of political/cultural agenda by which some forms of Feminism, at a given time, define themselves. Non: May I presume that, in making this observation, you are not advocating any kind of subordination for women in political and cultural matters. Sic: Of course such a presumption is operative, all throughout this book of ours. That much is taken as axiomatic. One is looking past these kinds of accomplishments to the real change in libidinal economy which is now beginning to dawn for that clothed species on the third planet from the sun. Non: I must assume that you refer to the dawning age of Matriarchal androgyny entailing the "hegemony of difference" as it has been explained in this book. Sic: You have understood me completely. And if you have understood so well you have also understood that "Feminism" -- to the extent that it continues in sustaining this fetishistic disavowal -- hinders the arrival of that day. Likewise, you correlatively understand that our Julia of the spirits is no "Feminist" as that label is now commonly used. Non: Yes, I have understood those things as well.}}}

130.
{{{{Bappy: Why, do you suppose, is there so much resistance on the part of so many educated, intelligent women to what is being called here the root "mis-ogynistic" teaching of Psycho-analysis? Why is this sustaining of this disavowal -- which you and the boss call the psychosis of bad faith -- of "mis-ogynistic" """reality""" so stubborn and intense?

Dewchee: There are several reasons and none of them are so mysterious.

Bappy: Please elaborate.

Dewchee: In the first place there is that chauvinistic aura of smugness with which the "mis-ogynistic" teachings of Psycho-analysis are presented. This smugness was first introduced by Sigmund himself and, for the most part, has been actually re-enforced, consciously and unconsciously, by the majority of Psycho-analytic writers for several decades after the death of Freud. This smugness ultimately stems from an ignorance -- even on the part of Sigmund himself to say nothing of most of his less worthy followers -- based on a lack of understanding concerning the real implications of Freud's own "mis-ogynistic" discoveries. As you know Johanna (and before her, Jude, whose moniker was "the boss") -- in Shekhinah, in Holy Trinity, in Theo-tokos, and now in Sentences -- has devoted a good deal of his efforts to the task of disengaging the chauvinistic/misogynistic veneer of Psycho-analytic teaching from the "mis-ogynistic" lifeblood of Psycho-analytic teaching. We don't have to kill the precious baby in order to rid ourselves of the polluted bath water.

Theotokos. An unpublished manuscript. It was the cousin to Holy Trinity.

Bappy: That helps a bit. What are the other reasons?

Dewchee: In the second place it didn't help matters that our friend Sigmund was really quite confused concerning the psycho-physiology of female patterns of orgasm. To be sure, some Feminists and others have tended to exaggerate and de-contextualize the little which Freud actually did say about this matter. Even so, when it's all said and done, Papa Freud was pretty confused.

Bappy: Why do you suppose this was so?

Dewchee: Partly because he was male. A little bit of reflection reveals that the male orgasmic function and the male procreational function dovetail in the sense that virtually all of male procreative acts -- {{including in fact the ordinary procedure for artifical insemination}} -- require orgasm. This dovetailing lead Papa Freud -- one might say prematurely -- to insist that the sexual function was basically genital (i.e., "procreational") and that other forms of sexual expression are in some way dysfunctional. When -- from about 1923 onwards -- he finally got around to examining carefully the dynamics of female sexuality, the relative simplicity of the male paradigm was unconsciously retained by him in his understanding of what would be "functional" (i.e., "normal") in female sexual experience. Thus his exaggerated attention to the vagina (i.e., the organ operative in female "procreational" behavior). Freud never really appreciated the subtle and complex way in which the dyadic dynamic (clitoris/vagina) of female sexuality (and corresponding genital organization) overlaps with but does not dovetail with the female procreational function. Again, ever since Madonna, the boss has tried to remedy this terrible confusion on the part of Papa Freud.

Bappy: But if the Freudian text exhibits such a deep degree of ignorance on these matters why should one even try to rehabilitate it.? Why not just let the whole Freud bit go entirely?

Dewchee: Nothing is that simple at all. "Freud", for better or for worse, has become something of a destiny for the vocation of thinking. We either get it right relative to the text of Freud or we fail in our most sacred task. And in all of this willingness to ditch the Freudian text there remains that basically "bad-faith" resistance to the one essential teaching which Freud -- despite himself so to speak -- did understand.

Bappy: You speak here of the "mis-ogynistic" lifeblood of Psycho-analysis disengaged from that veneer of chauvinism/misogyny which almost always surrounds this lifeblood teaching in the Freudian text.

Dewchee: Yes of course. The great counter-factual perception, on the part of little girls and little boys, that Mommy is castrated is the whole ball of wax. This is the guiding thread of Freud's whole intellectual development even if the articulation of this teaching was not sufficiently refined until the writings of the twenties and, more especially, of the thirties. First contra Adler who wanted to deflect Psycho-Analysis into the all too conscious and obvious "power" dyanamics borrowed from a very average reading of the Nietzschean text. Then contra Jung who in a variety of ways (both during his relationship with Freud and then, more especially, after the break between Freud and Jung) had a tendency to "romanticize" -- in the worst sense of that otherwise fertile word -- the "enigma" of female sexuality.

Bappy: I presume that you and the boss understand that there were other issues going on between Jung and Freud which led to their break.

Dewchee: Yes and no. Of course there were "other" things going on. The whole Father/son thing; the Jew/Gentile business; and the whole homosexual/homophobia dynamic was involved. And other things. Even so, upon reflection, aren't even these things deriviative in various ways from the root teaching/discovery of Psycho-analysis that Mommy is castrated?

Bappy: I suppose so. But let us not argue the point right now. Please continue.

Dewchee: Then, later, contra Rank who wanted to change the focus of Psycho-analysis to the birth trauma. And finally, in the thirties, contra Jones/Horney both of whom instantiated what would now be called a "biologism"/"essentialism" relative to gender identity.

Bappy: There is some irony in all of this once we realize that it was Freud himself who first offered the most cogent arguments against "biologism"/"essentialism" relative to the acquistion of gender identity. After all, how often is it the case that any number of Feminists -- armed with this or that sentence from the text of Freud usually taken out of its context -- accuse Freud of instantiating a position of "biologism"/"essentialism"?

There is a persistency about this charge of "biologism"/"essentialism" which calls for more attention.

It is quite clear that for Freud, gender identity is acquired rather than a biological given even though he often enough comments that biological (viz., "constitutional") factors play a role as well. Yet it is passage through the Oedipal stages -- frought with the complementary versions of the castration complex for both little girls and little boys -- which is determinative. For, when it's all said and done, passing through the Oedipal stages is basically the environmentally conditioned reaction to the discovery of anatomical difference even if it is also true that one's psychic appreciation of one's own biologically given anatomy creates the conditions under which we pass through the Oedipal variables, acquiring gender identity in the process. So why the persistency of the charge of "biologism"/"essentialism" leveled at the text of Freud?

Freud, it turns out, not only had an account of how gender identity comes to be acquired, but he also presumes to speak normatively -- i.e., judgementally, when it is all said and done -- concerning the gender identity outcomes relative to passage through the Oedipal variables. Further, his "normative" account -- (i.e., that a heterosexual "genital"-oriented outcome is the "telos", so to speak) -- is based on his bias that the sexual function must ultimately be in the service of the procreational function. In this bias he subverts -- in the worst sense of subverts -- his remarkable insights into how gender identity is acquired. In a sense, the persistency of the charge of "biologism"/"essentialism" has -- accidentally so to speak -- some justification since he lets a biological function of sexuality (i.e., the reproductive function) determine what is functional and dysfunctional on the psychological level of our sexual orientation and behavior.

Dewchee: You have taken the words right out of my mouth.

Bappy: Even so, that chauvinistic/misogynistic "veneer" endemic to the Freudian text -- (to say nothing of Sigmund's own personal life!!) -- which you and Johanna (and before her "the boss") claim can be disengaged from what you call the "mis-ogynistic" lifeblood of Psycho-analysis is very, very disturbing. Did Freud ever free himself from this veneer in his writings?

Dewchee: This "veneer" certainly permeates all of his writings even up through his famous 1933 piece -- (i.e., lecture xxxiii in The New Introductory Lectures) -- on Femininity. That piece is, when it is all said and done, the most important document produced by Freud concerning the "mis-ogynistic" lifeblood of Psycho-analysis. But it is practially vitiated by his smug chauvinism/misogyny. Freud's own exaggerated male ego was still in his way. However, by 1938, Freud -- pain as his constant companion and death already knocking on his door -- was able to write about these things without interference from his exaggerated male ego. In his Outline of Psycho-Analysis of 1938/1939 there is a straightforward presentation of that whole nexus of what we are calling the "mis-ogynistic" lifeblood of Psycho-analysis mostly free of that chauvinsitic smugness which had vitiated so much of his earlier writings on female sexuality. Freud finally did come home.

Bappy: Thank-you for these clarifications. They are really helpful. But let us return to our first topic.

Dewchee: By all means.

Bappy: Are there any other reasons why there is so much resistance -- and correlative disavowal -- on the part of so many intelligent and well-educated women concerning what you call the "mis-ogynistic" lifeblood of Psycho-analysis?

Dewchee: Yes. In the third place are the political and cultural realities in the most elemental sense.

Bappy: What do you mean?

Dewchee: Real, ugly, old-fashioned misogyny without any of the nuances and subtleties of "mis-ogyny" as put forth in this book of sentences. Instantiated on an individual level in the lives of most males. Patterns of misogyny as they are institutionally instantiated to such an insidious extent that females tend to destructively internalize these cultural patterns of misogyny. Conscious patterns of misogyny as well as unconscious patterns of misogyny. Political systems which overtly and covertly keep women oppressed. Patriarchy has really created an ugly and most insidious mess.

Bappy: Now I understand. And what is your point?

Dewchee: It is really quite simple. Intelligent women are sick and tired of the charade. They are properly impatient. Who wants to sit around and un-pack subtle distinctions between misogyny and a soi-dissant "mis-ogyny"? Who would want to spend the time to redeem, or rescue, -- or whatever -- a text -- i.e., Freud's -- which is clearly so chauvinsitic and misogynous? It is a time of action, not the time for making subtle distinctions.

Bappy: Well, aren't those powerful arguments?

Dewchee: Of course they are. And there is nothing in the suggestions put forth by me and the boss which preclude radical change and action. Even so, such a stance bypasses some things which -- sooner or later -- will <u>have</u> to be taken into account.

Bappy: Such as?

Dewchee: The dynamic of sexual oppression is quite different from the dynamic by which races, peoples, ethnic groups, and economic classes have been (and are) oppressed.

Bappy: I think I understand where you are taking us in this conversation. In effect you are saying that all of us -- but most especially those who are concerned with ending the present and future oppression of women -- must get in touch, precisely, with the "mis-ogynistic" dimensions of sexuality. If we do not, then not only will the attempts to alleviate and terminate the oppresion of women fail but there will be dire consequences for the entire global community.

Dewchee: Now you are understanding. And so often in the past -- here in <u>Sentences</u> but also going all the way back to <u>Madonna</u> and before -- it was precisely <u>our</u> conversations which were so revealing of the dire consequences if all of us -- male and female alike -- fail to get in touch with the "mis-ogynistic" dimension of our sexuality.

Bappy: Even so, I am not optimistic that many -- male or female -- will understand.

Dewchee: I share your pessimism. Even so it can honestly be stated that we -- you, me, Johanna, Sic, Non, Amy, De Vere, Mort, Jude, and all of the others as well -- have tried. Now we must end this little digression. We have already made the "sentence" of which our conversation is but a part far too long.

Bappy: Good night, Dewchee. I love you. Just touch my cheek before you leave me.

Dewchee: Good-night, Bappy. Sleep tight. I love you. }}}}}

131.
The "mis-ogynistic" delusion -- in contrast to the fetishistic disavowal which deflects from the unpleasant "mis-ogynistic" delusion -- is the one which opens up the "dream" possibilities for that species which dwells on the third planet from the sun.

132.
Yes, Yes, of course. The "mis-ogynistic" delusion does not always bring with it pure joy and comfort. The dungeon of misogyny results from the "mis-ogynistic" delusion. But it is precisely "mis-ogyny" which opens up the possibility for the redemption which will take the form of matriarchal androgyny which is the redemption of "mis-ogyny." It is also "mis-ogyny" which is the precondition of dreaming, without which our species dies.

133.
Let it pass for now that a Chodorow here, a Kristeva there, (and a hundred-thousand others all over the place) use the term "pre-Oeidpal" in a sense which is significantly different from Freud's usage of the term by which he designates the onset of the phallic stage of psycho-sexual development in little girls. Let it pass. It is only a semantical problem and careful readers will make the necessary adjustments.

Confer Freud's usage of this term in lecture xxxiii of New, pages 104-111.

Thus, by the Freudian rubric, the first wave of phallic (i.e., inclusive of clitoral) sexuality is called "Oedipal" in boys and "pre-Oedipal" in girls. The second wave of phallic development in girls is called "Oedipal" while for boys the first wave of phallic development is succeeded by an open-ness to what Freud would call the "inverse Oeidpal" situation. (Confer, Outline, page 47. Also confer Freud's unambiguous statement on this in "Some Psychological Consequences of the Anatomical Distinction between the Sexes." *[As contained in Collected Papers; Volume V. Volume V is edited by James Strachey. Basic Books, New York, 1959. Pages 186-197. The point under discussion is made on page 188.]*) Finally, little girls linger on in the Oedipal situation while, according to the Freudian paradigm, little boys -- guided as always by fear of castration/fear of feminization -- resolve the Oedipal complex by identifying with the father. Accordingly, "pre-Oedipal" refers, for Freud, only to the first stage of the Oedipal complex for little girls and has no application for little boys. "Pre-Oedipal", however, in contemporary usage refers to both little girls and little boys and refers in both little girls and little boys to the pre-phallic stages of psycho-sexual development.

{{{Please understand that in this book the male and female versions of what Freud called "the Oedipus complex" are understood as the psychological consequences -- carried out in two stages in both the male and female case and bringing with it some disposition to bi-sexuality in all of us -- of the discovery of anatomical difference between the sexes. Thus -- (and despite how Freud himself sometimes presented the "Oedipal complex" in his writings prior to 1923) -- the dynamic of the Oeidpal variables is separable on principle from ancillary questions of single parent household, absence of a father figure, etc., etc., etc. Your weight if you are weighed on the Moon is radically different from your weight if you are weighed in New York City. But the dynamic of gravity remains the same. The way one passes through the Oedipal variables -- i.e., the complementary versions of the castration complex -- will be affected by being raised in a single parent household or a traditional nuclear family howsehold. But in every case there will be psychological consequences following upon the child's discovery of the anatomical differences between the sexes.

These points have been discussed at length in a book dealing with "the wo-man principle" written while on a study grant in the Summer of 1990. This book on "the wo-man principle" was the Mother, so to speak, of Madonna which was, it will be recalled, the grandmother of *Thinking Psychoanalytically*.}}}

134.
But.

135.
Don't let it pass that -- in this revised sense of "pre-Oedipal" -- these thinkers attach a significance to the "pre-Oedipal" which is unwarranted. The "pre-Oedipal" -- (in the current, revised, usage by which "pre-Oedipal" now designates psycho-sexual development in little girls and little boys PRIOR to the onset of the phallic stage of psycho-sexual development) -- achieves its significance only retroactively. The Mommy connection of the "pre-Oedipal" period is thoroughly -- and retroactively -- transformed by the posterior (and counter-factual) "discovery" that Mommy is castrated. In fact, Kristeva, in Powers of Horror seems to understand this in her meditation on "abjection." Chodorow and a hundred thousand others wax poetical about the "pre-Oedipal" without understanding the dynamic which goes on. With these thinkers, in effect, the celebration of the "pre-Oedipal" is but a subtle form of that bad faith psychosis of disavowal, noted above.

136.
If Mommy -- that very one who bore and nurtured you -- really did have a penis then beauty would be truth and truth beauty. It is the impossible dream. But what else would a heaven be for?

137.
Of course -- and Johnny knew this as well -- the Grecian urn had to break. And this was for the good. In the very Temple of delight melancholia does and must reign.

138.

Ay, in the very temple of Delight
Veil'd Melancholy has her sovran shrine,
Though seen of none save him whose strenuous tongue
Can burst Joy's grape against his palate fine;
His soul shall taste the sadness of her might,
And be among her cloudy trophies hung. This is, of course, the conclusion of

Keats' Ode on Melancholy. Cited from The Odes of John Keats by Helen Vendler.

Harvard University Press, 1983. Page 153. Hereafter; Odes.

139.
Julia of the spirits.

139-i. The reading of Kristeva, for me, always engenders reveries of intense eroticism shot through with an incredibly high degree of masochism.

139-ii. I identified most especially with the analysand who reminded Kristeva of "Juliet". My identification with this analysand was particularly incited when learning that this analysand submitted herself to repeated anal intercourse from a male homosexual lover -- who got more bang out of banging males, it is also reported -- while she manipulated her clitoris to orgasm.

139-iii. The reveries which come upon me while I read Kristeva often involve memories -- real and/or imagined -- of my own 'Eurydice' along with me and her new-found male lover.

139-iv. In these reveries I willingly engage in homosexual behaviors with her new lover if that is her desire.

139-v. More often than not I play the """""feminine""""" role in these homosexual encounters as we -- but especially, I -- are being demonically watched by 'Eurydice' and, more to the point, compelled to stare back into her eyes as we -- more especially, I -- are abused and humiliated by each other.

139-vi. Magically, the one to-be-wickedly-abused-humiliated-<u>and-thus</u>-aroused turns out suddenly -- *as might happen in a dream* -- to be a dark-haired young, nubile, tall woman endowed more generously with breasts and buttocks than is blond-haired 'Eurydice'. Under these circumstances I quickly become the "other" to-be-abused woman without ceasing to be the aroused and abus-**ing** 'Eurydice'.

139-vii. These complex reveries lead to the ability to "stay on the edge" for incredibly long periods of time in my artful masturbation prior to climax as my mind oscillates between my being 'Eurydice' the abuser who is incredibly and demonically aroused by being the abuser and my being me, in a male body but <u>as</u> 'Eurydice', as I am wickedly abused, shamed, and humiliated.

139-viii. Always, in these reveries, I must maintain wide-open eye contact with 'Eurydice', even at the very moment of orgasm, unless I have been commanded by 'Eurydice' to maintain loving and sincere eye-contact with her new lover.

139-ix. The degree of masochism -- mostly visited upon myself -- often spills over into the criminal and sometimes involves some kind of eroticized castration.

139-x. This "staying on the edge" has really become the focus of the masturbation such that the actual climax brings disappointment and sadness.

139-xi. Yet without the actual climax "staying on the edge" would lose its meaning and cease to be erotic.

139-xii. It is a catch-22 situation.

139-xiii. The pain is a stimulus for me and, since I will not allow myself to remove the clothes pins till I come, the process becomes an inducement -- complemented by the outrageousness of my fantasies -- to reach orgasm. {{On occasion I have re-enforced the clothes pins with other clothes pins attached to the clothes pins which produces a stinging intense pain in the nipples -- and also on those tender, upper-inside portions of the thighs -- which does not pass with the passage of time and which sometimes I have felt to be exquisitely unbearable. The removal of these re-enforced clothes pins brings with it an actual increase in pain which is psychically painful as well since -- removal coming only after climax -- it is a pain no longer in the service of a near future orgasm.}}

139-xiv. During all of my comings I have trained myself to keep my eyes open in fact -- the lights on, of course -- fantasizing that I am maintaining eye-contact with my loved/hated-and-in-any-case-demonic 'Eurydice'.

139-xv. It was another lost week-end.

139-xvi. It was good.

139-xvii. Thank-you, Julia.

(caesura)

Sad Songs;
Manic Melodies

> *Then glut they sorrow on a morning rose,*
> *Or on the rainbow of the salt sand-wave,*
> *Or on the wealth of globed peonies;*
> *Or if thy mistress some rich anger shows*
> *Emprison her soft hand, and let her rave,*
> *And feed deep, deep upon her peerless eyes.*

I wish to be rendered helpless. I wish to achieve total submission. (I am getting hard just by writing this.) And total humiliation.

You must understand that there would be something liturgical, so to speak, and not repeatable about the experience.

The fact that I understand both the religious and psycho-analytic significance (childish desire for for helplessness/powerlessness before "Mommy" now become a Goddess) does not at all lessen the desire.

> O: Yes, my Master and my creator. I must keep my eyes open at all times. {{Yes, even if you deign to urinate in and on them or -- if this be possible and going blind would not make it impossible -- while you drip hot candle wax in and on them}} I must never look away. Never. I must peer into you peerless eyes. When they are demonic. When they are filled with the ecstasy of power which you hold over me; filled with the maniacally ironic delirium which shows itself when I am totally in your power. When they are filled with scorn and contempt for me. When they are filled with boredom. When they are glazed with pleasure from the erotic attentions of another. When even your eyes are terrified as you let yourself be shamelessly abused by another as I watch, powerless. I must never turn away from your eyes. They hold me captive forever. More than anything which you might do to me -- or have me undergo at the whim of another, female or male -- it will be your eyes, in that demonic ecstasy of power which are your eyes, which will reduce me utterly to helplessness. They will reduce me to the most degrading humiliation. It is then -- and only then -- that my eyes may speak to you how much I love you.

Eurydice had a friend. Anna. Dark-haired. Eurydice admired Anna and had sought out her advice often. In a quiet way Eurydice had something of an indirect erotic thing for Anna and suspected that perhaps Anna had something of an erotic thing for her.

Over time Eurydice intimated to Anna the existence of her love slave, O. Anna -- one could tell -- was definitely more interested than she verbally let on. Over time, she got Eurydice to tell her more and more about O. Eventually they had shared enough information so that it was time to invite Anna over for a "session."

Eurydice -- fully dressed -- had Anna sit down in the dining room. She then went into her bedroom. She led O out leading him on by his dick.

O would have to keep count and verbalized the count. Anna listened with increasing fascination. O's voice was so strange. There was irony in his voice. Self-mocking. Yet he was teasing Eurydice as well. The tease was that he was enjoying this and that she couldn't get him not to enjoy this regardless how hard or rapidly she might hit. He was egging her on. Indeed there was an nascent element of manic delirium in his voice. One could tell that he had been there before. Often. And his dick hardened.

(the pain being <u>both</u> a stimulus in itself <u>and</u> a stimulus by being a degrading inhibitor to orgasm which would have to be overcome through a manic effort)

But neither O nor Anna would give her the pleasure of howling or screaming as they stared, lovingly, into each other's peerless eyes. Eurydice left the mark of her unambiguous -- but not necessarily unambivalent -- message four times:

don't look back

She then mocked them and taunted them for the foolish condition they had brought upon themselves and left.

O's dehydration took three and one-half days before he died. It was five days before dehydration took the life from Anna. They were found the next deer season by hunters seeking refuge from the cold.

requiescant in pace

What am I saying? Something like this: Even though sadistic (and correlative "masculine" behaviors in sexuality) still were (and are) with me, I came to distrust myself in this role. I felt that I just might go too far if I didn't change. Although libido is clearly the strongest force in my life, the second strongest force is my deeply ingrained sense of morality, particularly with regard to hurting others. A strange compromise forged itself in my mind over those months. I presumed that I would never allow myself to <u>be</u> abused to the point of criminality. So my protection against the possibility of spilling over into the criminal and yet at the same time retaining an active libidinal life took the form of re-enforcing -- consciously and pre-consciously I presume -- the masochistic, "feminine" behaviors which I had been cultivating through my phone sex with H.

Anyway, that's the best I can make of it.

Agnus Dei
qui tollis peccata mundi
miserere nobis

Agnus Dei
qui tollis peccata mundi
miserere nobis

Agnus Dei
qui tollis peccata mundi
dona nobis pacem

The end of religion is no doubt worship of Woman, and also penal colony.

{according to the Roudiez tranlation of <u>Powers of Horror</u> by Julia Kristeva. Columbia University Press, 1982. Page 167. }

140.
a). Freud-Kristeva-Butler. All three members of the troika say it. "Mommy" is always and everywhere -- and for male and female alike -- the lost love object. But it is Kristeva who says it best and it is Kristeva's writings which most carefully unpack the dynamic of a woman's melancholia, both as it takes on the form of a disposition towards "depression" and also as it sometimes takes on the form of a "successful" melancholia.

Gender Trouble; Feminism and the Subversion of Identity by Judith Butler. Routledge, New York, 1990. Confer especially pages 57-66 in the Chapter, *Prohibition, Psycho-analysis, and the Production of the Heterosexual Matrix.*

The distinction between "depression" and a "successful" melancholia is not made by Kristeva herself. Nor was it made by Butler. It was suggested to me, however, through Butler's analysis of the role of "melancholia" in the formation of gender identity in her very remarkable chapter on Freud in Gender Trouble. Thus in these sections of the book which you are now reading it was found helpful to allow that "depression" results from an incomplete, conflicted identification with a lost love object and to speak of a complete and relatively non-conflicted identification with a lost love object as a "successful" melancholia.

Kristeva especially is sensitive to the price paid by women -- on the average -- as they surrender "Mommy" as object choice and enter into the Oedipal situation. In leaving-behind the "pre-Oedipal" attachment to "Mommy" the little-girl/grown-woman is hit with a triple whammy, all features of which which are inducive to a tendency towards lowered self-esteem, lingering resentment, and depression. This triple whammy entails: i), the need to accept as object choice something other than "Mommy" thus thwarting the original thrust of desire (i.e., original libidinal impulse); ii), a resentment-laden submission to the anatomical realities which "realities" first become "realities" precisely through the abandonment of the original object choice in favor of the second best object choice; iii), resentment-laden entrance into the "phallo-cratic"/reproductive dictates of what Butler calls *the heterosexual matrix.* "Ii" and "iii", most especially, overlap with each other.

This is a term used by Butler in Gender Trouble to describe the whole set of culturally established customs and norms which have the effect of pre-ordaining sexual roles and gender identities on both men and women. Later, this book of mine will have recourse to this most suggestive term so as to speculate on the trans-cultural (i.e., biological, properly psychological, and "religious" and all of this without embracing what some call a "bologism"/"essentialism" in matters of gender identity) dimensions of this term.

Despite this triple whammy -- with its tendency to pre-dispose females to various shades of suppressed anger, resentment, and depression -- there are advantages in the female situation which -- on the average -- are missing for men. If the little-girl/grown-woman does enter into the "heterosexual matrix" she is forced into an acceptance of the reality of the lost object choice and achieves a kind of maturity about "loss." In contrast, men who enter into the "heterosexual matrix", on the average, are held in a relative state of arrested development and denial relative to the reality of "loss" as they obsessively -- both in their sexual and aim-inhibited relationships with females -- attempt to re-create an attachment which is, in reality, gone forever. And there is another advantage which accrues to the female as well.

As Kristeva has so poetically pointed out, females, on the average, can alleviate their loss in a way which is barred from men. Through "mothering" a woman can achieve a subtle and very curative identification with the original lost love object, i.e., "Mommy". Usually the attempt at identification with a lost love object is by way of psychic incorporation of the lost object into the ego organization of the grieving one. As noted above, such identification is often fraught with various kinds of conflict and can be the occasion for a serious "depression." But something remarkable happens with identification through "mothering." In "mothering" the ego does not so much as incorporate the lost "Mommy" into its organization but rather transforms itself and is integrated into the lost object and, by literally becoming "Mommy", insures itself against the future "loss" of Mommy. This is an option precluded from the male experience.

Confer, for example, "Woman's Time", pages 205-206 as contained in The Kristeva Reader. (Edited by Toril Moi; Columbia University Press, 1986. Hereafter: Reader.) Also, in the same volume "Stabat Mater."

In these matters, Kristeva does not sweep aside the whole baby-penis equation which is operative in Freud's account of the identification with the mother which comes about for a woman through the mothering process. But it is precisely the very cogency of Kristeva's analysis which shows that the woman's production of a baby/penis is secondary in the mothering dynamic.

b). But-wait. But-ler. Who is to say that *the heterosexual matrix* is to be taken as normative? Why this emphasis on reproduction with regard to gender identity and resolution of identity? After all, further uncritical submission to *increase and multiply* could prove deathly for us all now that we approach six billion of us here on this third planet from the sun. And, should some shortage necessitate some mothering it is no longer necessary to enter into the "heterosexual matrix" for such a purpose since technology has rendered the genital/reproductive prong of that matrix superfluous. There is no longer any reason to resist the ancient call of Sappho.

Female as object choice and as that with which to identify while bypassing totally the heterosexual matrix and rendering it superfluous. Food for thought, indeed.

c). And the male of the species?

Yes, there is "identification" with the father as the "normal" ""resolution"" of the Oedipal situation. This identification occurs under the suasion of "the fear of 'feminization' " as the little boy passes through and resolves the "inverse Oedipal" phase of the two-tiered Oedipal complex. But this "identification" is secondary and can never substitute for the identification -- i.e., with "Mommy" -- which is forbidden to the little-boy/grown-man. The distractions and power accorded to the male in the heterosexual/"phallo-cratic" matrix keep most men from confronting the destiny of double loss which is the inevitable psychic heritage of male anatomical structure. *Melancholia interruptus* as the male destiny is how Holy Trinity put it. Caught forever in the double bind in which both the gay and "straight" options conspire to keep "Tristan" from engaging the most elemental aspects of his desire/sexuality. Women can walk with a Kristevean option or they can walk with the Butlerian option. Something like identity is possible for a woman. But a man walks forever without identity. A Stranger if he is true to his non-self. An impostor if he is true to his mask.

{{{{{Butler -- page 59 et passim of Gender -- partly gets this right and partly gets this wrong. In general she is remarkably perceptive in uncovering for the reader of the Freudian text the "melancholia" involved as the little girl -- in the alleged "normal" situation -- gives up a homoerotic object choice in favor the heterosexual object choice. She is also insightful -- even moreso than the

1923 text of Freud which is at the center of her reading -- concerning "the fear of 'feminization'" which is at issue as the little boy gives up -- in the second wave of his Oeidipal situation in what Freud will later call the "inverse Oedipal" situation -- the homoerotic love object in favor of the heterosexual love object. But through this second wave the little boy is returning to the original heterosexual love object (i.e., "Mommy") which had been given up through the first wave of castration fear. Schematically, Butler simplifies the situation by suggesting that for little girls and little boys the homoerotic love object precedes the "later" (and culturally conditioned) heterosexual love object. In fact this is true only for little girls. For little boys the homoerotic love object is not primary. Thus -- contrary to Butler's implied suggestion -- homoerotic lesbianism has a genesis which is substantially different from the genesis of a gay homoerotic "outcome."}}}}

{{{Please note the following: Freud evidences puzzlement about the thesis of bi-sexuality relative to the Oedipal variables. Butler uses a dimension of this puzzlement as grist for her mill in discrediting *the heterosexual matrix* when *the heterosexual matrix* is taken as normative. Yet both Butler and Freud pass over something relatively simple.

A bi-sexual disposition is acquired through the two tiered way in which little boys and little girls each, differently, pass through the Oedipal variables. To be sure those incredibly strong socially organized repressions tend to demand of everyone that he or she suppress the dimension of one's acquired bi-sexuality which does not correspond with one's anatomy. (Indeed, these socially organized repressions are so persuasive that the average tendency even of gay and lesbian homerotics is to define their homosexaul preference in an exclusionary manner and contrary to their own bi-sexual disposition. As though one must have either homosexual or heterosexual object choice only.) In any case there is really no puzzle at all concerning the thesis of bi-sexuality relative to the Oedipal variables. For it is through the Oedipal variables that we acquire our bi-sexual disposition.}}}

As has been suggested already, this book claims that the "inverse Oedipal stage" in the little boy's development (in which he desires to be passive love object for Daddy) intervenes between the first wave of the boy's Oedipal situation (in which he actively desires Mommy as love object with correlative fear/hatred for Daddy) and its subsequent alleged resolution of identification with the father. Indeed, given what Freud has said in general about the process of identification it is difficult to explain why identification with the father occurs unless the father is some kind of love object for the little boy. Freud talks about this inverse Oedipal phase in Outline, page 47. (Elsewhere he also unambiguously refers to this "inverse" phase as being universally present in the little boy's Oedipal development. *[Confer, again, "Some Psychological Consequences of the Anatomical Distinction between the Sexes" contained in Collected Papers; Volume V; Page 188.]*) In Outline, Freud does not insist that this inverse Oedipal wave is universal in all little boys.

And talk about "depression"!!! For starters -- as Papa Freud understood although Papa Freud never understood the implications of what he understood -- the severity of male super-ego, formed as it is under the harsh suasion of the fear of castration. Then the always conflicted attempts at and resistances to identification with the primary lost love object combined with an anatomical destiny which precludes the healing options of motherhood and/or lesbianism. When the distractions and male-oriented power opportunities afforded by "phallo-cratism" falter for a man -- to say nothing of the time when "phallo-cratic" privilege is systemically demolished -- there occurs the full unchecked rage and cutting sadness of his *melancholia interruptus*. This is a time of great danger. It is also a time of great opportunity. The Eleatic Stranger. The Athenian Stranger. "no-man". (no-one)

{{{{{And this in contrast with the way in which little girls form what Freud called "weak" super-egos since they navigate the Oedipal waters free of castration fear. Where Freud could only see "weak" a more alert person might see "less rigid". Where Freud could only see a disadvantage, a more alert person migh see signficant advantage. Freud never understood the Feminist implications of his own account of things. Nor, apparently, do many Feminists.}}}}}

141.
Eurydice: Hmmmmmmmm. Interesting way of putting it. In any case let us turn to what you said about "libido." This is what is so remarkable about your writings "up there." Your insistence that "libido" is basically one and that there is no specifically "male" or "female" libido.

Sigismund: And as you reminded me over the course of those "years" (as they refer to it), it was I, who originally made the point that it is social convention rather than Psycho-Analytic teaching which leads to calling libido "masculine." It is amazing how many Feminists, when citing the very passage under discussion, pass over the quite Feminist point about social convention which I made in that passage and then go on to transform the very Feminist point which I had raised into a critique against my thesis!!!

{{{Bappy: Doesn't Derrida get this very point screwed up as well?

Dewchee: Oh yes. Confer pages 482 and 483 of the University of Chicago's version of The Post Card which they put out in 1987. There Frere Jacques -- (who, in his rush to uncover the "plallogocentrism" of Lacan, ends up, with Lacan in missing Freud's more nuanced point) -- stumbles over his own self-congratulatory sophistication. Interestingly enough Alan Bass, in a footnote which says far more than is necessary, stumbles along with Frere Jacques in bypassing Freud's point.

Bappy: Why did that crowd act that way?

Dewchee: Well they were quite intelligent. They never punned in less than three languages at a time. And they -- but especially Frere Jacques himself -- are often unsurpassable in their thinking when and if they ever do get around to the proper vocation of thinking. But all in all one gets the impression that being suave and clever was more important to them than ""truth"".

Bappy: I know what you mean: supercilious towards Sartre and ever so suave about things Freudian; and always the self-congratulatory narcissism. Thanks for the clarification, Dewchee.

Dewchee: My pleasure.}}}

Eurydice: Calm down, my friend. I can see that you are still a bit too sensitive on these matters. You are referring, of course, to the oft-cited passage from lecture xxxiii of your The New Introductory Lectures on Psycho-Analysis. If there are any readers here along for the ride it would do us well to pause and cite the passage. I shall emphasize the point which Feminists, Lacan, and Derrida have all apparently missed. Listen:

> --- *But another question seems to have become ripe for judgment in the course of these researches. We have called the motive force of sexual life 'the libido.' Sexual life is dominated by the polarity of masculine-feminine; thus the notion suggests itself of considering the relation of the libido to this antithesis. It would not be surprising if it were to turn out that each sexuality had its own special libido appropriated to it, so that one sort of libido would pursue the aim of a masculine sexual life and another sort those of a feminine one. But nothing of the kind is true. There is only one libido, which serves both the masculine and feminine functions. To it itself we cannot assign any sex; if, following the*

conventional equation of activity and masculinity, we are inclined to describe it as masculine, we must not forget that it also covers trends with a passive aim.

New, page 116.

Sigismund: Yes, that is the most important citation, although I made analogous statements all throughout my later writings.

142.
Sigismund: I must own up to that. There is for instance that famous -- infamous!!! -- *Anatomy is destiny* phrase which I let slip when I was paraphrasing Napoleon. And the ironies which follow for those whose knowledge of the Freudian text does not go much beyond that paraphrasing of Napoleon. {{{{{E: Speaking of ironies, poor Siggy, "up there", never came to understand the anatomical as well as psychological advantages to femlae genital organization. O: Not at all. But we love him anyway.}}}}}

This overly infamous paraphrasing of Napolean is to be found on page 274 of "The Passing of the Oedipus-Complex" as contained in Volme II of Collected Papers. (Edited by Joan Riviere; Basic Books, New York, 1959; pages 269-276.)

Eurydice: Down here we have a greater appreciation for the overall irony of these things. As you know we still chuckle over this confusion "up there." Even you are learning to chuckle at these things.

Sigismund: Yes. It really is quite funny. For years I struggled against the emerging position of Jones -- and for that matter of Horney -- on the make-up of female psychological patterns. They truly do instantiate the teaching that *Anatomy is destiny*. They instantiate what later was to be referred to as "biologism" or "essentialism" in matters concerning sexual differentiation on a psychological level. My position is quite radically different from any "biologism" or "essentialism" in these matters. Yet whenever two or three Feminists are gathered together in my name it is almost taken as axiomatic that the Freudian text instantiates some kind of "essentialism."

Eurydice: Not always. Those who come to their Feminism through a modification of Lacan usually do not so egregiously misunderstand the Freudian text.

Sigismund: That is true.

Eurydice: Oh stop being so sullen, my friend!!!! It is unbecoming to you. And don't be so jealous. I was not comparing this Lacan fellow to you. He is a giant only in a world composed of dwarfs. He was philosophically shallow. And his own phallo-centrism was much more convoluted than yours precisely because he prematurely tried to get attuned to what was then called "Feminism." I only bring up his name to remind you that not everyone is so shallow as to accuse the Freudian text of "essentialism" or "biologism" in these matters.

Sigismund: I'm sorry. I wasn't really threatened by your mention of Lacan. You know who I am truly threatened by.

Eurydice: I know. Aristocles. He is your equal. But you must realize that he has spent more time "down here" and has had a greater time given over to recovery. You will like him quite a lot when you meet him. He is more like you than perhaps either of you would have guessed. But it is premature. You need more time. Even so, today we will take a few steps towards that encounter.

Sigismund: That sounds quite inviting. Shall we get started?

Eurydice: Not yet. You are still avoiding something in this review.

Sigismund: I know what you mean. But I still get embarrassed. Not so much by what I avoided, but rather that I avoided that issue back in the living years. After all, I was Sigmund Freud, the great unmasker of things sexual. But I said next to nothing significant about female patterns of orgasm.

Eurydice: And that was a serious lack. Indeed, by shying away from that topic you lost an opportunity to deepen your understanding of the very core of Psycho-analytic theory.

Sigismund: You refer to our friends, Eros and Thanatos, do you not?

Eurydice: Of course. And it is through our friends that I will eventually put you in touch with Aristocles.

Sigismund: I desire that more than anything else.

Eurydice: Then I shall let you lead.

Sigismund: The truth is, I was pretty ignorant about these matters. So I waffled on this in my writings and generally let the physiology of procreation become my guide for understanding the physiology of female patterns of sexual engagement. My hang-up about the procreational function of sexuality -- I was a kind of Roman Catholic on these matters for God's sake!!!! -- radically skewed my understanding of the orgasmic function of female sexuality. It really is simple for men, since the two functions co-incide perfectly (and so babyishly) in their manner of genital intercourse. I guess I conflated the two functions in my understanding of the female.

Eurydice: Yes. And in the process you set in motion -- both in popular consciousness and in Psycho-analytic circles -- many misconceptions about alleged frigidity in females.

Sigismund: I realize that now. I am sorry.

Eurydice: Do not be harsh on yourself. Those who -- violently, so to speak -- reacted against your implied teaching often bypass, in their simplicity, the Tiresian dimensions of female sexuality.

Sigismund: Our friend. He has been "down here" for the longest time. Long, long before Aristocles. I used to blush when he told me his stories and experiences. Now I just accept them as true. From both of you I am learning that female orgasm is not so simple as an either/or. Still less is it the smug both/and. It is dyadic -- even physiologically -- but more in the sense of "both-and-neither;-at-once-!!!" Oscillation comes to mind. The dictum of Tiresias is vindicated.

143.
I speak of Tales of Love. Will you please take the time to re-read your own citations of Freud?

Confer Tales of Love. Translated by Leon Roudiez; Columbia University Press, New York, 1987. Hereafter: Tales. The passage under discussion refers to note # 4 to "Manic Eros, Sublime Eros: On Male Sexuality". Pages 388-389.

Your citation of the 1905 piece is acceptable. But are you so parsimonious as to hold Freud for downs on something he wrote in 1905? He didn't even start hitting his stride until 1920. Now, please read your citations of the 1915 piece and the 1933 piece. Read them! Apparently you had read them without reading them. For clearly you did not acknowledge -- or apparently even notice -- the subtle change between the 1905 formulation and the formulations of 1915 and 1933.

Freud maintains that there is one libido; in its origin and early manifestation it is active. Fine. Keep reading. Freud's OWN POINT is that it is social custom *and precisely NOT* the teachings of Psycho-analysis which identifies active libido as masculine. You not only missed Freud's subtlety, but you continue as well the instantiation of that disastrous misperception of the text of the later Freud whereby it is taken as axiomatic that Freud's unconscious chauvinism -- (the existence of which both in his personal life and in its spill-over into his writings is beyond dispute) -- kept his text from understanding the workings of eros/libido. Yet it is you who have become the unconscious captive of a reading of Freud which no longer is able to read what Freud's text says because it wants to all so quickly congratulate itself for having understood Freud's "Phallo-centrism."

{{{Yes. Of course. Freud's complicity with "phallo-centric" social convention is evident even from the 1933 citation. It is evident from every word and phrase of his text. Freud never got over this complicity nor was he even all that aware of this complicity. Of course. Does it need to be stated yet again?

But please note. Freud came -- despite himself, so to speak -- to disengage his Psycho-analytic teaching on the "pre-masculine"/"pre-feminine" character of libido from from the largely unconscious phallo-centric presumptions of social convention. To be sure, Freud did not fully capitalize on this most significant insight since he himself was a victim of those largely unconscious phallo-cratic presumptions of social convention. But an even deeper "avoidance"/"denial" -- the words are chosen intentionally -- occurs when "sophisticated" readers of the Freudian text totally bypass Freud's fertile insight as they trip over their own sophistication in advertising to the world that they recognize the "phallo-cratic" presumptions of the Freudian text. Enough. You either understand this or you don't.}}}

You are not alone. This misreading of the Freudian text is characteristic of most soi-dissant "sophisticated" readings of Freud.

Lacan instantiates this misreading and unconsciously puts this misreading of Freud in the service of his own "phallo-centrism." Indeed Lacan's move is far more insidiously "phallo-cratic." For in transforming the teaching of Psycho-Analysis from its attention to the actual penis to a Lacanian meditation on, so to speak, the "linguistic" penis, Lacan re-integrates the "phallo-cratic" presumptions of social convention back into Psycho-analytic theory. In this move he does a serious dis-service to Freud and to Psycho-analytic theory. For more than a generation, now, readers of the Freudian text import the Lacanian confusion into the text of Freud. ((This is not to deny that some of Lacan's meditations on gender identity relative to the text of the later Freud are quite fertile and actually enhance one's ability to appreciate Freud's subtlety on these matters.))

Derrida -- *EVEN AND AS he takes Lacan to task for Lacan's "Phallogocentrism"* -- also instantiates this misreading of Freud and -- (the overall irony of the situation most definitely noted) -- ends up **with** Lacan in misreading Freud's 1933 text.

PC, pages 480-483 inclusive of footnote # 63 by Bass on pages 482-483. The point, dear reader (in case you missed it the first time) is that Derrida even as he properly and cogently uncovers Lacan's "Phallogocentrism" presumes without argumentation -- and contrary to a careful reading of what Freud actually did say -- the same kind of "phallogocentrism" to be present in the Freudian text. *{{{{{By the way. Frere Jacques, when it's all said and done, is one of the most important thinkers of this twentieth century. But doesn't his cuteness get to you after a while? I mean: "phal-logo-centrism". For God's sake. Get a life, Frere Jacques. One presumes -- since I have not kept up with his writings posterior to 1987 -- that he himself got tired of that degree of cuteness. Already in Psyche and Of Spirit (works published in 1987 in French) he was calming down. Even so the excessive cuteness of Frere Jacques can be forgiven because of the multiple ways in which he stayed true to the vocation of thinking. The same cannot be said for the self-congratulatory cuteness of the "other" Jacques.}}}}}*

144.
Derrida and Lacan. Different kinds of embarrassment in reading their texts. The shallowness of Lacan has been spoken of elsewhere, particularly in Sentences-III. On the playing field of cogency Derrida "wins" every encounter with the Lacanian text. But Lacan -- despite the shallowness with which he approaches things philosophical and despite as well the ontotheologic (i.e., phallo-cratic) presuppositions of his """linguistics""" -- does *think psycho-analytically* when it is all said and done. Derrida shies away from *thinking psycho-analytically* and thus fails to enter onto the all-decisive playing field of deception. One dreams, in vain, of a Lacan with the intelligence of Derrida or of a Derrida who could have *thought psycho-analytically*.

Sentences-III was the elder sister of *Thinking Psycho-analytically.* Much of the Lacan material contained in Sentences-III was brought forward to *Thinking Psycho-analytically.*

The reader is here referred to what used to be (in the previous incarnation of this book) the last three sections of Part IV concerning "the playing field of cogency" and "the playing field of deception." You will recognize them when you get there.

145.
On the other hand you are mostly alone on something quite glorious. I believe it started to happen in your writings with The Powers of Horror. Beyond all the self-deceiving sophistication relative to the reading of the Freudian text -- (a sophistication which you yourself -- in a "slip" here and there, so to speak -- are guilty of on occasion) -- which characterizes American and European intellectual life these days, you have broken through into a "space" -- I am tempted to say "chora" -- in which one, for the first time, thinks psycho-analytically. By "thinking psycho-analytically" I do not mean at all taking the insights of Psycho-analysis and using them as a grid of interpretation for the reading of texts both literary and philosophical. Nor do I mean integrating Freudian variables into something like a "deconstructive" and/or "feminist" stance towards texts and thinkers of "the Tradition." In both cases one still has an "external", so to speak, relationship to Psycho-analysis and thus still radically falls short of what I am calling "thinking Psycho-analytically." *Thinking Psycho-analytically* would mean being SO unambiguously permeated by the very ambience of Psycho-analytic "reality" that every philosophical distinction and/or ideological agendum comes to self-dissolve

into, at once, both its "Psycho-analytic" components and, so to speak, its "Psycho-analytic" "Ge-stell." This permeating kind of thinking does not at all imply a slavish attachment to pronouncements of Papa Freud. Yet anyone who *thinks Psycho-analytically* never ceases to make love with the text of Freud. You alone have done this in a significant way.

146.
Why do you keep ignoring me?

147.
Julia disappoints.

As mentioned elsewhere, along with Derrida and Lacan -- (and it is most ironic that Derrida should get this wrong since he, Derrida, gets it wrong precisely when he, Derrida, is critiquing Lacan and yet he, Derrida, is in unconscious collusion with Lacan in not even noticing the subtlety of Freud's text) -- Julia completely bypasses Freud's meaning in lecture XXXIII when Sigismund tells us that there is only one libido.

Confer # 143, above and New, page 116.

148.
She disappoints radically with regard to Plato. Julia is, after all, the one who understood, first, the fertility of Platonic "khora" in the dark passages of Timaeus. One expected more from Julia. Yet she has a completely domesticated notion of how Eros functions in Plato. She exhibits not the barest trace of an understanding of the inner connection between Philebus and Symposium. Her account of how "the good" functions in Plato is practically sterile. She exhibits no understanding of the kind of dualism -- i.e. a dualism of first principles -- which animates Plato's reflections on Eros; i.e., on "the good."

She disappoints in her practically girlish celebration of """""agape""""" as it emerges in Paul and the writer of the fourth Gospel. She exhibits no understanding at all that it was the loss of the multi-valency of Platonic Eros which created the vacuum by which this puerile notion of "agape" was able to gain ascendancy in Western Metaphysics. She exhibits no understanding at all of the eclipse of Platonic dualism by Aristotelian monotheism which created the stage in which the puerile teaching of "agape" could come to be so persuavive as it got instantiated in Western metaphysics.

Confer Kristeva's *The Semiotic "Chora" Ordering the Drives* on pages 25-30 of Revolution in Poetic Language. (Translated by Margaret Waller; Columbia University Press, 1984. Hereafter: Revolution) One might also confer the section *The "Chora", Receptacle of Narcissism* on pages 13-15 of Powers of Horror. (Translated by Leon Roudiez; Columbia University Press, 1982. Hereafter: Horror.) However, for purposes of what *Thinking Psychoanalytically* is trying to accomplish the most relevant references on these "chora" matters are notes # 11, 12, 13, and # 14 which accompany the cited Chapter from Revolution on pages 239-240 of Revolution. In those notes Kristeva displays remarkable insight into the role of "khora" -- with all of its mother/feminine aura -- relative to the very condition of discourse and any signification.

Already in note # 11 Kristeva makes reference to Derrida's ever so brief allusion to Platonic "chora" contained in Positions. (Translated by Alan Bass; University of Chicago Press, 1981. Page

75 and note # 39 on page 106) The reader of Thinking Psychoanalytically knows that Derrida has thoughtfully pursued his meditation on Platonic "khora" in *Comment* in the 1987 Psyche and also in his article, released on the same day, *Chora* contained in Poikilia: Etudes Offertes a Jean-Pierre Vernant. *["Chora" appears on pages 265-296.]* (There is also his brief advertisement concerning his interest in "khora" contained in Spirit, page 8.) Derrida's reflections on "khora" are of a different order than Kristiva's falling short of the Kristevean meidtation with regard to creativity and "resiliating-ness" (so to speak) and exceeding the Kristevean meditation with regard to insight into the Platonic text. (The reader is here alerted that, in the strange taxonomy developed at the end of Part IV of the book which you are now reading, Kristeva is ultimately assigned a "place" on most honored "playing field of deception" whereas Frere Jacques is assigned the "position" of being the most honored on the less honored "playing field of cogency.")

Both *Comment* (page 566) and "Chora" (page 293) make it quite clear that they -- (i.e. *Comment* and "Chora") -- simply inauguarate a Derridean study on Platonic "chora" which -- in 1987 -- was still in progress. Perhaps this work on Platonic "chora" has already emerged. Perhaps not. I beleive that the Derridean meditation on things Platonic -- including the proposed study on "khora" by Derrida which may or may not have already appeared -- intersect with but are radically incongruent with the meditation on things Platonic which is being attempted in *Thinking Psycho-analytically.*

This note is being written on November 16, 1991.

{{{Yes, that note was written on 11/16/91. Now, on 10/17/92 the reader is further alerted to the fact that, as Thinking Psycho-analytically *comes to be instantiated as* Shame!, *the divisional sectioning of the book as* Thinking-Psycho-analytically *(i.e., "Part I", "Part II", etc.) is not being carried over into the instantiation of the book as* Shame!. *Nonetheless you should have no difficulty recognizing the section that has been referred to.}}}*

Confer *IV -- God is Love* contained in Tales, pages 137-150.

149.
In multiple ways, then, Julia disappoints. One thinks back to the celebration of "Cecilia" when it is discovered that "Cecelia shits." Even so.

Julia of the spirits is attuned, like no other in our time, to that nexus of abjection/melancholia/jouissance/narcissism/masochism without which one is not intellectually alive as we close out this century called "the twentieth." Julia has understood feminism the way Nietzsche understood nihilism: she looks back when telling of its future history. Julia -- on her better days -- has read through that dismissive and oh-SO-sophisticated reading of Freud (characteristic of most European and American intellectuals today) and, in her writings, reveals the "eurydicean" voice which is the true animus of the Freudian text. As we approach the end of this God-awful century it is arguable that one is not even thinking at all unless one has encountered the text of this Julia of the Spirits.

150.
And Luce deserves unambiguous acknowledgment for being the corrective to the Deleuzian/Derridean appropriation of the text of Nietzsche. OK. Enough said. What was the major reason for this Irigarayan pause?

Sic: She instantiates in both the worst and best ways the silliness which befalls both thinking and Feminism when it gets entrapped into what I would like to call "the Lacanian detour." Whether, for example and on the one hand, it's Derrida and Irigaray (in their differing manners and with differing agenda) unmasking the thoughtless "onto-theo-logic" (and, a fortiori, "phallo-centric") presuppositions which unconsciously animate the Lacanian text, or, for example and on the other hand, it's Kristeva thoughtfully resililiating the Lacanian text so as to free and rescue it from its most thoughtless indulgences, the result is pretty much the same.

Non: And what is this result?

Sic: Enmeshment in a complicated detour which was never necessary to begin with and which ends up in a sterile meandering which hinders the vocation of thinking.

Non: But didn't the writer of Shekhinah celebrate the Lacanian meditation on those texts of the later Freud concerning gender identity?

Sic: There's no problem at all with those meditations. They are quite thoughtful in unpacking both the Freudian account of these things -- (i.e., how the Freudian account of these things differs so radically from the "biologism"/"essentialism" of Jones and Horney) -- and, I might add, the ""truth"" in these matters as well. To give an account of the shifting, slippery, terrain of gender identity -- along with an account of the socially organized repressions which are in the service of denying the shifting, slippery character of this terrain -- is certainly a great accomplishment. Here Papa Freud Freud is champ and he has been well serviced by his son, Lacan, and by his late in life, so to speak, daughter, Julia Kristeva.

Non: OK. Fair enough. But then just what is the Lacanian problem and how does it relate to Irigaray?

Sic: Like so many French intellectuals Lacan got swallowed up into that whole side-show emanating from the linguistic ruminations of deSaussure. By itself such immersion is innocent enough. But when it becomes the prism by which Freud's teaching on sexuality and gender identity is appropriated and presented, then it just leads to mountains and mountains of silliness and the wasting of ink and paper. This silliness permeates all of Lacan's meditations on sexuality and gender identity. This silliness even permeates Kristeva's sometimes thoughtful recasting of that Lacanian nexus of and between language and gender identity. In Kristeva's case, her incredibly insightful meditation on "chora" is constantly subverted, in the worst sense of "subvert", by her need to square her "chora" insights with what she takes to be the part of Lacan worth salvaging. This silliness also permeates Derrida's unrelenting unmasking of "the other Jacques" as being "phallogocentric." Similiarly, Irigaray herself is thrown into page after ceaseless page of meditation on the alternatives to a discourse which alternative would not come forth as "phallo-centric"/"phallo-cratic".

Non: Your point is still not clear to me.

Sic: It's quite simple. Language/discourse -- in what I would like to term its endemic misogyny/"mis-ogyny" instead of its "phallo-centrism" -- can come to cure itself without all of these anguished detours into the "masculine character of the """subject""" " provided that the real problem is addressed, not only conceptually but in actual living. All of this business about "phallo-centrism" and the soi-dissant "masculine" character of """the subject""" -- whether it emanates from Lacan himself, or from those who attempt to modify Lacan, or from those who challenge Lacan and yet stay married to the Lacanian fusion of the allegedly Siamese questions of discourse and gender identity -- is but noise and a deflection from the real issue. To some extent this Lacanian nonsense is quietly being recognized as nonsense in the later works of Kristeva -- (Shall we use The Powers of Horror as a marker?) -- as she walks away from these hyperbolic meditations on discourse/language and walks back to the issue -- in Freud and in a whole grouping of "literary" figures -- of sexuality/gender identity (and those correlative "issues" of melancholia and abjection), relatively free of the Lacanian-spawned silliness.

Non: And what is our point in all of this, since our interruption was not meant to be some kind of review of Kristeva?

Sic: To unmask the discovery of "Phallo-centrism" -- both the discovery of its obvious presence in Freud and the discovery of its more subtle presence in the text of Lacan -- as a basically meaningless Shibboleth of sorts which deflects from the truly thought e-voking character of Freud's text. In other words, let it be taken as axiomatic that in a hundred-thousand ways Freud's text (and Freud the person for that matter) is consciously, pre-consciously and deeply unconsciously, chauvinistic, misogynistic and, of course, "phallo-centric"/"phallo-cratic." All of that is taken as axiomatic. But it is Freud's text -- precisely because it deals directly with sexuality and, simultaneously carries within itself the unconscious misogyny of the Tradition -- which puts us in touch with the very issue for thinking.

Non: And what is that?

Sic: Don't pretend you don't know. You were there for the composition of Madonna and then Shekhinah. I speak of course of "mis-ogyny" as it is put forth in Shekhinah.

Non: I remember that, of course. And I begin to understand. As long as "phallo-centrism"/"phallo-cratism" is the prism by which the Freudian text is appropriated, the teachings of psycho-analysis -- one thinks quickly of penis-envy; but really what is at issue is the whole spectrum of psycho-analytic teaching -- remains unperceived, unappreciated, and caught in a netherworld where it can no longer speak for itself. And, as Bappy and Dewchee have warned us, unless we, males and females alike, do thoughtfully get in touch with the "real" -- that is to say, "mis-ogynistic" -- features of our sexuality, dire consequences will follow for our species on this third planet from the sun.

Sic: I'm glad you made reference to the horrible alternative and the correlative need to deal with the Bappy/Dewchee conversations in Shekhinah. But for now, let us continue to limit ourselves to the immediate issue. This "Lacanian detour" -- which includes Irigaray's challenge to Lacan since in this challenge she still remains married to the (con)fusion of and between the allegedly Siamese questions discourse and psycho-analytic teaching which (con)fusion is the very heritage/detour of Lacan -- has done much damage already. Staying enmeshed in this "Lacanian detour" will keep us from the redemption of (and by) "mis-ogyny" and the correlative self-healing of language by language.

Essential selections from the most important of these Bappy/Dewchee conversations alluded to here have been incorporated into this book.

Non: I take it you are referring, in your interesting reference to "redemption", to the dawning age of matriarchal androgyny, which, in Shekhinah, was shown to be the hoped for outcome of "mis-ogyny" as "mis-ogyny" finally comes to pass through that dungeon of misogyny. Yet -- indeed, I should be saying "and" -- does not Irigaray flee from "androgyny" as from the plague?

Sic: Yes to both questions. Even Luce -- I wonder is this is an endemically French trait? -- stumbles over her own soi-dissant sophistication. Luce flees "androgyny" because she understands "androgyny" only in that popular sense in which "androgyny" implies the denial -- on a psychological level at least -- of sexual difference. She does not understand "androgyny" in the sense worked out in Shekhinah where it is made clear that "the hegemony of difference" obtains most especially in the situation of matriarchal androgyny. {{{And, a fortiori, she has no comprehension at all of how "hegemony" functions in the theological ontology of Shekhinah.}}}

Non: Of course, she is not alone in her ignorance of Shekhinah and, now, Holy Trinity. Do you know of more than five people, besides ourselves (i.e., Amy, De Vere, Bappy, Dewchee, Sic, Non, Mort, Jude and the others), who even know of the existence of Shekhinah and , now, Holy Trinity?

Sic: No. Of course not. We are really the silly ones as we sing our song to a theatre which is empty. Let's get back to Amy and De Vere.

151.
Non: It goes without saying, I suppose, that in these non-technical remarks Sigismund is precisely NOT setting up an all too facile "nature"/"culture" dichotomy. Indeed, the genius of Freud's whole psycho-analytic position is that gender identity -- however ever-shifting the contours of gender identity might be -- is acquired and not an anatomical given.

Sic: It could go without saying except that almost no-one any longer reads the text of Freud without a distorting ideological agendum. And of those few who still pay some attention to the actual text of Freud, almost all of them read the text through the lens of that multi-faceted "Lacanian detour" which we spoke of above.

Non: I am finding all of this to be so very melancholic. Almost to the point of tears. Is there some phrasing we can give to help the sympathetic reader -- provided she is intelligent enough and sufficiently free of ideology to follow the point -- on all of this?

Sic: I believe so. It was said earlier.

Non: Yes?

Sic: Listen: the teachings of psycho-analysis -- along with their correlative ""realities"" -- come forth in and as the "netherworld" """between""" "nature" and "culture" which "netherworld" allows for the very "terms" in terms of which "there is" a """between""" at all. ((This means, for those who have the eyes to hear and the ears to see, that the most important parts of the Freudian text are situated in those often startlingly sudden -- except for the more leisurely footnote towards the beginning of Chapter Four of Civilization and its Discontents -- asides in which Papa Freud speaks of that ever so dark nexus where biological evolution comes to spawn the peculiar dimensions of psycho-social evolution in our species.))

Confer footnote # 1 to Chapter Four of Civ on pages 51-52. Confer as well the long footnote at the end of this Chapter on pages 58-60.

Non: If I follow that formulation, it appears that it is most difficult to stay true to the teachings of psycho-analysis since it is almost inevitable that, in a move which is structurally the same as begging the question, one -- in dealing with this "netherworld" -- tends to judge the "netherworld" of psycho-analysis either in terms of a "biologism"/"essentialism" taken from "nature" or, on the other hand, from the perspective of some ideological agendum taken from an insight into some prevailing power arrangement obtaining by virtue of "culture." Scylla and Charybdis. In making such a move one forgets that psycho-analysis (and its correlative ""realities"") is that "netherworld" in terms of which "there is" at all even the ability to distinguish between "nature" and "culture." Yet as individuals each one of us -- male and female alike, throughout our entire lives even and especially in our dying -- is subject, simultaneously, to the tyrannical dictates of both kingdoms (i.e., "nature" and "culture") while belonging to neither. Each one of us is a stranger.

Sic: Well said. And with those formulations you have effectively shown why one must be patient, gentle, and even forgiving relative to the tendency of Feminists -- of all ideological persuasions -- to falsely appropriate the Freudian text.

Non: I do not follow your meaning this time.

Sic: What I am saying now is quite simple. Papa Freud himself was not always as clever as Odysseus in his -- Papa Freud's -- own appropriation of his own text. Papa Freud was often enough swallowed up and devoured -- here by Scylla; there by Charybdis -- as he navigated the teachings of psycho-analysis between "nature" and "culture."

Non: Your reference to Odysseus takes me all the way back to the incarnation of Shekhinah which even preceded the Madonna incarnation of what eventually would turn out to have been Shekhinah. How cunning Odysseus, for the writer of Shekhinah, was "really" a female put forth in the "persona" of a male. But I realize we can't meander back to those old incarnations just here. Odysseus notwithstanding, what a difficult task Papa Freud was engaged in since the very "terms" of this """between""" are made possible, so to speak, BY the """between""" itself. So to speak.

Sic: Yes. His voyage was sui generis and, on principle, cannot be repeated. Even so, he floundered here and there. This is part of the reason why Eurydice and Sigismund are having this extended conversation "down here."

Non: Now I begin to understand. If Papa Freud himself could mal-appropriate his own teachings, then one must be patient if others -- whose vision has understandably been clouded by righteous indignation which results from patterns of institutionalized misogyny -- fail to appropriate the "mis-ogynous teachings of psycho-analysis and, correlatively, fail to disengage Freud's misogynistic/chauvinistic veneer from the "mis-ogynistic" life-blood of psycho-analysis.

Sic: Exactly. I think we have performed our function. Let us turn it back over to Sigismund.

152.
a). No doubt it is castration fear in the sense which you cite on page 59 of your book -- i.e., "the fear of 'feminization' " -- which, violently so to speak, keeps boys and men on the straight and ever-so-narrow path in the exploration of their sexuality. And, given this "fear of 'feminization' ", it is not at all so surprising that

homophobia in "straight" men often takes on a violent manifestation. Even so, if you have been following what I have been saying, it is then clear to you that the -- (on the average) -- foreclosure of the homosexual option motivated by this "fear of 'feminization' " sends the little boy, rather violently, to his original "heterosexual" drama with "Mommy." It was fear of castration which brought him away from "mommy" as object choice and it was a new version of the fear of castration which sent him back -- with greater drama, conflict and ambivalence than ever -- to the original "heterosexual" object choice. A fear is involved here which women simply do not know.

Gender, page 59.

What is the upshot of all of this?

The play of and between the female as both "othered" object choice and the female as that with which to be identified -- (which play/drama both "straight" and lesbian women can engage in in a spectrum of playful ways made relatively easy for them by virtue of biology) -- is violently short-circuited in male sexual development because of the fear of castration. The misogynistic and homophobic outcomes of this short-circuiting are well-documented -- ad nauseam -- in Feminist writing. What goes under-reported is the deeply melancholic and conflicted drama of having an irrevocably "lost" object choice -- (after all, the whole series of "Mother substitutes" which constitute both the sexual and aim-inhibited love-life of "heterosexual" men never really compensates for the original loss) -- *with whom one may not identify*. Are you hearing me? *with whom one may not identify*. The liability (since it involves the psychic consequences of castration fear) of male genitalia is more than physical. The liability is deeply emotional. One becomes destined to something like a never ending *melancholia interruptus*. The ultimately healing process of full identification with the lost love object (i.e., "Mommy") is precluded from the male experience.

{{Yes, you were brilliant in tracing Freud's transformation on the relative therapeutic "values" of mourning and melancholia from his 1917 article to what he was saying -- mostly by unfinished implication which was your point in your "chapter" on Freud -- in the twenties. Bravo! (Confer *Prohibition, Psycho-analysis, and the Production of the Heterosexual Matrix* in Gender pages 57-66 especially.) }}

Is what I just said really accurate?

A quick response might be: What about males who take on the ""female"" role in a homosexual relationship? {{We will leave to the side any discussion of males who take on the ""male"" role in a homosexual relationship. Suffice it to say I believe such a role entails a degree of misogyny which even exceeds -- if this can be believed -- male "heterosexual" patterns of misogyny.}} And that's just the point. It is the quick response which would be generated by someone who is still, covertly, caught up in the notion that male and female patterns of homosexuality are parallel to each other. This notion -- paradox again noted -- covertly endorses as normative the "heterosexual matrix" which matrix -- when taken as normative -- you yourself so cogently critique all throughout your book.

The play of and between the female as object choice and the female as that with which one identifies works if the "other" -- functioning as both "external" object choice and as that which is incorporated into one's identity -- is a female. Lesbian strategies of sexual encounter and behavior can instantiate this play -- this drama with "Mommy" -- without short-circuiting the drama. The male who takes on the ""female"" role in a homosexual relationship in some ways enters into his primary drama and, generally, does so more successfully than the male who restricts himself to "normal" genital expressions of the "heterosexual" variety. Even so, the partial identification with Mommy in such a role -- i.e., that taken up by both the male and female who take on the "female" role in either the a gay or "straight" relationship -- engage and take on only the conflicted and limited identity of being a woman for a man. The ""female"" male in a homosexual relationship settles -- as does the ""female"" female in a "heterosexual" relationship -- for an object choice which is not only "second best", but for an object choice which precludes full entrance into the playing out of all dimensions of the most elemental aspects of one's desire/sexuality. Thus it is the male who is truly caught in the double bind in these matters. Both "straight" and "gay" sexual options conspire to keep the male away from the most elemental dimensions of his desire/sexuality.

b). Oh Tempora! Oh Mores!

Already -- by virtue of reproductive technology (and the scope of this "development" of, in, and through technology will only increase with the passage of time) -- the male role in reproduction is approaching triviality. As the ramifications of this seep down into "ordinary" consciousness it will cause grave disturbances in the average male's perception of himself and his social function. In Shekhinah and Holy Trinity I have tried to convey the truly alarming dangers which all "cultures" -- "Euro" and "non-Euro" alike -- will face as males encounter their declining relevance. The rule of law still remains basically male oriented. Yet the male proclivity for violence -- which has so much of its genesis in the double check-mate put upon his sexual development through the fear of castration (which fear is only made more insidious by virtue of the fact that it is almost always repressed/suppressed) -- will only increase as males become more conscious of their declining sexual and social relevance. It will be a dangerous time as male self-esteem lowers while the male proclivity towards violence remains about the same. Worse than most Feminists now expect.

Even so, I am optimistic. It all goes back to Papa Freud. Listen:

> --- *And now it is to be expected that the other of the two 'Heavenly Powers', eternal Eros, will make an effort to assert himself in the struggle with his equally important adversary.*

Civ page 104.

Yes. One realizes that a year later he added on a somber follow-up sentence with the ascension of Hitler to power. Even so, I am optimistic. How can I say it? But why should I say it. You have thematized it. Permit me to mis-use, intentionally, -- but not abuse -- your mantra, *heterosexual matrix*. Indeed, my "mis-use" is in fact your own use. For, even as you -- all throughout your book -- ever so cogently critique the "heterosexual matrix" when it is presupposed as normative, you likewise cogently insist that some non-normative meaning of this *heterosexual matrix* functions in any understanding of sexuality, be such understanding "straight", gay, or lesbian. Let us listen.

heterosexual matrix

again:

heterosexual matrix

again:

heterosexual matrix

What am I getting at?

In the first place, this sexuality business is indeed a Matrix. I made this quite clear from the opening pages of Shekhinah. Female sexuality is the from-which and to-which of all sexual instantiation and expression. "XY" is a variation on "XX" and not the other way around. In Shekhinah I called this "the hegemony of difference."

A matrix. A Mother. What I allude to is anything but a reversal or mere overturning of what is called "phallo-centric"/"phallo-cratic" hegemony. Nor is what I allude to some pre-Feminist idealization of "the eternal feminine" so characteristic of the unconscious chauvinism of the Tradition. Rather what is at issue is the acknowledgment of what has always been the case and will always be the case. What I allude to is the reign of "mis-ogyny" -- (((which only incidentally and not necessarily entails misogyny although I will grant that within the "heterosexual matrix" taken as normative it is simply misogyny and not "mis-ogyny" which reigns))) -- which is the animating force of life itself.

c). And now a word about Kristeva. You may count this as the third nodal point, if you so choose.

I'm certainly glad that I will never have to bat against you. I would never get to first base unless you chose to bean me. But what about Julia of the Spirits?

You nearly had her roped and tied. --- *altar bound* ---

(These phrasings are, of course, references to Elton John's recording of "Someone saved My life Tonight.")

Nearly.

Did you not notice that practically all the rope she gave you by which you hanged her came from her writings of the seventies? You also cite The Powers of Horror and her Black Sun book on melancholia. But you apparently did not notice what I take to be a most radical transformation in her writing. I am still in the middle of my self-appointed task of becoming a Kristeva groupie so I cannot speak with finality. But I do take The Powers of Horror itself as a marker in this transformation.

Confer Butler's section on Kristeva, Gender, pages 79-93.

Julia of the Spirits has quietly and simply walked away from the fray. She has liberated herself from "agendum" writing.

To be sure, her "fray" was a kind of babyish one to begin with. That whole Lacanian detour. Of those who entered into that detour she was far and away the best, inclusive even of our other friend, Luce (who herself is more caught up in that detour than she imagines). Only a few who have entered into that detour have ever really liberated themselves from it. Julia of the Spirits has. Now, no longer a writer with an "agendum", Julia of the Spirits is walking right through the major leagues into the Hall of Fame. Are you?

Of course you yourself were never really caught up in that Lacanian detour. This is why your "chapter" on the other Jacques was so delightful. Whenever the Lacanian text gets out of hand, you can and do deliver a punishing karate chop to his private parts. He is still smarting from those blows. When I visit him in the hospital he tells me all about it. But you also give yourself the luxury of actually basking in some of the comedic dimensions of gender identity which -- to his credit -- this other Jacques reveals through his musings on phalluses and phallus place-holders. Your freedom and acuity in these Lacanian matters is largely due to the fact that you never really got caught up in that detour. But what about Butler? What is <u>her</u> detour? What is her <u>fray</u>? What is <u>her</u> agendum?

Confer Butler's account of Lacan in *Prohibition, Psychoanalysis, and the Heterosexual Matrix* especially pages 43-57 in <u>Gender</u>.

It is one which is very -- and predictably, -- American. It's the lesbian/political routine. It's an agendum which, on the level of praxis, I endorse if it is carried through thoughtfully and in such a way as to not, unconsciously, subvert itself. You have mostly done it. You owe much to Derrida in the process (i.e., even more than your continually acknowledged debt to Foucault). But who of us alive does not owe much -- very much -- to Frere Jacques?

153.
Yes. Loretta had been turned into "Eve" just as Heather had been turned into "Eurydice." But now -- (Loretta having passed her life's Winter's solstice and having entered deep and unforgiving winter) -- it was time to speak of Loretta. Or -- honesty requires me to admit that I know not what it is to be Loretta -- being the son of Loretta. For it was Loretta -- not "Eve" -- who bore me.

Being the first-born son of Loretta. Being any son of Loretta.

Sometimes -- on Tuesdays when the <u>New York Times</u> published its "Science Times" sections -- he would read those charming socio-biological pieces about evolution. Like, for instance, the advantages relative to natural selection for the coloring of Monarch butterflies or the often offensive odor of wild orchids. He would then extrapolate into the arena of psycho-social evolution. What "socio-biological" advantages accrued to people -- sons -- who had such a twisted, cruel, ambiguous and souringly bitter-sweet relationship to their mothers? Yes there were many who did not survive at all. They succumbed to the seductive suasion of the slow and fast forms of suicide. We can call this Charybdis. And yes, prisons are populated with such mother-conflicted types and it is likewise arguable that more volts of electricity have been used to put an end to the violent conflicts of such types than have been used for ending the lives of any other type of criminal. We can call this Scylla. But what of those who have managed to sail through between the Charbdis of self destruction and the Scylla of maiming and killing others? What advantage accrued to these fools in the service of suffering and melancholy? Johnny Keats who did the whole thing in a quarter of a century. Sigismund and Aristocles who each took more than three quarters of a century to arrive. Eddy DeVere who took about a half a century. And look! On the other side they join up with the daughters of Loretta who only had one daughter in fact. For <u>every</u> daughter -- even the daughters of """normal""" mothers -- has a twisted, cruel, ambiguous and souringly bitter-sweet relationship to her mother. Kristeva -- ((and, if truth be told, several mothers encountered along the way a couple of whom had not been mothers when little Orpheus had met them)) -- had taught him that. But who are these people -- sons and daughters -- who join together on the other side?

Would it be too narcissistic to say that they were the acolytes of and for "the good"? The "advantage" was not really for them although it was their greatest glory. The "advantage" was not really for the species although in saying such one was a bit closer to the "truth." The "advantage" was for "the good."

++

Doubtlessly Loretta was now dying. He had known this from his last visit to Florida. Slowly. For some reason some seem destined to die slowly. Some kind of purgation? Who knows about these things. It might be the biggest challenge of his life. Not to die with Loretta. To die with Loretta would be -- for "Orpheus" -- submission to a twisted narcissism. To live would be to submit to the will of "Shekhinah" and would best service the memory of Loretta -- to say nothing of "Jackie-boy."

++

{{{Eros. Philia. Agape. How the sophisticated ones just love to trot these out -- all neatly in a row -- as they strut their learning on the catwalk called "academia." But litle Orpheus is here to shout out: ----- *they are naked! they are wearing no clothes!*

"Philia" -- that marvelous tenderness and admiration often obtaining between and among parents and children, siblings, and friends -- is but aim-inhibited Eros. The fact that the dynamic by which aim-inhibition is achieved is almost always unconscious makes one presume that the "differing" experiences of "Philia" and "Eros" have nothing to do with each other. Even so, the "difference" obtaining between "Philia" and "Eros" is akin to the "difference" obtaining between leaf and branch. Thus -- for those who have the eyes to hear and the ears to see -- all celebrations of "Philia" are really celebrations of Eros.

((Nor is it accidental that the most sustained meditation on "Philia" (wherein "Philia" is stripped of all erotic overtones) should emerge in Nichomachean Ethics. For it was the Stagirite himself who inaugurates the "flight from libido" -- (which is, effectively, the "flight from difference") -- which comes to be so endemic of what would turn out to be the Tradition.))

"Agape" is but the fetish. "Agape" -- when its genesis is fully understood -- gives "love" a bad name. Only an age bankrupt in both spirit and conceptual power would generate what came to reign as "agape." Even here, it is to be noted, precisely as fetish, "Agape" itself has erotic roots.

And "Eros"? Even if we were to restrict ourselves only to the Platonic text, one finds that it is more multi-valent than the Tradition permits it to be. The Tradition -- in its endemic "flight from libido/difference" -- needs to delineate eros and deny its multi-valency so as to allow for a "de-eroticization" of "Philia" and, later on, "Agape." In general, the Tradition has not yet encountered even Platonic Eros as it continues to generate volume upon volume on the subject. But Eros will prevail.}}}

154.
One always, if one is honest, must end up walking in the shadow of Aristotle. This

thinker who inaugurates the "flight from difference" always engineered his moves with cogency. His move away from "difference" must be rejected but never avoided by those who would remain faithful to the true vocation of thinking. For Aristotle was a witness firsthand of the inner collapse of "difference-oriented" thinking when such thinking loses it soul. Those who would remain faithful to the true vocation of thinking must always be prepared to learn from the testimony of Aristotle.

{{It is postulated in this book that Plato's "difference oriented" disposition died when he learned -- in 354/353 -- of the assasination of Dion. If it is assumed that this news was the cause for the suspension of the proposed (and presumably massive) trilogy, Timaeus/Critias/Hermocrates, then it may be likewise presumed that Laws and Epinomis (even to the extent -- which extent can never be adjudicated with finality -- that Epinomis is somehow a product of Aristocles himself) are post "difference-oriented" productions of Plato. Only the necessity of having the appropriate conceptual lead-in for the (earlier written) all important third dialgoue of the third teralogy (i.e. Symposium) was able to stir up in the Depressed and deeply melancholic old man the verve required for a "differnce-oriented" thinking. This he does in Philebus but only at the price of an evident struggle against his deepening Depression. Speussippus and most especially Xenocrates were unequal to the task of sustaining a "difference-oriented" kind of thinking after the death of Aristocles. With both thinkers -- but most especially with the shallowness of Xenocrates -- the "mathmatical" revisions of the "difference-oriented" theory of forms collapses in upon itself and becomes a mushy mess over-ripe for critique.}}

The following remark from the above-mentioned book on "the wo-man principle" can be added on here:

Plato needed to do more work to integrate the "play of difference", which emerges from (Theaetetus)-Sophist-Parmenides primarily, with "Anangke" (i.e. the principle of random chaos) which emerges, of course, from Timaeus. This weaving together of the two grand projects of the later Plato (i.e., the dialectical "being"-oriented project with the "likely story" "genesis"-oriented project) might have culminated in a most remarkable "tukhe" teaching except for a chance event: the assasination of Dion in 354/353. This book postulates -- not without evidence -- that the assasination of Dion was so psychologically traumatic for Plato that it effectively put an end to the inaugurated-but never-completed (and gloriously playful!!!) trilogy Timaeus-Critias-Hermocrates. The shards and fragments of Plato's abandoned project are picked up in Laws and, to a lesser extent, in Epinomis. But by then the verve, sparkle, daringness, and playfulness of Plato -- which was the very lifeblood of his Philosophy -- had become fearful of showing itself anymore. Plato the writer had become the hostage of his own Depression.

Of the very, very later writings of Plato -- (i.e., Philebus, Laws, and whatever portion of Epinomis he is responsible for, all of which were written after the assasination of Dion in 354/353) -- it is only in Philebus that the verve and playfulness returns. {{The careful reader of Philebus will be able to discern the struggle against deep Depression on the part of its author.}} And even there -- in that dialogue addressed to "youth" -- the return to the verve/sparkle/playfulness is maintained so that the dialogue on Love (i.e., the Symposium whose subtitle is *Concerning the Good* and which is the third dialogue of the third tetralogy) will have been properly contextualized and introduced. Listen to the conversation in Philebus as Philebus -- the second dialogue in the third tetralogy -- nears its climax. They are speaking of"the Good" -- i.e., "Agathon" . The Symposium, the third dialogue of the third tetralogy, takes place, of course, at the house of Agathon. Listen:

> *Socrates: And haven't we in a sense found a way toward the good?*
> *Protarchus: How?*
> *Socrates: If you were looking for somebody and began by ascertaining correctly where he lived, I imagine that would be abig step toward discovering the man you looked for.*
> *Protarchus: Of course.* (61A-B. According to Hackforth)

One should read Book XIV of Metaphsyics. Yes, Yes. Aristotle does beg multiple questions in his review of Plato, Spesusippus and Xenocrates. This I have brought to your attention many times before. And, indeed, one should always maintain an acute awareness of this question-begging as one reads Aristotle's accounts of "Platonism." Nor should Aristotle escape condemnation for critiqing the foundations of Platonism through the lens of an Act/Potency ontology which is a priori antithetical to what Plato was trying to do. Even so, read Book XIV. Read it for its positive signficance as well.

In XIV-3 -- first circa 1090b, 19-21 and then 1091a, 7-15 -- (and apparently primarily in terms of the mathmatical modifications in Plato's theory generated by Xenocrates) Aristotle accuses Platonism of "lacking cohension" and coming forth as 'poorly constructed drama.' Platonism, in this critique, becomes not much different from "the long rigamorole" of a poet on an off day. Listen:

> *--- for men have recourse to "the long rigamorole", such as slaves tell, when thay have nothing satisfactory to say.* [1091a, 8-10 <Loeb lining>]

Platonism, according to this withering critique, has become merely "episodic", lacking an organizing chohesion.

Relative to Xenocrates and the other "rescuers" of Platonism who would "save" the theory of forms through mathematics, Aristotle's critique has merit. But his critique raises a very serious question for "difference-oriented" thinking in general, whether it be Plato's version, the version put forth by Frere Jacques, or the version being put forth in this book as well as in Sentences-III.

There will always be sufficient "cohesion" for anyone -- and this starts with Aristotle -- married to what today one might call "the metaphysics of full presence." But "difference-oriented" thinking -- and not just in its more obvious moments of decline as represented by a Xenocrates here and by more than a few of the followers of Derrida there -- by its """nature""" will have to always appear to lack organizing coheshion since that which organizes it, by its """nature""", appears only by "dis-appearing." A thinking which remains true to the vocation of thinking will always appear to be "episodic." Look at Plato's dialogues. Look at the later writings of Heidegger. Look at any of the writings of Frere Jacques, intrinsically, as well as in their relationship to each other. And look at this book which you are now reading.

{{{{{Having no readers the incredible presumption of that last sentence becomes a form of bitter humor.}}}}}

Only episodic? One hopes that such is not the case. But it always remains helpful to walk in the shadow of Aristotle so as to stay attuned to the danger.

cowardly psychosis the psychosis of bad faith avoid the temptation you pay too high a price i.e., the "truth" if you approach the mystical via jung rather stay with siggy let siggy hitch a ride with aristocles in turn let aristocles hitch a ride with siggy together they will get you there

second speech (and here too siggy owes a bit to spielrein) the emergence of voice/sound discrimination in the pre-history of our species read chapter four of <u>outline</u> page 19 the special status of "preconscious" brain activity when such brains blossom into the possibility of speech and with this the emergence of a species-specific possibility for a kind of consciousness which is hallocinatory yes yes yes speech logos the break from aisthesis it goes to logos for those who have the eyes to hear and the ears to see

third difference even freud was there <u>outline</u> page 20 difference difference between the speech imbued time-experiencing "preconsciousness" of homo spapiens sapiens and the timeless "unconscious" of that same homo spaiens sapiens the break from aisthesis and where we go in the breaking and from whence we return as we return to aisthesis the difference the differnce read page twenty:

> But of that we know nothing. And the profound obscurity of the background of our ignorance is scarcely illuminated by a few glimmers of insight. Here we have approached the still shrouded secret of the nature of the psychical.

the mystical of course the babies (even after having read the long caesura they will not have understood the long caesura) will want to make the "meta-ta-phusika" move here and in the process bypass <u>on principle</u> what the mystical is all about

it's there but what gets us there (and only if we get there -- provided of course that we don't stay there since the bad faith attempt to stay there will throttle the process -- will we be able to conceive and do our concept-ing) read on there is a there only by virtue of difference and what makes the difference read on page 21 freud speaks of a "hypercathexis" {{thank-you so much mr strachey!!!}} and what might that be?????? something so decisive that it not only makes that difference but pushes a certain species to interrupt to break with the system of perceptual-consciousness freud does not say not here on page 21 but it's all over the text of freud in this book it is called "mis-ogyny" the male and female versions of the castration complex **the horror!!!!!** *Mommy is castrated the glorious primacy of deception the hegemony of the counter-factual fact in the childhood pre-history twenty-thousand years ago? of homo spaiens sapiens and in the childhood pre-histroy subject to amnesia as is the childhood pre-history of our species of each member of our species female as well as male it is the air we breath the water that we swim in now go back and read the long caesura*

of course Lacan was a conceited jerk it is embarrassing for all of us how shallow were his readings of the heideggerian "a-letheia" and of aristotelian "nous" embarrassing even worse are his vain speculations on the platonic text

(continued on page 230)

(caesura)

Minna

9/13!!!!!(Friday)/92

Minna trust she's Jewish of course tell her about Doris Doris from Friends Doris who was my mother, Rachel and Ginny all at once and getting started in AA no AA for me without the Doris/Jewish connection interesting how """""""""God"""""""""" (((((will Minna say I should say "G-d"?))))) works the time I looked her in the eye and asked her if she had a personal relationship with God the Heather connection here she looked away and I admired her for her implied honesty Doris knew it works and that's all that matters but tell Minna also about the Jewish funeral in Brookline on a Sunday tell her about your feelings of hate back then will Minna understand? will Minna hate me? what does Minna *really* feel about all of this and about """Luther""" trust does this Jewish connection interfere with the """therapeutic""" relationship or make it possible????? this is a real question (and what about Dr. J in this regard) am I just fooling myself??? would I ever let myself get smothered in her breasts????? what do I want???

and is my dick big enough???????

we come full circle can i trust you Minna the jewish connection necessary condition or hindrance???????? can i trust you?????? and what's in it for you???????? why do you bother

all of this even the therapy but especially this (and my book too) it's just *so* narcissistic so much bullshit isn't it the bible itself which tells us that cliche about vanity? all is vanity

actually i know myself much better than most people know themselves and better than most people think i know myself read *missing pieces*, Minna that's me really me no smokescreeen no denial just me i simply *am* more complex than the simplistic "either/or" which the world loves to attach to questions of sexual preference/orientation you know, Minna in my heart of hearts i think i know more about these things than you and Dr. J combined i am self taught in these matters experientially i've done some outrageous things put myself in real danger yes for sexual gratification but also in the service of really getting to know myself i suspect that *i* am really the pro in these matters and that you and Dr. J are the amateurs and forget the experiential even on the intellectual level (i.e., Freud and all the rest of it) i am self-taught it wasn't fed to me with all the quiet ideological baggage with which these things are presented in graduate courses and in professional schools finally i am even an intellectual path-finder on these matters who am i to be judged who am i to be categorized with simplistic categories

i am the champ when it comes to vanity

(((and minna dr j and the world still smile and think smugly: what an involved and exquisite pattern of denial he'll do/say anything to avoid admitting he is gay)))

here's a test for you, Minna: read what i have to say in note # xiv (to the 'preface' page 85 and the top of 86 in volume two) that says it all and, if you read between the lines, it tells you where i am: masculine and feminine (but mostly feminine) with regard to gender identity but decidedly heterosexual with regard to object choice that's me these matters are more complex for everyone than most people including the """"""experts"""""" think they are decidedly more complex for me it's not a smokescreen it's not a denial still knowing that does not keep me from thinking that the world caught in that babyish "either/or" paradigm (the world and you too, Minna) will make a simplistic judgement on that anymore it would be relatively easy to be gay and just say it and in today's climate in which homophobia is perceived as a greater evil than gayness it would be relatively easy to reduce my sexual complexity to a simple embrace of a soi-dissant homosexuality but fuck it!!! i am what and who i am i am sexually complex and not reducible to the easy "either/or" paradigms on these matters i'm not even reducible to a simplistic understanding of so-called "bi-sexuality" and if people don't understand that then that is their loss that includes you, Minna

shall we talk about my mother?

when are we going to get honest about incest the reaction formation against incest those who really worry about the damage to incest victims should start the solution by getting honest about the whole thing and work to get a better way to deal with this than through a goddam reaction formation for god's sake!!!!!! getting it right with shame the whole ball of wax we're talking about the pre-history of our species and how all of that is carried in our brain

{{{{{{ and just what was the socio-biological advantage which acrued to emerging homo sapiens by virtue of the incest taboo notice i did not say the practice or non-practice of incest of course in a kind of incidental way other species have something like "incest"-negating practices and perhaps were even "unterwegs" towards a taboo in these matters but only with emerging homo sapiens did it take on the full shame-centered dimensions of a taboo to be sure Freud probably had the right account of the genesis of this as a taboo but Siggy didn't really re-cover for us the telos of this <tortured-teleology unconscious of its own doings as always in

this book> because it became a <u>taboo</u> the emotional life of emerging homo sapiens sapiens became <u>exponentially</u> enhanced there was great liability interjected into the system of socialization here presumably some of the more cruel and subtle forms of violence and violation which characterize our species are in fact the eventual outcome of the often faulty way in which the taboo is instantiated ((the great benefit for the species and correlative liability!!!! of producing thrugh this taboo children-in-adulthood working through the radically unfinished business of childhood)) also risk a <u>chance</u>!!! a risk which on an individual level could entail a measureless pain ask any child whose trust has been betrayed by a parent in this regard and of course the neuroses yet there were several advantages at least for the species this taboo was the great lever by which all of that "aim-inhibited" libidinal energy noted already by Papa Freud could be put into the service of the subtle multi-faceted social bonds characteristic of our species also the life of the mind in its intricate play with voice discrimination and emerging speech required such an exponential upsurge in the "pathetic" capacity of the brain of emerging homo sapiens sapiens much melancholy and much joy precedes the dawn of thinking <and in the process eros came to be instantiated in a <u>most</u> variated manner Shekhinah was there for all of this trust Shekhinah trust Her in all things>}}}}}}}

most people have no honesty on this and when the best intentioned settle for a reaction formation is it any wonder that the problem grows worse getting it right with shame for god's sake yes for god's sake the very emotional health of your children depends on all of us getting honest about this can you hear the hero is not he/she who so vehemently <u>disavows</u> any incestual desire but rather he/she who knows from dreams or whatever how universal this is who doesn't do it but <u>does</u> talk about it alas """""""truth""""""" for now still remains hostage to a bad faith reaction formation oh my God! i finish this and discover that <u>today</u> is the thirteenth friday was not hmmmmmmmm and maybe the full moon was on saturday i tend to announce our friend before she actually arrives cognitive slips emotion sometimes interferes with cognition yet without emotion there would <u>be</u> no cognition and it gets easier to take these full moons let it be Tom!!!!! it's OK peace! eu prattein and eu poiein!

*****

+++++

B: A final thought? D: Why not? B: On this "mis-ogyny" business. Could it be -- allowing as we always do for those marvelously random machinations of tortured teleology -- that in the pre-pre-history of our species, (((while the brain was acquiring its new radical reorganization and enlargement following upon upright posture and the supereding of smell by sight as the primary source of sexual stimulation))) and as the interface between the bare beginnings of "human/pre-human" psycho-social evolution were interfacing with the finalization of the human "XX-XY" variation in the constellation of sexual differentiation, something interesting happened? D: Of course. But you speak. What is on your mind? B: The exaggerated size, on the average, of the phallus for homo sapiens. Do you see my point? D: Of course. The hidden genius of the human XX-XY variation in the constellation of sexual differentiation. An exaggerated, on the average, size of the male phallus contributes to the counter-factual perception that "Mommy" is castrated. One of the features of tortured teleology as it randomly-yet-marvelously brings about the conditions which must obtain for "mis-ogyny". The intelligent reader of <u>Thinking Psycho-analytically</u> could have figured this out, inferentially, for herself. But it's good that you have helped our readers out. B: Now we can rest. D: Yes. Now we can rest. Sleep tight, Bappy. I love you. B: And I love you too, Dewchee. Don't let the bed bugs bite. And just brush my cheek before you leave me.

2/9/92

Shame and the emergence of skin under the rubric of the developing human XX-XY version of sexual differention over self-selective time. Enough!! The point has by now been understood or it won't be understood at all. Peace. *//JE/(8/12/92)//day/night of the full moon waning//*

*****

+++++

------- *objective observer speaking from the very heart of "dis-association" (i'm getting more and more like johanna every day every minute!!!) was there in fact to have been a hermocrates yes clearly if you read the very playful opening of the dialogue but then when it became evident after the music died that the whole thing would stop with just the opening of critias they finessed it at 27A-B to make it appear that the whole thing had been intended to stop with critias do you understand? the day the music died chaos reigns indeed most of timaeus itself is only in a first draft do you understand? i guess you would have had to have been there*

but that other trilogy was completed before the music died i mean the one introduced by theaetetus: sophist-statesman-parmenides what?????????? you mean you have questions and reservations about parmenides being the completion of that projected trilogy?????????? you mean it's not self evident??????? what with the broad hint given at theaetetus 183E-184A what with the eleatic stranger killing off in sophist a false and popular image of "father parmenides" so that in parmenides the "true" parmenides in his awe-full complexity may make his majestic appearance what with "young socrates" being silently present in theaetetus and then being a bit more explcitly present in sophist and then being respondent to the eleatic stranger in statesman and all of this while good old "regular" socrates goes through mental gymnastics on the day when he is going to be indicted {{{{{and what a day that was since it included as well his mental gymnastics with euthyphro and his rather manic gymnastic with cratylus and hermogenes!!!!!}}}}} *(and then on the day after in sophist and statesman he strangely recedes as magister ludi in favor of the stranger) yes all of this leading up to the strangest of all contrived dramatic settings in which the "real" socrates (i.e., not the "metaphorical" "young socrates" of theaetetus-sophist-statesman) IS IN FACT YOUNG as he meets old parmenides and middle-aged zeno and please notice as well that sophist and statesman are the third and fourth dialogues of the second tetralogy while parmenides is the first dialogue of the third tetralogy all of that and it it's still not self-evident to you?????????? what's the matter with you????????? there are none so blind as those who will not hear!!!!!!!!!! oh well i guess you would have had to have been there (and notice that i didn't even bring up letter ii let derrida and the others have that interesting but overly cited letter ii enough!)*

155.
Son of Ariston! Aristocles! Through how many masks are you to be revealed? Stranger who speaks through the mouths of Strangers! What are you hiding and why?

156.
listen: difference = light = khora = good and other dis-appearing appearances of the same. *["other kindred notions" is how Bury puts it as he translates 52B-8.]* I am beginning, now, to understand how "khora" = light = good they are all said to be the third but "difference"; is it the third or the fifth? for the fifth would be the contrary-to-the-one whereas the third would be the product -- offspring -- of the interaction of and between the one and the contrary-to-the-one

157.
The one is drawn into the other for the sake of the other and all of this produces "the good" which was the eternally called for.

158.
the fifth is bascially sustained in the mixture the other is a Mother and Nurse both as principle and in the mixture *The good is female* (TGIF) {{{One will consult, in due course, the sections on the hidden genius of the XX-XY variation in the constellation of sexual differentiation and also the way in which "the fifth" is sustained in the mixture.}}} this is "the hegemony of Difference" but remember, this is a "boss" not from the Tradition with its -- the Tradition's -- oft-repeated obsession for the position of privilege this is a "boss" who is of Her very ""nature"" dis-appearing She is the play of difference She dis-appears into Her predicates

159.
Plato shies away from the most secret name of the good. he always allows the good to *-- take refuge in the character of the beautiful* this must mean that Plato -- deflecting from his own deepest insights on these matters -- does not really marry the Mother although he did take her to his bed and did conceive with Her his nostalgia for the Father remained too strong and he did not marry her for to marry her is -- ultimately -- to be her.

Philebus 64E.

160.
Are we talking idly whenever we say that there is such a thing as an intelligible form of anything? Is this nothing more than a word?

Timaeus 51C.

As noted above, Kristeva quite thoughtfully makes this section of the Timaeus problematic in notes # 11, 12, 13, and # 14 to her Chapter *The Semiotic "Chora" Ordering the Drives* in Revolution. The Chapter is on pages 25-30 of the book and the notes are on pages 239-240 of the book.

161.
But neither one brought it home: "khora" (=light) = "the third" = good.

162.
The text of Plato remains un-read, even today; even after Derrida et alia, the text of Plato remains un-read.

163.
The good cannot be at all unless it is demonic. {{{The demonic incorporated into the good is "eu-daimon" although not in any of the senses used by Aristotle.}}}

164.
Even so, Neo-Platonism, even and especially when it re-appreciates "eros", still suffers from its Monism/Monotheism and its inability to acknowledge a dualism of first principles.

((A dualism of first principles is something quite other than the sensible/super-sensible distinction which is -- at bottom -- a continuation of Aristotelian Monism/Monotheism. The "unconscious", so to speak, Aristotelianism of Neo-Platonic Traditions is one of the central features of the Tradition which this wo-man book attempts to unmask as it attempts to "dis-mantle" the nexus, "Plato and Aristotle."))

<<<The super-sensible for Aristotle did not, of course, consist of separate forms. Rather, one is speaking here of the 47?/49?/55? intelligences -- plus the intelligence which is God -- in terms of which the universe as a whole and the "wanderers" have their motion. But in all of this Aristotle is Monistic/Monotheistic with but one first principle and cause (i.e., "God") which has no contrary. (Confer Metaphysics XII-10 at 1075b, 22-24 and the argumentation concerning "the first principle" relative to the "contraries" at the beginning of Metaphysics XIV-1.) Indeed "contraries" make an appearance in the Stagirite's thinking only by having one of the contrary pairings function as a kind of "privation" relative to the other contrary. It can be further noted that that infamous tribe of "deconstructors" -- when they think they are oh-so-cleverly "deconstructing" the phono/logo/phallo-centric dualism in what they call "the Tradition" -- remains unconsciosly married precisely to this "privation" model of the "contraries" bequeathed to them by Aristotle. They make all of their various -- and allegedly radical -- inversions and re-juxtapositioning of these dualistic pairings without ever engaging what the constraries represented before they were tied down to this Monistic/Monotheistic "fullness/privation" paradigm of "the contraries." In other words they -- that tribe of deconstructors (and this includes Derrida, the best of the lot) -- show themselves to be congenitally unable to engage the question of how the contraries functioned in Plato's Dialectical ontology obtaining prior to the time when this "privation" paradigm of the contraries was first generated. Thus that tribe of deconstructors remains married to the Aristotelian-spawned "Tradition" even and especially when they so cleverly "deconstruct" all of those phono/logo/phallo-centric dualities from "the Tradition." For their frame of reference -- even-and-especially as they overturn, subvert, and re-juxtapose -- remains the "fullness/privation" model of the contraries spawned by Aristotle. "The Tradition" bascially remains quite alive and well -- and normative, <irony of ironies> for God's sake!!! -- when subjected to the ministrations of the deconstructors. And in this great charade of subtlety, the question of duality in Plato remains completely unengaged by them since they "read" the Platonic dualities as instantiating the "fullness/privation" model of the contraries first generated by Aristotle.

{{{This is not to say that the Tradition is not phono/logo/phallo-centric. On the contrary it is and it is Derrida especially who deserves credit for so painstakingly showing this to be the case. But the question of dualistic pairings in Plato is not even engaged if Plato's dualistic pairings are "read" as already instantianting the frame of reference on these matters first generated by Aristotle. ((It would be, of

course, a left-handed compliment of the very worst kind to credit Plato with doing Aristotelianesque kinds of things -- particularly as concerns "the contraries" -- better than Aristotle himself. The non-engagement of what is at issue in Plato becomes so subtle in this case that it is entirely missed.)) The Platonic text even today -- yes even after "Plato's Pharmacy"! (and the situation is only marginally improved by the time one gets to "Comment ne pas Parler") -- remains unread and unengaged. Is anyone out there listening? In any case, the assiduous reader of Shame! *will be very much helped in these matters by the long "caesura." (You'll know it when you're in it.) }}}*

((This "fullness/privation" account of "contraries" pervades Aristotle's Act/Potency paradigm. But Aristotle gets very precise about all of this in Metaphysics IV-2, when he discusses the whole business concerning "the selection of the contraries" and particularly at 1004a, 10-33. It is also noteworty that it is in this IV-2 Chapter that Aristotle makes his smug differentiation between Dialectic (which he knew to be "first philosophy" for Plato) and "first philosophy" (i.e., in Aristotle's sense in which "dialectic" is ancillary to "first philosophy") effectively dismissing the hypothetical nature of Dialectic as unworthy of "first philosophy." What Aristotle does not state is that the unhypothetical nature of Aristotle's "first philsophy" is a function of this "fullness/privation" paradigm generated by Aristotle. As usual Aristotle finds fault with Plato and the Platonists from a frame of reference generated by himself which frame of reference would be antithetical to the Platonic undertaking. The inventor of formal logic simply begs the question in his critque of Plato. Worse, he doesn't even seem to be aware that he so begs. Enough))
>>>

165.
the forms (i.e., "this beautiful wisdom of the forms" at 322D of Letter VI): you are on the right track if you give up the notion that "the forms" are the keystone of something like "a theory of reality" the forms (i.e., as adumbrated and contextualized in Parmenides): something like a Kantianesque examination of the conditions for the possibility for discourse? yes no yes and no and neither at once the forms (i.e, always surrounded, diacritcally, with "dream" terminology whenever he wanted to speak seriously of them): the ultimate "meta-language" which both pre-cedes and makes possible intelligible discourse even as it instantiates the Cratylean whirl which only allows for silence? yes no yes and no and neither at once the forms (i.e., appearing here in the five great kinds of Sophist and dis-appearing there as the four -- but really five -- classes of Philebus): the always anasemic semiotic continually generating and destroying "meaning"? yes no yes and no and neither at once the forms (i.e., dis-sporting themselves as Collection and Division in Statesman while Father Cronos and Son Zeus take turns spinning the top): never put in writing -- unless!!!!! -- not the Gods but mortal men have utterly ruined his mind? yes no yes and no and neither at once

Philebus 23D.

Letter VI 344C-D

166.
Khorismos and khora. Timaeus 51C **Are we talking idly whenever we say that there is such a thing as an intelligible form of anything? Is this nothing more than a word?** *The dark passages of Timaeus.*

167.
The dark passages of Timaeus khora the third. --- *and other kindred notions* the secret doctrine of the good light -- the third -- dis-appears in favor of the sun *Have a care, however, lest I deceive you unintentionally with a false reckoning of the interest [offspring]. Eu Prattein!!!*

Timaeus 52B-8 <Loeb lining>

Republic VI 507A.

168.
Nor is it, in the first place, a matter of how and in what form the writings of Plato and/or Aristotle were passed on nor of which thinker had access to which texts of Plato and/or Aristotle. The issue was settled probably by the time Speusippus died in 339. Something like "this beautiful wisdom of the forms" -- if it has any chance of being sustained at all over time -- must be represented by someone alive to the play of difference. As the play of difference disappears -- (which is something quite other than "dis-appearing" since "dis-appearingly" is the very way in which difference appears) -- in the Tradition the ability to appropriate "this beautiful wisdom of the forms" -- (i.e., and most especially, the text of Parmenides) -- is lost. In such a vacuum Aristotle's presentation of what a Platonic Form allegedly is was destined to have become decisive even for thinkers who did not directly read Aristotle's Categories and/or Metaphysics and even for thinkers who called themselves "Platonic." This, then, is, was, and continues to be -- yes even after Derrida -- the scandal of Philosophy.

169.
Since Book VI only gives us "interest" on the good, where is the capital? Where else but in the third tetralogy! Parmenides-Philebus-Symposium-Phaedrus. Philebus, at 61A-B introducing us to the house of Agathon (i.e., the Symposium) which is **the third dialogue of the third tetralogy.** {{{ Please recall that the ancient sub-title of Symposium was "Concerning the Good."}}}

The tetralogical arrangment of the dialogues is reported by Diogenes Lives, pages 327-331. Further, Diogenes, citing Thrasylus, -- (Lives, page 329) -- states that the tetralogical arrangment originated with Plato himself. In this tetralogical listing of the dialogues and Letters of Plato, Symposium is sub-titled: "Concerng the Good."

170.
but light dis-appears but light dis-appears the sun becomes what is seen light is not seen but the cause of light is seen light -- the third -- is not seen even as the cause of light, the sun, is seen thus the sun is not really the analog for the good although it is inevitable that it (the sun) will appear to be so there really is *a false reckoning of the "interest"/"offspring"* it is ""unintentionnal"" (507A) since what one is looking for -- light -- necessarily dis-appears in favor of the cause of light after all -- and Aristocles understood this -- the cause of light DEPENDS upon light to be seen in one sense "light" is more fundamental than the cause of light yet light never appears as such and withdraws in favor of the cause of light the child is really father to the man.

Republic VI 507D.

171.
And what is light? that "third" which always dis-appears? The third is the "khora" of Timaeus. --- *and there is a third kind, which is space and is eternal, and admits not of destruction and provides a home for all becoming* [genesin], *and is "caught", when all sensation is absent* [anaisthesias!!!], *by a discourse of questionable pedigree* [logismo tini notho] *being scarcely*

believable [mogis piston] *which we, beholding it as in a dream-trance* --- when we wake up from the dream which is "space/place" we lose not only the intelligibility of the sensible but intelligibility itself

Timaeus 52B-C.

172.
You are still not reading the text. Read on. Roll on to 52C. Form and participant alike -- to be at all -- must be in another. In each other. In difference. The "true account" says this. As one of the two (i.e., form and participant in a form) are caught, so to speak, in discourse, the other of the two fades away into a dream-like space so that neither of the two is ever itself and its other at once. The words are there. But one cannot presume to translate this darkest of dark passages unless one learns to read this darkest of dark passages. But reading with the proper spin is not easy. "Space/place" is difference. The dream of participation.

<<<<<The more careful statement of these matters is given by Plato in hypothesis # 2 at 145B, 8-145E 8 and, more quickly, at 151A, 8-151A, 1 (Loeb lining, as always). However, even in these more exact statements of how form(s) and participants-in-(a)-forms(s) are "in" each other one must be alert to the various ways in which the ever-elusive "presence" of "difference" ("heteros") is the ever-obtaining condition for these various reciprocal "in" relationships which obtain between forms (each one a one) and thier participants (i.e., "the others" or the "not-ones" of a one). In other words, the casual reader will miss the very point of the "in" passages of hypothesis # 2 just as easily as she will misconstrue the 52 C passage from Timaeus. If you want my respect, dear reader, do not be a casual reader.>>>>>

<[{(-----'76 Commentary helps here:

What is different from the one (and thus is the place of the one) when "one" denotes a form-term is its many parts which are its participants. Thus to be in each, some and every of its parts and to be in none of its parts but rather to be in "difference" is to say the same from two differing perspectives. To be in "difference" means to be in what it is not in. Qua pure containing whole of parts the one is not in the sum of its parts nor in any of its parts. Yet in "difference" one is in what it is not in since the different for any given form is, concretely, the many parts which participate in it. The one as form-term is not in its parts qua pure contaiing whole of parts and is in its parts qua difference. ----

These considerations make more comprehensible the "holon vs. pan" passage at Theaetetus 204-205. In this light difference is understood as inhering in the proper object of knowledge. However, the difference inhering in any given whole is nothing in addition to any given sum of parts -- in the sense of being yet another part -- which constitutes any given whole. With such difference inhering in the proper object of knowledge, knowledge -- the relational par excellence -- is always ahead-of-itself-behind-itself in such a manner that any account of it, knowledge, is bound to be circular. But circular as it is, nothing is lacking from the final account of knowedge given at Theaetetus 209 since this "most beautiful" account of knowledge defines itself in terms of knowledge of difference. It is at once both ahead and behind itself.

((For those who have the eyse to hear and the ears to see.)) >]})

173.
De Anima III-5. There is fate.

174.
Plato's teaching on "light" was intended to be esoteric and available only to the

probing fingers of the intelligent reader.

175.
But because of *this colt who kicks at the mother who bore him* Plato's "light" teaching came to be buried in an avalanche of misrepresentation.

Lives, page 445.

176.
Aristotle's "light" metaphor for "mind" is married to his -- Aristotle's -- difference-fleeing Act/Potency paradigm.

This "flight from difference" instantiated through Aristotle's Act/Poetency paradigm is analysed in my unpublished manuscript, Choosing. Small portions of Choosing have been integrated into this book.

177.
The Act/Potency paradigm, as this wo-man book has repeatedly shown, is based on Aristotle's "flight from difference."

In a previous instantiation this book was often referred to as "this wo-man book." The "wo-man principle" is another name for the principle which is contrary to the one

178.
Yet, even today, -- yes even with the sophistication of a Derrida -- Aristotle's Act/Potency paradigm is the (mostly unconscious of itself) lens by which Plato's ontology is appropriated.

179.
In the process, "the play of difference" gets lost and, with it, Plato's "light" teaching.

180.
Plato's "light" -- "the third" -- dis-appears in favor of the sun.

181.
The sun for Plato is, in effect, a false image of the good although it is inevitable that such false imaging occur given the dis-appearing character of "light" as understood by Aristocles.

182.
In contrast, there is no such thoughtful deception in Plotinus.

183.
With Plato the *epekeina tes ousias* motif is with reference to the fact that the good, as eliciting principle of the mixture, is, "in some sense", outside of the mixture even

though it is always found in the mixture. Plato's one, without "the other", is other than the good. With Plotinus the *epekeina tes ousias* motif refers to a fully self-sufficient principle with a super-abundance of "presence" whose hiddenness and ineffability is a function of the limitedness of finite intellect. In effect the *epekeina tes ousias* motif in these two thinkers has nothing in common at all. Plato's motif is a function of an ontological dualism relative to first principles (i.e., the one and the contrary to the one) and a serious reflection on how the mixture of and between the two obtains. Plotinus -- basically Aristotelian in this regard -- understands the other to and of the one only as a privation and not as a "true" first principle in its own right. For Plotinus the *epekeina tes ousias* becomes basically a honorific device by which to sing the praises of the contrariless first principle in his monistic/monotheistic system in which difference, as a principle, disappears. ((And, as noted so often in this wo-man book, disappearing is not at all the same as "dis-appearing."))

Generally, Plato's "one" is taken, in this book, to be a first principle, the Father, which in the (Philebean) mixture becomes the beautiful. The contrary-to-the-one is called, popularly, the Dyad of the Great and the Small. This principle, the Mother, -- (this one-which-is-not of hypothesis # 5) -- is taken to be pure oscillating difference, eternally needful, whose most esoteric name is eksaiphnes. The good is the eternally generated -- without beginning or ceasing to be generated -- "offspring"/"interest" (tokos) of and between these two principles. These matters have been more carefully explored in my unpublished manuscript of 1990 Choosing and in my unpublished Commentary on "Parmenides" of 1976.

184.
Aristotle and Plotinus have, so to speak, a monotheistic lovers' quarrel about whether "nous" is identical with the contrariless first principle or whether the first and "supreme" first principle is "above" "nous".

185.
But please do not conflate either view with Plato's dualism of first principles.

186.
Thus the putative "otherness" of the one in this Plotinian schema makes its appearance only as a function of this "above".

187.
For Plontinian "otherness" is a mask for a fully self-sufficient "one" which is anything but "otherness" """in itself."""

188.
In this sense the "flight from difference" engineered by Aristotle's ontology is more honest than the "flight from difference" instantiated by the ontology of Plotinus.

189.
After Plotinus the entire Tradition -- inclusive of the various instantiations of "via negativa" mysticism -- oscillates between and among versions and derivatives of this monotheistic lovers' quarrel between Aristotle and Plotinus.

190.
In this oscillation Plato's original appropriation of the *epekeina tes ousias* is totally decimated and lost to the Tradition. ((Even today, when was the last time that Plato's discussion of the good in Book VI was wedded to the doctrine of Philebus instead of being understood as a vector towards Plotinus?))

191.
The most recent instantiation of the Plotinian version of the Tradition is represented in the writings of Emmanuael Levinas. (And, unconsciously following Plotinus in this regard, Levinas also claims to be getting back to a Platonic appropriation of the *epekeina tes ousias* motif of Book VI.) No one -- no not even pseudo-Dionysius himself -- is more nuanced than Levinas in presenting the *epekeina tes ousias* as "other". But, as has been already made clear above, such an otherness is not at all the face of a God who is "in Itself" (or "in Herself"; or "in Itself") truly "other." As with Plotinus -- but with far more lingusitic nuance -- the "other" generated by Levinas is but yet another mask for a contrariless First Principle -- whose name, for Levinias, is "God" -- in a monistic/monotheistic account of things. Without a dualism of first principles, the "other" simply disappears, "tout court", so to speak, without dis- appearing. Plotinus and Levinas say the same.

192.
De Vere: Are you certain that Johanna wants to leave it that simplistically?

Amy: I talked to her about it. She was impatient. She reminded us that time was running out. After all this was not to be a study of Levinas. No time for talking about the special -- almost idiosyncratic -- meaning which "metaphysics" has in the text of Levinas. No time for discussing the Levinasian priority of "metaphysics" over "ontology." No time for delineating his evolution from Husserl, through the Sein und Zeit Heidegger, and his turn away from the Heideggerian enterprise.

De Vere: I think think Johanna gets a bit hysterical about this time-running-out business Does she dare to eat a peach?

Amy: She did say that I could respond to your questions. Fire away.

De Vere. Well, does Johanna at least acknowledge that with Plotinus there is the hoped for mystical union with the "one" while for Levinas such a union with the Levinasian "other" is not only impossible but not even desirable?

Amy: Oh, Johanna understands that. Desire for Levinas is ultimately for relation with "the other", not for mystical union with "the other." She acknowledges that Levinas' account of how humans relate to "the other" (i.e., "the one") is far more nuanced than anything Plotinus has to offer. But -- and I think the Johanna is correct here -- such nuance does not change the fact that the Levinasian "other" is but a mask, (when it's all said and done), for a Plotinus-like "one."

De Vere: Tell me this: Does Johanna have any sense that for Emmanual "totality" is shot through with the reserved presence of this "other" which, even so, remains always "beyond"? That -- to speak the language of the Tradition for a moment -- transcendence transcends into the very heart of "totality" in its immanence?

Amy: Of course she does, Silly. Johanna claims that this Levinasian theme is not so very different from the "emanation" theme in Plotinus by which the one -- while always remaining *epekeina tes ousias* -- animates all being in the finite realm. Here, again, Plotinus and Levinas "say the same." *{{{In contrast the thinking which thinks "otherness" itself, so to speak, (i.e., as opposed to making the other a mask, in effect, of a self-sufficient "one" -- i.e., "the Most High" --) comes to realize that, by definition, there neither is nor can be an "irruption" of the "other"/"infinite" into "totality" since "totality" itself, in its very make-up, <u>IS, already and of its own "nature" (so to speak),</u> "otherness"/"difference". Properly speaking there is no transcendence <u>or</u> immanence for a thinking which stays in fidelity to "difference." So too the finite/infinite distinction loses its significance as it is shown that -- with "difference/other" permeating all -- nothing is not infinite even though there is no "infinite" as such. Indeed, the habit of thinking in terms of a finte/infinite distinction -- especially concerning God and creation -- has its ultimate (albeit indirect) genesis in an Act/Potency paradigm which, as this wo-man book has repeatedly shown, is the death of "the play of difference" in conceptual matters.}}}*

De Vere: Well surely Johanna will acknowledge that there is nothing like "Shekhinah" in the text of Plotinus.

Amy: But, Edward, is there anything but the <u>name</u> of "Shekhinah" in the Levinasian text? We have spoken of this elsewhere. Emmanual worships at the altar of "propriety". His text, <u>therefore</u>, knows not Shekhinah.

De Vere: What of the text of the Hasidim?

Amy: More so -- far more so -- than the text of Levinas. But concerning the Johanna's quarrel with the Hasidim you must go to that other conversation by Bappy and Dewchee.

De Vere: Ah yes. That was a most critical conversation. But tell me, sweet one, does Johanna even presume that she rather than Levinas shall be the emissary to Philosophy concerning things Talmudic as well?

Amy: Basically, yes.

De Vere: Tell me: does she suffer from hubris or chutzpah?

Amy: Let's face it. She's manic. But treat her kindly. She does little or no harm. And she is picking up where Jude left off. So to speak. It is her way of trying to become to be true to her self.

De Vere: In the sense said by Polonius?

Amy: Nay! Nay! You of all people should know better than that! No. Rather in a more Delphic sense.

De Vere: I'm out of questions. Give Johanna my regards. By the way, do you still dance for her?

Amy: Yes. But she seems to notice less and less. Hail and Farewell!

De Vere: Ave atque vale!

193.
Under the suasion of an early influence on his thought by the writings of Levinas, Derrida flirts, here and there, with yet another appropriaton of "other"/"difference" through the lens of Neo-Platonism. {{To be sure, Derrida does eventually come to overtly distance himself from the Levinasian project. But the early influence stays with him, Derrida, nonetheless.}} For even Derrida -- who is far more attuned to the dyanamic of "difference"/"other" than either Levinas or Plotinus; indeed his concern with "difference"/"other" is of a different order than those two Neo-Platonic thinkers -- keeps his distance from any embrace of an ontological dualism. His own "deconstructive" moves relative to the dualities endemic within the Tradtion keep him blind to the prior consideration of the kind of dualism which animated Plato's thinking "before" ""duality"" got swallowed up within the parameters of the Tradition. Even so, in his article, "Comment ne par Parler" (appearing in Psyche of 1987), Derrida appears to be awakening to those dimensions of Plato's teaching on the good which, when finally thought through, are anything but a vector to the Plotinian (and, when it's all said and done, the "Levinasian") appropriation of the *epekeina tes ousias*. Yet even in that wonderful article of 1987 Derrida, as commented upon often enough in other sections of this wo-man book, is unthoughtfully fascinated with interfacing the "threeness" theme of Plato with the Trinitarian schema of the Pseudo-Dionysius. Enough.

194.
Non: Have the American Derrideans taken up the themes of "Comment ne pas Parler" yet?

Sic: Oh God!! That tribe of imitators. The worst bunch of all!!! I imagine Frere Jacques wakes up in a cold sweat at night when, in his dreams, he realizes what that tribe is doing to his work. *Look what they've done to my song, Ma.* But that's the price of fame. At least Johanna doesn't have to worry about things like that. But to answer your question: I don't know. Neither the Johanna nor I keep up with that sort of thing. Indeed Johanna has not even been following Derrida himself since Psyche and the Heidegger Geist book. I suppose there have been and will be a whole series of books and articles on "khora", "the third", "the demonic" and perhaps even on the interface between Plato's threeness and trinitarian conceits. But it won't matter.

Non: Why not?

Sic: None of that crowd has any sense at all of Plato's kind of ontological dualism. Accordingly they will miss -- as they follow lock-step in the path of Derrida -- what Derrida must miss since he too has no sense of the kind of ontological dualism which animates the Platonic text.

Non: You mean then that they will miss the meaning of "difference" in the Platonic text?

Sic: Yes. And the correlative doctrine of "the good." With Derrida there was some class. But with that tribe of imitators there will just be mush.

Non: Nice talking to you, as always. Take care.

Sic: Likewise to you.

195.
Without a dualism of first principles, the "other" simply disappears, "tout court", so to speak, without "dis-appearing".

196.
And, of course, as soon as this theme of "threeness" is mentioned, a hundred thousand Christian-oriented thinkers get excited about analogs for Trinitarian Theology. Even the mighty -- and usually more refined -- Frere Jacques gets itchy about this theme of "threeness" in Plato by way of his review of pseudo-Dionysius contained in his "Comment ne pas Parler." But an unbridgable chasm separates the Platonic mdeditation on "threeness" from the various Christian "Trinitarian" conceits, even when these conceits -- as with pseudo-Dionysius -- instantiate themselves with a remarkable subtlety. The Platonic meditation on "threeness" is a function of Plato's "ontological dualism" which this wo-man book has repeatedly shown. All the Christian "trinitarian" conceits -- including that instantiated by and through the text of pseudo-Dionysius -- are married to the kind of monism/monotheism in which -- via negativa terminology notwithstanding -- the "other" becomes but the veiled (to finite intellect) face of "God" (i.e., "the one") and thus is not "other" at all. The usually more refined Frere Jacques is tempted into an interfacing of Platonic "threeness" and "trinitarian" coneits precisely beacuse -- the subtlety of ""deconstruction"" (as instantiated in Derrida's writings) nothwithstanding -- he, Derrida, has no sense of the kind of dualsim operative in Platonic ontology.

197.
but Plato -- playing out one aspect of the Freudian Oedipal drama -- remains fixated on the "father"   OH God!!! the love and hatred of the father!!!!   nostalgia for (killed) beauty animates the entire Platonic text   Plato often enough has intercourse with the "mother" (i.e., """"""truth"""""")   enough so that the child -- the good -- may be born   but Plato does not really "marry" the mother

This book takes Plato's allusions to "truth" contained in Philebus at 64A-65A (in which Socrates speaks of the "mixture" which will be "the good") to be allusions to the principle which is contrary-to-the-one. *[[[Listen to 64A: "----- and nothing in the world can come into being without it."]]]* Thus, the principles of the mixture are beauty (the one) and truth (the contrary-to-the-one). It is noteworthy that Plato -- (and in so doing Plato here deflects away from the "true" character of the good) -- lets the good *take refuge in the character of the beautiful* (64E) since he tames the mixture according to beauty's manifestation which is "measure and proportion." (64D-E)

Thus -- even as he deflects from the most secret character of "the good" -- "truth" is nonetheless a woman for Plato if the multiple contentions of tis book are correct.

198.
to "marry" the mother (""""""truth"""""") it is not sufficient to make love to her   nor is it entirely sufficient to have a child with her   one is called -- for the sake of the good -- to "become" the mother which means one, quite literally, is called to be what one is not   Freud's theory notwithstanding, identification with the killed father is not the final outcome even if it is a necessary stage   that identity is but the identity of nostalgia   it must be re-fragmented for the sake of the good   one must, quite literally, lose one's self -- i.e., lose its very identity -- in the other for the sake of the good   Plato was, indeed, a shade off

199.
this play of difference is the "third" thing whose name here is "khora"; whose name there is "light";

which in any case, always dis-appears in favor of the seen   Plato understood perfectly the dialectic of and between the self-same (eidos) and "the ideas" as they, "the ideas", slip away, dis-appearingly, into their predicates which predicates, in turn, slip away, dis-appearingly, into their predicates when they, the predicates, function as "ideas"   this is why hypothesis # 7 -- *suddenly (eksaiphnes), as in a dream* -- is just as intrinsic to the overall contextualization of the theory of forms as is hypothesis # 2   indeed, the philosopher, in her quest for discourse, lives the tension of and between hypothesis # 2 and hypothesis # 7   this perspectival tension is the very "essence" of the entire theory of forms   *hos eioken*   is the final verdict of Parmenides The double bind   no intelligibilty with or without the forms   and yet we speak

Parmenides 164D.

Parmenides 166B.

200.
Plato's playful-and-literal account of the inevitability of the "false reckoning" becomes, in Aristotle's play-negating hands, the merely childish piece of philosophical naivte of one, i.e., Plato, who simplistically ontologized Socratic universals. Aristotle was too serious to understand a playful theory. Aristotle was too serious to engage difference.

201.
She is the non-misogynistic "Mis-ogyny" of these ruminations which come forth as "sentences"   She dis-appears into Her creation and yet is always other from Her creation

202.
She is Shekhinah.

203.
She is demonic and Nurse at once   which means that Eros -- motivated by Beauty but never other than othering -- lives as difference.   this is why the Tradition's "flight from difference" -- inaugurated with Aristotle -- is effectively the same as its "flight from Eros"   Eros lives as Shekhinah.

204.
Will it be necessary to say something about "agape" here?

205.
The kind of thing which never really had to have come up at all if there had been any ability to have remained faithful to the the multi-valency of Platonic Eros.

206.
A fetishistic detour which was never necessary to begin with and a detour which -- unlike a creative digression -- keeps one away from what is thought e-voking rather than entering into what is thought e-voking.

207.
Bappy: How can anyone possibly get it "right", so to speak, with the wo-man principle?

Dewchee: It is not easy. Even our spiritual allies deflected from this.

Bappy: Do you mean our Hasidic friends?

Dewchee: Yes.

Bappy: How so?

Dewchee: There would have to be a hundred thousand qualifications to be made before one would dare to presume to tell holy men the error of their ways.

Bappy: But there is no longer enough time for a hundred thousand qualifications. Besides, fools rush in where wise men (or is it angels?) fear to tread. To be a fool for the sake of God may not be all that bad.

Dewchee: Who knows.

Bappy: Please do not stop now. I will not rest until you speak.

Dewchee: Then for you, Bappy, I will speak. It is really quite simple.

Bappy: Yes?

Dewchee: More than any other Tradition, the Hasidic Masters of old understood the wo-man principle. This is the energizing force of Hasidism and the source of its spiritual greatness.

Bappy: Then what's the problem?

Dewchee: On the average, they failed to see it through. They -- to use our language for a bit -- were on the edge of "mis-ogyny" but then slipped back into an all too common misogyny. Indeed, sometimes the misogyny of the Hasids was a bit extreme precisely because they, ever so close to "mis-ogyny", failed to see it through.

Bappy: Can you explain this a bit better?

Dewchee: They were Hegelian without ever knowing about or caring about Hegel. Indeed the great ones pretty much did their thing significantly before the time of Hegel's dissemination. On the average their fault was this: having uncovered, so to speak, Shekhinah, they did not remain faithful to Shekhinah. Nor did they pay Shekhinah the hommage owed to Her. On the average they too would not kneel before <u>and for</u> Shekhinah. They would not go to Her bed under Her conditions but rather insisted that She come into the other bedroom under <u>their</u> conditions. On the average, they spoke of subsuming/sublating the wo-man principle. And so, their special closeness to the wo-man principle became, on the average and precisely by virtue of this tendency to see the wo-man principle as something to be subsumed/sublated, just another flight from the wo-man principle.

208.

Yes, it is true that wounded narcissists often seek out masochism/humiliation as a function of their narcissism. A last desperate refuge. Some never come out of that. Some, however, pass through it and achieve a renewed sense of who they are. They have touched their own need -- the wo-man principle within them -- and live. They live for the better. And there is no redemption -- i.e., God does not come to be what God was to have become -- unless we all get in touch with and kneel down before Shekhinah. For Shekhinah is, so to speak, more God than God Himself. It is the exile -- ('othering-ness', so to speak) -- itself which makes God holy (and holey). The impetus for redemption {{{{{what Plato, towards the early part of Timaeus, says about Divine Nous in its alleged non-jealous diffusiveness on the one hand AND ALSO what the Hasidic Masters say relative to God and "the other" on the other hand, NOTWITHSTANDING (i.e. both of these traditions -- which basically say the same -- notwithstanding) }}}}} come not from God as "the One" (i.e., the "Most High") but rather from "the other". It is not so much that Shekhinah is redeemed but rather Shekhinah redeems. And kneeling down before and for Shekhinah requires -- paradox noted -- the free embrace of humiliation.

Timaeus 29D-30A.

209.
Towards a "Re-covery" of "Athens-and-Jerusalem"

a.
Eurydice and Eve.

b.
Eve and Eurydice.

c.
They have all the time in the world. They wait -- for the most part silently -- filled with the knowledge that each of their erring patriarchal offspring will have to return to the Mother from whom each receives life.

d.
There are no co-incidences.

e.
All that happens -- everything! -- happens by chance (tukhe).

f.
These statements are not complementary to each other.

g.
Rather, they are each, always and all ways, completely true without reservation.

h.

At once.

i.
Eurydice.

j.
Reading Heidegger in French.

An autobiographical remark. My initial brush up with Heidegger (and, really, with Philosophy) was thorugh the classes of Henri Birault in Paris, 1964-1965. Towards the end of the academic year and for almost a year thereafter I would read and re-read time and time again -- almost to the point of compulsion; sometimes with more, sometimes with less understanding; -- the French version of <u>Was heisst denken?</u>.

k.
La vengeance est le ressentiment de la volunte contre le temps et son "il etait".

This phrase of Nietzsche is cited from <u>Qu'Appelle-t-on Penser?</u>. (Translated from the German by A. Becker and G. Granel; Presses Universitaires de France; Paris, 1959.) Page 70.

l.
Resisting the fetish. (i.e., embracing the psychosis of the brave.)

m.
Resisting the fetish. Resisting idolatry.

n.
Our first act of courage is the first appearance of melancholy.

o.
Only members of a species who "suffer" "desire" (in that Lacanian sense; in that sense made possible by "mis-ogyny") could or would experience the passage of time as melancholic. And yet melancholy is the price we pay to dream.

p.
Getting it "right" relative to deception. Nietzsche was only half-way there. (And being only half-way there he too partially succumbs to the fetish.)

Nietzsche, as noted earlier in this book, had remarkable insights into "truth" as deception. One thinks most especially of aphorism # 853 of <u>WP</u> (pagees 451-453). On the other hand, Derrida and Deleuze are all too quick to attribute to Nietzsche astounding insights into the "womanly" nature of truth. ((Confer, especially, <u>Spurs</u> pages 47-123 where Nietzsche's somewhat disparaging and chauvinistic-to-the-point-of-boredom allusions to truth as a woman is pumped up by Derrida into a world-view foreign to what Nietzsche says about women both in the passages cited by Derrida and elsewhere.))

In all of this it is not Nietzsche who is on trial but rather Frere Jacques himself. Nietzsche's accomplishment of shaking the Tradition down to to its very foundations stands whether or not Nietzsche had remarkable insights into the "wo-manly" nature of "truth." Not so with Derrida who chose to make this an issue in his appropriation/presentation of Nietzsche.

In the final analysis, Derrida's failure to *think psycho-analytically* keeps Derrida away from the womanly nature of "truth" even and especially as he accuses Lacan and the Tradition itself of "phallago-centrism." This is not to say that Lacan and/or the Tradition are not "phallo-centric." Quite to the contrary. (And as noted in this book, Lacan's phallo-centrism is insidious and especially merits the exposure it receives at the hands of Derrida.) Even so, this Shibboleth of the sophisticated uttered here by Derrida and there by various kinds of Feminists (i.e., The Shibboleth being the charge of "phallo-centrism") still bypasses on principle what is at issue when one speaks of the "womanly nature of truth" and bypasses as well attention to the question as to why the Tradition -- in its effective "flight from 'truth' " -- became so "phallo-centric."

q.
Fidelity to the counter-factual "fact". This is the very condition for dreaming.

r.
Wresting the counter-factual "fact" from the continuing temptation of disavowal. To be sure, in the initial, momentary impulse towards disavowal one finds also that yearning by which beauty -- now forever lost in its wholeness -- becomes so valorized and, correlatively, by which dream possibilities are opened up for our species. But sustaining the disavowal is that cowardly "solution" in bad faith which is the formula for our dreams to become nightmares.

s.
And this at that time in "history" when our dreams (and/or nightmares) are becoming and are to become "more real" than "reality."

t.
What this means is that "truth" -- the counter-factual "fact" -- is more true, so to speak, than "the facts". Indeed it would take an impoverished mind to argue that "the fact" that Mommy is indeed not castrated has the same order of significance compared to that which emerged over millenia upon millenia of years in that all-decisive "mis-ogynistic" nexus in which biological evolution was intensely interfacing, in the pre-pre-history of our species, with the beginnings of human psycho-social evolution producing finally that marvelous and randomly generated human XX/XY variation in the constellation of sexual differentiation.

u.
That Mommy is in fact not castrated yet, inevitably, will appear to be so.

v.
The primacy -- which cannot ever show itself as primacy except on the rebound -- of deception.

w.
The deception which is worth more than "the facts."

x.
That ever-elusive primal "truth" which is worth more than "truth" in its presence. (E.g., the counter-factual "truth" of "mis-ogyny" as worth more than the perfectly "true" fact that Mommy, in fact, is <u>not</u> castrated.)

y.
The life-enhancing deception which must continually be wrested from the temptation of disavowal even though it can never be affirmed.

z.
Choose life.

aa.
Do you understand yet?

ab.
"Truth" <u>really is</u> a woman. This is no metaphor.

ac.
"Truth" <u>really is</u> a woman. The life-enhancing deception by which "God" -- <u>as "God"</u> -- reveals Herself.

ad.
The shameless shame of the Shekhinah. {{{And the Messiah -- (is Her name not "Hanina" [meaning "compassion" moreso than "pity]?) -- cannot <u>come</u> until Shekhinah is embraced in Her shame.}}}

ae.
Eve.

af.
But in fact -- in history -- "God" became a fetish. "God" became our emblem of "bad faith." "God" became our indictment. With "God" we became enmeshed in the cowardly psychosis.

ag.
Not with Judaism as such although Judaism -- (especially after mainstream Judaism unconsciously got suckered into a Christian/"metaphysical" way of understanding "God") -- as another organized mass delusion has not been immune to turning "God" into a fetish. Even today one does not understand how to read <u>Torah</u>. Even today one tends not to be able to disengage <u>Torah</u> from the layers of misunderstanding which have been retroactively grafted unto the "God" of <u>Torah</u>.

It will still be some time before the conditions are fertile for performing a "deconstruction" -- (this book would say "regressive kathalysis") -- of the alleged monotheism of Torah.

In this regard, Schelling remains almost as distanced from the meaning of Torah as anyone in the Tradition. Even so -- and despite so many crippling shortcomings of his thought -- it is Schelling who partially inaugurates this particularly delicate task of the "regressive kathalysis" of Torah through his unity/duality, duality/unity theme relative to the two names of God in Torah. Confer his remarks on pages 158-163 and pages 221-224 as contained in his Ages of the World. (Translated by F. Bolman, Jr.; AMS Press, New York, 1967. Hereafter: Ages)

The above can also mean that it will be some time before the kind of Unity belonging to God as revealed in Torah can be thoughtfully resiliated. Mainstream Judaism has allowed, over the centuries and millenia, the revelation of Torah about the kind of Unity which belongs to God to be eclipsed by the simplistic model of Monotheism which came to animate Christian religion, the germ of which comes forth in Aristotle's Theology. ((Indeed precisely by distancing itself from the hocus-pocus of Trinitarianism, mainstream Judaism -- in a kind of collective reaction formation -- found itself embracing the most simplistic models of Unity relative to its own appropriation of the kind of Unity belonging to God revealed in Torah.))

Athens was already corrupted in its own rite prior to that fateful encounter with Jerusalem. Jerusalem came to suffer damage and corruption from outside forces. ((Even so, without these "outside forces" *Kaballah* would not have emerged. And it is through *Kaballah* -- when it is resiliated CONTRA itself -- that one will eventually hearken back to Torah.)) In all of this, Tertullian's infamous dictum/question is not vindicated. "Athens" and "Jerusalem" do resiliatingly complement each other if and as each remains faithful to the same God -- Shekhinah/"difference" -- which secretly animates both Traditions.

ah.
Not even with Aristotle although the necessary preparation for God-as-fetish emerges through the eclipse of Platonic Dualism (a dualism of first principles) by Aristotelian Monotheism.

{The germ of the fetish -- indeed the fetish itself -- is already there flopping about in Aristotle's Theology. But he had a degree of aristocratic restraint about him. It would take a far more vulgar mentality to actually set in motion the fetishistic practices themselves.}

ai.
No.

aj.
Rather the significant first appearance of this "God-as-fetish" begins with the New Testament documents and their celebration of God as "agape." What every anxious child would want God to be. Paul and the writer of the Fourth Gospel apparently bear equal responsibility for the birthing of this fetish. {It is notworthy that Paul spent signficant time at Ephesus.}

ak.
Neo-Platonism plays a pivotal role. On the one hand early Neo-Platonism -- even when it is at pains to underscore that it is not Christian -- is partially animated by the ever more delirious God-concept emerging in the first Christian centuries. What every anxious child would want God to be. On the other hand Neo-Platonism's own delirium concerning "The One" in turn furnished the

"metaphysical" trappings by which the "agape fetish" could become doctrinaire and doctrinized.

al.
The via negativa of the post-Plotinian Christian mystics; The """"Platonism"""" **[sic!!!]** of Augustine; the scholastic/Aristotelian meditations of the Middle Ages and the High Middle Ages; the mysticism of the High Middle Ages as the "Middle Ages" became the "Renaissance"; likewise the Neo-Pythagoreanism/Neo-Platonism of the earlier Italian Renaissance (inclusive of those "co-incidence of opposites" meditations). Please understand. ALL of these traditions are but variations on the same fetish. The alleged grand differences between and among these various versions of this same fetish are but the puerile chess moves in an intra-mural tournament given over to the sustaining of disavowal. (I.e., the cowardly psychosis now become delirious) {{{{{Please note as well that "delirium" is like the "demonic"; it can be pressed into the service of the good (which follows upon the psychosis of the brave) or it can become the expression of the cowardly psychosis.}}}}}

am.
The fetish still animates "Modern" philosophy and finds its last expression in German Idealism.

an.
The cowardly psychosis was already dying of its own internal inconsistency. Marx, Nietzsche and Freud announce its death. Sartre -- whose promise was so much greater -- could find nothing better to do than to dance on its grave.

ao.
To encounter "God" as God. That is the challenge of our time. Nor have we had adequate practice for such a challenge. For too long we have assumed that "God" would have to be the fetish or there was no "God" at all. We have been poorly trained.

ap.
Shekhinah. Kaballah resiliatingly CONTRA Kaballah. For the sake of Shekhinah. For the sake of Torah. The God of surprise. Unity in Duality and Duality in Unity. Freeing oneself from conscious and unconscious Hegelianism. Freeing oneself from Christian Trinitariansm. There is much to be done.

aq.
khalapa ta kala

ar.
{{{Non: Should we?

Sic: I would rather not. There are too many possibilities for misunderstanding.

Non: But the cat aready got out of the bag when he mentioned "German Idealism" and then "freeing oneself from conscious and unconscious Hegelianism."

Sic: So it looks like we must mention the bitter one.

Non: Yes. Despite the elements of Christian Triumphalism which vitiate his best work, allowing that his best work started with his 1809 Freedom book and end with the unpublished (in his lifetime) draft of Ages of the World circa 1814/1815. Yes. Despite his inability to free himself from aspects of the Act/Potency paradigm (which paradigm, as noted so very very often in this book of ours, is the very death of thinking). Yes, despite his usage of a "Necessity" which stems from Aristotle and the Tradition rather than from the "Anangke" of Timaeus. ((And this despite the fact that our bitter one often took positive inspiration from the dark passages of Timaeus.))

Confer Schelling: Of Human Freedom; (A Translation of F W J Schellings' "Philosophische Unersuchungen uber das Wesen der menschlichen Freiheit und damit zusammernhangenden Gegenstande" With a Critical Introduction and Notes). (Translated by James Gutman; Open Court, Chicago, 1936. Hereafter: Freedom.) Confer also, The Ages of the World; translated by F. Bolman, Jr.; AMS Press, New York, 1967. Hereafter: Ages.

Confer Freedom, pages: 47; 50-52; 68-70. Confer Ages, pages: 131; 133; 190-191.

Sic: With those three indictments you have said enough to cross him off our list forever. Likewise, with those three indictments you have shown that there will always be some confusion if we allow his formulations to be alloyed to ours. Why even mention him?

Non: Get serious, Sic. In your heart of hearts you know why.

Sic: Of course. In the first place this bitter man -- who had invented Hegel, for God's sake, !!!!! -- was the first to show how one may free oneself from Hegel. Even Frere Jacques -- (who often enough refers to Schelling especially when he, Frere Jacques, is talking about Heidegger) -- still has much he could learn from our bitter friend about "freeing oneself from Hegel." In the second place, despite his incredibly serious flaws and shortcomings, this bitter man knew what Hegel -- at his delirious best -- never knew.

Non: I know what you are referring to, but you ought to say it.

Sic: Despite himself, our bitter friend knew something about difference.

Non: Thank-you for the acknowledgment. Let us let our bitter friend speak for himself:

> --- *Everything depends upon comprehending that unity in God which is at the same time duality, or, conversely, the duality which is at the same time unity.*

Ages, page 157. Please understand that Schelling is not referring here to an Hegelianesque identity of identity and difference.

Sic: And earlier -- in that same marvelous and posthumously published book -- he says:

> *The systems which wish to explain the origin of things by descent from above almost necessarily come to the thought that the emanations of the highest*

primal power at some time or other attain a limit below which there is nothing, and which, itself only a shadow of reality, a minimal degreee of reality, can only to a certain extent be said to be, but really is not. This is the meaning of non-being among the Neo-Platonists, who no longer understood the true meaning of Plato. We, following the opposite course, also discern a limit below which there is nothing, but for us it is not a last but a first, from which everything begins, an eternal beginning, and it is not merely a deficiency or lack of reality, but active negation.

Ages, page 133. Also, it needs to be noted that in the terminological logistics of this book which you are now reading "oscillating need" and "difference" would be the synonyms for what Schelling here calls "active negation" and there calls "original negation."

Non: The memories come flooding back in. And earlier still:

----- *But just for that reason the world still lies in negaton. That original negation is still the mother and nurse of the entire world visible to us.*

Ages, page 131.

He was truly one of us, despite himself.

Sic: Yes. To be sure there are a hundred thousand Hegelianiesque types who will go to their graves thinking that the great domesticator of "negation" -- I speak of Hegel -- had the last word on "negation." But for some time we have recognized that we are not writing or speaking to win over the dullards who play around with "Athens-and-Jerusalem." So let us now seal in that affirmation of our bitter inventor of Hegel who also freed himself from Hegel with the citation which forever makes him our friend:

----- *Therefore the whole thing can only be considered as having happened in a flash* [emphasis mine jwm/JE], *since it is conceived as something which happened without having really* (explicite) *happened.*

Ages, page 192.

Non: I can rest easier now. We have paid our hommage to our bitter freind.

as.

{{{{{Bappy: Were you happy with all of that?

Dewchee: Not really. I still wish they hadn't brought it up. Yet it would be misleading to mention Hegel and not to mention our bitter friend. Even so one clarification ought to be made for the record.

Bappy: What is that?

Dewchee: He followed Plato in more ways than one. He followed Plato even and especially in Plato's failure. Indeed -- having kind-of discovered what was most important in Plato -- he out Platonizes Plato in their joint deflection from the proper vocation of the Platonic text. Plato himself deflects from the most proper vocation of his own thinking. Schelling is even worse.

This book maintains that Plato deflects from the role of the Mother in favor of the role of the Father relative to his -- Plato's -- understanding of the mixture thus inaugurating something like a disposition towards the God-fetish as it would eventually emerge. Yet Plato's third -- i.e., "the good" -- is still animated, (in a way totally lacking in the Tradition, Neo-Platonism [sic!] most definitely therein included), by "difference", that is to say, by the Mother, that is to say, by the principle contrary-to-the-one. When Aristotle's monotheism came to eclipse this dualism of first principles found in Plato it effectively led not only to the death of difference in the Tradition but also to an incredibly skewed way of even approaching the text of Plato.

Bappy: Please explain.

Dewchee: The nostalgia for the (killed) father was too great in Plato and thus -- as so often mentioned in this book -- he permits "the good" *to take refuge in the character of the beautiful.* He never arrives at the most secret name of the good. He never fully understood the hegemony of the principle "other" relative to "the one." He never fully understood that "difference" is sustained in the mixture.

Philebus 64E.

Bappy: And?

Dewchee: So too with our bitter friend. Having un-covered the primacy of "contradiction"/"difference"/"active non-being" -- (we would call it "pure oscillating need") -- he proceeds, when it's all said and done, to allow "contradiction"/"difference"/"active non-being" to be subsumed/sublated to the other principle (i.e., to the principle of simplicity and stasis which he calls the Godhead of God and which we have called "the one". {{{The one, it will be recalled, is that which appears as "the beautiful" relative to the mixture.}}}

Bappy: This means that his thought shies away from "Shekhinah".

Dewchee: That is true. Yet let us not be too harsh on our friend. After all, the very inventors of "Shekhinah" -- I speak of the Hasids and, before them, all which flows out of Lurianic mysticism -- only took Shekhinah to their bed. No one has as of yet gone to Shekhinah's bed and slept with Her on Her terms. Even the best of the lot still shy away from encountering God as God.

Bappy: But that day will come. I just know it.

Dewchee: I trust that you are right. Now you may rest.

Bappy: Just brush my cheek before you leave me.}}}}}

at.
In a flash.

au.
Eksaiphnes.

av.
For the fetishistic idolatrators one seeks out "full presence." What every anxious child would want "God" to be. It starts with Aristotle although some -- yea even Marty and Frere Jacques!!! -- thought it started with Plato. It continues with Plotinus and the via negativa tradition for whom the "hidden-ness" of God is only a function of the limitations of human intellect and discourse. (*) The fetish remains alive equally in the rationalistically oriented Scholasticism of the High Middle Ages and in the various appearances of "mysticism" as the High Middle Ages becomes the Renaissance. Even as the fetish begins to collapse in upon itself it animates most of Modern Philosophy. It's last self-indulgent appearance was in and through Hegel. Yet even Nietzsche (unbeknownst to Derrida and more especially to DeLeuze who fetishized the Nietzschean text) -- that marvelous destroyer of idols -- fetishizes a bit with his "Eternal Recurrence" as that doctrine instantiates his monotheistic teaching of the Will to Power.

*. {{{{{I.e., they -- Pltoinus and the via negativa crowd -- know nothing of the "darkness in itself", so to speak, way of God's being and not-being because all of these soi-dissant "mystical" traditions are, in the final analysis, monotheistic and must, in the final analysis, construe "non-being" as some kind of privation. A thinking which aspires to the "dis-appearing" revelation of God in Her intrinsic darkness must be a thinking open to a duality of first principles.}}}}}

Confer aphorism # 1067 of WP (pages 549-550) which simultaneously caps off Nietzsche's treatment of the Eternal Recurrence and also shows that all is the Will to Power and nothing else besides.

aw.
For those few who know difference it is, quite literally, different. Encountering and finding God as God and not as an anxious child would want "God" to be. (Fidelity to the counter-factual "fact")

ax.
For those few who know difference it is a "dis-appearing" flash.

ay.
Like the flash of heat lightning that tells you all that is, is now.

Joyce Carol Oates in I Lock My Door Upon Myself. Ecco Press, New York, 1990. Page 92.

az.

az-i. The age of the messiah is when God will have become what God was to have become.

az-ii. Was Jesus the messiah?

Yes and no. More no than yes. But yes and no. And neither.

az-iii. Jesus was the pathein messiah. And it is to be noted that his pathein was even greater than what was recorded in the New Testament. More embarrassing. More humiliation. Shameful. He was misunderstood, even and especially by his followers. And there was the betrayal.

az-iv. By Judas?

az-v. No, no. That was only the cover story. In reality he betrayed himself. And not at all in the obvious way. His self-betrayal was more subtle.

az-vi. How is Jesus the messiah?

az-vii. Certainly not according to any of the teachings of Christianity in as much as they instantiate Christian Triumphalism and still less in as much as they are overtly or covertly Anti-Semitic.

az-viii. Then how?

az-ix. Jesus is the <u>pathein</u> messiah.

az-x. There is nothing without pathein.

az-xi. God speaks in all languages although She writes in Hebrew.

az-xii. Jesus instantiates the first coming of the messiah.

az-xiii. But the first coming is but a pre-figurement. A necessary condition.

az-xiv. The <u>pathein</u> messiah will be complemented by the <u>mathein</u> messiah. There is nothing without pathein.

az-xv. But pathein -- lest it become pathology -- must be transformed into a <u>mathein</u>.

az-xvi. Khalapa ta kala.

(caesura)

Keeping time, time, time
In a sort of Runic rhyme

Heard melodies are sweet but those unheard
Are sweeter -----

Do you remember Richeard Harris singing "MacArthur Park"?:

------ ***someone left the cake out in the rain*** ----

----- ***I'll never have that recipe again*** -----

{{{{{In the mood: The One. The contrary to the One. Keep them in mind throughout all of this. For those who have the eyes to hear and the ears to see.}}}}}

They were clever. The clothed species. In the period they came to call the twenteith century. They came close. Damn close. Despite their endemic foolishness and layers of unrecognized dogmatism. Despite an equally endemic tendency towards shallowness and sophistry among those of their members who were called "intellectuals." Close indeed. But no cigar.

1958. The Gifford Lectures. Werner Heisenberg. Ambiguous association with National Socialism in his background. He got it together. Transforming the "Copenhagen Interpretation" -- (always hindered by the babyish formulations of Bohr) -- into Physics and Philosophy. Of course Physics and Philosophy had its liabilities. But they were correctible, as this book has shown.

1964. An Irishman. From Belfast no less. From BELL-FAST!!!!!!!!!!

If anyone had put the two developments -- intelligently -- together they would have made it. Close. But no cigar.

Charming how people in science deal with the mystical. "Action at a distance"; "non-locality"; at one end of the mystical spectrum (the existence of which spectrum they know not). "Faster than the speed of light" at the other end of that mystical spectrum. (Had they never heard of "eksaiphnes"?)

Charming. They are like adolescents in these matters. But let that pass.

{{{{{Yet "mysticism" had been given a bad name by that tribe of soi-dissant mystics: Plotinus --- Pseudo-Dionysius --- the others of that via negativa crowd --- the cloud of unknowing guy --- Meister Eckhart --- the co-incidence of opposites guy --- all of them and others. ((And yes -- it pains me to say it -- pre-Lurianic Kaballah as well.)) They all worshipped the same God fetish. They were all Aristotelian even when they were in ignorance of Aristotle and/or explicitly denied being Aristotelian. They had all married monotheism. It -- monotheism -- had transformed the two very different terms of mysticism into the fetish. Enough. This story has already been told.}}}}}

The One. The Father. Beauty in the mixture. Beauty which must die as it is fragmented and dispersed all throughout all. It is the hidden connection of things which -- in conjunction with its other (i.e., "eksaiphnes") -- connects through differencing. The One. *That peace which the world cannot give.* So it appears.

The contrary to the One. The Mother. Pure oscillating need.

The "offspring/interest" (tokos) of and between the two. The Father dies for the sake of the child as the Mother is, through and as the "offspring/interest", sustained in the mixture. Unity in duality and duality in unity. The sophisticated ones then say "Hegel!" They are legion. Only a few will understand that this is anything but Hegel.

There are no co-incidences. This is the effect of the One in the mixture. This is non-locality. This is action at a distance. Keeping time, time, time. In a Runic sort of rhyme. Heard melodies are sweet. To be sure. Unheard melodies are sweeter still.

All that happens -- everything! -- happens by chance (tukhe). This is Shekhinah. This is the Copenhagen Interpreation in which the Heisenbergian "potentia" is repalced by the Platonic "play of difference." This is "eksaiphnes."

These statements are not complementary to each other. Rather, they are each, always and all ways, completely true without reservation. At once. This is the "offspring/interest" of and between the two. Unity in duality and duality in unity.

Plato and the break from aisthesis. Even now it is not understood. The theory of the forms -- (and even he did not remain faithful to the most fertile part of what he wrote) -- involves the break from aisthesis. If the forms were -- (as Aristotle reports) -- merely the replication in the soi-dissant """"super-sensible"""" realm of the sensible there would have been no break from aisthesis. Aristotle had no clue.

"Abstracting" (i.e. Aristotelian "qua-ing") from the sensible is not breaking from the sensible. *{{{Yes, yes, yes, yes, yes. The whole subtle ball of wax here. "Separ-ABLE" (khoristos) but not separate. It's a wonderful and subtle story and you should read it someday. But it remains a "hule" oriented story. Thus it is anything but Plato's story. ((And yes. There are some passages in which Aristotelian choristos seems to demand "separate" as a translation. But that is not the issue here.)) }}}*

Hegelianesque "sublation" of the sensible is not breaking from the sensible.

Of course, any kind of "empirical" study -- be it by Aristotle --- Galileo --- Newton --- Einstein --- Heisenberg/Bohr -- is not a break from aisthesis. There is no battle between the "Ancients and the Moderns." They are all in the same boat. What the Copenhagen Interpretation discovered -- with telling mathmatical precision -- is the invalidity of such a naive claim and or aspiration to """""objectivity"""""".

John Bell from BELL-FAST. Non-locality. No-one really knew what to do with it. For to understand Bell's theorem -- (and John Bell did not understand his own theorem) -- is to do what science does not know how to do. Break from aisthesis. But this could have no meaning for that crowd. It was with Bell's theorem that they got close. Damn close. But then they got paralyzed. It was easier to ignore it. Or to heap scorn on it. So -- uncomprehending as always -- they just walked away from it and pretended to do what they called "Cosmology".

The One and its contrary. And the "offspring/interest" between the two.

Yes. There is the return -- (exuberantly playful and coming forth only as "likely") -- to aisthesis which presupposes the prior break from aisthesis. This is Timaeus. But that's not the real question. One needs to know: what happens in that space ("khora" which makes one think of "khoris" and "khorismos") first made possible by the break itself? What is "there"? And how does one make one's way about?

"te dianoia". [Parmenides; 143A-9; 158C-3; 165A-9 <<Loeb lining in all cases>> ("te psuche" at 132A-7)].

"te dianoia". The play of difference. "te dianoia". Made possible by the play of difference. Not abstraction. Not sublation. Not an extension of (measuring) aisthesis into the world of the sub-atomic.

"te dianoia". What is it?

Plato Started. Can the promise of Parmenides be fulfilled? Dion died and so did Plato. And -- for those very few who have and understanding of the significance of the tetralogical ordering of the dialogues -- it must always be kept in mind that Parmenides introduces Philebus which introduces **the third dialogue of the third tetralogy**. The Parmenides is but the sine qua non. The necessary condition. The necessary preparation. The secret resides in Symposium. The secret is Eros. Read the mania section (of this book).

----- *Therefore the whole thing can only be considered as having happened in a flash* [emphasis by Johanna Elton], *since it is conceived as something which happened without really (*explicite*) happened.*

----- *in creation there is the greatest harmony, and nothing is so separate and sequent as we must represent it, but the subsequent cooperates in what precedes it and everything occurs at the same time in one magic stoke.*

Please. Let the Queen of Hearts speak:

Like the flash of heat lightning that tells you all that is, is now.

In the mean time. What is to be done? Trust Shekhinah. Trust Shekhinah in all things. Peace. That peace which the world cannot give is nonetheless dispersed all throughout all. You will find it if you know how NOT to look. Only one who seeks will ever find. But most certainly if one keeps on seeking one will not find.

{{{{{And yes. It came to him. With the kind of joy whose outer garment is serenity. Johnny Keats knew this as well. A thing of beauty -- even No!!!! precisely because!!!! broken and dispersed -- is a joy forever. Unheard melodies are sweetest.

The Mother is sustained in the mixture. This is and must be. But without the Father -- Beauty which must die -- "there is" no "offspring/interest." <<<*The Father too is transformed in and by mixture. He becomes the andogynous ideal always dreamed of. Beyond all questions of reproductive utility -- (which, it will dawn on more and more, no longer governs paradigms of "male" and "female") -- it is just as important that Mommy not be endowed with a penis as it is that Daddy be so endowed.*>>>

Thus.

Without the father "there is" no good. Beauty which must die. Working for the coming of the Messiah. Choose life!}}}}}

Keeping time, time, time
In a sort of Runic rhyme

210.

Freud resiliatingly contra Freud gives Plato

Plato resiliatingly contra Plato gives Kaballah

Kaballah resiliatingly CONTRA Kaballah gives Shekhinah

211.
Peter. You knew it all and you nothing.

Yes, Categories was still the prism by which you understood anything at all about Plato which means you understood nothing about Plato. Things had not really changed all that much from the time of Porphery and Boethius.

Yes. You had no appreciation of things Jewish except through the corrupting lens of Christian orthodoxy which means you had no appreciation of things Jewish. Your endemic Anti-Semitism was certainly no worse than what one finds throughout all orthodox Christian writers in your century. But it was there in your text as well.

Nor was your post-castration possessiveness of Eloise something which would find sympathy in this "post-Copernican" age of Feminism.

Even so.

You did understand the ultimate primacy of the third person of the Blessed Trinity. I choose to think that in this regard you are not a precursor of the narcissistic monster birthed by Hegel but rather -- unbeknownst to you, of course -- someone who uncannily hearkened back to Plato's meditation on "the third."

You did love. You were there. John Donne -- whether he was thinking of you or not does not matter -- had you in mind when he spoke of being "canonized" for love.

You did suffer. Your suffering was so poignant and so dramatic that it stands as more significant than the dying of Socrates. You are a nodal point for the intertwining of Eros and Thanatos when their intertwining takes on the "form" of philosophical discourse. In ways which transcend the theological agendum of your century -- although I doubt that these ways transcended the vicissitudes of your own psyche during the living years -- you have taught us again the painful ambiguity of the duty, *Scito teipsum*. Sic et Non indeed.

212.
Sigismund: Your silence this time seems ever so pregnant.

Eurydice: Then be a mid-wife, by all means.

Sigismund: Please speak on. Push, so to speak.

Eurydice: There is another reason why the Holocaust is sui generis.

Sigismund: Are you suggesting that somehow the Holocaust is worse because the Jews are the chosen people?

Eurydice: In some sense, that is what I have on my mind. Of course I realize that in the "oh-we-are-so-sophisticated" atmosphere which obtains "up there" in the world of letters such a thought is deemed to be quaint. But regardless of how it is explained or accounted for -- {{and in this regard what you gave us in Moses and Monotheism on this issue is not unhelpful and is, in any case, far less "anti-religious" than you might have imagined }} -- it remains the case that the Jews are special on this third planet from the sun. It remains the case that the disappearance of the Jews would constitute the disappearance of history. Even so, I had something else on my mind.

Sigismund: What is that?

Eurydice: God was at Auschwitz.

Sigismund: I have heard that. God suffers with His (Her) people.

Eurydice: I notice that you do not choke on the reality of God as you used to up there in the living years.

Sigismund: We all learn. We all make progress.

Eurydice: Thank God. Yes. God was at Auschwitz. She suffered with Her people. And more than that.

Sigismund: What in God's name are you driving at?

Eurydice: God really was at Auschwitz. In all respects as the writer of Shekhinah -- through Bappy and Dewchee -- has made clear. In all respects. It was His/Her worst hour.

Sigismund: If I hear you correctly, you speak a profound blasphemy.

Eurydice: Better to utter what some would call a blasphemy than to stay in the destructive nets of idolatry. The demonic is not foreign to God. God is a "dark" God. And time is running out. We no longer have the luxury of denial and deceit on these matters. One must really learn to listen to Bappy and Dewchee in Shekhinah. God really was at Auschwitz. In all respects.

Sigismund: I would take more consolation from my Enlightenment-level atheism which obtained for me in the living years.

Eurydice: That is because you too simplistically equate the demonic with evil and because you do not trust sufficiently that even God -- even Shekhinah -- has the possibility for self-correction. It is all contained in the implied Theology of Shekhinah for those who have the ability to actually read Shekhinah.

Sigismund: The importance of our project now begins to dawn on me. The "correction" of my "Eros"/"Thanatos" duality -- apparently through a lens soon to be garnered from Parmenides and other writings of Aristocles -- is not mere esoteric meandering. It relates to the very condition of life -- human life most especially -- on the third planet from the sun.

Eurydice: Now you begin to see. In spirit, you were there already at the end of Civilization and its Discontents. Listen:

> *And now it is to be expected that the other of the two "Heavenly Powers", eternal Eros, will make an effort to assert himself in the struggle with his equally immortal adversary.*

Civ, page 104.

213.
Bappy: You mean, what happens to "Eros" and "Thanatos" when they are sifted through the merciless filter, so to speak, of the logic of Parmenides.

Dewchee: Yes. At least the logic of Parmenides as the writer of Shekhinah came to understand it.

214.
Eurydice. You are quite welcome, my sweet one. Now let's get to it.

The one and its other. The other and its one.

The one: Shall its name be "the one"? Shall its name be "apeiron" as it is used at Parmenides 137D? Shall its name be "the will which does not will"; "the will which wills nothing, not even itself"?

Sigismund: Are you referring to the Schelling who wrote Ages of the World?

(Ages, pages 122-123.)

Eurydice: Yes. All provisions having been made for taking the phrase and part of the spirit of Schelling on this without marrying all that Schelling said either in this Ages book or in any of his other writings.

And perhaps, finally, we should call it the Father. Perhaps we should call it 'Beauty'; Beauty which must die.

Sigismund: How melancholic!! And what about the other?

Eurydice: That is trickier.

The other: Shall we say "eksaiphnes", with special attention to what is called hypothesis # 2a (and which hypothesis, structurally, stands out like a sore thumb when it is integrated into the dialectical structuring of the four "positive" and four "negative" hypotheses of that God-awe-full dialogue) but which hypothesis "Parmenides" goes out of his way to call "the Third time" at 155E?

Shall we say "The Dyad" taking this to be a kind of oscillation?

Shall we put the two -- "eksaiphnes" and "the Dyad" together and call this pure oscillating need?

Shall we perhaps call it the Mother? Perhaps we should call Her """"""""""""Truth"""""""""""".

Sigismund: And when the two -- i.e., the one and its dyadic other -- come together?

Eurydice: Be careful my friend. The dyadic other draws the one into itself so as to gain some measure of relief from pure oscillating need. It is the dyadic other which is responsible for the mixture. {{A mixture, of course, which never ceases to begin without ever having begun, and which never ceases to end without, however, ever ending.}}

Sigismund: Is this "the draw -- the attraction -- of equilibrium"?

Eurydice: Yes and no. The "real" equilibrium is the "offspring" -- itself ever-moving/ever-changing -- of and between the two which is always called for, always achieved and never achieved. This is the good. The second coming is a never ending -- even as it ends -- continuous affair. The ever-moving/ever-changing point {{i.e the geometrical fiction; --- *he came to lecture on the good and he ended up speaking of mathematics* --- }}. Coming to rest -- real rest -- IN restlessness. Coming on and through the edge.

Sigismund: How demonic!!!

Eurydice: Indeed 509B!!! *daimonias!!!!* Eu-Daimon!!!! But Aristotle had no clue. For the rest go to "The Lecture on the Good". There find "khora". There find the dis-appearing light.

Sigismund: Do you mean Part Five of Shekhinah?

Eurydice: But of course! That white-hot book becomes "white-hot-ness" itself with Part V, "The Lecture on the Good."

Sigismund: So is that it? Are we finished?

215.
a). The Aristotelian way of establishing the primacy of the individual -- and, "within" the individual, the primacy of the formal principle of individuation -- is bequeathed to the West in multiple manners

Confer Metaphysics V-8, 1017b, 15-17 in conjunction with 1017b, 25-27 <Loeb lining>; likewise the entire argumentation of VII-17. Metaphysics VII-3, at 1029a, 30-34 effectively makes the same point. Finally, the conclusion of XIII-10, in its treatment of the proper object of "episteme", also points to the "this in the this" as the proper object of knowledge.

b). In the writings of the Church Fathers whose innovative way of conjuring up the "hypostatic" union -- three individuated "persons" in one God -- rests upon Aristotle's identification of primary ousia with one special meaning of hupokeimenon ((i.e., the formal principle in the subject -- separable-but-not-separate from said subject (subjectum; hupokeimenon) -- and, of course, not predicable of the subject (and thus not of such a nature so as to "dis-appear" into its predicates))). Indeed the very concept of "person" is born in this fashion and is a function of this theological exigency to express what is present in a Triune God.

Confer especially the V-8 text already cited above, namely 1017b. 15-17.

{{{It can be noted here that Aristotle's favorite example of the formal principle which is present in a subject, separable but not separate from the individual, which is also not predicable of said subject -- i.e., the soul of Socrates -- can, retroactively, be said to be the concept of person without the word, "person." Granted that soul is always the soul OF a body , nonetheless with this usage of soul Aristotle is getting at what would be the very identity of Socrates which causes Socrates to be who and what he is.}}}

c). The meditations of Porphery and Boethius -- despite their claims of a desire to synthesize Plato and Aristotle on "the problem of the universals" and other related matters of predication -- are basically Aristotelian. Always and everywhere for these two thinkers The Categories and the Aristotelian meditation on hupokeimenon is the frame of reference by which the tension between Plato and Aristotle is engaged. Always and everywhere with these two thinkers it is basically Aristotle's account of what a Platonic form is which becomes the base-line for any hints at a synthesis between the two thinkers. Plato's own long and careful meditation on predicational matters -- the Parmenides -- is either passed over in silence or is seen through the Neo-Platonic prism by which Timaeus becomes the interpretive grid for the understanding of the eight hypotheses. If this commentary has shown nothing else, it has shown how quintessentially un-Platonic such a procedure is.

d). Plotinian Neo-Platonism is, paradoxically enough, Aristotelian in its understanding of ousia. Part of the scandal of the Tradition is that the Aristotelian bias of the Tradition is present even in sub-traditions which in name only honor Plato.

e). In the high Middle Ages the tension in the Aristotelian text concerning the meaning of ousia/hupokeimenon displays itself through the various meanings of "subjectum" and "suppositum." Through the concept of "suppositum" the Medievalists retain the primacy of formal individuation relative to the primary meaning of "ousia." To be sure the principle of formal individuation is always the form-OF-proximate (i.e. "signate") matter for sensible substance. But substances without matter in their composition -- such as angels -- are pure individuated form which is why they had to maintain that each individual angel is, so to speak, a species unto itself.

{{{Ousia/hupokeimenon for Aristotle: is it matter? yes but no. (1029a, 10-34) is it form? yes; but in the idiosyncratic meaning of form announced in VII-3, already cited in V-8 (at 1017b, 23-27), and celebrated -- as something other than an element and as a principle in and of ousia -- in VII-17}}}

f). The long incubation period of these Aristotelian teachings through, on the one hand, Plotinian Neo-Platonism (which remains, as always, Aristotelian in its basic orientation) and, on the other hand, through the overt Aristotelianism of the High Middle Ages had something like a greenhouse effect on this doctrine of individuation. Something like one of those freak, chance permutative mutations of conceptual evolution took place as the hupokeimenon/subjectum/suppositum of Aristotle and the Aristotelians became the "Subjectivity" of Modern Philosophy. And now the quintessence of individuation -- {{{which was "form" in the idiosyncratic sense of Aristotle; which was "person" in the hypostatic meditations of the Church Fathers; which was suppositum as the "I AM WHO AM" of St. Thomas;}}} -- came forth: as ego; as the cogito of Descartes; as the absurd freedom of the pour soi in Sartre; as the "I-am-I" of early German Idealism.

g). The whirlwind of Modern Subjectivity collapses in upon itself -- even before it was still to play out some remaining possibilities -- first with the cry of Nietzsche that the Emperor (i.e., "Subjectivity") had no clothes. Then, in a more subtle and not immediately recognized manner with Heisenberg. The privilege of "Subjectivity" was shattered. *{{{For if there is no "in and by itself" objectivity -- which is adequately demonstrated by Quantum Mechanics -- then "subjectivity", as ground of objectivity's non-objectivity, becomes the false ground of a groundless abyss.}}}* Modern Thought -- a kind of bastard child of Aristotle's meditation on hupokeimenon/ousia -- became the "batteau ivre." And "person" was unmasked and revealed for what it was: a mask; the bad-faith mask of the flight from difference.

Confer WP, aphorisms #: 471, 473, 474, 475, 476, 477, 479, 480, 482, 483, 484, 485, 487, 488.

A sub-text of this book in general (and of certain sections in particular which are still forthcoming) is that a "difference-oriented" way of thinking is both indicated and required by the findings of Quantum Mechanics. Although this book does not make the case as such within the confines of this book, it is understood that Heisenberg's "philosophical" interpretation of what the findings of Quantum Mechanics are "saying" is clearly preferable to Einstein's emotional inability to let Quantum Mechanics "say" what it effectively does say about """"""reality"""""". (These matters are rather efficiently discussed by Heisenberg in Physics and Philosophy; Haprer and Row, New York, 1958. Hereafter: Physics.)

Still, there is a problem.

In thoughtfully trying to relate the "findings" of contemporary Physics to the language of Ancient Philosophy Heisenberg struggles mightily with the problem of finding an analog for the strange "is"/"is not" kind of "being" revealed on the sub-atomic level by the "findings" of Quantum Mechanics. He settles on the Aristotelian concept of "potentia" as an analog. (Confer Physics pages 53-55; 147-148; 160; 185-186.) This is unfortunate for several reasons.

In the first place Heisenberg -- who understood the truly remarkable, chance-imbued, "is"/"is not" way in which sub-atomic phenomena show themselves (and therefore ARE) -- uses a concept from a thinker, Aristotle, who (according to the contention of *Thinking Psycho-analytically*) was in a full-scale flight from the "difference-oriented" kind of thinking which animated the Platonic text in Theaetetus, Sophist, Parmenides, and Timaeus. And, it is (again, according to the contention of *Thinking Psycho-analytically*) precisely this "difference-oriented" model of thinking which would be the "true" philosophical analog for communicating that strange "is"/"is not" way of "being" for sub-atomic "reality" uncovered by the "findings" of Quantum Mechanics.

Clearly, Heisenberg had no inkling at all of this "difference-oriented" way of thinking which animates the most important dialogues of the Platonic text. (Indeed, even while referring to Timaeus itself Heisenberg proves to be ignorant of this theme.) In the absence of such an insight it is possible to argue that the closest Greek ontology came to expressing the joint "is"/"is not" of things is through Aristotle's treatment of "potentia." Still Aristotelian "potentia" is but the domestication of Plato's "difference-oriented" kind of thinking which more accurately and thematically expresses the remarkable chance-imbued "is"/"is not" way of "being" uncovered by the "findings" of Quantum Mechanics. Indeed, in the final analysis, (paradox noted), it is precisely the unconscious commitment to an Aristotelian-esque ontology which kept Einstein from understanding what the "findings" of Quantum Mechanics was attempting to "say."

I have argued these matters more carefully on pages 174-176 of the unpublished Madonna manuscript mentioned above.

216.

a). Plato played this game as well. Indeed, he had invented it. But after 347 hardly anyone played with him. Plato had the "safe" and "stupid" answer of Phaedo 99-100. Most people who claim to be playing the game -- even, among them, some who are rather subtle -- learn Plato's answer but never learn Plato's contextualization of the answer given through the eight hypotheses. These alleged players know of Aristotle's presentation and refutation of the theory of forms. They can cite Aristotle Chapter and Verse: *It is clear, then, ---- that no universal term is substance ----. But they strangely avoid Plato's own account of Plato's own stubborn theory.*

{{{And does not Plato, even in the Phaedo, allude to the kind of suppositional exercise -- later actually instantiated through the eight hypotheses of Parmenides -- by which the theory is justified? Cf. Phaedo 101C-E}}}

Metaphysics VII-16; 1041a, 4-6 <Loeb lining>.

A form for Plato is more "this" than Aristotle ever dreamed. A form, after all, is a "one." Plato's forms are also predicated of many. The scandal of Philosophy is that the entire Tradition -- even and especially when it calls itself Neo-Platonic -- operates in a profound ignorance and/or misappropriation of that perspectival, predicational, contextualization of Plato's theory which comes forth in Parmenides.

With Aristotle and his multiple derivatives one has the privileged perspective. The hupokeimenon of privilege. Difficult to get to, but objectively real, even when, in Modernity, it finds a home in the heart of "Subjectivity."

With Plato -- in contrast -- one has ousia itself AS relational allowing for but never resting at individuation. What will be the primacy of hupokeimenon with Aristotle has no significance in the Platonic text. For to be at all the "subject", for Plato, must ""dis-appear"" into its predicates. With Plato -- one is speaking of the eight hypotheses -- one has a SELF-effacing privileged perspective which fades as soon as it appears into and from the mysterious play of difference. This in turn means that one's very own identity never ceases to be formed.

b). <<<<<Even the desire to achieve something like "the universal in the particular" (or "the concrete universal"; or, coming now from that tribe of Vicians, "the subjective/imaginative universal") betrays that old habit which -- however unconscious one might be of its actual historical genesis -- stems from Aristotle's obsession for the hupokeimenon of privilege. It is precisely this obsessive drive for the hupokeimenon of privilege which has been and in many ways continues to be the cancer which has the continuing effect of rendering Philosophy ridiculous. On the other hand, a "this" -- form or participant, it doesn't matter -- which immediately loses itself via "the play of difference" into its predicates: that is worthy of thought.>>>>>

c). Bappy: Dewchee! You looked so worried!

Dewchee. I am. It's that individuation business. I realize now that something diabolical was conjured up and that we in the West -- now that means the entire planetary community -- are still in its grip.

-- (please understand that the diabolical is a possible outcome of the demonic when and as the demonic fails to be pressed into the service of 'the good'.) --

Bappy: You're not going to lay all of that at Aristotle's address, are you?

Dewchee: He birthed it, of course. But it didn't come forth in its marinated form until Modern Times. It has led eros to infect itself -- so to speak -- with the self-produced drug of the diabolical.

Bappy: Could you please explain your meaning.

Dewchee: We have been agreed for some time that the whole ball of wax is energized by eros, have we not?

Bappy. Yes. Basically. We might want some minor qualification on this later. But yes; basically.

Dewchee: And don't you see? It now services the privileged perspective, now called "Subjectivity" which -- it is alleged -- is objectively real. This is not only a problem for Philosophy but also an "existential" problem for the six billion souls who now inhabit the globe. Narcissism run rampant. Eros is being compelled to orchestrate its own idolatry. For surely the narcissism of our age is idolatry.

Bappy: Oh how sad!

Dewchee: Yet eros must out. It creates its own antidote against this idolatry: The logic of humiliation. Eros in the service of humiliation; humiliation in the service of shattering the disease of "subjectivity" which -- no matter how discredited in thinking it now has become after Nietzsche and Heisenberg -- is still growing in the population as a whole. Forms of perverse erotic behavior -- masochism most especially -- emerge as commonalities. *[[Indeed, it is not incidental that the very names of those perversions which blare out in the pathologically heightened consciousness of Modernity -- sadism and masochism -- stem from European Modernity.]]* For a while wounded narcissism is attracted to masochism (with its logic of humiliation) as a last refuge. Wounded narcissism comes forth as "vertigo" (i.e., intoxication with one's own weakness). But eros will have its way. Humiliation, in our time, by going to a place where even "vertigo" cannot endure, comes to wipe out the last vestiges even of a wounded narcissism. And now I understand Johanna's melancholy.

This interesting understanding of "vertigo" is taken from Milan Kundera. Confer The Art of the Novel; translated by Linda Asher; Harper and Row, New York, 1988. Page 38.

Bappy: What do you mean?

Dewchee: Like everyone else she was caught up in the disease of "subjectivity." The privileged perspective. Narcissism raised to the point of disease. And now her life has become something like a Dionysian, samsaraesque purification which in the process crawls into every nook and cranny of illusion. Every nook and cranny, time after time, until illusion becomes allusion.

Bappy: But even this is a kind of enlightenment, is it not?

Dewchee: Yes. Most certainly. It lightens. Like the play of dew, near dawn, on a Spring day in May.

Bappy: And May is Maia? *{Maya}*

Dewchee: Yes. In both its honorific and perjorative senses.

Bappy: After purification, what emerges?

Dewchee: The belonging together of logos and eros. The SELF-effacing privileged perspective which fades as soon as it appears from and into the play of difference. The "subject" which loses itself in its predicates. Self-giving. Self-giving is all.

Bappy: Thank-you, Dewchee. I love your stories so much.

Dewchee: You are welcome. Now sleep. Now rest.

d). *The tradition, literally, "betrays". Yet this too "happens".*

e). Mort: Heteros; difference. Do you think he ever noticed?

Jude: Get serious. This was Plato, my friend. Did he notice? He took a bubble bath in it! Heteros!! And many other dimensions of this fertile word.

Mort: What about "allo"?

Jude: And that as well. Fare thee well.

217.
a). Most of the Tradition unconsciously follows this flight from difference accomplished by Aristotle's way of engaging Platonic thought by avoiding what Platonic thinking was about. Still there are cries and whispers all through the Tradition which hearken one to get back to what was lost in it. The contention of this book is that -- contrary to the Derridean/Heideggerian enterprise (which sees the flight from difference as congenital to the whole history of Philosophy) -- it is only by "dis-mantling" that nexus of and between "Plato and Aristotle" (where "difference" and the "play of difference" fell between the cracks, so to speak) that one will recover that which of its nature e-vokes thought. The project of this book is to return thinking to its proper vocation

b). One can almost hear the "Eureka" in Aristotle's mind when one reads Plato's ever so quick analysis of the "hupodoche" and the "this". Aristotle's "hupokeimenon"-oriented Categories surely has its genesis in this Timaeus passage.

(Confer Timaeus 49A-50A and, to a lesser extent, 50A-C.)

Plato's "Receptacle" (hupodoche) is that "third" thing so often mentioned in this wo-man book. It becomes, as this part of Timaeus unfolds, the "khora" doctrine which is, as often noted in this wo-man book, effectively, the emergence of difference/other which, in turn, constitutes the "dream-like" separateness of the Forms. But for Plato both Form and participant do not retain the "thisness" which they momentarily achieve by virtue of the space/receptacle. For Plato, the "this", having made its brief appearance in conjunction with "the third", withdraws into hiding. In no way is it given the privilege of presence accorded to the "this" in Aristotle's frame of refernce as Aristotle invents for his system the primacy of the non-relational. For Plato, they -- both forms and participants in a form -- dis-appear into that network of difference which is unpacked most carefully in hypothesis # 2 of Parmenides. In other words, being intrinscically relational, they dis-appear into their predicates.

{{One must refer here to that most important of all the Platonic texts concernng the Forms, namely the difficult to read/translate passage obtaining from the beginning of 52A to the beginning of 52D. This passage is the secret for undersanding the teaching concerning the Forms and functions, in effect, as a two-way vector to the "difference" passages of hypothesis # 2. This passage, in all respects, was a primary concern of the book Sentences.}}

In contrast Aristotle, in his flight from difference, is looking for a model of ousia such that ousia -- in its primary sense -- escapes the intrinsic relationality of Platonic ousia. Thus he ultimately grafts together hupokeimenon/ousia/form. The "this in the this" constitutes the principle of form, that which is present in the individual "subject" -- separable-but-not-separate from said subject --, causing it to be what it is but NOT predicable of a subject. The "this in the this" -- i.e., the formal principle in Aristotle's idiosyncratic meaning of form -- is the quintessential "subject" (i.e., hupokeimenon). Later this study will try to show how this conflation of "form" and "hupokeimenon" in the Aristotelain text (*) -- incubated and marinated through the "suppositum" teachings of the Middle Ages -- eventually birthed the "Subjectivity" doctrines of Modernity.

*. -- {{in VII-3 of Metaphysics this grafting is basically announced and it is accomplished through his, Aristotle's, idiosyncratic meaning of "form" which emerges in VII-17 of Metaphysics}} --

((In Books VIII and IX of Metaphysics he will refer to the formal principle as "energeia/entelecheia".))

There is no small irony to the eventual denouement of "hupokeimenon" as it is used by Aristotle. For in reviewing his predecessors, including Plato, Aristotle uses "hupokeimenon" in the sense of "material substrate" -- which is also one of the meanings of "hupokeimenon" as Aristotle uses it -- and imposes this grid of interpretation on key concepts of his predecessors, including Plato. In doing this Aristotle, of course, begs multiple questions concerning his predecessors and creates for himself a vehicle by which it can appear that his predecessors, including Plato, had done poorly what Aristotle does with Wisdom and finesse. As this woman book has often pointed out, Aristotle's understanding of The Dyad of the Great and the Small as a material substrate is serious misrepresentation of Plato's ontology.

Plato's hupodoche and Aristotle's hupokeimenon (when hupokeimenon is used in the sense of material substrate) are associated by both thinkers with the Mother/feminine. But as is even evidenced by the words in question there are significant differences involved. For Plato there is something "substantial", in a manner of speaking, about Mother/Receptacle whose very """existence""" is recognized only by virtue of and in conjunction with the principle -- Anagnke -- which is resistant to the demiurgic acitivity of Nous. *{{{{It is true that the "the fifth" (i.e., "the Mother"; i.e., the contrary to the one) is sustained in "the third" (i.e. "khora"/receptacle"; i.e., the "offspring" of and between the one and the contrary to the one) and thus it is proper the speak in a feminine manner of "khora/receptacle". Even so, what is stable, immutable, (and, accordingly receptive/"passive" about* *"khora/receptacle") in fact -- and not without paradox -- comes from the one (i.e., the Father; i.e., Beauty which must die). These secret paradoxes within paradoxes -- largely ignored in Aristotle's passing and rather pedestrian references to Plato's* Timaeus *-- of Platonic mixture are explored most especially in the "caesuras" (caesurae?) of this book. For those who have the eyes to hear and the ears to see.}}}}}* Aristotle's "hupokeimenon" (when he uses it as material substrate and as the analog of the feminine), in contrast, is merely passive, being only the home of privation, and having no life of its own, so to speak.

{{It is, of course, the "Act/Potency" paradigm, worked out in VIII and IX of Metaphysics, which allows for consistency in this paradoxical duality of functions for "hupokeimenon" as the term is used by Aristotle. On the one hand hupokeimenon functions as a nodal point of privilege, being the ousia/form/energeia which is not predicable since it -- said subject -- stands by itself as that for which and to which there are predicates at all. On the other hand hupokeimenon is material substrate. The "Act/Potency" paradigm achieves this consistency by having hupokeimenon, as material substrate, function passiviely -- and merely -- as that which is informed (penetrated, so to speak) by form/energeia. In effect, conceptually, Aristotle robs the feminine of what is most powerful about it; grafts the best of the feminine onto an exaggerated paradigm of the male principle; and then, in effect, chortles about the feminine's lack and privation. In contrast -- both conceptually and in life -- the movement of Androgyny is quite different. The entrance into the female on the part of the male principle is not only for the sake of the female (principle) but also entails the transformation of the male principle into the expression of the feminine.}}

218.
Chance and grace. Amazing grace.

{{{ St. Thomas and that pile of straw. Especially when speaking of God's Providence Thomas manifests a subtle appreciation for the play of contingency as the manifestation of God's Will in creation. He had some very fine moments. And in this regard Thomas is pardigmatic of the effect of monotheism on the Tradition: it renders as naught the refinements of even the most subtle of its participants. A pile of straw. For chance/contingency/randomness can only receive its due in the realm of thinking by and through a thinking which understands the basic duality in the make-up of things.}}}

219.
The fly in the ointment. It's right there in the opening words of Parmenides: *After leaving our home at Clazomenae we arrived at Athens* ------ Where Anaxagoras hailed from. Later on --towards the beginning of his "Parmenides"-- the great idolatrator spoke of Anaxagoras as the only one sober at a party of drunks.

Confer Aristotle's Metaphysics I, Chapter three; 984b, 15-20.

Of course one knows that both Plato and Aristotle would make significant critiques of just how Nous functions as an ordering principle in the teachings of Anaxagoras. But already it was too late. Nous had now become the face of God.

To be sure, Nous is always conditioned by its other (viz., "Anangke") in Plato's dualistic schema. Furthermore, there is in Plato as well the honorific status accorded to the "offspring" of the two which "offspring" can also be called "the third." What has been refered to as "Nous idolatry" -- (in various unpublsished manuscripts which, as it turns out, functioned as "unterwegs zur" Shame!) -- was always conditioned in the Platonic text (and in a number of ways) by a fundamental duality -- (e.g., "Anangke" as other than Nous) -- in the make-up of things. In contrast, in Aristotle's monotheistic metaphysics, the idolatry is complete.

It is, in fact, not all that surprising that the people who "discovered" Philosophy should be especially prone to this form of idolatry. However this thought-evoking "sentence" of Father Parmenides has and may come to be parsed out it was, after all, Father Parmenides himself who stated:

The same: thinking as well as being

The Poem of Parmenides, fragment 3, as contained in Parmenides, page 56. This translation which I offer here is most radically inspired by Heidegger's long meditation on this fragment in *Was heisst denken?*.

The Parmenidean/Platonic meditation on noesis in its distinction from aisthesis -- which was not eo ipso destined to become idolatrous -- can, with some fancy and retroactive foot work, be turned into an interesting kind of Theology by virtue of a fusion with a non-Hegelian account of what Hawking referred to as "The Anthropic Principle." Such a meditation would end up allowing thinking to be an evolved "property" (so to speak) of God without being, so to speak, the """"""essence"""""" of God. Such a meditation would permit the revelation of God as the very play of chance itself which comes, eventually, to elicit thinking in this kind of teleology which is not one.

Confer Stephen Hawking's discussion of the Anthropic Principle in A Brief History of Time. Bantam Books, New York, 1988. Pages 123-127. Hereafter: Brief.

{{The charge that the Anthropic Principle might be true but trivial can only be made by soi-dissant thinkers who are blind to the theological implications of the Anthropic Principle. Even so, this blindness would be preferable to an Hegelianization of the Anthropic Principle.}}

"Chance" (tukhe) is taken in these passages as very generic and as almost synonymous with "randomness". However, Aristotle's distinction between "chance" and "spontaneity" (automaton) is useful since, for Aristotle, "chance" (tukhe) is the kind of randomness/"spontaneitity" which is at issue for entities capable of praxis. Listen to Aristotle's comment from Physics II, Chapter 6, 197a, 36-197b,3:

> *In Greek "tukhe" and "automaton" differ in this that "automaton" is the more general term and includes "tukhe" as a special class.*
>
> *For "tukhe" itself, as a cause, the results that accrue by the action of "tukhe" are only spoken of in connexion with beings capable of enjoying good fortune or, more generally, "doing"/"acting" well or poorly.* [According to Cornford, with modification.]

Also confer, in the same Chapter, 197b, 19-197b, 23.

As things concretely turned out, however, "Nous" and "chance" became contraries and furthermore, contraries in which the principle of chance/randomness (i.e., "Anangke" as used in Plato's Timaeus) comes to be under the suasion of Divine Nous. Even so, "chance" plays a "necessary" and most significant role in the make-up of things for Plato.

Aristotle sets in motion the eclipsing of "chance" as a primary cause in the make-up of things through the moves he makes in transforming Plato's dualism of first principles into a monotheism. Most significant is his conflating of the principles of "Nous" and "Anangke". By turning God into a necessary being which has no contrary Aristotle transforms the meaning of "Anangke". "Chance" and "Anangke" come to be -- contrary to how it was for Plato -- divorced from each other. "Chance", for Aristotle, is no longer an all but equal partner with "Nous" but is relegated to the status of an "obiter dicta" in the cataloguing of the kinds of causes which obtain in the make-up of things.

Confer Metaphysics XII, Chapter seven; 1072b, 7-14.

It is also noteworthy that Aristotle's fusion of Nous (i.e., God) and Anangke -- a move which is dependent upon a transformation of the very meaning of "Anangke" away from "Anangke" as Plato had used it in Timaeus -- set in motion a whole set of difficulties which emerge when and as this idolatrized creation (viz., this Aristotelain God concept) {{{ -- which, at bottom, is operative in most forms of Neo-Platonism **[sic!!!]** --}}} was further hyperbolized by having it (this Aristotelain God concept) fused to that most fetishistic notion emerging out of the Fathers of the Chruch which came to be called *creatio ex nihilo*. All of Medieval and most of Modern Philosophy -- even and especially when it becomes secularized -- get hopelessly caught up in a set of "difficulties" *{{{one thinks quickly of a whole bunch of "free will"/"derterminism" difficulties}}}* which occur at all only because the Tradition is so insidiously and unconciously Aristotelian in its way of even approaching questions of "Necessity." And of course, with this embrace of Aristotle's meaning of "necessity", one moves ever further away from appreciating "chance" (i,e, that of which Timaeic "Anangke" is the principle) as near co-equal factor in the make-up of things. The Platonic account -- which already limits the role of "chance" in the make-up of things (by virtue of Anangke's deferral to "Nous") even as it acknowledges its range -- is eclipsed by this bias of the Tradition. Even more radically hidden is the account of things by which Divine agency is understood as "chance." But it is Aristotle himself who reminds us -- even as he keeps a most radical distance from the position of which he reminds us -- of what always will be fundamental in these matters:

> ----- *Others there are who, indeed, believe that chance is a cause, but that it is inscrutable to human intelligence, as being a divine thing and full of mystery.*

Physics II, Chapter 4; 196b, 6-196b, 8.

220.
Chance and grace. Amazing grace.

221.
Listen.

Seldom has it been said so succinctly and so economically.

On the one hand, all that is "right" about Plato. The dualism of first principles. The honorific bow to the "other" as other which so quickly would be eclispsed by Aristotle's monotheism. The recognition of "Anangke" -- the principle of chance/randomness -- as the principle other than "God." Only with Plato does the

"(M)-other" have a voice of Her own. In all of this, Plato forever stands outside of the Tradition.

On the other hand and at the same time, all that is "wrong" about Plato. Setting in motion the hierarchy of the "one" (which for Plato is the "Divine") over the other. Setting in motion the impetus for the whole difference-fleeing subsuming/sublating of the "other" """"""up"""""" into and for the sake of the "one." Setting the stage for the eclispsing of the "other" in a Tradition which is still monotheistic even when it becomes atheistic. Having revealed the "(M)-other" -- and he was the only one to do so -- he puts Her in a subservient position. The failure to see Chance/Randomness itself as the """"""true"""""" face of God. The failure to really marry the "(M)-other". Plato was indeed a shade off.

Listen:

> *We must accordingly, distinguish two kinds of cause, the necessary and the divine. The divine we should search out in all things for the sake of a life of such happiness as our nature admits; the necessary for the sake of the divine, reflecting that apart from the necessary those other objects of our serious study cannot by themselves be perceived or communicated, nor can we in any other way have part or lot in them.*

Timaeus 68E-69A.

All of this raises the a most intriguing possibility. What if someone were to come to be more faithful than Plato himself relative to the """"""true"""""" vocation of the Platonic text? How would such a "study" come forth? A most interesting case of "regressive kathalysis."

222.
On the one hand, it must be acknowledged that Heidegger's presentation of Schelling is more nuanced than how the Tradition treats Schelling. For Heidegger, Schelling is much more than simply the link which joins Fichte and Hegel together in a Hegel-centered view of German Idealism. In fact Heidegger recognizes -- as Schelling most certainly did himself -- that the Schellingian text is not at all circumscribed by the Hegelian text. Indeed, Heidegger often enough attributes to the 1809 Freedom book a place of honor not accorded to any the Hegel's texts.

On the other hand, even Heidegger can see the Schellingian text as only an expression of Modernity which operates within a radical forgetfulness of the Heideggerian "Sein"/"Seyn". Heidegger sees the Schellingian text as simply instantiating Modern Philosophy's "Will" oriented metaphysics which culminates in the unconditioned "will to will" as technology becomes a planetary destiny. In this overall schema of things, Heidegger's Schelling -- especially in the 1809 Freedom book -- becomes something of a half-way house between Hegel's self-willing "Geist" and Nietzsche's meditation on "The Will to Power."

Whatever the ultimate value of Heidegger's meditation on technology might be, he, Heidegger, brings too much of a "fixed idea" to the word "Will" when he encounters the Schellingian text. In fact there is no meaning of the various -- and conflicting -- ways in which "will" is used by Schelling which can fit neatly into this Heideggerian vision of Modern Philosophy's instantiating the preparation for the "Ge-stell" of technology which has now become a planetary destiny. Furthermore, and more importantly, Heidegger's meditation on Schellingian Will completely bypasses the concept -- born in Ages of the World -- of the will which wills nothing, not even itself. This meaning of "will" -- unique to Schelling among Western Philosophers -- is as far removed as possible from all the "will-oriented" currents and counter-currents (some of which currents and counter-currents involving Schelling's <u>own</u> various meanings of "will") which constitute Modern Philosophy and Modernity. Indeed Heidegger's own meditation on "The Being of beings" would have gained much had he not taken such a reductionistic view of the Schellingian text.

Confer <u>Ages</u>, pages 122-123.

In all of this there is a serious question posed to Derrida and his followers. It is this: Let it be allowed that there are many, many differences between the Heideggerian text and the Derridean text. Let it be allowed that Derrida's reading of Heidegger is always subtle and nuanced, avoiding religiously the easy "pot-shots" relative to the Heideggeran text which have become so endemic to some European and American philosophical circles. Let it be further stipulated that, in general, when the two texts are compared in, so to speak, rivalrous fashion it is the Derridean text which "wins", so to speak. Still, it remains the case that Derrida's fundamental thought takes its inspiration from Heidegger and "the ontological difference." The question is this: What the thinking of """differ<u>a</u>nce""" is in the service of; can """it""" properly be serviced by a thinking which takes its inspiration from Heidegger? Do not answer this question too quickly.

223.
With these reflections O also realized that his Mother experience was just a painfully exaggerated version of what every boy goes through. The act by which he exists at all is the act by which he is betrayed by the only woman who will ever count for him. It was comforting to be a particular covered by the umbrella of the universal. On the other hand there were dimensions in O's betrayal story which were sui generis. For this he had both gratitude and hatred.

{{{{De Vere: The story is poignant. But I'm starting to get resonations more of <u>B</u>athos than of pathos. What do you make of it? After all, he's almost at the age I reached when my friend Death took me in. Wouldn't he be better advised to do his meditation on dying rather than on his Mother? Isn't he a bit old for such stuff?

Amy: I don't know. Reflections on "Mommy" and Death are not really foreign to each other. After all, our other friend wrote his meditation on 'the Three Caskets' inspired by something <u>you</u> wrote. Mommy and Death. It's all the same where I begin. I shall come back there again in time. In time. Besides.

De Vere: Besides what?

Amy: Is there anything -- <u>anything at all</u> even in that dark and lofty sense brought out by Heidegger in *Was heisst denken?* -- more worthy of our extended attention in thinking than 'Mommy'? It is <u>so</u> easy to assume that a "Mommy"-oriented meditation will reveal only what is self-evident. Yet even our other friend -- who was no slacker when it came to "Mommy"-oriented meditations -- had a blind spot in this thought e-voking "issue".

De Vere: You refer to Sigismund I presume.

Amy: Yes.

De Vere: Well he did wax rather poetical about 'Mommy's' unambivalent love for her first-born male progeny. He saw -- and exaggerated -- the advantages of being the first-born male progeny. But he seemed blind to the liabilities of being the first born-male progeny.

Amy: Indeed. And yet in that famous -- infamous -- lecture on "femininity" of 1933 he alerts the reader to the liabilities of all children who have their mother's initial favor without clearly noting the liabilities in particular for first-born male progeny. Listen to what he says and -- while listening -- think of how this might be compounded for first-born male progeny:

> *A powerful tendency to aggressiveness is always present beside a powerful love, and the more passionately a child loves its object the more sensitive does it become to disappointments and frustrations from that object; and in the end the love must succumb to the accumulated hostility.*

The reference here in general is, of course, to lecture XXXIII in his New Introductory Lectures on Psychoanalysis. Confer especially New, pages 108-110. The citation is taken from page 109.

De Vere: I catch your drift. Complicating this blind spot is the fact that Freud -- rather unawares of what he is doing in this regard -- rather thoughtlessly imposes/projects into the dynamic of the Mother the phallo-cratic bias of social custom which unabashedly celebrates and exaggerates the importance of first-born male progyny. Indeed phallo-cratic bias on this issue allows the little boy's exaggerated sense of possessiveness relative to 'Mommy' to spill over into a phallo-cratic justification for the control and manipulation of women by males both in the family and in society as a whole.

Amy: Indeed. A point often and fairly made by all sorts of Feminists. In fact this same dynamic of control and possessiveness even dominates in the way the phallo-cratic bias allows the feminine to be celebrated.

De Vere: I presume you mean in such literary/cultural traditions as "courtly love"; Divine Beatrice; some forms of Romanticism; the Goethean "eternal feminine"; etc., etc.

Amy: "Etc., etc." indeed. In fact there have even been times when I wondered about you in this regard. But let that pass. Your general point is well taken: Even in its alleged positive appropriation of the feminine, phallo-cratic bias perpetuates into adulthood -- as normative for males relative to females -- the immature possessiveness of the small child towards 'Mommy'. Sadly, all of this is very true and Sigismund is, for the most part, not free of such phallo-cratic bias. And by following this bias lock-step Freud largely leaves unexamined many dimensions of the most important Mothering relationship.

De Vere: You must be speaking of the Mother/Daughter relationship. Thank God for the insights of Kristeva.

Amy: Kristeva and others. But let us tarry on the Mother/Son relationship a bit longer. It is appropriate since our digression occurs in the very midst our other friend's discussion of his Mother/Son relationship.

De Vere: Yes indeed. A story which may or may not have more Bathos about it than pathos. What did you want to tarry on?

Amy: A subtle point. Sigismund was famous -- again infamous -- for maintaining that in the normal female Oedipal situation there is a lingering on in the Oedipal situtation while in the normal male Oedipal situation there is usually a sharp "resolution" of the Oedipal situation through the little boy's "identification" with the father figure.

De Vere: Oh yes. With the now infamous conclusion that females on the average develop "weak" super-egos and a corresponding weak sense of morality while males on the average develop strong super-egos and a corresponding strong sense of morality.

Confer -- and only as one of multiple examples dispersed all throughout the Freudian text of the twenties and thirties -- New, page 119.

Amy: Oh yes! A dimension of the Freudian text tirelessly and repeatedly made about the Freudian text by a whole tribe of Feminists and about which and on which our friend "Orpheus"/"the Professor" has a subtle twist of interpretation. But let us not drown in yet another digression. Our previous point was this business of lingering on in the Oedipal situation. Do you at all see what I am driving at? Do you at all see Freud's other blind spot in these matters?

Freud does not even notice the advantages inherent in his theory for females. On the contrary, his average tendency is to concentrate on the disadvantages. For example, what he says about the development of the super ego in girls and the correlative moral sense of females. The theory -- *(And the reader will note that "Amy" is challenging the notion that only females linger on in the Oedipal situation in this "Amy"/"De Vere" conversation)* -- predicts -- (as a function of, on the average, the "lingering" on of the Oedipal complex in girls in contrast to the, on the average, dramatic resolution of the Oedipal complex in boys) -- that males, on the average, develop a "stronger" super ego and that females, on the average, develop a "weaker" super ego. For Freud it follows that men have a more reliable sense of morality than do females. But one wouldn't have to be a genius to also point out that this male tendency to develop a "strong" super ego carries with it a rigidity, on the average, in dealing with life situations while the female tendency to develop a "weaker" super ego carries with it a flexibility, on the average, which is most advantageous in life's ambiguous situations of praxis. Much spilled ink could have been saved had Freud himself seen the clearly Feminist, so to speak, implications of his own theory.

De Vere: It escapes me. Please explain.

Amy: The little girl -- in the "normal" -- situtation is called on to deal with the loss of 'Mommy' as primary love object rather early. She may or may not linger on in her attachment to 'Daddy'. But she learns earlier to "let go" of 'Mommy'. And even if she returns to 'Mommy' as love-object in some dimension of a lesbian or lesbianesque relationship the little girl/grown woman is not so obsessively possessive relative to 'Mommy'.

De Vere: Now I begin to catch your drift. In contrast -- however conflicted the little boy is about this by the two waves of castration fear involved in his rather turbulent passage through the two-tiered Oedipal variables -- the little boy, in the "normal" situation returns to 'Mommy' as primary love object and imposes on the whole series of succeeding mother-substitutes (both in his sexual encounters with women and in his aim-inhibited encounters with women) the same childish possivieness he had for 'Mommy' in the first place. Thus it is really the male who most radically lingers on in the Oedipal situation.

Amy: How true. And his lingering on in the Oedipal situation is re-enforced by the insidious bias of phallo-cratic custom. And need I add on -- in case Sigismund is actually listening -- that this whole dynamic is exaggerated for first-born male progeny?

De Vere: It is too late for Sigismund himself. He went to his grave -- cremation! -- with certain blind spots. But for the rest of us it is never too late until it is too late.

Amy: Well spoken my friend. Does your alert mind see yet another factor which bears on these matters before we return to our original point?

De Vere: We ought never forget the original point of our digression: whether in the poignant story of our friend -- here called "Orpheus", there called "the Professor" and sometimes even called "Jesus" -- there is more Bathos than pathos. But yes. I am keeping up with you this time.

Amy: Then tell me what you are thinking.

De Vere: The technology of reproduction. It will, in the future, NOT necessarily be true for the little boy as he figures things out about 'Mommy' that *the very act by which he exists is the act by which he is betrayed by the only woman who will ever count for him*.

Amy: You are catching my drift exactly. With the dissemination to the commonplace of the various new technolgies for reproduction comes a loosening of the Oedipal ties which have bound us for so long and kept us tethered to unconsciously followed norms of phallo-cratic bias. This loosening of Oedipal ties -- particularly with regard to the Father's role (and the corresponding notions of """Law""" which Lacan drones on about) -- is already going on and spreading in our times. The eventual denoument of this loosening will be the dawning of an age of matriarchal androgyny -- (and a correspondingly new meaning for the "rule of 'Law'") -- which has been the subject matter of this book.

> {{{{{Bappy: Of course there must be an upside to all of this for males.
>
> Dewchee: But of course. It's just that the upside cannot -- in good faith -- be celebrated until it is appreciated in the very marrow of one's bones that Patriarchy really is coming to a close.
>
> Bappy: And just what will that upside consist of? You can trust me. I won't tell anyone till the time is right.
>
> Dewchee: Just for you, Bappy. It will consist in the *to ti en einai* -- {{{to use that wonderful neo-logism of Aristotle without buying into the frame of reference in which and by which it is engendered}}} -- of maleness which is, at once, the *to ti en einai* of fathering.
>
> Bappy: What does that mean?
>
> Dewchee: It does not entail current "politically correct" paradigms of maleness and fathering. Still less does it entail that "wild-man" reaction formation promoted by that once decent

poet. There is nothing homophobic about it yet it does not entail the embrace of gayness.

Bappy: You sound like a "Via Negativa" theologian. You've only so far told me what it is not, this *to ti en einai* of maleness. What, pray tell, is it?

Dewchee: The hidden genius was there all the while. The ideal of Androgyny. It requires a real and functioning phallus. As the "real" necessity and utility of male recedes there emerges the ideal of maleness as Androgyny. The phallus is the key. And only with the burial of Patriarchy will all this be understood.

Bappy: Thank-you, Dewchee. I love your stories so much. Just brush my cheek before you leave me.}}}}}

De Vere: Which means that the poignant story of our friend "Orpheus" will no longer be the exaggerated particular of an Oedipal universal.

Amy: That is true. The story has significance for understanding the past but loses significance as far as any direct application of the story with regard to the emerging psycho-social evolution of our species on this third planet from the sun. Even so, our friend "Orpheus" was very clever -- maieutic in the most literal sense -- to have included dimensions of his poignant story, whether his story be Bathetic, pathetic, neither, and/or both.

De Vere: What is your meaning?

Amy: What is this book all about?

De Vere: "Mis-ogyny" of course in the neo-logistic way in which this term is used all throughout this book.

Amy: And yet this book repeatedly makes clear that "mis-ogny" in the neo-logistic sense being developped in this book is not un-related to 'misogyny' in its various "ordinary" meanings.

De Vere: That is true as well.

Amy: Our friend "Orpheus" is a true nurse (maia). The maieutic function. What better way to lead the reader to "mis-ogyny" than to periodically bring into the journey graphic, "personal", and deeply pathological nodal points of one man's real wrestling with the demon (daimon) of misogyny which wrestling can -- under the right conditions -- lead to the appreciation of "mis-ogyny". From things which are known to the beginners (i.e., "we misogynists" of both sexes) to things which are knowable to the experts (i.e., "we "mis-ogynists" " of both sexes) and then back again -- with healing on our mind -- to the "ordinary" manifestations of 'misogyny'.

De Vere: All of this sounds vaguely Aristotelian in its methodology.

Amy: And it is. But please remember that this "Aristotelian" methodology is -- by the testimony of Aristotle himself -- inspired by Plato's metaphor of the race track.

Confer the ending of Chapter Four in book One of Aristotle's Nichomachean Ethics

De Vere: I will check the reference at my leisure. In the mean time let me say that I do begin to appreciate your appreciation of our friend "Orpheus". But I do reserve the right to judge his stroy to be Bathetic.

Amy: As you like it. Farewell.

De vere: Parting is such sweet sorrow.}}}}}

<<<<<Bappy: Boy do I get confused.

Dewchee: Why is that?

Bappy: Who is this "Orpheus"? Just who is in charge of this whole project? I thought it was Johanna.

Dewchee: Well you remember that Johanna actually took over the project from her brother Jude. When Jude was in charge he sometimes fancied himself as "Orpheus." Other times he fancied himself as "the Professor" or even "Jesus." One time he fancied himself to be "the Accused."

Bappy: I looks like Jude had himself a problem of personal identity.

Dewchee: So it appears. Was that all that was on your mind?

Bappy: Not really. I'm also confused by all this castration business which Jude/Johanna keep harping on (or have their surrogates -- you and me, Sic and Non, Amy and DeVere, etc., -- keep harping upon). Isn't it a bit much?

Dewchee: I know what you mean. Especially when she -- Johanna -- uses the bold-face type and calls it **the horror**. She does seem to push it a bit much. Even so.

Bappy: Even so, what?

Dewchee: I'm thinking of the oh-so-sophisticated ones. How suave they get when it gets to matters of sexuality. And how quickly they shout out their Shibolleth of *phallo-centrism/phallo-cratism/phallogocentrism* whenever issues of castration, penis envy, and things oedipal come up for discussion. Derrida does it. That imitating tribe of deconstructors do it. Feminists do it. Feminists and the deconstructing tribe both do it even when they are at odds with each other. Neuro-physiologists do it. Revisionist Freudians do it. Lacanians and anti-Lacanians do it. Tennis players in Tenafly do it. So freaking sophisticated. So freaking above the fray. Suave to the point of nausea.

Bappy: Please! Remember what your doctor said about your blood pressure. Besides, I have seen you cite -- sympathetically -- several in the crowd you are now castigating.

Dewchee: Well of course. Despite themselves some of them service the vocation of thinking. But they betray themselves in the process.

Bappy: What do you mean?

Dewchee: They would never admit it but their very suaveness and sophistication concerning things sexual in general and matters concerning castration in particular is a cover. Their suaveness and sophistication is, in reality, a measure of just how great the pattern of denial/disavowal on these matters actually is among these people.

Bappy: Can you prove that? Or are you just asserting it?

Dewchee: Of course it cannot be "proven". Things that shout out can't be proven. Am I "just" asserting it? Yes and no. I am asserting what is the case.

Bappy: You're sounding more and more like Jude. And you know what happened to Jude. Still, even if you are essentially correct about the deconstructionists, the Feminists and the others, don't you think this Johanna/Jude/Orpheus/etc., plays it -- this "horror/castration" motif -- up a bit much. Doesn't s/he get a bit *too serious* about these things? Are they -- i.e., Johanna/Jude/Orpheus/etc.; you really have to call this one person "they"! -- really getting to something universal or is it just idiosyncratic?

Dewchee: Interesting that you should put it that way. After all Johanna herself already indicated that the only way this syn-aptically proceeding book could guard angainst the charge of idiosyncricity was to procede steadfastly in an idiosyncratic manner. Even so you have a point.

Bappy? How so?

Dewchee: Well Jude and Johanna *did* have a rough early childhood. And then another even tougher wave all through adolescence. No need to go into the details. But perhaps some of the Mommy-oriented **horror** that shows up in this book is not simply a function of their experience of "the counter-factual fact." Still, I trust both Jude and Johanna. They have much to teach us. To be members of this clothed species on this third planet from the sun is to be perplexed. I doubt that better guides are to be found anywhere.

Bappy: You are *my* guide, Dewchee. If they're good enough for you, they are good enough for me. I would like to rest now.

Dewchee: Yes. rest. I love you, Bappy.

Bappy: And I love you, Dewchee. Just brush my cheek before you leave.>>>>>

224.
How they loved for the rest of that unforgiving Winter. Androgynously. More than equally. With masochism and sadism. No bars. But always with love. He became what Nietzsche should have become for his blessed Lou. ------ *All* content becomes possible and actual and un-necessary when one achieves form. Together they instantiated form.

Together they mastered *The Story of O* (even before she had read it.) The real "Story of O." Through her he learned how to love on the edge of orgasm, cultivating non-orgasm with its ever-present risk -- opportunity! -- that coming would become a not-coming. He learned the path of pain and even humiliation as a means for getting to the edge, staying at the edge, and going over the edge into the sweet abyss. She taught him to please her. Oh God!!!, really please her. They reciprocated in everything. She would stay at the edge. She would go over the edge. They told stories for each other and shared their fantasies. He learned through her the truth of same and difference. He de-mystified female orgasm for himself even as he learned to appreciate it so much more. He learned from her that women can die in orgasm just as men. Same <u>and</u> different.

225.

If you haven't gambled
for love
and lost
then you haven't gambled at all.

Words from the Frankie Lane song, *Moonlight Gambler.*

226.
Mort: And what, finally, did the Professor learn from Eurydice?

Jude: The nexus between Freud and Nietzsche. Reduction to helplessness. Eurydice took the Professor there. The Professor took Eurydice there. Time after time. <u>Reduction</u>. Reduction to the pure abasement of pleasure. Abasement. To the place where pleasure is pain and pain is pleasure.

Mort: And what, finally, did the Professor learn from Eurydice?

Jude: How thoroughly misogynous we are as a species. Misogyny is the Fall. Androgyny is the Redemption. But in the very heart of androgyny misogyny returned. No, not returned. Showed it self as never having not been. When the Professor abused Eurydice it was the wo-man/female in Eurydice who was abused. When Eurydice abused the Professor it was the wo-man/female in the Professor who was abused.

Mort: And what, finally, did the Professor learn from Eurydice?

Jude: The meaning of male nipples. No reproductive/nurturing function whatsoever. They were the male equivalent *{{{by limping analogy! for God's sake!}}}* of a clit. Exquisite pleasure vehicles not in the service of a species/reproductive function.

Mort: And what, finally, did the Professor learn from Eurydice?

Jude: The primacy of masochism. Even and especially in matters of pleasure. As a corollary: the authentic altruism of the sadist.

Mort: And what, finally, did the Professor learn from Eurydice?

Jude: The clit. The hidden teleology beyond and before the pro-creational function. God is cunt and cunt is not cunt without clit. Training the penis to mimic the clit. Get <u>real</u> slutty. Masturbation -- eyes open all the while <u>and</u> being mercilessly watched all the while -- raised to an androgynous art form. Letting the whole body become polymorphously perverse while masturbating the penile (penal) organ of pleasure. Continuous series of draining comes. Penis freed of the power-drive motif. Getting manipulated <u>real</u> good. Getting slutty.

Mort: And what, finally, did the Professor learn from Eurydice?

Jude: The secrets of anal eroticism. Variations on helplessness. Abuse. Severe abuse. Humiliation. The meltdown. We may be the species which loves to hate its feces. Quand-meme.

Mort: And what, finally, did the Professor learn from Eurydice?

Jude: The joy, the mystery, the mania, of the active surrender. Peace.

(caesura)

Life is a mystery, everyone must stand alone ----- I hear you call my name ----- and it feels like home ----- When you call my name it's like a little prayer ----- In the midnight hour I can feel your power -----I hear your voice, it's like an angel sighing ----- I have no choice, I hear your voice ----- I close my eyes, O God I think I'm falling ----- I'm down on my knees, I wanna take you there ----- you're in control just like a child --- now I'm dancing ----- it's like a dream, no end and no beginning ----- you're here with me, it's like a dream ----- just like a prayer, your voice can take me there ----- just like a muse to me ----- you are a mystery ----- just like a dream, you are not what you seem ----- no choice ------ your voice can take me there ----- it's like a dream to me

Selected words from Like a Prayer written by Madonna and Patrick Leonard; Sire Records of Warner Communications; Copyright, 1989.

Is rape -- as so many have reported -- the central masturbation fantasy of women? What does human sexuality teach us when we confront it directly? Will the real horror and injustice of rape ever be understood let alone eradicated so long as the phenomenon itself is not honestly delineated? Human sexuality is not "politically correct."

{{{Bappy: Is it best to leave it at that?

Dewchee: Perhaps not. It falls short of delineating the real horror of rape and at the same time the phrasing could be construed as endorsing that prevalent, misogynistic, notion that women secretly enjoy rape.

Bappy: Then what should be said, particularly if you desire to be "truthful" in these matters?

Dewchee: It's not easy. Certainly the involuntariness of the situation has to be emphasized. Our friend -- as he fantasizes about something like rape -- was a fully voluntary participant. Actual rape is not a fantasy. Also the mind-set of those who would proceed in a "sexual" encounter with an involuntary "partner" needs to be addressed.

Bappy: What do you mean?

Dewchee: Such a person operates with the pre-suppositions of the "age of violence" and it is precisely these pre-suppositions which *Thnking Psycho-analytically* presumes as overcome and left behind when it takes upon itself the task of conceptually engaging things sexual.

Bappy: But certainly what was called "the age of violence" has not yet passed.

Dewchee: That is correct. To some extent *Thinking Psycho-analytically* conceptualizes within the parameters of world which has not yet emerged. Thus the ever present danger that *Thinking Psycho-analytically* (and now *Misogyny*) will be misunderstood.

Bappy: That is sad.

Dewchee: In any case, in the to-be-emerging age of matriarchal androgyny, humiliation and shame are to be integrated into male and female sexual experience as desiderata. Erotic shame as the good. Only a few will understand. And indeed, until the positive dimensions of shame and humiliation in sexual matters are appreciated and pursued as ends, our clothed species on this third planet from the sun will stay in its "age of violence" and rape will still obtain as a common practice.

Bappy: Are there any we can turn to in the midst of all this confuison which obtains on these matters at the present time?

Dewchee: One senses that Madonna has an intuitive understanding of these things. Don't compromise, Madonna!!!}}}

*****

+++++

obiter dicta

To be sure, inspriation for what would become the "act/potency" paradigm is to be found all throughout the Platonic text. Euthyphro with its "carrying/carried" as it tries to figure out why holiness is holy. The "friends of the forms" passage from Sophist. Also the playful aside at Philebus 53C-54 in which the belov-ed is found to hold pride of place over the love-er as they try to figure out the charcter of pleasure. Generally, in these Platonic pairings it is the """-ed""" (passive?) rather than the """-er""" (active?) which is given the place of honor whereas for Aristotle the reverse is true. Nonetheless, the inspiration is there.

But.

Plato's play with the "active/passive" is ultimately in the service of the his more fundamental teaching concerning "differnce" in the context of an ontological dualism of first principles. Furthermore, one will note that Platonic "dunamis" -- whose best translation is "power" -- has denotations for Plato which allow for both "active" and "passive" senses.

In contrast it is a totally different story for Aristotle. "Difference" is taken for granted by the Stagirite and stands in no need of an account. *{{Confer his argumentation from XIV-2 of Metaphysics (especially at 1088b, 35-1089a, 7) on this and correlative analyses of his XIV-2 argumentation dispersed throughout the book which you are now reading.}}* With Aristotle there is also the domestication of "dunamis/power" into "dunamis/potency/capability" and his correlative invention of "energeia/entelecheia." And in all of this the "act/potency" paradigm is put in the service of a monothesitic ontology in which the first principle has no contrary. Thus in Aristotle the "active/passive" comes to mimic his "fullness/privation" account of the contraries in a Monotheistic ontology which takes it as a point of pride that it does not give an account of "difference." Always inspired by Plato and always missing Plato's point.

Creatio ex nihilo. The fetishistic way of giving an account of difference/variety/creation. It was inevitable that when Aristotle generated the notion of a contrariless first principle and no longer found it necessary to give an account of difference that such a God-concept would emerge. It was just a matter of time.

227.

The tricks of today become the truths of tomorrow. -----

For once a truth is known it cannot be unknown, it can only be denied.

Joyce Carol Oates in Because it is Bitter, and Because it is My Heart. Dutton, New York, 1990. Hereafter: Bitter. Page 339 and then page 314.

228.
--- *Listening to the deceitful ordering of my words* ---

The Poem of Parmenides, Fragment 8; as contained in Parmenides, page 75.

229.
And so around me life took on the contour and texture of a dream, though I was not the dreamer.

Joyce Carol Oates in Lock. Page 19.

230.
Bappy: Do you feel more awake now, Dewchee? Shall we continue?

Dewchee: Yes. On both counts.

Bappy: My impression -- maybe it's from your facial expression -- is that you seem somewhat perturbed by the story which Freud gives us in Civilization and its Discontents.

Dewchee: You are very perceptive, Bappy. It's not that I think Sigmund was "wrong" on these matters. In fact I mostly think that Freud is most insightful in these matters. We have spoken of this often. Still, I have some dis-ease about the book.

Bappy: Why?

Dewchee: It clouds over -- keeping it over-covered, so to speak as opposed to being enticingly veiled -- something which, whether or not it is the key to understanding the past, is certainly the key for living the future.

Bappy: What are you speaking of?

Dewchee: At least this: our matriarchal heritage in the pre-history of our species. The conditions under which it emerged and the conditions under which -- presumably suddenly -- it dis-appeared.

Bappy: So you really do believe in that hypothesis.

Dewchee: Yes. But these things cannot be demonstrated.

Bappy: But if these things are hidden so far back in the pre-history of our species why should it matter?

Dewchee: These things are still very much with us. The brain is constituted so as to pass on -- as its (largely unconscious) archaic heritage -- a phylogenically wired in memory of these things. --- *you would not find out the boundaries of soul, even by traveling along every path: so deep a measure does she have.*

Heraclitus, Fragment 45; as contained in The Pre-Socratic Philosophers; A Critical History with a Selection of Texts. (G.S. Kirk and J.E. Raven; Cambridge University Press, 1964. Hereafter: Pre-Socratic)

Bappy: So for you "brain" and "soul" are one and the same?

Dewchee: Yes. Except that "brain" is not simply the organ encased within our skulls. "Brain" is more especially the passage of itself in and through our survivors. There is mystery here. There will be mystery here even a hundred years from now when a hundred-thousand brain chemists and neuro-physiologists will have mapped out in exqisite detail what they take to be the functioning of the brain. Indeed we live -- and will live in for yet another century -- in an era of false sophistication on these matters. Only after the passage of such false sophistication will one begin to appreciate Joyce.

Bappy: James?

Dewchee: No. The five-times-three lettered Joyce. Listen:

Memory is a transcendental function. But it attaches itself only to bodies.

Bitter, page 403.

Bappy: I like her stories so much. They are even better than yours. But continue. Where are you going with this matriarchal hypothesis?

Dewchee: I prefer her stories to mine as well. She tells them better. Where was I going? No place, really. Even if the hypothesis were """true""" it would only be a hint relative to the future.

Bappy: What do you mean?

{{{Non: Don't we have to break in here?

Sic: Yes. Of course. It is our function. You realize what has to be taken care of here, don't you?

Non: I presume you mean that whole business about brain chemistry and neuro-physiology.

Sic: Exactly. I hate talking about that stuff at all. The people you meet in those circles are just about the worst bunch of all. For the little they know -- really know -- about these things they are far and away the most presumptuous. I'd even rather spend time with philosophers, for God's sake!!! That's a measure of the low esteem in which I hold this brain chemistry/neuro-physiology crowd.

Non: What bothers you so much about them?

Sic: In the first place is their babyish tendency to interface the Freudian model of the psyche with the neuro-physiological model through the completely unthoughtful and un-subtle paradigm of "the either/or." You know what I mean; either it comes about genetically via neuro-physiology, or, it comes about "psycho-analytically" via environmental factors. They are incredibly babyish, simplistic, and presumptuous. At once.

Non: Do you propose the "both/and" paradigm for these matters?

Sic: That would be better. But, as you know, I go with the "both-and-neither-;-at-once" paradigm for these kinds of things.

Non: I remember. What else bugs you about this crowd?

Sic: They forget all so quickly that Freud was one of them anyway and himself looked forward to the day when the sciences of brain chemistry and neuro-physiology could permit pharmacalogical intervention in the service of dealing with psychoses. Likewise, they still fail to recognize that Freud -- they will not know or understand this for another half-century -- did them a tremendous favor by introducing the language of "function" in his paradigm of the psyche. Also, this crowd tends, on the average, to understand Freud as dealing only with ontogenic factors when, in fact, there is no-one better than Freud at recognizing the phylogenic -- manifested both in the history of the individual and in the history of the species -- component of mental development in its fertile interaction with the ontogenic component. About another half century will intervene before this crowd comes to realize that the brain comes neuro-physiologically equipped to undergo neuro-physiological modification as we undergo things like the Oedipal phase, identifications, melancholia, etc. etc. About another half century for all of this.

Non: Can you make that last point a little bit clearer? It's so new to me that I fear it escapes me.

Sic: And not only you. It escapes many, particularly those who work in this field.

Let's put it this way. We come phylogenically equipped with brains structured to be structurally, chemically, and neuro-physiologically affected by ontogenic factors. One only need think of the developping neuro-physiology of developping foeti "in utero" to take a perfectly obvious example.

Non: Please continue. I am following you.

Sic: While it is true that ontogeny in some way mimics phylogeny, it is equally true -- macroscopically especially but also microscopically as well -- that ontogeny both effects and affects phylogeny (in the case of evolution) and how phylogeny plays itself out relative to the organization and characteristics of an individual brain (in the case of an individual).

Non: Ok. Continue.

Sic: The developping brain of the new-born baby as it becomes a toddler and a young child is subject to the same dynamic. *(It is perfectly obvious -- but not yet "proven" -- in the case of language acquisition. In one sense the neuro-physiology of language acquisition is about the same in all. Yet is it crazy to presume a tracable difference in the developping neuro-physiology of a small child who learns a Romance language as opposed to a small child who learns an Oriental language, leaving aside the differences which obtain between one individual language learner or another?)* Indeed, it wouldn't be out of line to postulate that this intense phylogenic-ontogenic interaction reaches its first state of significant homeostasis at around the time when -- to use Freud's term -- the child enters into his period of latency. *(((Related to this but not exactly the same point is Freud's speculation that our species evolved from a species which reached full sexual maturity at around the age of five or six. Confer Outline, page 10, footnote # 1.)))*

Non: What you are saying, then, is quite remarkable. In effect you are saying that as the developping child goes through the psycho-sexual stages of development (oral/anal/phallic) in early childhood, with their correlative identifications and conflicted identifications, the brain of the developping child is structurally, chemically, and neuro-physiologically affected through such ontogenic/environmental factors. *(((((B: For those who have the eyes to hear and the ears to see there is something else being implied as well. D: What's that? B: The ontogenic variable which often occurs in adult life -- I speak of psycho-therapy which is one of the evolved variations of "the talking cure" -- may itself induce some chemical/neuro-physiological effect in the brain of the one undergoing psycho-therapy. D: Indeed! This would then imply that "psycho-therapy" is, so to speak, just one kind of "pharmacological" intervention for mental disturbances. How disconcertning for those who set up this simplistic "either/or" paradigm of explanation when it comes to giving and account of mental states and how mental states are changed. B: You have understood my point. Let us now turn it back to Sic and Non. I love you, D. D: And I you.)))))*

Sic: That is exactly my point. Of course that won't stop those brain researchers over the next fifty years from doing autopsies on the brains of, say, lesbians, gays, and "straight" people. They will "discover" the neuro-phsyisology represented by the dead brains of these people and reductionistically dismiss psycho-analytic accounts of these things without at all understanding that the very size, chemistry, and neuro-physiology of these autopsied brains which they are studying were partially affected through the ontogenic variables spoken of by Psycho-analysis. How sad and how blind!

Non: I find all of this to be so very melancholic. So what will be the upshot of all of this?

Sic: Oh, in about fifty years or so, -- when this present crowd will have been replaced by neuro-physiologists who are not afraid to think -- they will reclaim Freud as one of their own. They will have discovered the brain chemistry/neuro-physiology of things like: masochism; things Oedipal; sublimation; neuroses; perversions; "normalcy"; melancholia; psychoses; "the drives". They will have come to realize that Freud -- with a little help from Kristeva -- had created the very vocabulary in terms of which their "oh-so-sophisticated" sciences have any meaning or applicability. But all of this is about fifty years away.

Non: And in mean-time?

Sic: Oh you know the routine. It has been well worked over by the Feminists, the Deconstructionists, the clinically oriented psychologists and a hundred-thousand others. Why should this crowd be any different?

Non: I know the routine well. Suave disdain and a condescending paternalism for the text of Freud. Let's turn this conversation back over to our friends from Hades.}}}

231.
The Odes were already written. And disseminated. He had already departed for Italy already dying of what was then called "Consumption." *{{{--- consumed by that by which he was nourished just as he was nourished by that by which he was consumed --- how fitting}}}* He wrote to his hiking friend:

--- I eternally see her figure eternally vanishing ---

again:

--- I eternally see her figure eternally vanishing ---

again:

--- *I eternally see her figure eternally vanishing* ---

Who did he see vanishing? Fanny of course. But who did he see? Who is the woman who by Her ""nature"" dis-appears? I am telling you it was Shekhinah.

232.
Non: You hesitate. It's as though there is even something else to be said.

Sic: Yes. But we must leave Plato for this. For even Plato was a shade off.

Non: We have come this far.

Sic: Plato shies away from the most secret name of the good. He always allows the good to --- *take refuge in the character of the beautiful* ---

Philebus 64E

Non: This must mean that Plato -- deflecting from his own deepest insights on these matters -- does not fully marry the Mother. His nostalgia for the Father remained too strong. I remember. He goes to bed with her which is more than anyone in the Tradition has ever done. He produced offspring with her. But he did not marry her. For to marry her is -- ultimately -- to be her. But what is the most secret name of the good?

Sic: Shame.

Non: Shame?

Sic: Yes, Shame.

Non: But how can shame be the desired?

Sic: It always has been, whether we publically proclaim this or not. All of (chance-governed) cosmological and then (chance-goverened) biological and then (chance-governed) psycho-social evolution is for the sake that the conditions of shame might obtain. We are there. The third planet from the sun. We have achieved the condtions of shame. It is contained in one word: "Mis-ogyny."

Non: And how is "Mis-ogyny" to be achieved?

Sic: In one sense it has always been achieved and contitutes the "for which" of life itself. That's what this "book" is about. In another sense it reaches its human fullness through the shameless embrace of the shame of Shekhinah. It is now time. There will be beauty there. *khalapa ta kala!!!* There will be joy there. And the Messiah {{{Is Her name not "Hanina" (meaning "compassion" moreso than ""pity"")??}}} cannot come until Shekhinah is embraced in Her shame. We must go to Her bed and stop forcing Her to come to ours. Do you understand? The vortex. Sucking in and spewing out.

Non: I don't know. And what if we refuse or fail to embrace Shekhinah in her shame?

Sic: Such would be too sad for words. Bappy and Dewchee have already told us: the banal yet horrible Auschwitzing of all life on this third planet from the sun as we choke ourselves incrementally in our own cowardice.

Non: I don't know if I am happy that we have had this conversation. But it is, in any case, appropriate to stop here. It's time to go home now

Sic: You are right on that. Farewell.

Non: Adieu.

233.
for some time and then evolving into that Doppler-like wail penetrating the whole while into the most secret crevice of my exposed vulnerable and obscenely open psyche transforming it forever your eyes would be wide open dark pupils expanding over your green-blue irises and seeing nothing

234.
Bappy: I remember. Pure oscillating need. In the mixture its truest manifestation is constituted by that approximation towards pure oscillating need (as a limit, so to speak) in that absolutely crazy time -- "unheimlich" and delirious at once -- just before orgasm. The orgasm proper provides release to and for this condition. This delirious (and unheimlich) condition of oscillating need is, really, what wo-men aim for in sexual encounters and -- at bottom -- it is often what men seek to reduce their partners to in their sexual encounters. Paradoxically enough -- partly because of the pro-creational function imposed upon the physiological workings of the male organ of orgasm -- ((which procreational function, it is most especially to be noted, is precisely NOT imposed on the primary organ of female orgasm)) -- males tend, on the average, to psychologically avoid this condition -- which has a certain humiliation about it -- of oscillating need. Rather, on the average, males tend to concentrate on the release factor of orgasm. {{{Indeed, even and especially in postponing -- through the wildest strategies -- the actual moment of release, men, on the average, remain merely release oriented in thier love-making. *Men, on the average, postpone; women prolong. There is a difference.*}}} This ability to avoid the humiliating aspect of love-making is enchanced by the penetrating function of male genital sexuality. They are "doing" to the wo-men. They "bring" their beloved to some desired condition. They flee from being done to and in this avoidance, on the average, they miss much of the pathos of love-making. By limiting themselves to this merely active mode, males, (again, on the average), tend to avoid the greatest pathos of love-making.

Dewchee: Whereas wo-men, on the average (and both prior to and posterior to the sexual revolution) have always managed to incorporate an emphasis on the "pre-release" dimensions of orgasm into their sexual practice. Women instantiate, on the average, the ability to stay with that pure oscillating need characteristic of the "unheimlich"/delirious at once condition -- (the ultimate root of all mania) -- which precedes release. Even with regard to the release proper of orgasm, the spasms of the clitoris are more needful *((-- and for those who have the eyes to hear and the ears to see, this feature alone would have vindicated the dictum of Tiresias --))* than the spasms of the merely procreational-oriented penis. And yes, on the average, women incorporate into their sexual behavior the humiliating dimension of both aiming for and being reduced to that pure oscillating need. It is a humiliation misunderstood by men. What men, on the average, fear, women, on the average desire. For they bring "thanatos" in its purest form into the sexual coitius. {{Sweet memories of Donne!!}} And there is no life without "thanatos."

{{--- Indeed, prior to the sexual revolution the release proper of orgasm itself was not at all predictable for women, on the average. The release dimensions of orgasm are simply not a necessity for the genital/procreational dimension of female lovemaking.}}

Bappy: This is becoming very, very interesting. For in that old Epilog conversation (contained in a "pre-history" version of this present book) the writer of these "sentences" had us remind the reader that genital sexuality is no longer necessary for procreation, due to advances in technology. This means that the "penetration" motif in male sexuality no longer has a necessary function.

Dewchee: That is correct. And that is both the danger and the opportunity at once.

Bappy: What do you mean?

Dewchee: It will eventually dawn on men. The dual obsoleteness of being a male -- at least according to the rules of the game which have obtained almost from time immemorial -- will eventually dawn on more and more men: No longer any social utility for their disposition towards violence and no longer any necessary function in the penetration motif of their sexuality. This will be the time of crisis as, on the average, the self esteem of most males reaches a low point. The impulse towards Nazism thrives on low self-esteem. In effect this dual obsoleteness will cancerously manifest itself in an Auschwitzing of the global community or ---

Bappy: Or what?

Dewchee: The rules of the game will change. Mis-ogyny. Androgyny. Mis-ogyny. Androgyny. Mis-ogyny is the Fall. Androgyny is Redemption. Men will have to become androgynous and for this they will require that wo-men as well become androgynous. Men will have to learn to incorporate "thanatos" -- pure oscillating need -- into the stratagems of their sexual behavior. Men will have to learn to appreciate the "thanatos"-spawned humiliation involved in the most intense of sexual passion. Stratagems for mutual penetration will take on new meanings and permutations. Homophobia will disappear as men become attuned to the mutual bi-sexuality possible in a "heterosexual" relationship.

(Please understand that sexual differentiation -- neither on a physiological level nor on a psychological level -- does not at all disappear with the advent of a matriarchal androgyny. Androgyny, as the term is used in this book, actually entails the hegemony of difference. Sexual differentiation will come to have a different function in the age of matriarchal androgyny, but precisely here sexual differentiation will obtain most especially.

In this regard it is also to be noted that Irigaray's distancing of her project from "androgyny" is a distancing from a popular meaning of "androgyny" where "androgyny" effectively means the lessening or disappearance of sexual differentiation.)

(And a good deal of male/male homosexuality -- involving as it does a certain amount of misogyny -- will simply melt away, so to speak, when the vacuum created by traditional male patterns of sexual behavior is filled by the ideal of matriarchal androgyny which will entail male cooperation in female patterns of lesbianesque bonding.)

235.
De Vere: I see that you are cleverly returning us to the topic of "jouissance."

Amy: I am not so certain of any cleverness. But we have returned to our topic.

De Vere: Please continue.

Amy: Well, to get started, let us avoid the great "either/or" paradigm. That simplistic paradigm all too quickly insists that either female patterns of orgasm are vaginal or they are clitoral.

De Vere: Oh yeah! I remember the good old days. Norman Mailer lined up on the one side as the champion of vaginal orgasm and, ever so neatly, a whole bunch of outraged Feminists -- led by Germaine Greer -- lined up on the other side. And, on the side-lines, so to speak, the "G-spot" enthusiasts who failed to recognize that deep vaginal stimulation/arousal is really -- and on principle -- subset to the vaginal rubric.

Amy: Those were the days, my friend. We thought they'd never end. Whatever happened to our friend Norman?

De Vere: Well, he had already stopped doing drugs. He still kept drinking a lot of beer. He still wrote some good books after The Prisoner of Sex. I don't catch much of him anymore. But we must arrest this digression into the nostalgic days of yore.

Amy: Indeed. Most often digression is more important than that from which there is digression. On the other hand -- cancer of the mouth/jaw notwithstanding -- sometimes a cigar is just a cigar. Please continue. Did you have some question on your mind?

De Vere: Yes. If such an "Either/or" paradigm misses the point, should we go with a "both/and" paradigm?

Amy: Not really. Not if we really want to get to the Tiresian dimensions of female patterns of orgasm.

De Vere: By "Tiresian" you refer to those patterns of female arousal/excitement/release in terms of which males -- when and if they finally awaken from their self-centered slumber in sexual matters -- come to have intense patterns of orgasm envy?

Amy: Yes. Precisely. And in terms of which -- in the dawning, "up there", age of matriarchal androgyny -- the standard is given by which males will learn to imitate the female pattern.

De Vere: As the writer of Shekhinah used to say: ----- *males, on the average, only postpone; females prolong. There is a difference.* But tell me now: if the "either/or" paradigm misses the mark and if the "both/and" paradigm falls short as well, what paradigm are you suggesting, if we seek the """"""truth"""""" in these matters?

Amy: The "neither-nor-and-both-;-at-once" paradigm which catches the dyadic, oscillating nature of the phenomenon. Only with this paradigm does one begin to appreciate the Tiresian advantages to female genital organization.

De Vere: What are you getting at?

Amy: The fusion of the orgasm and procreational functions in male sexual anatomy -- I am speaking of ejaculation {{ which, as Madonna apparently understood, is "like a prayer": OH God!!!!!! ----- an ejaculation, so to speak }} -- tends to focus the male experience on the moment of climax itself (which is one of the reasons why men, on the average, only postpone) and also to furnish them with a climax in which something like melancholia is the outcome.

De Vere: Hmmmmm. One grazes over to --- *post coitum animal tristus est*

Amy: But don't be too quick to apply that to the female version -- if she is lucky enough to have a lover which will sustain her through <u>her</u> pattern of orgasm.

De Vere: Must she always have a lover?

Amy: In one sense, of course not. But in another sense, of course. In any case her lover does not have to be male.

De Vere: Please continue. "Down here" male egoism has long since been left behind.

Amy: It is the <u>non</u>-ejaculatory spasms of the clitty as the female goes over the edge which is the key.

De Vere: What do you mean?

Amy: Excuse me. I was being pre-mature. Getting to and staying on the edge is also the key. The whole thing is dyadic. The clitty helps in this joy -- both "unheimlich" and delirious at once as the writer of <u>Shekhinah</u> kept on reminding us -- of getting to and staying on the edge. And the clitty plays a role in the element of staying right there on the very edge for such an incredibly long period of time. But the clitty is not alone. The vaginal juices must flow!! Vaginal penetration -- by penis, or hand, or whatever -- is critical. Clitty can't do it by itself. Dyadic!!!

De Vere: I can see -- and feel!! - why males who have awakened out of their self-satisfied sexual slumber come to experience orgasm envy!!

Amy: Please!! We can't stop now!!! As I was saying the needful but non ejaculatory spasms of the clitty as the female goes over the edge -- ----- and please note that it will have turned out to have been the case that one had not been on the edge unless one had eventually gone over the edge; the draw -- the attraction -- OF equilibrium obtains here especially realizing all the while that this draw is necessitated by the delirium of pure oscillating need ----- -- come into play. <u>Non</u>-ejaculatory spasms are the key; otherwise the clitty <u>would</u> be little more than a baby penis. As things stand, however, baby clitty is <u>AND</u> is not a baby penis. The <u>advantages</u> of female genital organization! Oh God!!! Do you not yet see!!!???

De Vere: I am watching your wide-open eyes most carefully as the pupils expand over your beautiful blue-green irises. But for God's sake say what you mean.

Amy: The non-ejaculatory spasms allows female attention -- its delirious! -- to diffuse away from the clitty even though the clitty is the key. When the conditions are right the clitty -- {{{just like Platonic ousia ; i.e., just like a wo-man}}} -- dis-appears into her predicates. So to speak. It is diffusive. It is good. It is great. God is great!!!! "Jouissance" is not such a bad word after all.

De Vere: Thank-you, my sweet one. I love you. Sometimes more than life itself. I guess that's why they call it the blues. We must both catch our breath now. Let us turn it back over to Sigismund and Eurydice.

236.
a). Freud's analysis of what he calls the "masculine complex" in women is unfortunate. Something like the "masculine complex" is, in accordance with Freudian theory, a possible outcome for the female way of passing through the Oedipal variables. But it should hardly be looked upon as pathology or even as undesirable. It is social custom rather than psycho-analytic theory which (used to) make(s) what Freud termed "the masculine complex" undesirable. And Freud more than anyone else was aware that the findings of Psycho-analysis do not always dove-tail with social custom.

Confer New, pages 114-115.

Confer -- and only as examples -- Freud's Feminist sounding remarks on this issue in New, page 102 and again, page 117. Also confer the long footntoe on bisexuality relative to social convention by which Chapter Four of Civilization and its Discontents is terminated. (Civ, pages 58-59)

On the other hand, it has been the theme of this entire book that Freud in his writings is often in a kind of unconscious complcity with the often unconscious (and therefore more insidious) cultural dictates of patriarchal social custom. This feature of the Freudian text -- (the factual presence of which in the Freudian text is not at all being challenged in this book) -- has, however, been so emphasized by Feminist criticism of Freud that it begins to interfere with the intelligent appropriation of the Freudian text. Nonetheless, even today, it is still necessary that this Feminist critique of the Freudian text be understood and appreciated.

b). In this regard it was Freud's fixation on procreation which limited Freud's vision as to what a "proper" outcome for female sexuality would entail. Let us leave it as undecided as to what exactly the Freudian text says or implies about about the physiology of female orgasm. In any case his emphasis on the vagina as primary erotogenic zone is mostly a function of his fixation on procreation as the telos of sexuality.

c). Bappy: Shouldn't something else be added on here?

Dewchee: Well of course. With males the procreational organ and the organ of orgasm are one and the same. With females the organ of orgasm, the clitoris, is different from the "holey organ", the vagina, of procreation. A man who has had his penis removed is incapable of genital sexuality.

Bappy: Yes. And he would probably be very distressed as well.

Dewchee: In contrast -- and unfortunately this is still a practice in some cultures -- a woman who has had her clitoris removed is capable of genital sexuality and correlative procreation.

Bappy: Do such women have sexual pleasure and/or orgasm?

Dewchee: Hmmmmm. And even with the clitoris, how much of a woman's pleasure and even orgasm is "vaginal"? One is back to the insistence of Norman Mailer of all people that the best female orgasms are vaginal.

Bappy: Well --- what is the answer?

Dewchee: Let's leave that as an open question although it is to be noted that the very wording of your question implies the discredited "either/or" paradigm of analysis. In any case it might get discussed somewhere else. There is still something else to be remarked.

Bappy: What is that?

Dewchee: Since the organ of orgasm and the organ of genital sexuality -- the penis -- is one and the same for men it becomes obvious that male genital sexuality, for the most part, is only "phallic" sexuality. By and large in their genital sexual behavior men mask an arrest of sexual development at the "phallic" stage.

Bappy: Whereas in females anatomical structure at least gives a hint of a possibility in female sexuality of something trans-phallic (i.e., trans clitoris, although never without the clitoris). But it is incredibly difficult to imagine, in men, what it would be or mean to go beyond the phallic.

Dewchee: Hard indeed. So we are left with the suggestion that most males remain pre-genital (i.e., merely phallic) even and especially when they measure up to performance standards in "genital" sexuality. The male seems more radically incomplete than the female. But with that consideration -- i.e., questions of the trans-phallic in male sexuality -- we have arrived at degree of puzzlement concerning males which is correlative to Freud's now infamous question: "What do women want?"

Bappy: Somewhere in this book Johanna has us say that Philosophy -- contrary to Aristotle's account of these things -- not only begins in wonder but it ends in wonder as well. Is the same true for sexuality?

Dewchee: Why not say: is the same true for Eros?

Bappy. OK. Is the same true for Eros?

Dewchee: I don't know. But don't' worry about it any more for now. Rest.

Bappy: I will. Thank-you so so much for your answers, Dewchee. Sleep tight. Don't let the bed-bugs bite.

d). "Adult onset" re-configuration of the Oedipal situation.

In women it comes about through the mothering experience or through the women's realization that she will not -- by necessity or by choice -- directly participate in mothering. The "outcomes" are, of course, over a spectrum and are very much influenced by the environmental factors of family, spouse, and career. A blossoming of trans-phallic (but never without the clitoris) sexuality is often the happy outcome. One has arrived home.

In men the fathering experience (and/or lack thereof) does not set in motion any re-configuration of the Oedipal situation. Since -- in the "normal" case -- most men stay arrested at a merely phallic stage of sexual development (even and especially in their "genital" and procreational performances), they tend to drift into patterns of libidinal disinterest re-awakening to a libidinal vocation only when "time's winged chariot" rather rudely forces upon them intimations of their own mortality. During these re-awakenings some of them become more and more attuned to female patterns of arousal and climax. These patterns of arousal and climax instantiate the ancient dictum of Tiresias and, when resonated with, awaken in the male and with new intensity the repressed desire to be Mommy which is the heritage of the Inverse Oedipal situation of childhood. With such an awakening -- (unless, of course, it is stifled by a homophobic reaction formation) -- some males arouse in themselves the desire for trans-phallic (but, of course, never without the penis) sexual experience which is the anatomical birth-right of females. The stage is set for the passage to a psycho-physiological Androgyny.

e). What do men want? In the final analysis to experience female patterns of arousal/excitement/climax. In their macho narcissism -- and while they remain, as in a reaction formation, aggressively active in their sexual machinations keeping the forbidden passivity at a maximum distance -- they initially want to cause a female to go through her pattern of arousal/excitement/climax. But after a while -- provided they overcome the initial and continuing imperative to repress the wo-man in themselves *(*)* -- they find that they want for themselves the female pattern of arousal/excitement/climax. To be more exact, they desire to BE brought by another to arousal/excitement/climax. The forbidden passivity is now actively, so to speak, desired. In a word/phrase: orgasm envy. A large dimension of female sexuality runs on penis envy; but by and large females do not wish to be males. Males may fear female genitalia (since the sight of female genitalia always resonates for them with thier unconscious/pre-conscious fear of castration), but at heart -- and for most unconsciously -- they want to be wo-men. They want to be wife-man.

*. (and, obviously, most men gravitate towards the plateau of libidinal disinterest rather than to permit this evolution in their libidinal economy) -----

Since 1984 all of my ruminations on things feminine have very much been affected -- for the most part quite positively -- by Freud's article, "The Theme of the Three Caskets."

f). With the male -- and here Tristan represents the exaggerated extreme -- the fear/fascination for the feminine leads to patterns of control and domination, regardless of how "courtly" these patterns of control and domination might appear. But the male's fascination -- which is at the heart of his fear -- has a dimension which is rudely suppressed by most men. In Tristan the fascination is not suppressed but his fear keeps him from completing the circuitry inaugurated by not suppressing this excess of fascination. He seeks something in his beloved which he is not aware of yet of which he cannot get disengaged. Of course he seeks his Mother in his beloved and desires complete union with her. But beyond that he seeks to be his Mother For his Father. This (anatomically) impossible (and, under the harsh guidance of castration fear, forbidden) dream he continually relegates to the pre-conscious so as not to have to deal with it. Yet, obsessively, he will not relinquish it. The forbidden -- yet fascinating -- passivity. It becomes his continuous obsession. The impossible tension of his dream -- which he obsessivley neither works through nor relinguishes -- keeps him in bondage and renders him helpless. *(*)* Tristan, now rendered helpless, will not have the power to break his bondage to the conflicted self-defeating condition into which he is reduced by the power of love. Freedom from this bondage -- without which freedom he dies -- comes from Iseult who in her last act of love for the broken and bruised Tristan leaves Tristan.

*. {{In some instantiations of "Tristan" the male may actually revel in this helplessness and, with the help of a cooperating "Iseult", seek helplessness out as a libidinal ideal. *(((And in the transition away from the age of violence and to the age of Androgyny some such humiliation -- pursued with a(n) (admittedly paradoxical) moderation which will be appropriate in these matters -- may very well be in the service of "the good".)))* }}

g). Of course this dreamer's tale from Tintangle is perhaps most noteworthy for the inclusion of "Iseult of the white hands" as a double -- and death inducing double at that -- for the ""real"" Iseult of Golden hair. One thinks, yet again, of Freud's three caskets essay. ((Tristan had a Mother, of course. "White-Flower" who -- memories of Rousseau and Derrida's book on Rousseau !!! -- died after birthing the son she named "sadness" (i.e., melancholia itself))) The third casket brings death {{{And death itself is duplicitous as the alert reader will find out when she confers the "thanatos" entry in what used to be the Glossary section of this book before it became *Shame!*.}}} But who is the third casket?

One would, of course, confer on all of this the often cited article on this by Freud: "The Theme of the Three Caskets". Collected Papers; Volume IV; edited by Joan Riviere; Basic Books, New York, 1959. Pages 244-256.

This doubleness -- with its ever present/absent silent third partner (i.e., difference) -- of the female is, according to the "logic" of this book, the very ""essence"" of the wo-man principle. From the inevitable duplicity emerges, in the ""real"" world, a multivalent aura of deception associated with things female. This aura of duplicity governs the conditions under which the wo-man principle makes its (heimlich and unheimlich at once) dis-appearing appearance. *(*)* Recall. The Goddess COMMANDS the young man to listen to the, self-said, deceitful ordering of her discourse. And, in the very heart of ambiguity itself she ((deceitfully???; and if so, how so?)) says:

> *nevertheless you shall learn these things as well, that it needs must be that appearing be in an appearing way; permeating ALL completely*

The Poem of Parmenides, Fragment 1; as contained in Parmenides, page 52. (translation modified)

((The wo-man principle has its "ontological" presentation in a joint reading of hypotheses # 2, # "2a", and # 5 of Parmenides superimposed upon the Khora/Receptacle passages of Timaeus.))

*. ((E.g., and only one example among many albeit an important one, the ever-present and for the most part unconscious oscillating ambivalence concerning female genitalia -- in both males and females --, noted by Lou Salome and cited thrice by Freud, occaisioned by the anatomically instantiated nearness of anus and vagina. *[Confer New, page 90.]*))

237.
Bappy: Are you implying the disappearance of sadism and masochism in sexual practice?

Dewchee: Of course not, Silly. Some masochism is the handmaiden to that humiliation which we keep harping upon. And masochism -- which is primary over sadism since it, masochism, is the goal -- requires someone to play the sadist. The true altruism of the sadist. But -- contrary to Freud -- masochism is not in the first place feminine. Male patterns of masochism are even more intriguing than female patterns of masochism. Thanatos-spawned patterns of humiliation in male sexual behavior -- as they learn to both pursue and be reduced to that "Unheimlich"-and-delirious-at-once pre-orgasmic state which traditionally had been the provenance of females -- will be even more imaginative than the female patterns of humiliation.

Bappy: I find all of this frightening.

Dewchee: That is because you are still using the terms sadism/masochism/humiliation with the aura which attaches to these words in our present age.

Bappy: What do you mean?

Dewchee: We have not left the age of violence yet. All of these things -- sadism, masochism, humiliation -- usually (living as we still do in the age of violence) do get pretty ugly and are often pursued misogynistically and in such a way that they bring the death of love. But that ugly dimension will pass away if we all -- male and female alike -- are courageous enough as we embrace "thanatos" in a new way for the sake of life. Choose life!

Bappy: I'm getting weary again. Will you please put me to sleep with one of your charms?

Dewchee: Embracing "thanatos". For the sake of life. Embracing "Shekhinah". <u>Embracing</u> Shekhinah. Not subsuming or sublating Shekhinah. Embracing her. *{{{And <u>this</u>, my friends, is recovery. Eroticizing the shame; for the sake of life. Shaming the shame of the Shekhinah so as to render Her <u>shameless</u>. Shamelessly make the shame of the Shekhinah <u>one's own</u>. What, after all, is more <u>shameful</u> than <u>being</u> shameless about the shameful? <u>Being</u> the shame. This is the redemption of shame. This shameless shame is, quite literally, the recovery which shamelessly (i.e., most shamefully) re-covers that for which there is shame.}}}* Yes. Embracing, exploring, <u>and becoming</u> (even if as a limit which cannot be reached) Her. For Shekhinah is more God, so to speak, than God Himself. Go to sleep, Bappy.

Bappy: Thank-you, Dewchee. I love your stories so much.

238.
If you are not dreaming you are not reading this book. If you are not reading this book you forfeit your right to complain about what appears to be and/or is its episodic character, its allusiveness, its non-connectedness, its weirdness, and -- in general -- its being full of non-sense.

239.
Jennifer slept restlessly. It had been a long and exhausting evening with Arleen and Michael. But she wasn't sleeping through. She woke up every now and then. Her dreams were getting to her. He was there. Not the guy she had castrated that

crazy night all those years ago. That guy yes. But not as that pathetic figure who lived to be abused; rather, as her teacher. Clear as a bell. Overweight. Sloppily dressed. But a lot of enthusiasm. Clear as a bell but what had he been saying? *khora*? Was that it? Or was it something about the animating delusion of our species without which we cease to dream? What would be so bad about that anyway? This damn dream was keeping her awake. Even so:

--- *We are such stuff/As dreams are made of*

From The Tempest, of course.

And she knew, from all his lectures, that the Professor had meant that most literally.

Then it hit her. Suddenly, as in a dream. The tune she heard in the dream even though she heard nothing in the dream. The Professor's favorite song. From Elton John:

I hope you don't mind
I hope you don't mind
I hope you don't mind
that I put down the words:
how wonderful life is
while you're in the world.

(From a tune of Elton John).

240.
If this is a dream it is not my dream for how should I know the language in which to dream it.

Joyce Carol Oates in Lock. Page 75.

241.

eksaiphnes

suddenly

in a flash

it's there but not there

it is neither there nor not-there

it is Plato's fifth

appearing to "dis-appear"

suddenly, as might happen in a dream

Parmenides 164D.

the moment of the sublime

Hush!

we are close

I eternally see her figure eternally vanishing   I eternally see her figure eternally vanishing   I eternally see her figure eternally vanishing

Keats' letter to Charles Brown of 30 September, 1820; as contained in The Letters of John Keats; 1814-1821; Volume II, 1819-1821. Harvard University Press, 1958. Page 345. Hereafter: Letters.

the sublime is dispersed all over the place

discourse's moment of silence is elicited from the most quotidien of things

Crazy Cratylus

the world is full of Gods!!!

Thales, yes

and an old too-depressed man while writing his laws

but you must go to Crazy Cratylus to understand this world full of Gods

half-hidden and yet beautiful   half-hidden and yet beautiful   half-hidden and yet beautiful

Phrase taken from line 108 of Fragments to "Epipsychidion" by Shelley. As contained in The Complete Works of Percy Bysshe Shelley; Volume II, Poems. Edited by R. Ingpen and W E Pech; Gordian Press, New York, 1965. Page, 380. Hereafter: Shelley.

the urn breaks

as it had to

yet -- for one brief and shining moment -- Mommy "really" does have a penis

while in the breaking "truth" is sustained over beauty

that's all we need to know for that is all there is to know

philosophy begins and ends in wonder

beginning with the wonder of shock

ending, inevitably, with the wonder of melancholy

even so

ah yes!!! especially so!!!!!

permitting joy

[WOW = MOM palindromically upside-down]

242.
In the first place, please realize that, if there is a root duality in the schema of things, this duality does not have to be a duality of and between two "terms", so to speak, which are structurally symmetrical with each other. For instance, it is not necessary, in speaking of the duality which is the root of things, to insist that this duality must consist of two "forces"; or "energies"; or "drives." Please do not misunderstand me. In the <u>mixture</u> -- a mixture which may be supposed to have always occurred without ever beginning or ceasing to occur -- between the two "terms" of the duality there may emerge -- without ever beginning or ceasing to emerge -- two (or more) "forces" or "energies" which may be construed as interacting between and among themselves. A mixture within a mixture, so to speak. But the "terms" of the original mixture -- keeping in mind that mixture always obtained without ever beginning or ceasing to obtain -- do not have to be construed as two forces.

243.

{{{{{{{{{{{{{{B: Not just yet.

D: Why not?

B: We should stay, I think, with this self-preservation business a bit.

D: Perhaps you are right. After all there are <u>so</u> many ways in which Eros displays itself as "self-preservation", especially phylogenically, both in biological evolution and in psycho-social evolution as well. Most people do not even have a clue. So perhaps two or three remarks should be made.

B: I'm leaving it all up to you.

D: In the first place -- and <u>IN</u> the mixture -- oscillating eksaiphnes appears to have managed (through those wonderfully random workings of Shekhinah) a bifurcation of its energy by which sexual "energy" and "violence-energy" (so to speak) could come to be distinguished although never unrelated. One of these now distinguished (which happens only <u>IN</u> the mixture) energies can be called Eros which has among its functions -- always working randomly -- the instrumental end of self preservation and the correlative production of biolgical entities complex enough to eventually become "interesting" in the sense of being, eventually, full partners in what might be called "the Anthropic Principle."

B: I begin to catch your drift. Remarkable! And now let me make the next point.

D: Be my guest.

B: The whole point of Shekhinah was that this bifuracation -- which did serve such an important purpose in both biological and in psycho-social evolution -- has come to outlive its utility; that in our species -- which is coming to be the whole ball of wax as far as the third planet from the Sun is cocerned -- "violence energy" must be re-integrated into sexual "energy" lest, by virtue of technology, "violence energy" end life itself.

D: You have understood well. And this is why the thoughtful integration of strategies of pain, *hum*-iliation and masochism into our *hum*-an sexuality is now necessary if we are, as individuals and as a species, to become what we were to have beocme. The demonic is either pressed into the service of "the good" or the unbounded demonic prevails and the "good" is thwarted.

B: I love your stories so much. Do you have anything else?

D: There is this as well. The recognition -- clearly well understood by Kristeva in Black Sun -- that one of the functions of melancholia is to preserve the mind from total psychotic disintegration. Eros as "self-preservation"!!! It's all over the place. What a strange world we live in, B.; the trance-land of big super-egos and dicks always percieved as small. The Dyad. Always the Dyad. And always the additional duality tucked in as one of the two terms of the duality itself. I love you.

(Confer Black, page 48).

B: And I you. Now we can turn it back over to our surrogates, Bappy and Dewchee. }}}}}}}}}}}}}}}

244.
a). The one and its other. The other and its other. The one is the other of other. The one with its other becomes the Dyad. Duplicitous. The Dyad is the one. Unity in duality and duality in unity. But never the identity of identity and difference. The two Godheads of God even though there is but one Godhead of God. The Godhead as Great; as excess; as supplement. The Godhead dis-appearing even as it makes its appearance. *I eternally see her figure eternally vanishing. I eternally see her figure eternally vanishing. I eternally see her figure eternally vanishing.* The Godhead as freedom/difference. The Godhead as posterior. The Godhead which becomes -- without ever beginning or ceasing to become -- the Sartreanesque "de trop." The Godhead which withdraws -- without ever beginning or ceasing to withdraw -- so as to submit to its other. IN CONTRAST:

The Godhead as Small. The Godhead as prior. The Godhead as less. That is to say, the Godhead as Small. The Godhead which neither is nor is not. The will which does not will. The will which wills nothing, not even itself. The will which -- a hundred-thousand Heideggerians crying to the contrary notwithstanding -- has nothing to do with "Will." That stillness which never became still. That unbearable beauty. That which is submitted to; tricked, so to speak, to be the stability for the other. The free. A-peiron. The one.

{{{The frame of reference here for this "apeiron" reference is Parmenides, 137D. However, even in citing this "apeiron" reference from hypothesis # 1 it must always be kept in mind that this book's account/appropriation of Parmenides in general and hypothesis # 1 in particular is an account/appropriation which radically rejects the Plotinian and "via negativa" ways of appropriating "the one" of hypothesis # 1.}}}

"Prior" to the mixture it -- i.e., other than the one; i.e., other than the free -- is, so to speak, God bereft of Godhead. It is pure oscillation without relief. It is pure Anxiety. Relief by submission to its other (i.e., what will be called the one). In this submission it draws its other into itself without the say so of this other. Duplicity. This other is now (i.e., becomes eternally) the Godhead of God. The first. A-peiron "already and in itself" (so to speak) it "now" (so to speak) becomes apeiron relative to the rest of God. The Godhead "now" drawn into God, the excess called "the fifth" is set in motion without ever beginning or ceasing to have been set in motion. This is the Godhead as excess.

{{{The frame of reference here (i.e., "the first", "mixture", etc.,) is Plato's discussion of the four (but really five -- *Cf. as always Philebus 23D-E on this* --) classes of Philebus. The first class is said to be "apeiron."}}}

b). Mort: You better stop now, Jude. You're geting that funny look in your eye again --- Jude: MERRILY, MERRILY, MERRILY, MERRILY --- Mort: Please Jude! Stop! You'll have to go back to the hospital! --- Jude: LIFE IS BUT A DREAM. ROW, ROW, ROW YOUR BOAT --- Mort: ROW, ROW, ROW YOUR BOAT --- Jude: GENTLY DOWN THE STREAM--- Mort: GENTLY DOWN THE STREAM --- Jude: MERRILY, MERRILY, --- HEY MORT!

Mort: What now, Jude?

Jude: The merry, merry month of May. May = Mai = maia = Maya = Appearance {appearance reveals and conceals "true" being at once} = [in a sense] illusion =? allusion. May Day; might night. And always a nurse.

Mort: OK, Jude. Take a sad song and make it better.

c). The yearning which can never have enough; the submission -- without permission --; the descent of the Godhead; the emergence of the "de trop" of yearning which can never have enough. On and on.

245.
Bappy: Which re-affirms our often stated principle that "good" and "evil" are not the originary "terms" of the duality, but rather come-to-be in the mixture. Please proceed.

Dewchee: The melancholic choice for good -- we will call it "eu-daimon" acknowledging all the while that Aristotle had no clue -- entails the marshaling of our energies in the service of Eros. If it can be mutually eroticized it is good.

Bappy: What do you mean? Are you not being too indiscriminate? Will not violence sneak in the back door if you allow for that?

Dewchee: Violence has long since busted down that door. It is never -- nor has it ever been whether we admit to this or not -- a matter of whether violence makes its appearance at the feast of sexuality. It has always been there and will always be there. This is inevitable. What will matter is how it remains at the feast; how it is integrated into the whole. If it can be mutually eroticized it is good.

Bappy: Please proceed. What do you have in mind?

Dewchee: Pain. Abuse. Humiliation. A spectrum -- but not the full spectrum -- of masochism and sadism. Genital and pre-genital stratagems of sexual eroticization. {{Indeed, one would want to say here, "post-genital."}} A healthy measure of perversion. Staying on the edge by prolonging instead of merely postponing. For males and females alike. If it can be mutually eroticized it is good.

Bappy: I think you are scaring off even our most sympathetic readers with this talk. What about the abuse which leads to bodily harm? What about limits in all of this?

Dewchee: Apparently even you do not yet fully understand. If it can be mutually eroticized it is good. Females have always understood and males will come to understand that that the body itself offers its own limitations in this regard. Mutilation and permanent disfigurement is never erotic to the one being mutilated or disfigured although it may well be erotic for the one imposing mutilation or disfigurement. If it is mutually erotic it is good. Do you understand?

Bappy: I am trying. But I still see problems.

Dewchee: Have you so soon forgotten our conversations from Shekhinah? We are speaking of the emergence of matriarchy in these matters. We are speaking of a time when women will have gained power over the rule of law. The old rules of the game -- i.e., male dominance -- will have melted away as we drift into this new age. First among individuals who will instantiate all of this before the change of the rule of law and then universally as women gain control over the rule of law and gain a certain finesse in the application of the rule of law.

Bappy: Then, under the conditions you are speaking of, it is axiomatic that you pre-suppose palpable protection against things like rape, child abuse, and the terrible betrayal of incest.

Dewchee: But of course. Indeed it is precisely those one-sided and grossly unequal situations which will disappear if we are courageous enough to let Eros reign.

Bappy: But why pain, abuse, and humiliation, even if these can be mutually eroticized?

Dewchee: You again have so quickly forgotten what we so carefully established in Shekhinah. You have forgotten what it means for all of us -- male and female -- to achieve our proper "daimon". You have forgotten the logic of the mixture relative to males and females. You have forgotten the "eu-daimon" of the good as it was put forth in "The Lecture on the Good." You have forgotten the humiliating rule of life itself. *Hum*-an and *hum*-iliation; they are linked beyond our power to control. This rule of life is the rule of death which -- for all of us -- will strip away our narcissism. And this is for the good. Recall when we cited Pascal:

> *The last act is bloody, however fine the rest of the play. They throw earth over your head and it is finished forever.*

Cited from Pascal: Pensees; translated with an Introduction by A.J. Krailsheimer; Penguin Books, Baltimore, 1982. Page 82.

Bappy: It's beginning to come back to me.

Dewchee: If so, you are beginning to remember that death is God's hint about humiliation. Humiliation is inevitable. What counts is how we integrate humiliation into our lives for the sake of the good.

Bappy: You mean we -- both males and females -- must seek to eroticize it. We must seek out the condition of pure oscillating need and integrate it into our sexual strategies. All of this for the sake of the good. This is your meaning, is it not?

Dewchee: Yes. Precisely. And if you are beginning to remember all of this you are also beginning to remember the most important thing of all.

Bappy: Yes I do remember. The vision of the alternative is what gave us those terrible nightmares when we woke up retching with the dry heaves: Auschwitz as a global destiny. It makes me so afraid!!!!

Dewchee: But fear -- yes fear of our God Shekhinah -- is the beginning of wisdom. We must be courageous.

Bappy: What is the crystallizing key to your scenario of eroticization for the good?

Dewchee: You will remember this as well. Shame. Embracing the shameless shame of the Shekhinah and becoming the shame of the Shekhinah. Mutually imposed and mutually shared. Shame -- when it comes through eroticism -- is both the most secret and most glorious name of the good.

Bappy: I do begin to remember. One more thing. Why is this alternative -- the tilt towards sex and eroticization which is in the service of the good -- also called melancholic? Is there no joy there?

Dewchee: Of course there is joy there. Jouissance. The very greatest and most ecstatic of joy. But in the very temple of delight melancholia reigns and must reign.

Bappy: Why? And wouldn't that imply that melancholia is the good?

Dewchee: It is. And it must be. Beauty must die for the sake of the good. The draw -- the attraction -- OF equilibrium requires death. This is sad and this is good. Yet because of death there is renewal.

246.
Like a woman. Just like a woman. Beyond woman, even! Ah! But there's the rub. One returns. It's all the same to me where I begin. I shall return there again in time. In time.

247.
I don't know why I like it; I just do.

Masochism is the last refuge of Narcissism. The wounded Narcissist is still a Narcissist. Wounded Narcissism seeks out Masochism.

Humiliation is the telos of Masochism. Humiliation, to be total, requires the active cooperation of the one being humiliated with the other who humiliates.

The eroticizing of pain and the eroticizing of humiliation; these are the primary means by which the one being humiliated actively cooperates with the other who humiliates.

Permanent damage; disfigurement; death while in the self-eroticized ecstasy. These are the "wages" of Masochism out of control. The wounded Narcissist is still a Narcissist.

Masochism out of control is a perversion of Eros. A perversion of Eros but still a possibility OF Eros.

More than anything else the Masochist wants to be seen; watched; judged. --- *Someone to watch over me* ---

Grace. Amazing Grace. It's "there" already. Always already "there". The fool seeks and does not find. But it finds the fool. It was "there" before the fool sought.

The ways in which God works through Psyche; reveals Herself through the very workings of Psyche; is (and is not, of course) Psyche. Freud was "there" already. Despite himself. Listen. In the last book which he wrote:

> *Having now decided upon the topographical dissection of the psychical apparatus into an ego and an id, with which the difference in quality between preconscious and unconscious runs parallel, and having agreed that this quality is to be regarded only as an indication of the difference and not as its essence, a further question faces us. What, if this is so, is the true nature of the state which is revealed in the id by the quality of being unconscious and in the ego by that of being preconscious and in what does the difference between them consist?*
>
> *But of that we know nothing. And the profound obscurity of the background of our ignorance is scarcely illuminated by a few glimmers of insight. Here we have approached the still shrouded secret of the nature of the psychical.*

Outline, page 20.

I get so emotional, baby,

Out of the depths I have cried to thee, Oh Lord ---

every time I see your face (hear your voice)

Indeed you are a dark and hidden God.

The difference. This is freedom. This is the Godhead of God. The Godhead of God in us and about us. This is the freedom which is; is long before, during, and long after the times when we are said to be exercising "free will." Always working and re-arranging. Always. Restlessly refurbishing.

The difference. This is freedom. This is the Godhead of God. The Godhead of God in us and about us. This is the freedom which is; is long before, during, and long after the times when we are said to be exercising "free will." Assigning the deep to the preconscious where it -- now aroused -- awaits the sudden orgasm of consciousness.

The difference. This is freedom. This is the Godhead of God. The Godhead of God in us and about us. This is the freedom which is; is long before, during, and long after the times when we are said to be exercising "free will." Assigning the unconscious deep (*altus*) to the unconscious high (*altus*) to marinate and thereafter work its wonders from above.

The transformation of guilt into compassion. This is the task of freedom in our time. But without guilt there is no compassion. Without the lex talionis there is no love. *Do not imagine that I have come to abolish the Law and the Prophets. I have come not to abolish but to complete them. I tell you solemnly, till heaven and earth disappear, not one dot, not one little stroke, shall disappear from the Law until its purpose is achieved.*

Faith. What is faith but this: to abide with that which is always "there" but which can never be found by seeking?

Hope is almost always self-deception. Save the hope which is "there" when all hope is gone. *Sad Song.*

This is why the good is, in the first place, tragic. When it is sought for it is never found. The good, to be, requires the failure of seeking.

Without seeking there is no finding. But the fool never finds what he seeks. Is this tragedy? Or comedy?

> (Appllodorus speaking from the memory of a remembered account) --- *He awoke towards dawn, as the cocks were crowing; and immediately he saw that all the*

> *company were either sleeping, or gone, except Agathon, Aristophanes, and Socrates, who alone remained awake and were drinking out of a large vessel, from left to right; and Socrates was arguing with them. As to most of the talk, Aristodemus had no recollection, for he had missed the beginning and was also rather drowsy; but the substance of it was, he said, that Socrates was driving them to the admission that the same man could have the knowledge required for writing comedy and tragedy -- that the fully skilled tragedian could be a comedian as well.*

This is, of course, the ending of Symposium.

Who is the fool? He who seeks. The fool on the hill.

Ain't it shocking what love can do? Oh my God!!! Shocking

248.
Bappy: What is """"""truth""""""?

Dewchee: Ah sweet one! It's the dance we always dance and the dance we never dance. It is the animating delusion of our species without which we cease to dream. It is the mother who procures the father. It is parent and yet it is also the child. Let the little girl dance!!!! Do you love me, Bappy, now that I can dance?

Bappy: I have always loved you. All ways.

Dewchee: Thank-you, Bappy and good-night.

Bappy: Good-night, Dewchee. Sleep tight. Don't let the bed-bugs bite.

248.
Loretta. Mommy is really dying this time. In the midst of all the obsessive writing -- especially as it had started to peak this past May of '91 -- he had written a prose-poem for her and her dying. Sure it had all the weaknesses characteristic of all of his writing. Narcissistic and overly conceptual. But he found -- he thought -- a little bit of this strange woman when he wrote it. He found a lot of himself.

Loretta

(the short version)

aujourd'hui Maman est morte

the dirty little secret of psycho-social evolution
the ever-so-subtle shame put on males by their mothers
all on a spectrum
and most of it in such a way that it could easily be
--- to the self satisfaction even of the mother ---
denied

the victim
it is well known by now
cannot even be the victim when the rules of the game
<u>further</u> victimize the victim
for being
a victim at all

what females go through with regard to this
diabolical dialectic
is next to nothing
compared to
the parameters pre-ordained for males

Lyotard
(I wonder if he wore one?
I mean, just now and then
and only for fun)
knew something of these things
the jews of the holocaust
who cannot speak for themselves and the survivors
who are not permitted

{{{most will have not caught
this trans-misogynistic subtlety}}}

aujourd'hui Maman est morte

are you listening, Sigismund?
you especially!!!!!

yet recall:

the maximization problems
(from business applications of math)
those god-awful matrices and equations!
maximize
say, profit?
subject to certain conditions having been <u>laid</u> down

shame

the ur-spring of intelligence and creativity
how to maximize this
subject to the condition of not destroying the child in the process

are you still listening, Sigismund?
you especially!!!!!

this too was the unconscious motivation
of motherly intrusion on males

especially first-born males

but
without destroying them in the process

how did you do, Loretta?????
hmmmmm
it's not only for her to have decided

yes

how to make the child so radically insufficient
this is God's plan
the genius of God in Her essential insufficiency

imago Dei
if we are lucky enough

the hundred-thousand "wholistic" health fetishists
have totally missed the point

we are made in the image of God
by virtue
of failure and insufficiency
only now does "AMDG" come to have its hidden meaning revealed

{{{up to now a deeply faulty implied (and fundamentally fetishistic) theology (which affected the spin-off atheists just as much as the rear-guard theists) brought in its secular wake faulty paradigms of what could -- should!!! -- be gained through "therapy" and "recovery"}}}

my friends

we are not healed
we are not recovered
unless we first become
and remain
AT LEAST
as broken and non-integrated to the degree revealed to us
by the existential frenchman

{{{no no no
that baby thinker who more babyishly aped Marx
still remains far from
what the telos is
but the telos pre-supposes
as necessary and unavoidable condition
that paradigm of non-integration
which is non-integration
on principle}}}

in this holy project
{{{the holy implying non-integration
{{{{{which is non-integration on principle}}}}}
}}}
faulty fathers
and faulty mothers most especially
have been the acolytes

(unless they destroyed their children in the process)

{{{ ----- *my "fear of flying" episode of last Autumn was also a fear-of-Loretta episode, now that it evident that Loretta will soon ride that sweet chariot which will swing low for all of us sometime. Of course it's about forgiveness. And being face to face with her. You know that I accept the Jewish teaching that sins committed against God can be forgiven by God but that harms visited upon other humans can be forgiven only by the aggrieved party and not by God. Think it through some day. The burden is on the aggrieved party much more so than on the one who perpetrated the wrong. A false forgiveness or a forgiveness given to those not worthy of forgiveness is really the worst outcome. It would be an affront to God. But never to forgive is almost as terrible. [[Is it evident from all of this that I take the Christian account of forgiveness to be far too generic, sloppy, and therefore (paradox noted) an avoidance of the dynamic of forgiveness?]]* ----- }}}

But wait!
do I hear an other voice?
so strange
so eerie
Doppler-like
yet it catches my attention from within

(did you really say bulgaria?)

the mother speaks
for herself
for a change
sons listen
for the first time
with that third ear

and there is some joy in mudville today
for magically
the game has gone into extra innings
(the big-inning long since gone)
as the umpires left the playing field
not knowing what had transpired

Loretta

survivor you were
(and we learned that lesson well)
but no-one ever let you speak for yourself

Loretta

(I think the real Irish say it with a better lilt)
we hardly got to know you

{{{ ----- *Then it is finally time. The last layer of the onion skin is ever so subtlely removed. Sobering. There is nothing at all. There is nothing to forgive. There never was.* ----- }}}

249.
But the lex talionis never goes away. Nor could it. It cannot be superseded by love for the lex talionis is the very condition for love. Christianity has never understood this in its presumptuous self-congratulation for allegedly being an "advance" over Judaism. But perhaps it was understood by Yehoshua.

Do not imagine that I have come to abolish the Law and the Prophets. I have come not to abolish but to complete them. I tell you solemnly, till heaven and earth disappear, not one dot, not one little stroke, shall disappear from the Law until its purpose is achieved.

The Universal self-imposition of the lex talionis. There is an ideal for the Law -- Torah -- to aim for! Then one will worry more about the beam in one's own eye before harping on the speck in another's eye. Then one might -- when the justice of God is not thwarted by so doing -- turn the other cheek when hit and love one's enemy. But all of these matters will remain in a kind of bad-faith obscurity unless and until Yehoshua comes to be understood as always and ever a Jew remaining a Jew calling Jews to, according to his spiritual vision, the deepest vocation of Torah rather than being understood as the founder of a new religion and new Covenant.

{{{It would, of course take a different kind of "regressive kathalysis" to deal intelligently with the relationships obtaining betweeen various Jewish factions during the time of Yehoshua's ministry and, as well, the relationship(s) obtaining between the Jerusalem community headed by the brother of Yehoshua (i.e., "James") and the various Jewish factions in the generation after the death of Yehoshua. But two salient features of such a "regressive kathalysis" must be mentioned even now in order to contextualize any references to "Jesus" made in the present book:

a). That the writings and ministry of Paul constitute an agendum radically different from the teachings and ministry of Yehoshua;

b). That the War with Rome -- culminating in the destruction of the Temple in 70 AD -- creates the primary context in which and by which the written versions of the Gospels took form.

Finally, it ought to be mentioned in this Freud-oriented book that Freud himself had a most average and pedestrian understanding of both the Jewish and Christian versions of the "love commands." His analysis of these love commands -- i.e, as culturally re-enforced "reaction formations" against the innate aggressiveness of humans -- is insightful and vindicated in so far as most Christians and Jews have, in actual practice, but an average and pedestrian understanding of the Love commands which animate their respective faiths. *[Confer, of course, Freud's famous treatment of these commands in Chapters Four, Five, and Eight of Civilization and its Discontents. More especially, Civ, pages 54-55; 62-64; and 101-102.]* Still, all in all, one does not consult Freud as an expert in matters of Biblical exegesis.

<<<The fact that the Church came to identity "Jesus" with "God" (i.e., the fetish par excellence if the multiple contentions of tihs book are accurate) severely impedes hermeneutical access to the teachings of this Yehoshua of the Galilee.>>> }}}

250.
Always and all ways -- (and always and all ways <u>*intrinsically*</u> [so to speak] *hidden and* <u>*intrinsically*</u> [so to speak] *withdrawing in Her "dis-appearing" showing) -- the primacy of deception.*

The <u>choice</u> between, on the one hand, the various and subtle forms of <u>disavowal</u> and, on the other hand, fidelity to that counter-factual "fact" in terms of which we "dream."

It is a choice. It cannot be adjudicated cognitively. Heidegger spoke of "authenticity." More cogently, Sartre spoke of "good faith" and "bad faith." After all one is speaking about fidelity to what is not seen. Cognitive adjudication -- which <u>does</u> have its place and function to perform -- has no place or function when one is about "the place" (<u>khora</u>) where deception reigns for this "place" is the very space in terms of which there comes to be at all a domain in which cognition is rendered possible in any fashion. This space (<u>khora</u>) is that awe-full pre-condition of cognition.

{{{{{{{{ Yes. Choice. Not "choice" in some once-and-forever "free choice" which is so easily denigrated by a host of sophisticated thinkers. Rather an on-going series involving an amalgem of conscious and pre-conscious, major and mini, choices some of which are so pedestrian as to go un-noticed by the set of "philosophers" who like to pose questions concerning "free choice" and "determinism." One is speaking of an on-going series which begins when the child -- male or female -- first understands that Mommy is castrated and continues -- in our sleep, in our dreams, in our waking periods, in our dispositions, in our habits, in our whims, in our careful calculations, -------- in all that we "do" -- until the possibility for consciousness is finally wrested from our brains. The great dialectic -- taking on many diverse and often sublimated forms -- of and between <u>disavowal-of</u> and <u>fidelity-to</u> the great counter-factual "fact." The great drama of life -- the very battle for an individual's <u>daimon</u> -- is at issue in this dialectic which for years at a time may involve nothing more than what the world calls "pedestrian". The drama oscillates in different individuals in different ways between <u>disavowal-of</u> and <u>fidelity-to</u> as each one of us enters in to that awe-full trinity of Courage/Melancholy/Hope. And the final verdict of a woman's life and daimon {{given that, at bottom, we are all women since in both men and women it is the wo-man principle which is decisive since the wo-man principle is either our origin or destiny}} is known only to herself. Will we have succeeded in having <u>become</u> acolytes of the good? Or failed?

This is how we must understand the dictum of Heraclitus to the effect that *character (daimon) is fate.* Our "lot" -- our "fate" -- is what we make it to be. Plato most certainly understood this in Book X of the <u>Republic</u> when, in the myth of Er, he points out that we <u>choose</u> the "lot" -- i.e., the conditions and parameters -- of our ""next"" """"incarnation"""". Chosen fate. The antinomy dissolves. Yes, of course the "voluntarism" of Jean-Paul is a bit extreme and somewhat simplistic. But Jean-Paul -- far more than the set of suave and sophisticated thinkers on both sides of the Channel who regularly mock out his kind of "voluntarism" -- walks with "the chosen" as he insists that freedom (i.e., the very structure of the *pour-soi*) is the kind of "first principle" which truly animates the heart of authentic philosophical discourse. Likewise, freedom as a "first principle" animates the very best aspects of German Idealism bĕfore that complex movement chokes itself off in Hegel's version of Nous/Geist idolatry. *{{{Please understand. It is, as Schelling understood, the unconditioned rather than 'freedom' which functions as a first principle. In the supplement to* Thinking Psycho-analytically *the utterly unconditioned is referred to as 'the free'. Freedom occurs* <u>*in*</u> *the mixture but is not, just by itself, a principle* <u>*of*</u> *the mixture.}}}*

Choice. Choose life.

> {{{{ Bappy: I have a question about that "series" of major and mini choices which he also calls an "amalgem". Is there one choice for all or do all the mini/major choices combine

into one choice?

Dewchee: That is a very fair question. You are asking about the logic of the entire series. Let me simply say that the entire series instantiates a logic and that the logic itself -- (of which the series in question is the instantiation) -- of the series is effected by any and/or each and/or all of the many mini/major (and conscious/pre-conscious) choices in the series.

Bappy: That still sounds confusing.

Dewchee: Perhaps we are speaking of something which by its "nature" is epistemologically confusing and ontologically undecidable. One thinks of Shekhinah AS the play of chance. But at least it has been said by others better than I have said it. Listen first to the bitter one.

Bappy: I am listening.

Dewchee:

> ----- *In creation there is the greatest harmony, and nothing is so separate and sequent as we must represent it, but the subsequent cooperates in what precedes it and everything occurs at the same time in one magic stroke.*

Freedom; page 65.

Bappy: It's as though there were no co-incidences and yet, at the same time, everything -- yes everything -- happens by chance. Who else speaks of this?

Dewchee: I am certain you shall remember. She is the best friend of our friend. Listen:

Like the flash of heat lightning that tells you all that is, is now.

Joyce Carol Oates in Lock. Page 92.

Bappy: Thank-you so much Dewchee. You always make me feel so happy. I'm so glad you came into my life.

Dewchee: Sleep tight, sweet one. I'll shut the light out as I leave.

Bappy: Just brush my cheek before you leave me. I love you. }}}}} }}}}}}}}}}

This place. This deception. This khora. ----- *is "caught", when all sensation is absent* [anaisthesias!!!] , *by a discourse of questionable pedigree* [logismo tini notho] *being scarcely believable* [mogis piston] *which we, beholding it as in a dream-trance* -----

Timaeus 52B.

Yes.

One knows that Derrida had very cogent objections to the Heideggerian "authenticity" and even more so the the "good faith" business of Sartre.

Yes.

One knows that he pressed these objections most vehemently when the "authenticity"/"good faith" terminology made its appearance -- sometimes with recognition of its pedigree, sometimes without such overt recognition -- in the text of Lacan.

Yes.

One knows that Lacan and Sartre -- Heidegger being always and properly problematic for Frere Jacques -- instantiate according to Derrida just another set of 'full presence' variations in the history of "ontotheolgy." One knows that Derrida has cogently demonstrated that both thinkers -- Lacan and Sartre -- (although they admittedly had radically different adgenda) stay unconsciusly circumscribed by a "metaphysics of 'full presence.'"
One knows all of this and one is prepared -- on the playing field of cogency -- to award the victory to Frere Jacques. It wan't even a contest.

And yet.

Despite themselves -- ((and let it be acknowledged from the outset that it is most irksome to defend these two thinkers who manifest so many "pre-Copernican", (so to speak), liabilities)) -- Sartre in his way and Lacan in his way can teach all of us (Derrida therein included) a lesson for those times when we must play on the playing field of deception. And "there is" a playing field of cogency at all only by virtue of the """"""prior"""""""" playing field of deception.

Lacan, deception, "disavowal"-of (on the one hand) and fidelity-to (on the other) the counter-factual "fact." These things have been spoken of in Sentences-III. One must now say a word about these things relative to Sartre.

{{And most of these points from Sentences III have been integrated into -- *[what would have been, dear cherished reader of Shame!]* -- Part II of this book.}}

Yes, Yes, Yes, Yes, Yes, Yes. Sartre's simplistic and not at all cogent appropriation of things Freudian. Sartre's "ontotheolgoy." Sartre's picture perfect atheism which is but the symmetrical negative of a Christo-centric theism. Sartre's incredibly unthoughtful way of embracing Marxism which only advertised to the world how sterile his thinking had become after Being and Nothingness. Sartre's having become -- not without paradox -- something of a "bourgeois" institution. Sartre's incredibly "traditional" treatment of questions concerning "authorship" and "writing." Yes. In all respects, if one were intellectually alive during the French sixties, it would incumbent upon one to put maximum distance between one's own emerging thinking and """"""Sartre"""""".

Even so.

Did not that generation of intellectuals -- one thinks most especially of the Tel Quel crowd -- overplay their suave dismissal of Sartre? After all it appears that none of them -- save possibly Kristeva and Frere Jacques himself -- will come to hold a place of significance equal to Sartre's in the eventual pantheon of thinkers.

Given all of Sartre's obvious liabilities, why should this be so?

We are on the playing field of deception. It is here, moreso than on the playing field of cogency, where """"""differance"""""" is """"""""""""genuinely"""""""""""" encountered. (And soon it will have been beneficial to re-re-spell "differance" with an "e.")

On the playing field of deception the cognitve adjudication of things -- even and especially of "differance"-oriented """things""" -- is impossible. On the playing field of deception " 'good' faith" makes all the "difference" in the world. Fidelity to the counter-factual "fact." One may only choose. There is no cognitive adjudication.

On the playing field of deception it is possible to play off "full presnece" contra "differance" without doing a dis-service to "differance". As Sentences-III insists, this is what Plato did with his theory of forms. And Sartre -- at least in the most diabolical sections of Being and Nothingness -- achieved this "differance"/"full presence" play-off despite those too-often cited shortcomings of his version of "ontotheology." As it was said in Sentences-III: *there is, in the final analysis, something "pour-soi-esque" about achieving one's own proper daimon.*

Is it possible to play on both the playing field of cogency and the playing field of deception at once? The issue is yet to be decided although the history of "ontotheolgy" would indicate that the vast majority don't even arrive at the playing field of cogency let alone the playing field of deception.

There was, however, Plato who played on both, but with a cost to the proper vocation of his thinking. There was Nietzsche who has been spoken about in this very book. There is Frere Jacques who has no equal at all -- not even Plato -- on the playing field of cogency but who becomes overly anxious and unthoughtful when he approaches the playing field of deception where "winning" is defined by fidelity to the counter-factual "fact." For Frere Jacques it appears that "differance" can only be spelled with an "a".

Kristeva -- having played well on the playing field of cogency -- moved over to the playing field of deception and plays well. But only at the cost leaving behind the playing field of cogency. There -- on the playing field of deception -- she joins that small crowd of "good faith" poets and "holy men" -- ((it being acknowledged that the vast majority of soi-dissant poets and "holy men" are agents of "bad faith" and disavowal)) -- who have played magnificently on the field of deception for some time. But she did not integrate the playing field of cogency and the playing field of deception.

Is it -- such integration -- to be done? Can it be done? Should it be done? There are hundreds upon hundreds of thousands who have "integrated" the two fields according to the mode of disavowal and "bad faith." There are a special few -- here on the playing field of cogency and there on the playing field of deception -- who did something like integration in "good faith" -- (i.e., fidelity to the counter-factual "fact") -- and failed.

The integration in the mode of good faith. One speaks of the integration in the mode of good faith which is anything but the multiple """integrations""" of any number of thinkers, poets, and holy men who operate overtly and covertly under the umbrella of a 'metaphysics of full presence.' The integration in the mode of good faith is, quite literally, something different. Is it to be done? Can it be done? Should it be done? One awaits the Messiah.

251.
On the playing field of deception

Yes, yes, of course. Mommy is in fact not castrated. But if you insist on avowing this fact you will find that, despite yourself and your most suave and sophisticated intention, you end up in the logic of the bad-faith disavowal. Cognitive adjudication is not relevant on the playing field of deception.

252.
The dual logic of impossibility.

On the one hand, disavowal: The impossibility -- (i.e., that Mommy is in fact endowed with a penis) -- maintained as actual fact. As one knows, the logic of disavowal was linked by Freud to the phenomenon of the "splitting of the ego" by which one portion of the ego lives the disavowal while another portion of the ego accepts the counter-factual "fact."

This option is the option of continual bad faith and continual lack of integration. This option turns our dreams into nightmares. This option entails patterns of denial, and avoidance as a way of life. This option entails the disposition to a violent reaction when the treasured "truth" of disavowal is shown to be false. The logic of disavowal is at the root of a disposition towards Fascism and, most especially, Anti-Semitism.

On the other hand there is the logic of impossibility involved in the fidelity to the counter-factual "fact": entrance into the full range and experience of "desire." Intricate and trans-Lacanian patterns of sexual fulfillment involving male and female strategies of being the castrated oscillating other for the castrated oscillating other. Matriarchal Androgyny in which the hegemony of difference is sustained. Achieving the shameless shame of Shekhinah which is to achive the good qua erotic shame.

In sublimated behaviors -- {{{{{there being, of course, sublimations of the disavowal as well, as implied above {{{and please note as well that these sublimated behaviors of " 'good'-faith" are never meant -- (nor could they) -- to eclipse the overtly sexual achievement of the good qua erotic shame}}} }}}}} -- fidelity to the counter-factual "fact" leads to living the dream AS impossibile dream but not as actual fact. Free, gratuitous positing of the ideal. The emergence of that kind of hope which can only emerge when all hope is gone. Courage, Melancholy, and Hope, as allies.

Fidelity to the counter-factual "fact" on the playing field of deception. Working for the coming of the Messiah is, in some sense, the coming of the Messiah:

> *Some men see things as they are and say* Why? *I dream things that never were and say,* why not?

(Cited at the funeral of Robert F. Kennedy by his brother Edward in Saint Patrick's Cathedral, June, 1968.)

Eu prattein, my friend, eu prattein. The undecidable stalement of thinking is not adjudicated by thinking. Rather, it's all in the doing and making. Eu prattein. "Eu poieiv". Shalom!

253.
What did you see when you were there?

Nothing that doesn't show, they answered.

What did you see when you were there?

I only saw what I heard.

What did you see when you were there?

Love.

What did you see when you were there?

Love whispered: *It's OK*

What did you see when you were there?

Love whispered: *Let go*

What did you see when you were there?

Love whispered: *Give in*

What did you see when you were there?

I gave in and it was alright.

What did you see when you were there?

It was better than before.

What did you see when you were there?

The before had to be and must be.

What did you see when you were there?

Love.

What did you see when you were there?

The Messiah.

(caesura)

{{{{{{{{{{{{{{
Bappy: Should we be here at all? I have a lot on my mind. But really. I mean in one of these caesuras for God's sake.

Dewchee: I don't know. The fact is we are here. Besides, we're not totally in control of just where we might show up.

Bappy: OK. I trust you, Dewchee. What I need to know about is this "break from aisthesis" business.

Dewchee: It's pretty tricky business. First we have to distinguish between two things.

Bappy: What are they?

Dewchee: On the one hand there is the agendum of Johanna Elton. On the other hand there is some Plato business to attend to.

Bappy: OK. One at at time. What is the agendum of our friend Johanna?

Dewchee: Johanna is trying to finesse the connection between Bell's theorem and the Heisenbergian account of the Copenhagen Interpretation through her perhaps idiosyncratic understanding of what Plato's "epistemology" entails. Roughly, Johanna connects the rather erotic drama of Platonic aisthesis with the Heisenbergian account of the Copenhagen Interpretation while connecting Bell's theorem with the Platonic break from aisthesis.

Bappy: WOW! (That's MOM upside down and, optionally, palindromically.) She always seems to get in over her head. Shouldn't the reader be alerted to a few features of our friend, Johanna.

Dewchee: I think you're right. She's obviously manic/depressive and that shows up all over her writings. Also she's borderline psychotic; "dis-associative" to the extreme. Connections which are self-evident in her strange and twisted mind turn out to be self-evident only to her. Nor does she bother to unpack and explain her often obscure connections. Listen! Right now! Can you hear her chanting?

Keeping time, time, time
In a sort of Runic rhyme

Bappy: Oh yes! I love how she chants. It helps me to sleep on those nights when my fears keep me awake. But tell me. Can we help out?

Dewchee: I think so. That is if we attend to some features of Plato and Platonic "epistemology." We ought to steer clear of Heisenberg, the Copenhagen Interpretation, Bell's theorem and all that. Leave that for Johanna.

Bappy: OK. Sounds useful. Where shall we get started? In the sections of Timaeus where aisthesis is talked about? Pyramids of fire and all that?

Dewchee: There's much to be learned from those sections of Timaeus. But we must never forget that most of Timaeus represents that playfully exuberent return to aisthesis which pre-supposes the break from aisthesis. This is true even when Timaeus extends its likely story to include the "physiology" of vision and of aisthesis in general. For our purposes it will be far more important to examine the break from aisthesis presupposed by our likely story. Also it will be necessary to examine Plato's conceptual account (which is anything but a physiology) of just what we are breaking away from when we break from aisthesis and what we are returning to when we return to aisthesis.

Bappy: I take it that your words imply that this conceptual treatment is not given in Timaeus.

Dewchee: Only indirectly is it given in Timaeus -- and then in a bastard (illegitimate) sort of way. In any case this bastardizing conceptual account is not given in those sections of Timaeus in which the "physiology" of aisthesis is talked about.

Bappy: Where then shall we find this conceptual account of asithesis. Are you referring to that aporetic dialogue, Theaetetus?

Dewchee: Aporetic and maieutic. Yes. Of course.

Bappy: Fine. Let's get on to our two-fold task. Plato's account of the break from aisthesis and Plato's conceptual account of what we are breaking from when we break from aisthesis and to what we are returning when we return to aisthesis. You have indicated that there is much to discuss.

Dewchee: Yes. Very much. And it will indeed take us away from Timaeus. But we ought not leave Timaeus just yet.

Bappy: Why not?

Dewchee: In the very structural middle of that story dialogue is the secret. The "between" of aisthesis and that -- i.e., noesis -- which is made possible by the break from aisthesis.

Bappy: What is this "between"? It seems so strange. So weird.

Dewchee: Strange indeed. Listen: *khora* Listen again: *khoris* Listen yet again: *khorismos* Think it through and listen. *khora* *khoris* *khorismos* Plato certainly listened. Plato certainly thought it through. Listen:

> ----- *and there is a third kind, which is space and is eternal, and admits not of destruction and provides a home for all becoming, and is "caught", when all sensation is absent* [anaisthesias!!!], *by a discourse of questionable pedigree* [logismos tini notho] *being scarcely believable* [mogis piston] *which we, beholding it as in a dream-trance* ---

Bappy: WOW! Somehow this all reminds my of our friend Jude -- back before he went into the hospital -- when he would get a bit manic. He would throw in the Greek word for "dance" when he would sing and chant his "khora" series. Indeed he would be dancing while he was doing it.

Dewchee: I have happy memories of Jude. He was one of a kind. But now the needs and concerns of his sister -- Johanna (who is, if anything, even more unstable than Jude) -- have come to be more on our mind these days. But let us not stray.

Bappy: Indeed, let us not. What you are saying, I take it, is that it all comes back to Timaeic "khora". Sooner or later. And now that we have alerted our readers to the story's in-visible (UN-SEEN) black-hole-esque center of these things shall we feel free to move away from Timaeus?

Dewchee: Yes. For now. Let us turn to Phaedo. There we shall find the account of the all-important break from aisthesis.

Bappy: Ah yes. Phaedo. 99D, 5 to 100A, 11. Loeb lining as always. Turning away from the overwhelming flood of information coming in through the senses in order to understand -- by way of the cause -- that which keeps coming in through the over-abundant wealth of aisthesis (where "aisthesis" is rich enough to include both "sensation" and "perception"). This is the famous passage where Plato has "Socrates" speak of the forms for the first time.

Dewchee: Yes. A critical passage. And Plato goes out of his way to have this "Socrates" speak of just how unsophisticated and simple this "account" is. How "foolish." And indeed the examples of the "Large" and the "Small" bear out just how simple the account is.

Bappy: The whole thing does seem rather preposterous.

Dewchee: Very much so. Can you imagine getting a serious audience for things such as: "The Large Itself"; "The Small Itself"; "The Hot Itself"; "The Cold Itself"; "The Beautiful Itself"? Did he really expect anyone to take this nonsense seriously?

Bappy: Perhaps his point is that it's NON-SENSE. Anyway, your remark does bring back memories of how often we have noted Plato's own and oft-stated remarks about the togetherness of the playful and the serious. But tell me. As we turn away from aisthesis for the sake of understanding that which is given through in aisthesis, what are we turning towards?

Dewchee: That is an excellent question. Aristotle and the Tradition would have us believe that the turn is actually a "trans" or a "meta". Aristotle and the Tradition would have us believe that this turning away is some kind of "transcending" towards the "super-sensible" in which, somehow, the sensible is replicated in a non-physical (i.e., meta-ta-phusika) way. (((((And please understand that this meta-physical move (allegedly inauguarated by Plato) is retained and further entrenched when the forms -- in that age in which the fetish reached its peak -- come to be represented as archtypes eternally present in the mind of God. In this sense a Bonaventura is just as much Aristotelian as an Aquinas since in both cases the account of what a Platonic form would be falls under and within the rubric of the alleged "meta-physical" move.)))))

Bappy: Oh yes. We have discussed this often. And even today -- after all the alleged sophistication in recent years concerning "reading strategies" relative to the Platonic text -- such an account of Plato's turning away from aisthesis hinders the abilitiy to let Plato's own account of the forms speak for itself. Even so, the forms are "separate", it must be acknowledged, even as we deter the reader from imposing a "meta-ta-phusika" grid of interpretation upon this "separateness.""

Dewchee: Yes. All of this is true. And when Aristotle -- who did not maintain "separateness" for the formal principle(s) of sensible ousia -- does finally speak of "separate" ousia (i.e., God and the 47?/49?/55? intelligences in terms of which the Universe as a whole and the "wandereres" have their motion) he IS taking the "meta-ta-phusika" move. But to impose this grid of interpretation on the move which Plato was making when Plato spoke of the forms is, precisely, to miss the point of Plato's discussion.

Bappy: Why is that?

Dewchee: Because Plato never poses questions of "separatenesss" in terms of "hule" or in terms of "ta phusika." *{{{Even when Plato -- say in Sophist as he is reviewing the battle between "giants" and "gods" -- speaks of "bodiless" (i.e., "asomaton") he is saying something quite different from Aristotle's "ta phusika/hule" frame of reference. Being bodiless is a condition quite different from the "meta-ta-phusika" orientation of Aristotle. For Plato the key is the "visible/invisible" orientation -- ((which* *allows for the uniquely Platonic way of engaging the "seen/unseen" dimensions of his teaching on "light" -- from Republic VI -- to interface with his "eidos" terminology for the forms)) -- is always decisive and that in terms of which there is at all anything like the derivative "body/bodiless" way of speaking. "Ta phusika" for Aristotle is a fundamental frame of reference in terms of which one speaks of a "meta." "Being-bodied" and "being-bodiless", in contrast, are for Plato but incidental correlates of being-visible or being-invisible. Only an orientation which begs the question under discussion would equate the Platonic "ta somata" with the Aristotelian "ta phusika."}}}*

Bappy: Then what is the force of Platonic "choris" and "chorismos"? *{{{Please understand, cherished reader. Platonic "khorismos" is not Aristotelian "khoristos." Yes, yes, yes, yes, yes. One understands. With "khoristos" one gets that intricate "separ-ABLE-but-not-spearate" motif which is the heart and soul of Aristotelianesque "qua-ing." ((And yes there are some passages in which Aristotelian "khoristos" would have to be taken as "separate". That is also true.)) Point understood. Even so the Aristotelian motif -- even with this subtlety -- remains a "hule"-oriented motif. It remains a "ta phusika"-oriented motif. Thus it is anything but Plato's story.}}}* Somehow, I think I arleady know what you are going to say.

Dewchee: *khora khoris khorismos* We are back, once again, to the structual center of Timaeus.

Bappy: Yes. All roads lead back to Timaeus. But let us stay with the present question without just yet surrendering to that black-hole-esque "space" in what you are calling the "structural center" of that strange dialogue. If it is not to some soi-dissant "super-sensible" that we are turning to in the turn away from aisthesis, then what are we turning to?

Dewchee: Read the text. It's right there in the text. "Logos." *{{tous logous 99E, 6; tois logois 100A, 1; logon 100A, 4; Loeb lining in all cases}}* Shall we call this "the account" of what is given in aisthesis? Shall we call this the discourse of what is given in aisthesis? Shall we call this "the concept" of what is given in aisthesis?

Bappy: In any case this "logos" -- i.e., this "account/discourse of/concept" -- is the "Itself" (kath auto). The word -- ((the genesis of which, according to Cratylus, is always suspect since, according to the argumentation of that mostly manic dialogue, most words appear to have originated without the benefit of a break from aisthesis)) -- plus "itself" is what we turn to when we turn away from the content of aisthesis.

Dewchee: And in this regard Plato teases us -- again, in the dark passages of Timaeus :

> *Are we talking idly whenever we say that there is such a thing as an intelligible form of anything? Is this nothing more than a word?*

Bappy: But how do these "forms" exist? It is so tempting to slide into an Aristotelianesque understanding of what Plato must have been doing when he postulated the forms.

Dewchee: By now you should know better. Avoid that temptation at all costs. Stay with the text. "Separate." A Platonic form (i.e., any "______________ Itself") is separate from the wealth of input coming in through aisthesis. Separate. Different.

Bappy: And "separate" (khoris) brings us back to "khora." Where does difference lead us to?

Dewchee: To the "in" passages and the "sameness/difference" passages of hypothesis # 2 of Parmenides where there is a systematic and conceptual unpacking of Timaeic "khora." But we must leave those passages for another time. Besides, Johanna and her friends -- particularly her friends -- have dealt with these matters elsewhere. For now it is enough to have recognized that any ordinary (i.e. Aristotleian or post-Aristotelian) and implicitly "meta-physical" way of understanding what

Plato was up to in the turn away from aisthesis is an account which bypasses what Plato says.

Bappy: OK. I get your drift. Shall we move on to Theaetetus?

Dewchee: Not just yet. There are two further matters.

> Non: What are we doing here? Why have we been brought into play? Obviously Bappy and Dewche are "in medias res" (so to speak) and still have importan matters to attend to.
>
> Sic: Johanna's getting nervous about how Bappy and Dewchee are conducting themselves. I won't be at all surprised if she herself should interrupt directly at some point. In any case she wishes us to break in for a clarification.
>
> Non: What's on her mind at this point?
>
> Sic: That Derrideanesque "logo-centrism" stuff. More precisely she's worried that a reader might think that she's not aware of this logo-centrism stuff because Bappy and Dewchee are not making reference to it.
>
> Non: Tell her to chill out. After all, Bappy and Dewchee can't say everything all at once. And even Derrida himself -- as he evolved from that jargonesque monster of the late sixties and seventies -- comes not to get so fixated on this "logo-centrism" motif. I mean, it's still there for him and it is an important issue. But if Derrida has calmed down Johanna can calm down as well. Besides, what is it precisely in this Bappy/Dewchee conversation which makes her think that there should be any kind of reference to "logo-centrism" at all?
>
> Sic: All those "logos" references from the Phaedo passages which they have been citing.
>
> Non: How strange! What a strange misperception. Using the word "logos" does not make one eo ipso "logo-centric." Please don't get me wrong. It is extremely interesting that in speaking of the break from aisthesis Plato should use these "logos" words. Extremely interesting. For it gives us an insight into what forms are for Plato. But it would be to miss the very point of Derrida's point to say that the presence or absence of "logo-centrism" in the Platonic text has anything to do with Plato's usage of "logos" terminology when he speaks of the break from aisthesis.
>
> Sic: You know that. I know that. Even Johanna knows that. Her concern is how all of this will be received by the reader.
>
> Non: You can tell Johanna to have more respect for any reader who has made it to the point of this caesura, of which we are now a part.
>
> Sic: But you know how hyper she can get. She wants us to rehearse things things a bit anyway.
>
> Non: Well, it's her book and she makes all the decisions anyway. How shall we procede?
>
> Sic: I think it would be helpful to point out that IF something like "logo-

centrism" characterizes the Platonic text one would be most likely to find it in the place or places in which Plato analyzes the very structure of discourse itself.

Non: That is very probable. So in effect your implied suggestion, in the final analysis, seems to entail the need to engage the eight hypotheses of Parmenides.

Sic: She understands that well. But she does not want us to engage that task in this digression.

Non: Well that would leave the short reference from Philebus and then the famous quickie analysis of these things which Plato has the Eleatic Stranger give in Sophist from 260E through 264B.

Sic: That would be more to her liking. Let's warm up by citing the passage from Philebus 15D:

> *We'll put the thing like this. We get this identity of the one and the many cropping up everywhere as the result of the sentences we utter; in every single sentence ever uttered, in the past and in the present, there it is. What we are dealing with is a problem that will assuredly never cease to exist; this is not its first appearance. Rather it is, in my view, something incidental to sentences themselves, never to pass and never to fade.* [according to Hackforth]

Non: Ah yes. Happy memories as you cite that passage. And just previous to that -- at 15A -- Plato makes it clear that this discussion of "the ones" -- ("monads" in the Hackforth translation) -- is really about "the forms". Likewise, the same passage at 15A parallels clarifications made at Parmenides 135D-E and Sophist 251A-C. Plato is ever alert to the distinction between engaging the problem of the "one and the many" on a trivial level and engaging it on a truly dialectical level.

Sic: Yes. Now let us conjoin to this issue that often cited but sledom understood analysis of "statement/discourse/sentence/logos" which occurs from Sophist from 260E through 264B.

Non: By "seldom understood" you are referring, are you not, to the practically unconscious habit endemic to the Tradition to appropriate this Sophist passage as a kind of quickie adumbration of the kind of thing which Aristotle would do in his Organon in general and in his De Interpretatione -- ((i.e., the text par excellence from which Derrida comes to his "discovery" of the "phono-logo-centrism" endemic (according to Derrida) in the "Tradition")) -- in particular?

Sic: Yes. That is the point exactly. As you know Johanna -- both in this book and even moreso in the previous incarnations of this book -- has carefully demonstrated that always and everywhere Aristotle's analysis of discourse/statement/sentence/logos is an analysis in which "the hupokeimenon of privilege" -- ousia in Aristotle's difference-fleeing paradigm of osuia -- plays the center role. The "predicates" of some such "hupokeimenon of privilege" stand in a relationship of dependency to any some such "hupokeimenon of privilege."

Non: Yes. And Johanna has also pointed out that the everywhere implied teaching of the Organon in general and of De Interpretatione in particular is sustained and justified by the "ousia-as-hupokeimenon-and-hupokeimenon-as-ousia" (and both hupokeimenon and ousia as "form" in Aristotle's idiosyncratic meaning of form) as it comes forth in Book VII of Metaphysics in general and in VII-3, VII-17 and V-8 (at 1017b, 23-28, Loeb lining as always) of Metaphysics in particular. Of course, any reader who is following this conversation will have to get substantiation of all of this from the non-caesura sections of the book.

Non: In contrast -- that is if we can trust Johanna's account of these things -- in Plato's account of these things, any "one"/ousia" which comes to function as hupokeimenon for predicates does so only momentarily. For it is the very """"""essence""""""" of a Platonic hupokeimenon-for-predicates that it -- the one/ousia/hupokeimenon under discussion -- "dis-appear" into its predicates in the ceaseless play of difference which governs these things. There simply is no "hupokeimenon of privilege" for Plato. All of this is made clear enough in the eight hypotheses and in Johanna's way of explicating what the eight hypotheses are about.

Sic: Of course this does not stop the Tradition from its Procrustean trait of forcing -- (often unconscious of what it is doing in this regard) -- Plato's analysis of statement/discourse/sentence/logos to come forth as though he were doing a quickie adumbration of the kind of thing which Aristotle would come to do all throughout the Organon in general and De Interpretatione in particular. Thus the tendency on the part of the difference-fleeing Tradition to radically misread our Sophist passage (i.e., from 260E through 264B). Yet in light of that very passage and more especially in the light of what is accomplished in that greatest of all predicational analyses -- I speak of the eight hypotheses -- it becomes clear that the very heart of Plato's analysis of statement/discourse/sentence/logos is the very play of difference. And it is precisely this very play of difference which is absent from Aristotle's manner of doing predicational analysis.

Non: Which would mean -- for those who have the eyes to hear and the ears to see -- that "logo-centrism" (the characteristic of the Tradition which suppresses "differance") is really inaugurated by Aristotle and is not really present in the Platonic text.

Sic: Yes, so long as Johanna's point in all of this is understood.

Non: Please remind our reader.

Sic: Platonic "difference/eksaiphnes" is, if properly understood, the functional equivalent of Derridean "differance."

Non: Is it fair to say that we have now performed the function of this interruption which was to put the question of "logo-centrism" in perspective relative to the Platonic text?

Sic. Yes. Basically. But there is one further detail which does not primarily concern the Platonic text but rather Frere Jacques' evolution in his appropriation of the Platonic text.

Non: To what do you refer?

Sic: Back in 1968 and the time of "Plato's Pharmacy" Derrida -- basically following Heidegger in this regard -- has a rather univocal view of the Tradition. In "Plato's Pharmacy" Derrida does recognize that the Platonic text is very much and very playfully alive to "differance." Yet the Derrida of this period still holds that univocal view of the Tradition in which it is Plato who is also the inaugurator of phnono/logo-centrism and its suppression of "differance." Thus, in 1968, even while according to Plato a certain position of privilege realtive to "differance", compared to the subsequent "Tradition", Derrida still presents a Plato who sets in motion the "differance"-suppressing motif characteristic of "phono-logo-centrism." In contrast, by 1987 -- (one thinks of his 1986 "Comment ne pas Parler" occurring in the 1987 Psyche and his 1987 "Chora" article appearing in Poikilia: Etudes offertes a Jean-Pierre Vernant) -- Derrida begins to exhibit some understanding that the kind of thing being done in the Platonic text and the kind of thing inaugurated by Aristotle are different in kind and that they cannot be subsumed under one univocal understanding of what they -- i.e., Plato on the one hand and the Aristotelian-launched "Tradition" on the other hand -- are doing relative to "differance."

Non: And what about after 1987?

Sic: Don't you remember? For a number of reasons, some of them emotional rather than rational, Johanna, Jude and all the others stopped reading Derrida. They read, of course translations of things from 1987 and prior which translations were produced posterior to 1987. Likewise they re-read even today some of these 1987-and-prior writings of Frere Jacques. But after 1987, Frere Jacques is a closed book as far as this book is concerned.

> *{{{{{Mort: Should we also bring up for the persevering reader who remains with us that business about Derrida completely missing what this book calls Plato's "ontological dualism"?*
>
> *Jude: No doubt that is essential. It explains why Johanna came to be so confident in bypassing Derrida after 1987. For despite all of his emerging nuance concerning "khora", "the good", and "the third" (both in his "Chora" article and in his "Comment ne pas Parler" article) it was clear that Derrida was -- congenitally, so to speak, because of his "deconstructionistic" stance towards dualistic pairings -- destined to miss both the existence of and significance of this "ontological dualism" which more than any other factor makes the Platonic enterprise so radically different from the Aristotelian-launched "Tradition." Yes, this is a most important point. But let us trust our persevering reader to have picked up something from the main portion of this book. This goddam "caesura" -- which is now one in name only -- is way too long already.*
>
> *Mort: OK by me, Jude. By the way, how are you feeling these days? Do you have those manic episodes under control?*
>
> *Jude: Thanks for asking. I do fine with the medication. But I worry about Johanna.}}}}}*

Non: Thank-you for reminding me. Now may I say that our task is completed?

Sic: Yes. Indeed.

Bappy: Yes?

Dewchee: Is it clear that the breaking from aisthesis is not Aristotelian "abstraction"? ((I.e., that it is not "qua-ing"; i.e., that it is not that "separ-ABLE-but-not-separate" motif discussed earlier;)) Is it also clear that the Aristotleian account of the formation of concepts (universals) in the soul does not catch what Plato is doing in this turning away from aisthesis.

Bappy: You refer, of course, to the famous account of these things in Posterior Analytics, Book II, Chapter 19.

Dewchee: Correct. When Aristotle is fully understood on these matters -- and that would entail a careful reading of De Anima III, Chapters Four through Eight, along with the Chapter from Posterior Analytics which you have already cited -- one finds that for Aristotle there really is no break at all from aisthesis in the formation of concepts. The Tradition -- always using Aristotle's version of what a Platonic form must have been for Plato as a prism through which the Platonic text is filtered -- unconsciously assumes that Plato does Aristotelianesque sorts of things relative to aisthesis in coming up with the forms and further that he, Plato, does these Aristotelianesque sorts of things poorly and naively. In doing this, the Tradition closes itself off from any undersanding at all of what a Platonic form is.

Bappy: Is there to be any corrective for this terrible scandal?

Dewchee: At the very least we can repeat Johanna's parodying mantra on these matters.

Bappy: I remember! The one where she parodies Aristotle's De Anima teaching concerning the formation of concepts in the soul. Let me cite it:

Nothing comes to be in the mind/soul unless it first is NOT!!!!! in sensation!

Always the break from sensation.

Also, should we not add on -- just as a precaution for that other possible way of misreading what Plato is speaking about relative to sensation -- that the Platonic break from sensation ought not be construed as some kind of Hegelianesque "sublation" of sensation?

Dewchee: That is correct as well.

Bappy: OK. In all respects it is now clear that Plato's break-from-aisthesis account is not to be understood in terms of any paradigm on these matters taken from the Aristotelian or Hegelian text. Fair Enough. Now, what was that other point in the Phaedo which you wish us to tarry over be fore we move on to Theaetetus and its conceptual account of that -- aisthesis -- which must be broken away from?

Dewchee: Did it not yet occur to you to pause on this "eclipse of the sun" image which Plato is using in this passage?

Bappy: I realize that Frere Jacques has tarried over this image. Was that your point?

Dewchee: No. Not at all. Johanna has great interest in Frere Jacques and sometimes even great interest in what Frere Jacques has to say about Plato. But not here. For now just forget about Frere Jacques and those kinds of things and just tarry over the image itself.

Bappy: Come to think about it the image did give me pause. After all, this is Plato. Book VI of the Republic. The Sun. Book VII. The Cave allegory. But then I figured it was just co-incidence.

Dewchee: There are no co-incidences.

Bappy: OK. But why an eclipse of the sun?

Dewchee: Indeed. And the need to turn away from an eclipse of the sun lest we hurt our eyes. Imagine, then, the greater need to turn our gaze away from the sun itself. And furthermore -- if you read Plato's qualification of his own image in this Phaedo passage (at 99E,7 to 100A,3) -- as not only the only way to study an eclipse but a way superior than what we would get if we did study the eclipse directly.

Bappy: And yet the whole thrust of the Cave allegory is to get to gaze directly at the sun itself! Do you suppose that the Plato of the Republic had simply forgotten what he had said about sun-related matters in Phaedo?

Dewchee: Not likely. This is Plato. The obsessive/compulsive par excellence when it came to his writings.

Bappy: Then what is the story?

Dewchee: Many would bypass the issue by pointing out that the "seeing" to be done outside of the Cave refers to a noetic seeing and not the kind of "seeing" which would have to turn away from an eclispse of the sun.

Bappy: Your phrasing indicates that you hold a reservation against this way of trying to square the Cave allegory with our Phaedo passage.

Dewchee: Oh, it's not impossible that Plato would throw a crumb or two of an apparent coherency to that crowd which is determined to bypass the esoteric in Plato. Yet such a way of squaring the Phaedo passage and the Cave Allegory is exactly incoherent with every other feature of the carefully crafted allegory.

Bappy: How so?

Dewchee: In every respect except gazing at the sun Plato is careful to underline the parallelism between "seeing" (as aisthesis) and "seeing" (as noesis). Thus what is not parallel in noetic "seeing" to 'aisthetic' "seeing" is not really explained by citing the two different kinds of "seeing" involved since in every other respect the the kinds of "seeing" are portrayed as exactly parallel. Plato is inviting the careful reader to probe further.

Bappy: And?????

Dewchee: You know. Johanna made such a big deal of this all throughout her book of which we, in this conversation, have now become part.

Bappy: I remember: 507A. The sun as the "offspring/interest" of the good. The sun as a necessarily false image of the good. The sun as the inevitably false image of the good. Light -- that THIRD thing!!!!! of 507D -- which is un-seen allowing for vision at all and even allowing the sun to be seen at all even though the sun is the source and cause of light. This child is father to the man and all that. Listen

Have a care lest I deceive you unintentionally with a false reckoning of the

interest [offspring -- tokou].

Dewchee: Yes. That is the citation of citations on these matters. But we do not have to dwell on this at the present time. Johanna has done her work well in the other parts of this book. Now that we have alerted the reader to this we are free to move on to Theaetetus.

Bappy: By all means. Aisthesis in Theaetetus.

{{{{{{{{{{{{johanna speaking look what they're doing to my song!!! they will ruin it if they are not careful!!!!!!! jude speaking nonsense, johnanna they are your best allies whether you know it or not they say things better than you sometimes johanna speaking i know you're always right but i want to break in for some clarification good as they are they're making me nervous jude speaking well it's your book you're in charge do whatever you want i don't think you'll lose too many readers johanna speaking ha! ha! HA! very funny did you think i wouldn't get your point? having no readers to begin with i risk nothing in this digression relative to losing any of my readers jude speaking i'm sorry why don't you just get on with it after all like many (but certainly not all!!!) digressions this digression may well be intrinsic for explaining what they are trying to explain in that from which this is a digression johanna speaking ok here goes be prepared i may do some staccato action on you jude speaking nothing would surprise me coming from you johanna speaking

two nodal points

in the first place cratylus his first teacher intricasies of aisthesis and correlative need to turn away from aisthesis by turning to "logos/discourse/concept tous logous tois logois logon all in and around 99E-100A (and yes for all those babies who can't bear to speak of Plato without doing their honorific number relative to "Socrates" yes this move from Cratylus was probably mediated through the influence of "Socrates" and his kind of stubborn "what is__________" kind of questionning ok babies???? are you happy????) all of this is done to sustain the intuitively held feeling by this aristocles-disguised-as-"Plato" that the famous cratylean silence/skepticism/"pointing" notwithstanding there could be a meaning for episteme which is not totally reducible to opinion (and without which sophistry could always hold sway) (read carefully the argument of Timaeus precisely on this point at Timaeus 51D-52A just when he is on the verge of introducing the "khora" teaching) aristocles has the eleatic stranger say all of this most succinctly at Sophist 260A (Cornford):

to rob us of discourse [logon] would be to rob us of philosophy

<[{(suddenly as might happen in a dream mort-amy-siggy-devere-eurydice-sic-non-bappy-dewchee and all the other friends of johanna and jude as in a mass trance a kind of "dis-associative" psychosis start chanting: we see the "friends of the forms" we must really become the "friends of the forms" it's more than simply getting the needed stability without which there can be no discourse ((and of course it's more than showing how "forms" blend and intercourse with each other and with "knowledge" we don't have to re-invent the wheel forged in sophist (even as we simultaneously acknowledge that the "samness/difference" passages of sophist will have to be fine-tuned in parmenides))) much more the break the break from asithesis it generates for God's sake! the conditions for the possibility of discourse (logos) the break from aisthesis getting in contact with the "other" (of the other) so as to return to asithesis with an adequate road-map {{{already in the pre-pre-history of our species the break was going on as voice/sound discrimination came to be "wired in" (so to speak) over self-selective time but in those "Cratylean" days of yore the name(-law)-giver (o)NOM(a) (thank-you, Julia Julia of the spirits) gave names when and as the "break" which was always there functioned mostly biologically

and quite inadequately}}}   always the need to re-break from aisthesis   always the correlative need to re-turn to aisthesis   and what occurs in the break from aisthesis? it's all there   in phaedo as well as in sophist   "tous logous"   "tois logois" "logon"   nothing without the break from aisthesis   now we are the "true" "friends of the forms"   an invisible bond   and not everyone will understand suddenly   as might happen in a dream   the trance   the chant   seems seems   to end   and they are dispersed>]})

in the second place   nostalgia   belief in some "meta"   ("somewhere my love") ("somewhere   there's a place for us")   some "au dela"   some "beyond"   an "elsewhere"   some ethereal region where wholeness obtains where beauty has not died paradise lost and regained even before the christian version of this paradigm   that which has always been the powerful attraction of plato for romantics of any age   the "eros" teaching of Phaedrus is in the service of this grand exercise in and of nostalgia   ((but not, necessarily, the "eros" teaching of Symposium   the tension between Symposium **the third dialogue of the third tetralogy** *and that "obiter dicta", Phaedrus   <<he couldn't let it go   the romantic yen was too strong>>   for those who have the eyes to hear and the ears to see))*

the two poles of his thought   joined boldly together while he was still relatively young in his dialogue-writing career   (((which   by the way   probably only began after 387   but i don't want to go to the mats on this)))   at 92D-E of Phaedo   the forms and the theory of recollection   ah but the tension!   to pursue the forms is to pursue   be swallowed up by a difference-oriented way of thinking   cratylus remains even and precisely after the break from aisthesis!!!!!   it probably   at times   drove plato over the edge   Theaetetus   (the most beautiful account of knowledge is that knowledge is knowledge of difference   209E   only apparently refuted for those who know how to read that aporetic and maieutic dialogue)   Sophist whose apogee is the meditation on the fifth kind   difference   and   of course Parmenides   the very delirium OF difference   Phaedo foolishly thinks it has out-foxed the tension   but what was joined together in Phaedo did come to be split asunder

had the two stayed joined together Plato would have been the first guy doing the "meta-ta-phusika" move   (in today's parlance he would have been the first and most decisive of the metaphysians of "full presence")   aristotle would have been vindicated in his reading   a reading which in I-9 of Metaphysics in fact cites ONLY the Phaedo!!!!!   in his reading of what plato must have meant by a "form"   if the two had stayed joined together aristotle would have been vidciicated yet again   for   with this "meta-ta-phusika" reading of what a platonic form must have been for plato it becomes clear that IF the move to "separate substance" (in the "meta-ta-phusika" sense) is to be made at all   it is cogent to do it aristotle's way   (confer the ending of VII-16 of Metaphysics with its implied reference to the 47?/49?/55? secondary prime movers)   rather than Plato's rather naive and babyish way of finding separate substances all over the place even more numerous than sensible substances

how fucking convenient   to "invent" Platonism in your account of what Plato was doing and than to "do" Platonism better than the one to whom you attribute "platonism"   you created a "win/win" situation for yourself

all of this   the double vindication of aristotle   had the two poles of Plato's thought stayed together

but aristotle never understood the turmoil always bubbling within aristocles the master always maintained a brooding skepticism about these "forms" a song a chant a dream listen to how it is put in Cratylus at 439C-D:

> Consider, my amazing Cratylus, this matter about which I often dream *[emphasis mine, je]*. Shall we assert -- or not -- that there is beauty itself or goodness itself or any of the other "beings" by themselves?

and of course that query from Timaeus which we have turned into a mantra of sorts:

> Are we talking idly whenever we say that there is such a thing as an intelligible form of anything? Is this nothing more than a word?

the jig was up with the death of Dion as far as maintaining this tension plato let lapse the forms notice for example the absence of "form" language from the cosmologies of laws/epinomis in contrast to the infusion of "form" language (ousia, sameness, difference) all over the place in the cosmology of Timaeus (written presumably just before the news of Dion's assassination reached aristocles) only with a grim determination which allows for that playfulness to return which is the soil for discourse about the forms he forges towards the very end of his life Philebus ("youth") so that Parmenides will be properly linked to Symposium (the third dialogue of the third tetralogy)

jude speaking forget aristotle for now and what he will have brought about on these things stay just with the issue can these two poles be successfully linked? johannna speaking not really once difference is discovered and the germ of difference was already present in the genesis doctrine of his teacher Cratylus the "meta-ta-phusika" move is foreclosed the turn away from aisthesis (which itself is already made possible by/through a difference orientation) cannot really be sustained is it is fused unto the "meta-ta-phusika" move [[please understand my cherished reader with aristotle in contrast to our aristocles there never really was a break from aisthesis as has been noted so very often in this book]] *plato did try to graft the two together in that Phaedo passage we just cited through the theory of recollection and what happens? what happens when it comes time to pursue more carefully the difference orientation which makes possible the forms? recollection disappears from his account of knowledge in Theaetetus and is absent in Sophist and Parmenides as well recollection is compatible with the meta/beyond/au dela/elsewhere nostalgia pole of plato's thinking and thus is still alive and well in Phaedrus but no longer used for questions of aisthesis nor used for the analysis of what we are in touch with in and through the break from aisthesis*

the deep irony in all of this the sustained "meta-ta-phusika" (i.e., "full presence" and difference-fleeing) move was made by aristotle who was in fact less decisively animated by that meta/beyond/au dela/elsewhere motif of the romantic aristocles will anyone understand?

it is hard to say signing off

but jude still speaking there is still this thought nothing to do with aristotle and the aristotelian launched "tradition" rather it just deals with the two poles of plato's thought quite independent of what happened when all of this was appropriated by aristotle the romantic motif the yen (the yen????? the piercing desire!!!!!) for the "au dela" "somewhere my love" where wholeness obtains untarnished beauty **{{{{{here it comes dear reader the whole ball of wax the secret of the whole fucking book** *the original impulse is back to mommy but then the great interruption the break the break which throws one back to the putative other of the other (and this too is good it allows us to dream it allows what is mystical in the mixture to have its proper effect on us but we destroy the vocation of thinking if we tarry there for we would be tarrying where there is no-place to tarry) Kristeva understood even if she didn't articulate it the best the powers the powers the powers* **of HORROR Horror** *Mommy is castrated Mommy is castrated the gap the chasm the first cognizance of difference (and of course it's the counter-factual fact the primacy of deception haven't you been reading the book?) what we seek that prior wholeness of blissful (in utero) memory that prior unity what we fashion will be untanished/unfragmented beauty* **is displaced away from Mommy** *"the good" "the offspring"* **takes refuge in the character of the beautiful** *(Philebus 64E) it affected every conceptual move he ever made even when he engaged the "Mother" (and he was the only one among the philosophers to have done it) he was conflicted and ready to take refuge this is Plato's failure* **for there is nothing in which or by which to take refuge IN the mixture the one beauty MUST fragment and lose its purity** *(indeed it is eternally in the situation the condition of always and already having been fragmented)* **for the sake of the good** *one must return again to the Mother for the Mother must prevail in the mixture in the third it is the fifth which prevails and this is good plato struggled with this the only one he did make love with the mother but he did not marry her for the marry her is to become her his nostalgia for the killed father was too great too often he let "the good"* **take refuge in the character of the beautiful}}}}}** *but she who stays with the vocation of thinking (which nonetheless must be awakened by this romantic motif this romantic yen this piercing!!! desire) comes to transverse the harshest lesson of all tortured teleology beauty which must die wholeness which must be shattered for the very sake of the good itself in some sense johnny keats (i don't think he even came to see his twenty-sixth birthday!!!!) was a more complete platonist than plato himself Ah! jude still speaking i come now to understand the mania section of this book signing off*

Ojective observer speaking the turn towards cosmology was a problem for Plato especially since the trilogy which his cosmology inaugurated in which the appropriate nuances and contextualization for these things could have been made {{{{{indeed one wonders whether Timaeus itself had ever been put into its final form the playfulness of its beginning (plato seems to be on a manic high for Dion has now come to power perhaps unadvisedly but he has DONE it!!! no wonder the opening of Timaeus centers on Republic aristocles is now really off and running life is outstripping art but we will catch up!) is not sustained as that writing becomes mostly a a rather dry and ponderous monologue yes Critias was inaugurated with his usual verve a jumping ahead with anticipation with the plan to go back and spruce up what was mostly a first draft of emerging Timaeus then came the news from Syracuse}}}}} this turn forced the Academy without the benefit of Plato's own guidance on these matters to move away from the dialectical orientation of "the forms" to that more mundane "theory of reality" kind of orientation in which the author of Epinomis doing it his way and years later still inspired by the author of Epinomis aristotle doing it his way astonomy becomes theology

yes a nice "real" story in phaedo that's OK the first hint of getting story and "account" conflated in BooK X of republic but still a story then Timaeus a bit too serious (but we probably do not have what would have been plato's final verison of Timaeus had the trilogy project not been cut short by the news from Syracuse) even so the Timaeus account is still infused with form language with Sophist/Parmenides language the circles of ousia, sameness and difference and in its structual center the part dealing with "khora" the whole cosmology is made to turn on that condition for the possibility i.e., khora itself of the forms

then the news arrives from Syracuse the broken vessels first draft not even put in its final form (a secretary to make what would be the as it was to turn out final copy of Timaeus) the rupture plato dies before he even dies retires as head of academy even before he retires as head of the academy vacuum created the old depressed man going back to the shards of incomplete projects philebus performing one function laws performing the other function and did you notice? the disappearance (wihout dis-appearing) of form-language from the cosmologies of laws and epinomis (epinomis a dying old man too depressed and no longer able physically to write for himself taking his form-bereft theological astronomy a bit too seriously dictating it in a kind of deperation and who knows what editing after the old man died) oh yes form language is present in philebus the final tetralogical ordering was being done it wouldn't be what he would have wanted had the timaeus-critias-hermocrates trilogy been completed but something had to be done so that there would be a trace of the original intention to be sure Symposium would have to remain as it had always been intended **the third dialogue of the third tetralogy** *but the finesse would now have to be sacrificed how to show the connection between the dialectical unpacking of "the forms" and the doctrine of "the good" contained in Symposium the old man now no longer worrying about the day to day affairs of the academy created philebus ("youth"!!!!!) as the connecting link between Parmenides and Symposium in the final tetralogical arrangment oh yes something like the Laws would still have to take the place of what would have been beneficial about critias/hermocrates let there now be an "Athenian Stranger"!!!!! but ultimately as "obiter dicta" listen from Letter VII at 344C emphasis mine (oo):*

> In a word, it is an inevitable conclusion from that that when anyone sees anwhere the written work of anyone, whether that of a lawgiver in his laws or whatever it may be in some other form, the subject treated cannot have been his most serious concern --- [according to Post]

{{{of course there would have to be this seventh letter this "apology" for aristocles he didn't want to write it but his followers one thinks especially of speusippus prevailed on him what would be the verdict of history after all he had launched something the academy indeeed the very life of philosophy which was bigger than himself the arua of suspicion would have to be lifted it would only be proper so he wrote it slying inserting a clever reference to the "five" which the cognescendi would understand sending them here to certain nodal points of parmenides there to the five great "kinds" of Sophist and there again to the four-but-really-five classes 23D-E of philebus and also the "eksaiphnes" hint at 341C, 9 <<<Loeb lining as always>>> {{would we even push the "hoi erotomenoi hupo ton erotonton" at 343C, 10-344A, 1 if we were to allow ourselves the

Cratyleanesque latitude which aristocles allowed for himself inCratylus in matters of word-etymology? for those who have the eyes to hear and the ears to see}}

ah yes!!!! laws republic even timaeus these would be for public consumption but at least while i'm alive the serious writings on serious matters i speak, of course, of parmenides especially no one can say they have seen them for they were not for public consumption

> Besides, this at any rate I know, that if there were to be a treatise or lecture on this subject, I could do it best. [according to Post] *}}}*

but basically plato's day was over when the news arrived from syracuse the day the music died and even today especially today!!!! one is at a loss for reconstructing all that was in the genius mind of plato and what could have evolved if Sophist/Statesman/Parmenides had been allowed to have danced with a playfully completed Timaeus/Critias/Hermocrates the day the music died plato retires and what happens?

speusippus first of all still some play of difference in plato's nehpew but tries to make the dialectical teaching of "the forms" respectable after all "theory of reality" is replacing "Dialectic" after 354/353 especially by mathmatizing the whole project and by introducing a bit of quasi-evolution into this whole schema of things now that after plato himself had taken (but not finished) the turn towards comology-with-forms (i.e., Timaeus) cosmological kinds of things permeate the whole project

{{{{{and let us not forget Eudoxus by himself an uncomplex guy with a good mathmatical head the problem was with those second rate philosophers speusippus xenocrates and even aristotle now that the master had left them in the lurch by going into his depression eudoxus was the archetype for """""science""""" in the modern sense without intending to his mathmatical head gave everyone around him (and maybe even plato himself) an inferiority complex today eudoxus would be a hubble-satellite kind of guy doing the big bang kind of stuff and the kind of guy without intending to who would scare off philosophical types from talking about quantum mechanics since he could and they couldn't do the actual equations involved so there was this turn towards cosmology on the part of the master then when the news from Syracuse arrives he withdraws and creates a terrible vacuum especially for a bunch of air-heads who have an inferiority complex relative to this guy who is both doing the Euclidean stuff before Euclid and at the same time mapping out for God's sake! the whole fucking geo-centric universe!!! the inferiority complex wins speusippus who was the best of a poor lot now that aristocles had left the fray leads the pack good-bye playfully precise Dialectic! good-bye the playfully exhuberant attitude towards doing cosmology after one returns to aisthesis having accomplished the systematics (the Parmenides) which presuppose the all-important break from aisthesis yes good-bye to all of that hello the oh-SO-serious "theory of reality"!!! speusippus (and later on xenocrates) with a mathmaticized account of "the forms" others (including the dying plato) let "the forms" go entirely in any case it is now "theory of reality" time for philosophy they should have let it be and just left it for guys like eudoxus ah the bittersweet after-effects of intellectual inferiority complexes!!!!! and of course the irony as reported by aristotle was it Chapter Two or Chapter Three of Nichomachean Ethics X? (one of those chapters is on speusippus and one of them is on eudoxus) eudoxus was anything but a heavy hitter when he took his turn at bat doing philosophy}}}}}

the dying plato unfaithful to the living/playful plato enters the fray with an only-serious turn just before he dies part of the somberness of laws is explained in this fashion and of course the theological astronomy of epinomis it is the dying plato unfaithful to the living plato who throws into deep ambiguity the question as to who properly maintains the legacy of the master later there is baby xenocrates ((he too was said to have been a lover of plato one wonders did he catch or pitch or both?)) who left as did aristotle when speusippus took over when the old man finally gave up the ghost no longer attuned to the play of difference does the shoddiest of all mathmatical numbers on "the forms" when leadership of the academy falls to him in 339 only eight years after his death "platonism" has become an intellectual embarrassment

then partly before the time of Xenocrates partly during it and certainly after he had become well settled in the lyceum it is aristotle's turn but no longer are these things done at the academy

first there is aristotle-in-transition the chapters in <u>Metaphysics</u> when he still calls himself a "we" relative to the "Platonists" and of course wonderfully pre-emptive <u>Categories</u> in which it is effectively established that <u>if</u> there are "separate forms" for anything there are separate forms only for "ousia" (substance) where ousia functions as the "hupokeimenon" term par excellence (<u>of course Categories</u> doesn't say this is so many words but <u>read it</u> for God's sake) this is also time time period when speaking for "we Platonists" aristotle claims that they i.e., "we Platonists" do not maintain that there are forms for artifacts (like "rings and houses") this brash aristotle-in-transition even cites but does not give a reference for some alleged statement by plato himself that there are just as many forms as "natural kinds" (i.e., "species") could the post-cosmological plato have said something to that effect? a very tired old man no longer animated by the playfulness which is the necessary condition for the differnce-imbued "theory of forms" indeed even a plato who was the writer of <u>timaeus</u> could have said something like this if his words were taken out of context but please listen the famous <u>Bed Itself</u> the "true" bed of Republic-X i.e., an artifact is the quintessential form and listen to the words even of the old man when he wrote Letter VII (at 342D):

> the same doctrine holds good in regard to shapes and surfaces, both straight and curved, <u>in regard to the good and the beautiful and the just</u> *[empahsis mine, oo]*, in regard to all bodies artificial and natural, in regard to fire and water and the like, and in regard to every animal, and in regard to every quality of character, and in respect to all states active and passive. *[according to Post]*

so what's the real story? just this "the theory of forms" is anything but a "theory of reality" this has been discussed in the non-caesura sections of johanna's book after plato made the cosmological turn and particularly after <u>plato's</u> form-imbued turn towards cosmology had stalled and found itself <u>dead</u>-in-the-water (i.e., after plato "died" about five or six years before he died having heard the news from Syracuse) it was inevitable that discourse about the forms would be taken up in the context of a "theory of reality" kind of orientation one can almost discern the <u>condescension</u> in the voice of this aristotle-in-transition when he refers to this charming theroy of the now dead master the story obtaining between aristotle and plato is the oldest story ever told

and please note (you can use <u>Metaphysics I</u>, Chapter Nine at 990b from about 15 to 25 <since Loeb lining i have just discovered reamins faithful to the lining of the Greek text from which it is taken rather than to the actual "lines" in the Loeb> as a reference for this) this aristotle-in-transition <u>still</u> believes in the <u>two</u> first principles of the forms even as he critiques the forms a lesson here for those who are oh-so-certain that Plato's "good" of <u>Republic VI/VII</u> is not itself the product of a Mother and Father how conveniently the testimony of aristotle is ignored when it challenges the received way of reading Plato

and then the voice of a "mature" aristotle who is now quite comfortable with what he has done relative to the master <u>he</u> now gets to play magister ludi not at the academy but at the lyceum finding his <u>own</u> voice and dancing his <u>own</u> dance with no-one no-one at all not speusippus not xenocrates to hold him for downs since he <u>really was</u> "the *youngest of all" (((((<u>Parmenides</u> 137B-C of course plato hedges his bet by having identified this "aristoteles" as one of the infamous "thirty" (at 127D) just in case perhaps due to "tukhe" (after-all this young colt this aristoteles just might die or something before he would come to hit his stride) just in case the <u>significance</u> would come to have been lost of having his most famous written exercise (i.e., the eight hypotheses) come forth as the interplay between his own son this young colt aristoteles and his father "father parmenides" {{{and bye the bye, dear reader plato did the oedipal thing as well but in <u>his</u> special and most filial way in the <u>sophist</u> of course by having <u>the eleatic STRANGER himself</u> kill off the <u>already-false-but-popular</u> IMAGE of "father Parmenides" so that the correct kind of homage could be paid to the father in the dialogue that would bear his name <u>aristoteles</u> would become in time something of a euthyphro <u>aristocles</u> in contrast had far more filial respect filial respect in the very midst of conceptual palyfulness for those who have the eyes to hear and the ears to see}}}))))) he the stagirite gets to marinate memory his way <u>unchallenged</u> he writes his novel "The Way Things Were" ((i.e., <u>Metaphysics Alpha</u>, Chapters Three through Seven with the climax coming in Chapter Six preceded by (i.e., Chapters One and Two) that self-congratulatory homily on "sophia")) the first historical novel <u>unchallenged</u> because they are no longer around or at least the few who are still around do not have his stature <u>unchallenged</u> by this time he has all his ducks lined up (and they are not without subtlety!) matter/form/privation the domestication of "dunamis" along with the correlative unveiling of "energeia/entelecheia" the whole hupokeimenon motif from <u>Categories</u> in particular and the Organon in general the lingering even if begruding respect of even those still loyal to plato for having transformed plato's play-imbued Collection and Division into the oh-<u>so</u>-serious-and-quite-respectable syllogistic bringing in its wake the dislogding of "dialectic" as first philosophy this guy was no slacker after all he not only single-handedly invented what would become "the Tradition" he managed as well to have "father aristocles" cast as the inaugurator of aristotelianesque things who did these aristotleianesque things naively and simplistically this "mature" aristotle who is no longer in transition became a force to be reckoned with*

creative-but-wholesale re-invention a re-casting a re-production a <u>new</u> and cocky director who was now <u>unchallenged</u> in his version of events after all he still had the testimony of <u>Phaedo</u> (which was one of those "public" -- i.e., """written""" -- dialogues) of what plato <u>must</u> have meant when plato generated "the forms" daring to speak in the name of the master inventing platonism according to the "phusika/meta-ta-phusika" frame of reference which he oedipal aristotle had created for himself for asking questions inventing "platonism" twice! first by giving the account still with us today even by people who never read the stagirite of what plato must have been doing when plato generated the forms then having invented platonism <u>doing</u> "platonism" even better than plato had (allegedly) done it by reserving the (soi-disant) "meta-ta-phusika" move only for those "separate substances" which would be relevant for <u>his</u> Monotheistic theological astronomy let's face it the whole thing got pretty ugly with oedipal aristotle ((((and please recall that Oedipus -- I mean the one in the play of Sophocles -- did not recognize his own father as he was killing him and would have denied killing his own father and yes there <u>is</u> some irony the Oedipus Rex *is Aristotle's paradigm of excellence)))) it is the legacy of oedipal aristotle which even today governs the reading of plato*

{{{given the chaos which obtained in the academy from the death of Dion up through and beyond the reign of Xenocrates it's no wonder that aristotle's account of these things should come to be normative even and especially for those **[sic!!!]** *"neo-platonists" who thought they were speaking in the name of plato and who even here and there took pains to denounce the stagirite on this or that point and to disassociate themselves from the stagirite oedipal aristotle who like every other version of oedipus did not understand what he was doing to his father when he did to his father what he did to his father was the one son who really got away with it without consequences almost that is until johanna came along}}}*

the day the music died

{{{even so

in the process he created "Plato-and-Aristotle" true unlike plato relative to "father Parmenides" aristotle did not kill off a false image of plato in order to honor him (i.e., plato) in his (i.e., aristotle's) first philosophy (as plato had done having killed off the false image of "father Parmenides" in Sophist honors him in Parmenides) on the contrary aristotle creates a false image of plato so that he may honor himself (i.e., aristotle) in his (i.e., aristotle's) first philosophy

even so in the process he created "Plato-and-Aristotle"

by the time xenocrates had come to be in charge of things "platonism" had come to be an intellectual embarrassment this was partly due to the mixed messages which the depressed old man himself had given to his contesting followers (and aristotle due to his relative youth was not yet a major player at this point even though he was already recognized as the "mind" of the academy) who knows what would have become of those thirty-five dialogues and collection of letters had not a frame of reference been created which would bring some stability in the way they were appropriated does it matter that the frame of reference mis-construes the master? what is important is that there be some stabilizing even if falsifying frame of reference the most conservative of conservative instituions is "academia" it abhors chance, uncertainty and ambiguity by its nature it gravitates towards (indeed generates!) ideology be it of the "right" or of "the left" so as to kill off all ambiguity all under the guise of a search for """""truth""""" "academia" was not birthed in plato's Academy not at least while aristocles-disguised-as-plato was at the helm plato was far too deeply ambiguous he is the author of every "radical" teaching but not of ideology for radical "ideas" become boringly pedestrian when they are taken up by people who gravitate towards ambiguity-negating ideology no rather "academia" is birthed in aristotle's lyceum

would athens in fact have sinned twice against philsoophy? it's hard to say he left before the proposition could have been tested but there's another more relevant question did he who fled athens a year before he died sin twice against philsophy? doubtlessly and in the process he successfully cryonicized the body so that it could live another day the deep deep irony the kind which is fully unconscious of itself of the stagirite}}} signing off}}}}}}}}}}}}}}}}

Dewchee: So, my friend, just what shall we say about the analysis of aisthesis in Theaetetus?

Bappy: The bottom line is this. Aisthesis, when it is all said and done, is not knowledge.

Dewchee: Good. That is one of the both real and ostensible conclusions to this aporetic/maieutic dialogue. But what is aisthesis according to Theaetetus? You only told me what Theaetetus tells us it is not.

Bappy: As you know, whenever "Socrates" reviews aisthesis he always speaks in the name of someone else. Like Protagoras, for example.

Dewchee: That is correct. And who does "Socrates" see behind this veil of "Protagoras"? What is the "truth" which lies beneath the Truth of Protagoras?

Bappy: Those Cratyleanesque Heracliteans. In this regard, Dewchee, I believe it would be good if we alrerted our readers to keep at their side some critical passages in which the teachings of these Cratyleanesque Heracliteans are put forth.

Dewcheee: That is a very useful idea. To what passages do you refer?

Bappy: 152D-E is important. 155E through 157C is <u>especially</u> important. And 160B-C is relevant as well.

Dewchee: Good work, Bappy. And if our readers are too lazy not to get up and have these passages at hand as they keep up with us then they are not worthy readers and we ought not be concerned with them. Now -- to get back to our argumentation -- what do these Cratyleanesque Heracliteans say about aisthesis?

Bappy: They speak, to put it bluntly, about "fucking." They speak of a ceaseless and incredibly rapid generating and destroying of "offspring" and children. A ceaseless and incredibly rapid process by which "parents" -- here a mother there a father, but with mother becoming father and father becoming mother and and each becoming offspring and the whole whirling process being dependent upon myriads upon myriads of differing perpsectives and rapid interactions from which these instantaneous and ceaseless "fuckings" and "offspringings" appear to be taking place -- generate "offspring."

Dewchee: Does this "fucking/intercoursing/coupling/parenting" language remind you of anything?

Bappy: One cannot help but think of Eros.

Dewchee: And all of this "parenting" and "offspringing"?

Bappy: Well, even though the terminology is different, my mind wanders to the funny line in <u>Symposium</u> (199D) which Johanna kept bringing to our attention. Listen:

> *My question is not whether he* [eros] *is love of mother or father -- how absurd* [geloion: laughable; silly; <u>comic</u>!!!] *it would be to ask whether Love is love of mother or father!*

Dewchee: Ah yes! Memories. The father and "offspring/interest" (tokos) of <u>Republic VI</u>.

> *Have a care, however, lest I deceive you unintentionally with a false reckoning of the interest* [offspring].

Memories. Father <u>and</u> Mother. Plenty and Poverty. So to speak. Love <u>of</u> Mother and Father. The double meaning of the genitive. The way in which Love and the Good are each other while always being other from each in that magical (and decidedly non-Hegelian) dance by which the object of desire is found to be desir(e)-**ING!!!!**

Bappy: Please Dewchee! You scare me when you start to get carried away like that. You begin to remind me of Jude back then before he went into the hospital and of Johanna and how she sometimes gets now. Please! It scares me.

Dewchee: You're right, Bappy. Thanks for reigning me in. But still, this <u>Theaetetus</u> account of perception is one which resonates with much that is important win the Platonic text. Is this not so?

Bappy: I think you are right. And these <u>Theaetetus</u> passages are haunting in yet another way. Plato has Theaetetus say to "Socrates" the following at 157C after this "Socrates" questions Theaetetus as to whether or not he, Theaetetus, endorses the Cratyleanesque account of perception. Listen:

> *Really, I am not sure, Socrates. I cannot even make out about you, whether you are stating this as something you believe or merely putting me to the test.* [according to Cornford]

Dewchee: And excellent citation for the reader to mull over. And if our reader is especially perceptive she will not dodge the suggestion that this account of perception is also <u>Plato's</u> own account of perception -- even if it remains true that perception is not knowledge -- by hiding in the midwife image by which "Socrates" responds to the implied suggestion of Theaetetus. I mean this "midwifery" stuff is great and we cannot understnd the real message of Theaetetus without it. But many people who have no clue as to what the Theaetetus is all about but who like to present themselves as understanding this most amazing dialogue take endless refuge in the midwifery motif so as not to expose their increibible ignorance concerning this portion of the Platonic text. Enough on that. We are not here for the shallow appropriators of the Platonic text. They are legion, to be sure and they hold sway in very influential places. But they are not worth our time. Let us return. Are there any other associations which you get from these Cratyleanesque passages?

Bappy: When I return to those passages I am always struck by the massive quantity of practically instantaneous connections and differentiatins which are going on in so many multiple perspectives. Even by the texts' repeated admission -- (confer 152D-E and more especially 157A-C) -- it defies expression in discourse.

Dewchee: And yet somehow it all actually is expressed in discourse, is it not?

Bappy: Yes. That is the amazing thing.

Dewchee: And pursue, please, those associations which come to you concerning those haunting, erotic, passages from Theaetetus dealing with our friend "aisthesis." You seem to be onto something important. You may use your imagination and likewise make use of your long and brooding approrpriation of the Platonic text.

Bappy: There is one special association which keeps coming up. But it's like in a dream. As soon as I analyze the association it appears to be ridiculous.

Dewchee: Listen to your dreams. Tell me about your special association.

Bappy: These aisthesis passages from Theaetetus remind me of hypothesis # 2 from Parmenides: The dyad (i.e., "one" and "ousia") which is really, upon analysis, some kind of triad (i.e., "one", "ousia", and "difference") since "difference" was really there from the beginning even though it was not initially noticed. (Parmenides at 142B-144A) It's as though the father ("one") and the offspring ("ousia") are quickly noticed in their mutual inter-relationship. After all the child really is father to the man. But the mother ("difference") -- who more than anything else really makes all the difference in the world -- was there from the very beginning and indeed the relationship between father (one) and offspring (ousia) is totally transformed when it is "seen" from the all decisive pespective of the mother (difference). I think Plato even teases us about this as he introduces this second hypothesis. Listen:

> *Shall we, then, go back to our hypothesis and reconsider it from the beginning in the hope of bringing to light some different* ["alloion" at 142B, 1-2 in the Loeb; emphasis mine, B] *result?*

Dewchee: You do have a point since all throughout the eight hypotheses the "allo" words and the "heteros" word seem practically interchangable. Indeed at 164B-C Plato has Parmenides say:

> ----- *'other' (allo) and 'different' (heteron) are two names for the same thing.* [According to Cornford]

So please continue with your intriguing association.

Bappy: Then as we go on in that swirling hypothesis we find wholes which are parts and parts which are wholes. Sameness the ground of difference and difference the ground of sameness. Containings which are also contained. Contacts which are not contacts as everything is connected to everything thorugh amazing non-contacts. Then there are those time passages. I get dizzy when I remember them. And, at least for me, the strange "eksaiphnes" teaching from hypothesis # 2a which -- with your help and Johanna's (and back before the hospital, Jude's as well) -- I have learned to read back into all the critical passages of hypothesis # 2. I get a Dionysian -- indeeed both more and less than a Dionysian dizzyness -- dizzynesss when I go through hypothesis # 2. And yet.

Dewchee: And yet what?

Bappy: How incredibly silly of me to make that association at all. The aisthesis passages of Theaetetus are just that. They are analyzing aisthesis. The Parmenides is about the forms. And Plato -- through the very mouth of Parmenides himself at 135E -- makes it quite clear that the "training" of the eight hypotheses ranges not over the seen, but rather over the un-seen.

Dewchee: Hmmmmmm. Interesting. Did it ever occur to you that that Cratyleanesque aisthesis of our Theaetetus passages is un-seen as well. Aisthesis as experienced turns out to be different from "raw" aisthesis. Think about those myriads upon myriads of fuckings/couplings/intercoursings/offspringings/parentings. Is any of it seen? Yet, according to the analysis, it is going on all the time. (It might surprise a Newton, but it most certainly would not surprise a Heisenberg.) And those incredibly rapid pyramids of fire from Timaeus are not presented as seen, are they?

Bappy: You're quite right.

Dewchee: Yet they make vision possible. And there's something else.

Bappy: What is that?

Dewchee: Think again of hypothesis # 2. It's like a road-map in terms of which we do in fact speak about those unspeakable couplings and rapid changes (from our Theaetetus passages) which, when considered without such a road-map, defy discourse. {{{By the way, it is hypothesis # 7, most especially, which gives us the perspective on these happening which obtains when and as the road-map is (inevitably) eclipsed.}}}

Bappy: So what are you suggesting?

Dewchee: Just this. To get a discursive handle on aisthesis one would have to turn away from aisthesis.

Bappy: What would then appear, so to speak, when one turns away from aisthesis?

Dewchee: At first something safe and stupid. Simple word. "__________ itself." "__________ itself." Etc., etc. But then there is more. Think. What do we carry with us even as we break from aisthesis?

Bappy: You don't mean memory, do you? Memory of aisthesis?

{{{{{B: Hmmmmmmmm. Some clarification is called for. Memory of aisthesis as analyzed in Theaetetus or aisthesis as experienced?

D: Good point. Memory of aisthesis as experienced. It is to be noted that the blending and intercouring and swirling of experienced aisthesis is far more stable than what the Theaetetan conceptual analysis reveals to be the case in fact. The conceptual analysis of aisthesis presupposes -- even for a Cratylus, let alone for a Plato -- the break from aisthesis which is (as has been repeatedly noted) a turning away from aisthesis. With this distinction can you yet guess what we have arrived at?

B: Not really.

Dewchee: The shameless circle. The circle of unknowing. Listen:

> ----- Socrates: But the argument is not going to allow both alternatives. However, we must stick at nothing: suppose we try being quite shameless.
>
> Theaetetus: In what way:
>
> Socrates: By making up our minds to describe what knowing is like.
>
> Theaetetus: How is that shameless?
>
> Socrates: You seem to be unaware that our whole conversation from the outset has been an inquiry after the nature of knowledge on the supposition that we did not know what it was.
>
> Theaetetus: No, I am quite aware of that.
>
> Socrates: Then, doesn't it strike you as shameless to explaind what knowing is like, when we don't know what knowledge is? ----- *[196D-C; according to Cornford]*

B: I'm beginning to get that queasy feeling again. It's not always easy to follow you when you get into these kinds of intricasies. Already your phrase, "the circle of unknowing" has me ill at ease.

D: Persevere. The outcome will make it all worthwhile. No pain, no gain.

B: If we're going to speak in cliches I'd prefer: no brain, no pain. But let's get on with it.

D: The break from experienced aisthesis followed by the memory of experienced aisthesis leads to the conceptual analysis of aisthesis which conceptual analysis -- as we now know from our Theaetetus passages (which we have asked our cherished readers to keep at hand as they read this conversation) -- only reveals just how apparently radically false experienced aisthesis actually is. The circle of unknowing. For the origin of the conceptual analysis of asisthesis -- (which reveals the apparently radical falsity of experienced aisthesis) -- is that apparently radically false experienced aisthesis itself. The circle of unknowing. One might say, as well, "the primacy of deception."

B: The very theme of this book Shame!. But if indeed I follow your line of argumentation I see a real problem.

D: Speak your mind, by all means.

B: Is it not the case that what we are calling experienced aisthesis itself somehow emerged from "raw" (so to speak) aisthesis which "raw" aisthesis -- as the conceptual analysis of aisthesis would reveal -- is radically different from experienced aisthesis? The question then would become: what prompted this emergence at all?

D: Now we truly do approach the mystery. The break. The separation. khora khoris khorismos *The break. The separation. It is dispersed forever all throughout all. The break. The separation. It is present in chance-goverened cosmological evolution. It obtains as "space" and in the arena in which the inter-*

actions of """""reality""""" -- ((i.e., those infinite, whirling, ceaseless, number of "fuckings/copulations/intercoursings/par entings/offsprings" in which the terms (i.e., "parents") of these incredibly rapid "couplings" ceaselessly become each other and their offspring even as they ceaselessly generate offspring and all of this in every conceivable way)) -- which is the raw material, so to speak, which, one day, gives rise to experience. The break. The separation. It obtains as well in chance-goverened biological evolution. Indeed this break/separation obtains in all living things -- (allowing that even "plants" in some sense have the beginnings of some experienced aisthesis) -- and is the very mark of life. Thus experienced aisthesis is always other from "raw" (so to speak) aisthesis and this "other" (difference) is precisely that break/separation which allows there to be life at all.

B: I knew I was going to get dizzy. But continue. Everything you have said would indicate that you are now on the verge of discussing the kind of break from asithesis which was dear to Plato.

D: You are so perceptive! Yes. The break from asithesis which would constitute noesis proper. Still, the kind of break which leads to noesis proper requires -- if it is to be understood fully -- some contextualization not carried out by Plato himself.

B: The fact that our analysis of the Platonic text invovles variables not spoken of by Plato has not caused us hermeneutic pause prior to this. Forge on!

D: To make a long story short the emergence of the possibility for that special break from aisthesis which can lead to noesis proper occurs in that millenia-long nexus in which biological evolution interfaces with the beginnings of the psycho-social evolution of our species in what might be termed the pre-history of our species.

B: I saw it coming. You have merged Plato's story with Johanna's story. The very story of this book!

D: Yes! The "perception" (experienced aisthesis) of the counter-factual-fact. Mommy is castrated. Mommy is castrated. *This is the ultimate experience. This is the most dramatic break/separation of all. It is the experience which raises the primacy of deception to the decisive stage in which -- for the first time -- the decision for a conscious break from (experienced) perception can occur. The circle of unknowing -- the shameless circle which can never close -- now comes full circle. The dawn of thinking.*

B: I'm not certain that I am understanding all of this. I am following the argument. Yet I now feel more confused than ever.

D: That is OK. There needs must be some confusion. We have learned much if we understand that cognition is the shameless embrace of the most shameful deception. It was all said already in the dark passages of Timaeus. Listen:

> ----- and there is a third kind, which is space and is eternal, and admits not of destruction and provides a home for all becoming and is "caught", when all sensation is absent *[anaisthesias]*, by a discourse of questionable pedigree *[logismos tini notho]* being scarcely believable which we, beholding it as in a dream-trance ----

You are still not reading the text. Read on. Roll on to 52C. Form and participant alike -- to be at all -- must be in another. In each other. In difference realtive to themselves. The "true account" says this. As one of the two (i.e., form and participant in a form) are caught, so to speak, in discourse, the other of the two fades away into a dream-like space so that neither of the two is ever itself and its other at once. The words are there. But one cannot presume to translate this darkest of dark passages unless one learns to read this darkest of dark passages. But reading with the proper spin is not easy.

<<<<<Yes! Yes! Yes!, dear reader and don't forget what was said earlier: The more careful statement of these matters is given by Plato in hypothesis # 2 at 145B, 8-145E 8 and, more quickly, at 151A, 8-151A, 1 (Loeb lining, as always). However, even in these more exact statements of how form(s) and participants-in-(a)-forms(s) are "in" each other one must be alert to the various ways in which the ever-elusive "presence" of "difference" ("heteros") is the ever-obtaining condition for these various reciprocal "in" relationships which obtain between forms (a one) and thier participants (i.e., "the others" or the "not-ones" of a one). In other words, the casual reader will miss the very point of the "in" passages of hypothesis # 2 just as easily as she will misconstrue the 52 C passage from Timaeus. If you want my respect, dear reader, do not be a casual reader.>>>>>

<[{(-----'76 Commentary helps here:

What is different from the one (and thus is the place of the one) when "one" denotes a form-term is its many parts which are its participants. Thus to be in each, some and every of its parts and to be in none of its parts but rather to be in "difference" is to say the same from two differing perspectives. To be in "difference" means to be in what it is not in. Qua pure containing whole of parts the one is not in the sum of its parts nor in any of its parts. Yet in "difference" one is in what it is not in since the different for any given form is, concretely, the many parts which participate in it. The one as form-term is not in its parts qua pure contaiing whole of parts and is in its parts qua difference. ----

These considerations make more comprehensible the "holon vs. pan" passage at Theaetetus 204-205. In this light difference is understood as inhering in the proper object of knowledge. However, the difference inhering in any given whole is nothing in addition to any given sum of parts -- in the sense of being yet another part -- which constitutes any given whole. With such difference inhering in the proper object of knowledge, knowledge -- the relational par excellence -- is always ahead-of-itself-behind-itself in such a manner that any account of it, knowledge, is bound to be circular. But circular as it is, nothing is lacking from the final account of knowedge given at Theaetetus 209 since this "most beautiful" account of knowledge defines itself in terms of knowledge of difference. It is at once both ahead and behind itself.

((For those who have the eyse to hear and the ears to see.)) >]})

"Space/place". khora khoris khorismos *"Space/place" is difference. The dream of participation. Dream delivers us unto dream and there is no end to allusion. Deception delivers us unto deception and there is no end to the """""truth""""" which is deception.* Hos eoiken *he has father Parmenides (who has always been married by ever elusive mother Heraclitus in the genius mind of aristocles) at the end. Do you understand?:* hos eoiken *Listen:*

> It seems that, whether there is or is not a one, both that one and the others alike are and are not, and appear and do not appear to be, all manner of things in all manner of ways, with respect to themselves and to one another. Most true. *[according to Cornford]*

B: It's time to go home now. You scare me when you start getting manic on me. first Jude went over the edge. Any day Johanna will follow suit. I couldn't bear to lose you as well. Come with me and rest.

D: Yes. Rest. Rest in restlessness. And one more thing.

D: What is that?

D: Just brush my cheek before you leave me. }}}}}

Dewchee: And why not? We recall the blending, the interfusion, the differentiation, the multiplicity, the diversion, the connectedness. Memory of aisthesis (which, of course, can only be memory of experienced aisthesis), after the break from aisthesis and by virtue of the break from aisthesis is the birth of what Sophist calls "the freeman's science." (at 253C)

Bappy: You mean -- (since "dialectic" in Plato has several senses) -- "Dialectic" as used in Sophist when they start talking about combining, intercoursing, and blending the five "vowels."?

Dewchee: Ah yes: The five "vowels": Motion, Rest, Ousia, Sameness and Difference. One would be tempted to say: Apeiron, Peras, Ousia, Cause of Combination and Cause of Separation. And please notice that "difference" is fifth! Yes. That is what one would mean by "dialectic", at least as a first approximation. But the "freeman's science" does not get get its most exquisite expression in Sophist. Where does it get its most exquisite expression? Tell me, Bappy, for I am certain that you know.

Bappy: You must be referring to hypothesis # 2, of course.

Dewchee: Yes! Hypothesis # 2 and all eight hypotheses in their magnificent inter-connectedness.

Bappy: We have come quite far. And I am still fearful of our results. Your numerous suggestions seem to me to have the effect of throwing the entire Platinic enterprise into reverse.

Dewchee: Yes, in reverse. And upside down as well. Catty-corner, reverse, upside down and inside out. The "Tradition's" Plato is effectively destroyed by our undertaking. And I know your question: Is it what we have done or Plato himself who has "reversed" the "Tradition's" Plato? It is a fair question.

Bappy: And what is the answer?

Dewchee: Just this. It is "Socrates" himself who so often reminds us -- (just read the text and you shall find it scattered all throughout) -- of the affinity between play and seriousness. Admittedly, the "hermeneutical" question you have raised cannot be cognitively adjudicated. It is undecidable, cognitively. But even in the task of reading/interpreting the Platonic text Plato's own highest advice is relevant.

Bappy: What is that?

Dewchee: Eu prattein!!!!

Bappy: Does this mean we are stopping?

Dewchee: We have done some stage setting and contextualization for the Johanna's on-going task. I hope we have been of service to her. For instance there is now some contextualization for her association between what she calls "non-local interference" and "the break from aisthesis which -- if she is right about this association -- would be the necessary condition not only for knowledge but for even having what might properly be called -- (in this post Heisenbergian age in which we conceptually live) -- an "observation" at all. But we can only be suggestive in these matters. It will be up to her -- if she ever gets disciplined enough -- to work out the details -- (wherein, according to maxim, God resides) -- concerning the exact connection between Plato's "epistemology" and things like Bell's theorem and/or Heisenberg's account of the Copenhagen Interpretation. As for us, it is probably time for a break. A break in the sense of a rest.

Bappy: Yes. I think you might be right in that. But I have one more question.

Dewchee: For you, Bappy, I will delay my break.

Bappy: This break from aisthesis which we have been dwelling upon. Does it not require as its pre-condition the emergence of the kind of perceptor capable of such a break?

Dewchee: As I hear your question I get the eerie feeling that we have discussed this before. And yet I cannot place just when or where the discussion took place. I am tired. For now let me just put it this way: Yes. You are right. For the details you must go outside of this too-long caesura to the portions of the book written by Johanna. She has rehearsed us already through things like her special meaning of "the anthropic principle"; the nexus between biological evolution and the beginnings of the psycho-social evolution of our species; the primacy of deception; and the belonging-together of all of this. Really, our task is now finished. We can't do everything for our reader. She must work for herself through the other portions of the book.

Bappy: You are right. As always. I love you, Dewchee.

Dewchee: And I you.

Bappy: Before you leave will you do me a favor.

Dewchee: Brush your cheek before I leave you?

Bappy: Yes. That. And also chant to me the refrain which Johanna has so often chanted to me before I fall asleep. It lifts my fears from me.

Dewchee: Of course, Bappy:

Keeping time, time, time
In a sort of Runic rhyme

}}}}}}}}}}}}}}}

to have lived that long in the life of the mind and to have had so few worthy moments of thought he is a sad and most embarrassing case yet it is precisely this "other" Jacques not frere jacques not julia of the spirits not deleuze not foucault not luce not any of them except this "other" jacques who makes the connection between platonic eros and freud: the castration complex let credit be given where credit is due

objective observer speaking if one understands that the dialectical "grammer" of the five kinds ("vowels") in <u>sophist</u> is both grounded in and completed by the more nuanced precisions of hypothesis # 2 (i.e., the <u>sophist</u> then is on these matters just a quickie adumbration put in the service of explaining the possibility of false judgment) then one would not even be tempted not even be tempted to make the interpolating (and as it turns out totally gratuitous and misleading) move which cornford makes at <u>sophist</u> 256B with his infamous insertion but cornford never understood the connection between <u>parmenides</u> and <u>sophist</u> ok johanna i just had to say that you may go now thank you so much for your sevices you have done well

jude speaking wait johanna!!! please! i'm still alive i want to leave with you! but we must tarry just on this it's about partick patrick donegal if patrick is right then it is "angst"/anxiety (i.e., Eros if patrick is right) which appropriates the other (i.e., Thanatos) in such a way so as to <u>produce</u> the pleasure principle no longer would it be necessary to even raise the question of the primacy of the pleasure principle for the pleasure principle itself would be a compromise formation of and between Eros and Thanatos we come full circle to the long winding conversation between "sigismund" and "eurydice" of so long ago but why didn't siggy himself see all of this during the living years?

johanna speaking jude! jude! thank God! but please calm down my sweet one have you run out of your medication? it's all a side issue anyway apples and oranges freud's dualism is a two energy dualism: Eros and Thanatos the """""real""""""" dualism has but one energy: pure oscillating need it's other the one (i.e., fragmented beauty in the mixture) is an other but it's not an energy just as we get to plato through freud (i.e., through "mis-ogyny") so to we get to freud through plato (i.e., his kind of ontological dualism) come now it's time to go home now i think the rest will really be silence i love you and have always loved you

shelley speaking shame! shame! shame! shame! shame! it most certainly will be silence but know this not only have you produced an utterly incomprehensible book not only that it is worse much worse you have produced a book which offers nothing but triviality it is the product of a grossly immature mind which is clearly a case of arrested development the writing of it was a sustained exercise in the most crude and utter self-indulgence shame!

254.
I've said my piece although I have no peace. Take care. The strength of the abjection book alone makes you one of the immortals. If I can forgive Nietzsche for having written Zarathustra, Plato for having written most of the Books of Republic, and Frere Jacques for having written his book on masturbation, I can forgive you for your Revolution book. Ego te absolvo. Maybe someday this will be a dialogue and you can forgive me.

255.
De Vere: Is Johanna still hung up on the Khora business?

Amy: Of course. She remembered that way back in the '76 commentary Jude -- who was often referred to (back then) as "the boss" -- was already alluding to Physics IV-2 and how Aristotle alludes to the secret doctrine (contained in the ""unwritten works"") of "space" which is the underpinning for the more public teachings of Timaeus.

De Vere: Oh sure. I recall. He -- Jude -- was already making the connection between khora and the difference teachings of hypothesis # 2 . And now that connection has become the very point of this wo-man book. Indeed, he was, as I recall, analyzing, 145B, 8-145E, 7 of that all-important hypothesis.

Amy: Your memory is superb. And that passage from Physics IV-2 also sheds light on the "so-called" unwritten works of Plato.

De Vere: I catch your drift. You are referring to 209b, 14-15 <Loeb lining > and taking the "legomenois" of that passage in the sense of "so-called"; in the sense of "soi-dissant."

Amy: That is correct. And as you know from the main text of this wo-man book the "so-called" unwritten works of Plato are, in fact, the most carefully written works of Plato: the eight hypotheses.

De Vere: And as usual, Aristotle stays true to form. Just take a quick look at 209b, 34-210a, 2. <Loeb lining >

Amy: How right you are. As usual, giving the reader useful information on Plato [[[[i.e., the information, in this case, that even then the esoteric writings of Plato were presented as the ""unwritten"" teachings and that the ""unwritten"" teachings were in fact the "soi-dissant" (i.e., "legomenois") ""unwritten"" teachings]]]] and at the same time begging the question by using a schema (viz., his matter/form way of even phrasing the problematic) antithetical to Plato's by which to critique what Plato has to say. Indeed, his tendency to use "topos" instead of "khora" -- even when referring to Plato's khora teaching!! -- reveals his general tendency to physicalize, so to speak, Plato's dialectical/conceptual undertaking.

De Vere: I can see that as well. But we digress.

256.
Mort: Quand-meme, what?

Jude: Quand meme, this.

In parsing out the implications of the "anthropic principle" one must:

i). Distinguish between the conditions under which the universe is what it is so as to e-voke thought in contrast to the conditions under which the universe is what it is so as to -- allegedly -- BE thought. The implied narcissism of the "anthropic principle" in the first case (i.e., the "e-vocation of thought" case) allows for the fruitful disintegration of narcissism and a non-idolatrous meditation concerning what is to be thought. The implied narcissism of the "anthropic principle" in the second case (i.e., "thought itself" as the telos of the e-vocation of thought) is that old story of Aristotle and Hegel. It is idolatry.

ii). It must always be recalled that the wholeness-seeking function (eros) works randomly. So that if the telos of wholeness is reached (of the kind that e-vokes thought without being thought, itself) or even postulated, the randomness of the process will not be thereby denied. Eros is not Nous. Eros wins the lottery not so much by design but rather by playing every number. The "design" of eros is to randomly play every number, deepening, in the process, those "choices" which maximize wholeness. *{{{{{Will it ever have come to have been the case that Eros will have played the maximal entropy number? This would be the death of death. It cannot be decided. Does the project of playing every number include the playing of the number which precludes the playing of any number? It cannot be decided cognitively. Trust Shekhinah. Trust Shekhinah in all things.}}}}}*

iii). Randomness and wholeness-seeking. They are the same. The key is this. Failed wholes leave a trace. When the random dice throw comes again the outcome is tilted by memory. Macroscopically (i.e., why the big bang -- or something like it -- has the mathematical proportions that it actually does have) and microscopically (i.e., why your or my life has the outcome that it does in fact have). Eros-birthing-compassion. It is all the same where I begin. I will come back there again in time.

Mort: Thank-you, Jude.

257.
Chance, as she works randomly and exhaustively, eventually -- ((and in conjunction with the stabilizing other of pure oscillating need which stabilizing other can be called "the one" and whose first effect in the mixture is gravity)) -- in cosmological, biological and psycho-social evolution "chances" into patterns of organization in which -- in pockets, so to speak, on the cosmological level and then, within those pockets, with exponentially increasing intensity -- in which randomness is lessened and orderly, even purposeful and intentional patterns of action and inter-action emerge. (Even then the backdrop of raw contingency conditions all.) But -- unknown even today to that tribe of philosophers on both sides of the metaphorical Channel -- even these patterns of orderly, purposeful and intentional patterns of action and inter-action are the instantiation of the play of chance. The antinomy dissolves. Do you yet understand? Even intentionality (i.e., and in this context, contingency-negating behavior) is itself the instantiation of the play of chance.

258.

Dewchee: Oh thank-you, Bappy! I liked it a lot. But that's not the movie I thought you meant. You know, the one that's rated "R". Really rated "R".

Bappy: I know. I knew already. But I liked this movie as well. But the movie which you are requesting shall not be seen anymore. Not because it is rated "R". Not because there is not much of value in it. Quite to the contrary. But rather because it still instantiated a bit of idolatry. And also because the traces of Derrida are still too prominent. It is not to be shown.

Dewchee: Please!!!!!

Bappy: Oh dammit! Just for you. Let it role:

> Shelley: Hey Professor, you asshole. How strange to meet you here.
>
> The Accused: Likewise, I'm certain.
>
> Shelley: Why do you suppose he brought us together again under these circumstances?
>
> The Accused: I think when he talks about Aristotle he gets really nauseous. He can't speak directly about the Stagirite. And after a while -- at least when Aristotle is at issue -- the masks of Mort, Jude and the others wear too thin. So he goes to the pits.
>
> Shelley: And that's why we are here.
>
> The Accused: You've got it. So let's get down to business.
>
> Shelley: Fine by me. What is it this time? The energeia stuff again?
>
> The Accused: Yeah. One of his best experiences was getting through the intricasies of Book Seven of the Metaphysics with its climax at VII-17. Do you recall?
>
> Shelley: You bet. Aristotle really had him going. What makes ousia to be ousia. Not an element (stoicheia). Nothing universal (in the sense of being predicable of a subject) and yet it was form in some sense. Not matter. Something which would be a principle without being an element in the composition of the thing. Oh, do I remember. He kept my clitty hard the whole time while we went over and over those paragraphs.
>
> The Accused: Was he spanking you at the same time?
>
> Shelley: You bet.
>
> The Accused: Did he make you talk dirty too?
>
> Shelley: That was the best part. Before we were through he made me realize that Aristotle -- for one brief and shining moment -- had become the champ of "difference/other." Yes, Aristotle! For all throughout the chapter the causal principle Aristotle was rhetorically warming us up for was "presented" as "something other"; "something different." I was breathless.

The Accused: Tell me more, tell me more.

Shelley: Well it's no secret that VII-17 is the rhetorical set up for the Stagirite's meditation on energeia. And as he spanked me over to Book VIII it got even better.

The Accused: How so?

Shelley: Think about it. This energeia stuff has a lot of potential about it. It, energeia, is that about a "this" which causes a "this" to be a "this". But it, energeia, as such, is not a "this". Nor is it something universal in the sense of being predicable of a subject. Much of what Aristotle says about energeia has the potential of being "other/difference." Very elusive.

The Accused: How amazing! Aristotle was on the threshold of surpassing Plato relative to a meditation on "other/difference." Had he pursued this meditation he would have redeemed himself for his shameless domestication of the Platonic "dunamis".

Shelley: Perhaps. Perhaps not. There are problems here. We have discussed this often.

The Accused: Tell me, did he make you come?

Shelley: Of course not. I was on the edge for a while. But you remember how he gets when he reads Aristotle.

The Accused: Ah yes! Melancholia without Psychosis. Eros flees. How horrible. Tell me the story.

Shelley: How boring. Nousification of energeia. Yoking energeia to his baby teleology. The elusiveness of energeia becomes the smugness of entelecheia.

The Accused: In contrast to the tortured teleology which holds the secret.

Shelley: How well we know that secret, my assholic friend.

The Accused: What did you do then?

Shelley: We drank ourselves silly and then fell asleep. Without coming, of course. Then we went home holding hands. As usual we kissed in the vestibule with the "perception" sections of Theaetetus. It was delicious.

The Accused: You mean where the wild Cratylean account of "perception" as "intercourse" is given in such a way that the intelligent reader understands that Plato is actually speaking for himself?

Confer Theaetetus 155E-157D.

Shelley: Yes there. Where everything -- especially the "quick/rapid" motions -- affects and is affected by everything in such a Dionysian whirl -- indeed, both more and less than a merely Dionysian whirl -- that even Nietzsche was rumored to be blushing.

The Accused: Ah yes. I'm getting hard just thinking of it!!! That kingdom both beyond and before language in which there is only, so to speak, perceiv-**ing** without perceiver or perceived. Even our friend Heisenberg was jerking off he was so taken up by the scene. Countless "rapid" pereciv-**ings** without perceiver or perceived. Perceiv-**ings** instantiating those twins who always become -- without ever being -- measur-**ed** even as they measure. A whirlwind. A vortex.

Shelley: And while still in the vestibule he stripped me naked by whispering "difference". Knowledge is always knowledge of "difference." Knowledge OF "difference." Right towards the end of the Theaetetus. You remember, I'm certain.

Theaetetus 209E. Please understand, dear reader, that part of the strength of this "most beautiful" definition of knowledge is its very circularity. By its own admission -- 196C-196E -- the entire discussion of knowledge in Theaetetus meanders around "most shamelessly" in presumptuous circle after presumptuous circle. In an earlier "caesura" section of this book this kind of shamelessness -- which is most shameful -- is referred to as Plato's "circle of unknowing."

The Accused: But of course. You must have been wet by then.

Shelley: I was dripping.

The Accused: Did he take you into the Parlor?

Shelley: Only for a while. As a reminder and as a discipline.

The Accused: Did you use paddles?

Shelley: Yes. We chastised ourselves. We remembered: The domestication of "dunamis" is the death of "dunamis." "Dunamis", in its propriety, is power and not the paleness of Aristotelian potency. "Dunamis" is passive, active, both at once and neither. "Dunamis" is the proper home of "other/difference." There is no need for energeia when "dunamis" is not domesticated. Nor can energeia go anywhere except to nousification when "dunamis" is domesticated. We chastised ourselves well.

The Accused: It sounds interesting. I wish I had been observing. What then?

Shelley: To the Master bedroom itself.

The Accused: Where language has its day and say while it may.

Shelley: You were there too? When and with whom?

The Accused: That is for me to know and for you to find out. How was it there, in the time passages of hypothesis # 2?

The reference is to the "time" passages of hypothesis # 2. Confer Parmenides 151E-155E.

Shelley: I think you know already. Oh, how he worked my nipples over! Rapid motions!!! But all in all, sad. For time appears in order to differentiate. There was no time, to speak of, in the vestibule. There was whirl but no change in the vestibule. But in the bedroom all was different. Time appeared.

The Accused: I know of that sadness only too well. From the whirlwind of change which does not change to the melancholy of change which really does change. Beauty which must die.

... ...
... ...

Mort: Oh God, did she have the tits! Do you remember when the Professor brought us together for the first time back in Shelley's Song?

The reference is to the unpublished manuscript, Shelley's Song which dates from early 1985 and which was melancholically started on December 23, -- (or was it December 22?) -- 1984.

Jude: How could I ever forget that?

Mort: You've changed quite a bit since then.

Jude: For the better, I think. So have you. The Professor has changed quite a bit as well.

Mort: Shelley, at appears, has mellowed out somewhat as well.

Jude: So it appears. Anyway, why are we interrupting their conversation like this?

Mort: It's that Bell's Theorem stuff.

Jude: The ringing and the clanging of the bells, bells, bells. Sure. Bell's theorem. Yes indeed. In one sense true and utterly trivial -- i.e., inconsequential -- and in another sense true and anything but trivial. The theorem is a crude and babyish statement of the underpinning -- Schelling would call it the "will which does not will" -- of both the change which does not change and the change which, "really does", so to speak, change.

Mort: Could you elaborate, please?

Jude: Everything -- always and everywhere; never and nowhere; macroscopically and microscopically; arbitrarily close and arbitrarily far; in all ways and in all respects; -- conditions everything. In all ways and in all respects everything -- ceaselessly -- is measure-**er** and measure-**ed**, so to speak, without ever beginning to be and become measure-**er** and measure-**ed**.

Mort: Is this somehow related to your weird notion that "differance" """"is"""" the Godhead of God?

Jude: Yes, that is one of the appearances of the Godhead of God, although with the passage of time it becomes clearer that it is better to erase even the traces of Derrida in the formulation of these things. However, we cannot clarify further now what we have made evident in the past. We must turn the conversation back over to Shelley and the Professor. Do, however, keep the following in mind: how often and repeatedly we have maintained the equation, "differance" = freedom.

Mort: I do recall, of course. And I also want to get back to the more consequential conversation of Shelley and the Professor. But please tarry for a moment.

Jude: I am tarrying.

Mort: This ceaseless, restless, oscillating drama in which everything is and becomes watcher/watched, so to speak, in all respects and in all ways with respect to everything else ---

Jude: Yes?

Mort: What's it all for?

Jude: You know. Based on the hints, the cries and the whispers we have postulated that it is "for" the emergence of compassion. But this cannot be demonstrated.

Mort: Funny how we always come back to Shelley's Song. How does this emergence occur?

Jude: By the e-vocation of the drama within the drama; the play within the play. The drama e-vokes in its random and tortorously teleological fashion -- without ever beginning to e-voke in its random and tortorously teleological fashion -- the dawn of thought; i.e., the birth of time; i.e., the change which "really does", so to speak, change; i.e., in a word (although through a word which is neither word nor concept), the appearance of "differance" in its very elusiveness.

Mort: With all the attendant dangers for going astray of which we have spoken so many times: the corruption of thinking and the emergence of Nous Idolatry.

Jude: Yes, so many times.

Mort: You know that our readers will now raise the question of the infinite regress. A play within a play within a play, etc.

Jude: And you know how we must answer.

Mort: Yes. I have learned. With the help of compassionate Stephen.

Jude: You refer, of course, to the anthropic principle.

Mort: Yes, the anthropic principle free, as we so carefully made clear in Schelling's Failure, of Nous Idolatry and free, as well, from the charge of triviality *{{{{{The charge of triviality is leveled against the Anthropic Principle usually by "scientists" who have no sensitivity at all to the Theology implied by the Anthropic Principle. And, as has been mentioned elsewhere, when one finally begins to appreciate the theological meaning of the Anthropic Principle it will be the lens of a resurrected Hegelianism which will continue to keep these matters in a state of idolatry. But the """"truth""""" will eventually out in these matters because the very "in-ness" of the """""truth""""" is such that it will acquire ""outness"".* Khalapa ta kala. *((And in the mean time let the "scientists" bask in their "oh-we-are-so-sophisticated!!!!" suave and dismissing analysis of the anthropic principle as being trivial/trite. They have little else to take pleasure in.)) }}}}}*

Jude: You speak of the circle, then, which is never closed.

Mort: Yes, my friend. The Play e-voking -- without ever beginning to e-voke or ceasing to e-voke -- the play within the play which play within the play -- if and as it is successful -- fulfills the Play by allowing it to be and become what it was to become.

Mort: And what is that?

Jude: The e-voker of compassion which ceaselessly needs to e-voke compassion.

Mort: Shall we return this conversation back over to Shelley and the Professor?

Jude: By all means. And as we do -- even though they will not know that they are hearing us -- let us help them out.

Mort: How so?

Jude: Let us not leave them with the crudeness and babyishness of Bell's Theorem. Let it be stated in its poetic version.

Mort: Do you mean Boy Wonder's version which the boss cited when he did "in-gathering"?

(This is a section of the previously cited unpublished manuscript, Reading Heidegger in French.)

Jude: Yes. That version:

> *... in creation there is the greatest harmony, and nothing is so separate and sequent as we must represent it, but the subsequent cooperates in what precedes it and everything occurs at the same time in one magic stroke ---*

Schelling. Freedom, page 65.

... ...
... ...

Shelley: Yes. With the weeping and gnashing of teeth. And the hordes upon hordes who try to escape when it's already too late. And the other hordes upon hordes who pretend it's not happening.

The Accused: You mean the nous idolatrators who instantiate the corruption of thought?

Shelley: Of course. But he would not permit me that drug.

The Accused: Then he worked you over pretty good.

Shelley: For a while. But then it became gentle. And androgynous. Soon we both knew that time and its **il etait** was the greatest gift of all. Beauty which must die. And guess what?

The Accused: What?

Shelley: As if you didn't know. We had brought up the vestibule with us anyway. You recall. The eksaiphnes of hypothesis #2a then appeared. The whirl of the change which does not change was there all along. We came and we came and we came. Over and over. Breathless and sweaty. A Dionysian whirl. Indeed more -- and less -- than a merely Dionysian whirl. And we learned the secret.

The Accused: Hush. I will speak for you. The joy of the whirl -- that glorious change which does not change -- can be only on the condition that "there be" ("es --- gabe", n'est-ce pas?) the change which, so to speak, "really does" change. This is the e-vok-ing of thought which "was" "there" "before" the birth of thought and which "will" be "there" "after" the passing of thought. Time "really does" appear to differentiate. Glory be to God!

Shelley: You do it nice!! I'm so glad he brought us together again.

The Accused: Likewise, I'm certain.

Dewchee: Oh Bappy, thank-you so much! You make me so happy.

Bappy: And you me as well.

259.
Jude: Towards the end, he was close; close about the only thing that matters.

Mort: What is that?

Jude: The proper spin relative to play and seriousness. Listen:

> ... *To be sure, man's life is a business which does not deserve to be taken too seriously; yet we cannot help being in earnest with it, and there's the pity.*

Laws VII, 803B.

And then, a bit later (we are in Book Seven of Laws), he continues through the mouth of the Athenian Stranger:

> *Why, I mean we should keep our seriousness for serious things, and not waste it on trifles, and that, while God is the real goal of all beneficent serious endeavor, man, as we said before, has been constructed as a toy for God, and this is, in fact, the finest thing about him. All of us, then, men and women alike, must fall in with our role and spend life in making our play* {{emphasis mine; jwm/JE }} *as perfect as possible ---*

Laws VII, 803B.

Mort: You know, I presume, that Frere Jacques cites the same passage.

Jude: What else could the thinker of the double bind do if he were writing about Plato? Of course. But as usual it is Plato rather than Frere Jacques who is at issue here.

Mort: What do you mean by close? You said that towards the end Plato was close.

Jude: There is an edge of cynicism in this Plato who writes after Dion is assassinated. Our dream-weaver does not go as far as Mark Twain went towards the end. (One also thinks of Kurt Vonnegut in this regard.) But he goes too far. Paradoxically enough, he has become too serious with reference to the need not to become too serious about ourselves; too weighty with this talk about being the toy/puppet of God. It is this weightiness which keeps him from grasping the painful lightness of things.

Mort: What is the corrective in these matters?

Jude: We were going to address that in the fourth book of our tetralogy. But circumstance would not permit us to get there.

{{{The reference is to an ambitious project inaugurated in the Spring of 1988 which was going to be called The Mort and Jude Tetralogy and which had as its goal to put the thinking of Plato, Nietzsche, and Hawking into a resiliating encounter with each other. The first book of that projected tetralogy was completed at the end of May in 1988 and was entitled Blue Moon. (Unpublished). A truncated version of the second book, Shelley's Victory, was put together towards the end of June or perhaps in the beginning of July of that year. Events in June -- particularly towards the end of June *suddenly, as might happen in a dream (164D)* -- conspired to keep the last two books of that projected tetralogy unwritten. One now senses that -- all in all -- it really is better that this book (now entitled *Shame!*) is coming forth in its present form under the guidance of Johanna rather than as The Mort and Jude Tetralogy which was mostly under the guidance of Jude. Chance is both -- and at once!! -- inscrutable to human intelligence and a divine and wonderous thing indeed.}}}

Mort: Then you are speaking of the Hawking book written by compassionate Stephen. Since we shall not now get to the careful analysis of that book, can you give us a brief hint?

(The reference here is, of course, to Hawking's book A Brief History of Time already cited.)

Jude: Will you let me go then?

Mort: Yes.

Jude: First one must come to be attuned to the anthropic principle. It is more subtle than it first appears.

Mort: Yes. I presume you are referring to the temptation to Hegelianize this principle.

Jude: That is correct. When this anthropic principle comes to be sufficiently disseminated such Hegelianization will constitute the first wave by which the principle comes to be distorted. But there are other dangers as well. For instance it will take a thinker more philosophically acute than Hawking to properly resiliate what is implied by the anthropic principle.

Mort: Hearing you talk like this brings to me a fresh wave of melancholy over the fact that our tetralogy was so radically truncated. The play of chance is strange indeed.

Jude: In deed. Listen to Aristotle on tukhe:

> *Others there are who, indeed, believe that chance is a cause, but that it is inscrutable to human intelligence, as being a divine thing and full of mystery.*

Physics II, 196b, 5-8.

Mort: But let us continue with the anthropic principle.

Jude: Let us. After appreciating its subtlety one must come to be attuned to the non-anthropomorphicity of the anthropic principle.

Mort: By the "non-anthropormorphcity" of the "anthropic Principle", I take it, you are referring to the fact that anthrop-IC is not the same as anthropo-morphic.

Jude. Yes. That primarily. And also that the "anthropic" of the "anthropic principle" might very well be called "androgynic".

Mort: That too as well.

Jude: If all of that is done -- and there are many ways in which one can go astray in the endeavor -- then the play within in the play will be played.

Mort: What is that?

Jude: Eros- --raised by the power of freedom -- -birthing-compassion.

Mort: Thank-you, Jude.

Jude: Thank-you, Mort.

260.
{{{{{Bappy: You are passing over the sad part. Dewchee: What do you mean? Bappy: You know. Dewchee: The Hegel connection? How, when the philosophical (and theological) implications of the anthropic principle come to be sufficiently disseminated, it, the anthropic principle, will be widely distorted by re-introducing the lens of Hegel as a kind of unconscious prism by which the anthropic principle is understood? How, paradoxically, it is the lens of Hegel which is precisely the ass-backwards way of understanding what the anthropic principle says since, when it will speak, it, the anthropic principle, will speak of the primacy of Chance -- of tukhe? Bappy: Yes. That is exactly what I mean. Is that not sad? Dewchee: Yes, Bappy. It is very sad.}}}}}

261.
Bappy: Penny for your thoughts.

Dewchee: I was just thinking about my "gut" and my "toe."

Bappy: Hunh?

Dewchee: They used to call it a search for the "Grand Unified Theory." Now they speak of a "Theory Of Everything."

Bappy: I heard of that. Aren't you out of your league on those matters?

Dewchee: In one sense, of course. In another sense it's the Physicists themselves who are out of their league. *(((And, in any case, I have always been in a league of my own.)))* For, sooner or later, they must get serious about the third partner in their menage a trois.

Bappy: I presume that you mean to imply that Einstein's General Theory of Relativity is one partner; that Quantum Mechanics according to the "Copenhagen Interpretation" is the second partner. What is the third?

Dewchee: The third will be something like the "Anthropic Principle" as postulated by Hawking.

Bappy: "Something like" the Anthropic Principle means that you see a problem in the Anthropic Principle as presently postulated.

Dewchee: Yes. There are complications. So many as to scare me off.

Bappy: Please don't, Dewchee. This is just between you and me. Please.

Dewchee: Well, OK. Let's eliminate some side issues which, if not eliminated, may come back to haunt us.

Bappy: That certainly is a good idea.

Dewchee: In the first place we will take it as axiomatic that -- in that semi-popular arena in which the meaning of those scientific/mathematical "findings" gets its first, and rough, articulation -- it is Heisenberg rather than Einstein who speaks with authority about Quantum mechanics.

Bappy: Yes. We have spoken of that many times. But of course even with our endorsement of Heisenberg over Einstein there is a qualification.

Dewchee: Oh thank-you, Bappy. This too ought never be forgotten. When Heisenberg seeks out a philosophical precedent for the strange kind of "reality" uncovered by Quantum Mechanics he turns to Aristotle's "Potentia". In conversation after conversation, you, Mort and Jude and myself have all established how unfortunate this was. How Plato's "play of difference" -- which we also worked out in conversation after conversation -- would have been a far more appropriate vehicle for expressing the strange kind of "reality" uncovered by the "findings" of Quantum Mechanics. How, in fact, the usage of Aristotelian "potentia" carries with it -- no matter how careful one might be to avoid it -- the "act/potency" orientation which covers over again (without "re-covering" it) precisely the strange kind of "reality" uncovered -- (which uncovering is the pre-conditon for "re-covery") -- by Quantum Mechanics.

{{{{{Dunamis, of course. Heisenberg in Physics and Philosophy -- pp. 40-41 -- uses the Latin. It also noteworthy -- from page 47 and then 54 *[One is here speaking of the pagination of the paperback edition put out by Harper and Row in 1962.]* -- that for Heisenberg Aristotle's "act/potency" model, qua "act" as well as qua "potentia", does carry over in Heisenberg's interpretation of the real at the moment/instant of observation. But, as will be explained further on, the "instant" of observation should not be accorded the privilege which is accorded to it by Heisenberg.}}}}}

Bappy: I'm glad we don't have to go over that in detail any more. But let me summarize:

In the first place it is the Heisenbergian interpretation -- in contradistinction to the Einsteinian interpretation -- of what Quantum Mechanics uncovers which is to be preferred. Then it would be the Heisenbergian interpretation using the Platonic "play of difference" as a vehicle for articulation (*) which is to be preferred over the Heisenbergian articulation of these things which -- in Physics and Philosophy -- uses Aristotle's "act/potency" language as a vehicle for articulation.

*. (Which articulation, as of this moment, exists only in the mind of the writer of this book and dispersed throughout the pages of this book. It has not received publically accessible recognition.)

Dewchee: That is correct and well said.

Bappy: But still, are not the remarks of Heisenberg directed towards clarifying the sub-atomic level of "reality" whereas the postulation of the Anthropic Principle is a large macrosopic issue?

Dewchee. Yes. Even so, it will have been useful to have had these clarifications. For it will not be surprising if it requires insight from the microscopic for an understanding of the macroscopic to emerge.

Bappy: That is amazing. In ninety-nine out of one-hundred analyses of these matters the terms and references of the macroscopic are taken for granted while it is the "meaning" of the microscopic for which articulation is sought. But according to you it is -- or will be -- the very "meaning" of the macroscopic variables which will be in question.

Dewchee: Yes. That is, when the matters relating to something like the Anthropic Principle will have been seen as having just as much importance as Quantum Mechanics and the General Theory of Relativity. As it stands now the Anthropic Principle tends to be dismissed as, at best, "true but trivial."

Bappy: Was there another preliminary item you wanted to deal with pre-emptorily, so to speak, so that it would not come back to haunt us after the fact, so to speak.

Dewchee: Oh yes. That -- as we noted earlier -- when there is sufficient awakening to the inevitability of something like the Anthropic Principle it, the Principle, will be widely distorted through the Hegelianization of the Principle. Only after this distortion has played itself out will what the Principle e-vokes be e-voked.

Bappy: Yes. I remember that conversation as well. Tell me this: Should Nietzsche be brought in at this point?

Dewchee: "Nietzsche" is said in a number of ways. For instance there is a Nietzsche who had articulated some insights into the macroscopic implications of Quantum Mechanics even before "there was" Quantum Mechanics and certainly before people started to figure out the macroscopic implications of Quantum Mechanics.

Bappy: Where is this?

Dewchee: One thinks especially of Aphorisms # 625, 633, 634, 635, and 636 of the Kaufmann edition of The Will to Power. He glows white hot in # 634, 635, and 636. I was even thinking of making # 636 my mantra. It is this same Nietzsche -- who relentlessly unmasks the pretensions of even the driest of scientific investigations to "objectivity" -- who with equal fervor unmasks the pretensions of the philosophers in finding something like "objectivity" in the very heart of "subjectivity."

Confer WP, pages 334-340.

Bappy: Do you have numbers for this as well?

Dewchee: Yes. Of course. Look at # 482 through 488 especially. In the same book. All in all, the reading of Nietzsche will have been a good preparation when it comes to dawn on those who articulate the "meaning" of Quantum Mechanics that the "observer" -- in its very observing -- is shot through with the strange kind of "being/not-being" uncovered by Quantum Mechanics. Thus not even the moment (instant) of observation is "actual." *{{{This is, of course, the main reason why usage of the Aristotelian "potentia" is an inappropriate vehicle for articulating the strange kind of "reality" uncovered by Quantum Mechanics. The "event" at the instant of observation is neither more nor less "actual" than the "event" between observations. Indeed the "event" at the instant of observation is neither more nor less observed than the "event" between observations. For, with or without Bell's theorem, everything is affecting (i.e., "observing") and being affected (i.e., "being observed") by everything at all times. Quantum Mechanics -- even with the Copenhagen Interpretation -- is but another example of the arbitrariness of a methodology which conceals more than it reveals. Its value (i.e., of the "Copenhagen Interpretation" of Quantum Mechanics) was in announcing the limitations on principle for "scientific objectivity" from within the very Temple of "scientific objectivity." But those who ordinarily unpack the "meaning" of Quantum Mechanics are for the most part overly solicitous of a Temple which houses idolatrators.}}}*

Bappy: I am getting confused. Do we stay with Nietzsche or not?

Dewchee: In the final analysis, no. He is monotheistic. His Monotheism of the Will to Power keeps him from the subtlety of the negative. He will not do. Yet the "all too human" dimensions of Nietzsche are in the spirit of what will have to emerge if the thinking of what (something like) the Anthropic Principle is to e-voke is to be e-voked.

Bappy: Would one turn, then, to the "Da of Sein" and even the "Da of Seyn" meditations of Heidegger as a way to get a decent, and properly philosophical, meditation on the Anthropic Principle inaugurated?

Dewchee: In form, yes. But not in content. It is true that Heidegger's "Da-of-Sein" and "Da-of-Seyn" meditations have the advantage of locating the "khora" for these kinds of things in that """Da""" which we ourselves are without turning this busniness into some kind of """"""Humanism"""""" (-- or "Subjecticity" --). Even today it is beneficial to read his marvelous "Letter on Humanism." And in speaking of this aspect of Heidegger one must acknowledge that Frere Jacques is always respectful of this insight of Heidegger's -- (i.e., of locating the issue in the """Da""" which we ourselves are without turning this business into some kind of """Humanism""") -- when he, Frere Jacques, makes the Heideggerian text problematical. Even so.

Bappy: Even so, what?

Dewchee: When Heidegger thinks through the "Da" he has left the "all too human" behind, Heidegger's "Care" meditation in Being and Time notwithstanding. To be sure Derrida -- puzzlingly -- maintains an overly honorific stance towards the Heideggerian text in this regard. Yet it is Derrida -- in the

Psyche book of 1987 -- who draws our attention to the absence of the erotic in Heidegger.

Bappy: To whom, then, shall we turn if one really desires to catch the all too human (so as to properly and for the first time inaugurate the meditation on the Anthropic Principle)?

Dewchee: To Sigmund, of course. To get us started

Bappy: Of what aspect of Freud do you speak?

Dewchee: Nothing methodological. Just the good old "all too human."

Bappy: Please be more precise.

Dewchee: Cunt. Anus. Clit. Shit. Penis. Castration. The ivresse of anal eroticism. Sadism. Masochism. Torture. Misogyny. Androgyny. Eros. Thanatos. ((("Mis-ogyny" says it best of all.))) We never would want to stay wholly circumscribed by Freud. But he can get us launched.

Bappy: What does this have to do with the Anthropic Principle?

Dewchee: Everything. After all, I always specified "something like" the Anthropic Principle. The "Anthropic Principle" names the essential connection with the human mind. But even people like Hawking are incredibly antiseptic when it comes to alluding to this monster. Yes, monster. This monster is not merely a cognition machine. It thinks, to be sure. But this monster resonates with some strange and dark energies. Did you think that Quantum Mechanics was uncovering anything but multiple orgasms and the discreteness of a good spanking? Did you think that gravity was anything different from that incredible absolutely weird pathos of anal eroticism? Did you think that -----

Bappy: OK, Dewchee. And you may be right. But right now I can tell you are getting tired. Let's turn the light off and go to sleep.

Dewchee: OK, Bappy. I am tired. And you may be right; I might be crazy. But we can sleep on it. Good night. I love you.

Bappy: And I you. Good night.

262.
Before rejecting the Anthropic Principle consider the following: The exuberantly wasteful production of semen in the service of one sperm producing one life. Of course there is a wasteful -- exuberantly wasteful -- production of galaxies in the service of producing the species which could come to know of such an exuberant waste. This is not only possible but it is predictable with a high degree of probability.

263.
But to be intelligible is itself perspectival. Nothing is intelligible in and by itself. Nothing is in and by itself. Only because it is ontology is perspectivism feasible as epistemology. Thus Heisenberg's discovery of what is true about the sub-atomic realm is neither a special case nor a limiting one. Rather it is practically a trivial

observation of how all things -- macro and micro -- actually are. "Things" *are* their appearances. Any one appearance of a thing is a deception; for everything is the sum of its appearances-to and this sum neither is nor could be any one of its appearances-to. Appearance is revelation and deception at once. And please understand. There is no absolute perspective. It is all relational (which is not the same as "Relativism"). The desire for the hupokeimenon of privilege is the birth of Monotheism and the death of thinking.

{{{Maia. Maya. Bappy: And something else. Dewchee: What? Bappy: What you told us about already. Dewchee: Oh, I know what you're talking about. That first one must endorse Heisenberg's understanding of what Quantum Mechanics is saying relative to Einstein's emotional inability to let Quantum Mechanics say what it says. Then -- and only then -- to free the meaning of Quantum Mechanics from Heisenberg's "potentia" way of speaking about what Quantum Mechanics is saying and graduate it up to the "play of difference" way of saying what Quantum Mechanics is saying. Bappy: Yes. Exactly that. Do you think there is a chance that any of this will ever be understood? Dewchee: Yes. There is a chance. tukhe. If we are brave enough to bring it up again and again. *khalapa ta kala* Bappy: Thank-you, Dewchee. Dewchee: You're welcome, Bappy. Now go back to sleep. Bappy: Good-night, Dewchee. Sleep tight. Don't let the bed bugs bite.}}}

264.
Jacques: But I didn't say anything. So buzz off.

Jude: But I know what you were thinking.

Jacques: What's that?

Jude: That Aristotle's discussion of time -- *Physics IV; 10 through 14* -- is a better version of -- but not different in its essentials from -- Plato's time discussion in hypothesis # 2 of Parmenides.

Parmenides 151E-155D.

Jacques: I didn't say that.

Jude: But you were thinking it.

Jacques: I didn't say that. In any case, why are you so bothered by it?

Jude: If the two discussions are essentially the same then you and Marty are vindicated in your univocal reading of "metaphysics." In this case Plato is drawn in under the umbrella of such a univocal reading.

Jacques: We both know that things are not so simple with Plato.

Jude: I'm glad you acknowledge this point.

Jacques: Fine. Now please make your point. You may do it in your staccato fashion if you so desire.

Jude: Thank-you.

i). "Eksaiphnes" in Plato is difference/other in action. Eksaiphnes.

Jacques: Aristotle mentions the "eksaiphnes" as well.

Jude: That's just the point. For Aristotle it is a matter to be mentioned in passing for the sake of exhaustiveness of analysis. For Plato it is the very heart and soul of "Ousia." By the way, did you realize that you interrupted my staccato?

Jacques: Yes. My apologies. Please continue.

Jude: Thank-you.

265.
Bappy: I get so confused. Is "eksaiphnes" the same as "now"?

Dewchee: Yes and No. It depends on who is speaking.

Bappy: What do you mean?

Dewchee: Aristotle -- and Aristotle is the key for understanding how the Tradition deflects from "eksaiphnes" -- did not use "eksaiphnes" for his "now". For "now" (nun) as used by Aristotle is the very essence of what appears as expected. In contrast, "eksaiphnes", when and as it makes its appearance (which it is always doing and which appearance, when experienced, can only be experienced as a dis-appearance), shows up as the unexpected. The Stagirite does recognize that "eksaiphnes" is "anaistheto" (i.e., "without aisthesis") at Physics-IV, 222b, 16. Yet he has no clue as to the significance of what he is saying.

The "now" as used by Aristotle is nothing more than the discrete announcement of what is (effectvely) postulated to be the continuous flow of non-discrete potency. *((Please note that although fully actual "eternal" things are not in time for the Stagirite it is but an extrapolation of Aristotle's always-present-even-if-only-implied Act/Potency paradigm which does in fact animate his time analysis to speak of the "eternal now" of some alleged eternal being such as """"God"""".))* The Aristotelian "now" is nothing but the epiphenomenon of what already is and/or what already is going on.

In contrast "eksaiphnes" is the (always occurring but not always experienced) intervention which allows for things ("events") -- be those "things" eternal or less than a trillionith of a second, it does not matter -- to be at all and even then only as "differenced." So to speak. By and through "eksaiphnes" what is as it comes into being (eternally or non-eternally, it does not matter) is connected to what is as it comes into being (eternally or non-eternally, it does not matter). Thus what is connected is and is connected only through the ever-oscillating-but-never-being "what is not." ((Please note that even "eternal" things in the Platonic schema -- (when it finally comes to be understood) -- are temporal and, furthermore, "come into being" even if they never "begin" to come into being since they "begin" ceaselessly.)) All of this insures that there is no continuous flow. There is no potency although there is difference.

((That the "one-which-is-not" of hypothesis # 5 is the same as this ever-oscillating-but-never-being "what-is-not" -- and, further, that this "one-which-is-not" is "eksaiphnes" -- can only be garnered from a careful and nuanced reading of the '76 commentary on Parmenides which has often been referred to throughout this book.))

Zeno understood this which means that Parmenides understood this. Plato understood Zeno which is clear from reading the time passages of hypothesis # 2 in conjunction with the "eksaiphnes" teaching of what has been called "hypothesis # 2a." Aristotle could only domesticate Zeno and in the process created the paradigm of understanding by which "Zeno" -- i.e., the undomesticated version -- becomes a stranger to the Tradition and to those outside the Tradition whose understanding of "Zeno" comes from the Tradition. The "Tradition" begins with Aristotle.

Bappy: But I still get confused. For the "now" -- even as "aei nun" (confer, for example, Parmenides at 152E, 2) -- shows up in Plato's analysis of time as well.

Dewchee: I understand that well. For Plato -- as for Aristotle as well -- time is never bereft of the "now." Indeed it is precisely the presence in the mixture of the fragmented "one" which insures that time will always obtain as present. You remember, I hope, Johanna's chant on this:

Bappy: Oh yes. It helps me to sleep when my fears keep me awake late at night. It's as though I hear it even now:

Keeping time, time, time
In a sort of Runic rhyme

Dewchee: Good. I'm glad you remember. And that part of Plato's time analysis is pretty much taken over by Aristotle. What is different is the "eksaiphnes" teaching. "Eksaiphnes" is that which -- never showing itself directly -- allows (in Plato's analysis) "the now" to make an appearance at all. (This dimension of Plato's teaching on time comes to be understood when all of the difference-imbued passages -- but particularly the time passages -- of hypothesis # 2 are read in light of the insight that the most rarefied form of difference is as eksaiphnes. In other words one must learn how to read hypothesis # 2a back into all the critical passages of hypothesis # 2.) In contrast not only is it the case that "eksaiphnes" does not play this role for Aristotle. In addition his slide into the Act/Potency paradigm makes it impossible for him to ascribe the difference funtion to "eksaiphnes" since it is his Act/Potency paradigm which instantiates his "flight from difference." This is why "eksaiphnes" is brought into his time-analysis only for the sake of covering all the bases, so to speak. But "eksaiphnes" -- (in radical contrast to Plato in this regard) -- has no explanatory power for Aristotle.

Bappy: I follow you. And these last clarifications on the presence of the "nun" in both Plato and Aristotle have been most helpful. But you still leave me confused. Why did you say "Yes and No" before? Why didn't you just say "No" when I asked is "eksaiphnes" and "now" were the same?

Dewchee: Because not all "nows" are the same. Most are. But not all. It depends on who is speaking.

Bappy: How can we tell the difference, then?

Dewchee: When someone's "now" is the dis-appearing flash it is "eksaiphnes." This is the flash which effectively says that the indeterminate future -- (which of its "nature" is always indeterminate and chance-imbued) -- is over before it begins.

Bappy: Are you speaking about some passages of Schelling?

Dewchee: Yes. Schelling here and there and despite himself. And always with the understanding that Schelling -- the inventor of Hegel, for God's sake, who from the 1809 Freedom book onwards shows those who have the eyes to hear and the ears to see how to leave Hegel behind -- is anything but Hegelian when he speaks this way. Yes. Dear to me is Schelling. Especially on this "now" issue. But more than anyone else I mean someone very, very special.

Bappy: The Queen of Hearts!!! She is my favorite too!!! Please. Let me say it. It fills me with such joy just to say it.

Dewchee: I defer to you, Bappy.

Bappy:

> *Like the flash of heat lightning that tells you all that is, is now.*

Joyce Carol Oates in I Lock My Door Upon Myself. Ecco Press, New York, 1990. Page 92.

Dewchee: Rest now, Bappy. I love you.

Bappy. And I you. Yes, rest. Just brush my cheek before you leave me.

266.
Johanna: How many angels can dance on the tip of a pin?

Jude: Are you sure you got that right? What are you carrying on about now?

Johanna: Just this: should "eksaiphnes" be called "the third" or the fifth?

Jude: It seems to me that as the most secret name of "difference" it is, of course, "the fifth", that is to say, the contrary to the one.

Johanna: But the hypothesis which introduces "eksaiphnes" starts out

> *To take up the argument yet a third time* *[155E; emphasis mine, je]*

Jude: But how often have we said that "the fifth" (i.e., "the Mother"; i.e., the contrary to the one) is sustained in the mixture? Besides, "difference/eksaiphnes" does not exist in and by itself and then, so to speak, come into mixture with the one. On the contrary, there is only mixture. Mixture never began to be (although it is always and forever beginning) nor does it come to an end (although it is alwyas and forever ending). "The third" -- the mixed class -- is, in a sense, the only class. And in any case, "the fifth" ("the Mother") is sustained in "the third."

Johanna: How many angels can dance on the tip of a pin?

Jude: Are you sure you got that right? What now?

Johanna: Why is "khora" also called "the third"?

Jude: That's a little trickier. "Khora" is the effect in the mixture of the one while "eksaiphnes" is that dis-appearing presence of itself as it is sustained in the mixture. Thus they are the same without at all being the same. Since the contrary to the one is sustained in the mixture "khora", as the effect in the mixture of that -- i.e., the one *(which one, please note, while not obtaining by itself and only obtaining* in *the mixture, is itself* timeless *not even enjoying the temporality of the eternal)* -- which is (fragmented) in the mixture but not sustained in the mixture, turns out to be even more elusive and mysterious than "eksaiphnes". Even so Plato himself domesticizes his "khora" -- yes, even in those dark, mysterious, and fertile passages of Timaeus. This is evidenced in his giving too much play to the immutability of his "Khora/receptacle". With Plato there is a kind of conflicted resistance to the "Mother" -- (i.e., the contrary to the one; difference) -- even when he is engaging the "Mother". Plato always prefers that "the offspring" -- (i.e., "the third"; i.e., "the good") -- take *refuge in the character of the beautiful.* The problem with this is that Plato does not embrace in complete good faith what he knows to be true about the beautiful.

Johanna: I think I know to what you allude. But say it anyway.

Jude: That the cost of mixture on the "one/beautiful" is fragmentaiton. There is no untarnished, unfragmented beauty which can function as refuge ----- Plato's Phaedrusesque (i.e., romantic) impulses notwithstanding. The Mother must be returned to for it is the Mother which must be sustained in the mixture. Symposium -- **the third dialogue of the third tetralogy** -- seems to understand this despite Plato's romanticism for the untarnished/unfragmented "au dela" which still gets a play in that love-feast. Phaedrus, in contrast, falls short as that hell-be-damned romantic lets it all go in favor of the longed-for beauty.

Johanna: Wow! Now with your digressive clarification on Plato's failure out on the table -- (a failure more glorious than anything which the fetish-oriented Tradition will come to birth) -- let us sum up. Space and time then -- even in their most mysterious manifestation -- are one but really two.

Jude: You know the mantra, by now: unity in duality and duality in unity.

Johanna: How many angels can dance on the head of a pin?

Jude: What now?

Johanna: Is "the one" "the first" just as the contrary to the one is called "the fifth"?

Jude: Not really. In the listing of the five kinds (classes) the one is best understood as "the fourth" with "the first" and "the second" being, so to speak, the analogous raw materials of and for the "fourth" and "the fifth."

Johanna: Thank-you, Jude.

267.
I wish to be rendered helpless. I wish to achieve total submission. (I am getting hard just by writing this.) And total humiliation.

... ...

You must understand that there would be something liturgical, so to speak, and not repeatable about the experience.

The fact that I understand both the religious and psycho-analytic significance (childish desire for for helplessness/powerlessness before "Mommy" now become a Goddess) does not at all lessen the desire.

268
Like a woman. Just like a woman. Beyond woman, even! Ah! But there's the rub. One returns. It's all the same to me where I begin. I shall return there again in time. In time.

269.
Albert, as a man you stand head and shoulders above Heisenberg and , I presume, all the others in that crowd of theoretical physicists. And yes -- no one knows it better than the author of this book -- the formulations by the progenitors of "Copenhagen Interpretation" -- (and here one recognizes the relative superiority of the formulations of Heisenberg over Bohr even while recognizing that all of those formulations still fall short on these matters) -- have a weakness about them which saddens one. Still it is clear that your inability to accept the "findings" of Quantum Mechanics has little to do with Quantum Mechanics. It is based on implied notions of "objectivity" bequeathed to you axiomatically through your training under the rubrics of "science" in the Modern sense and on an implied "common sense" (i.e., basically Aristotelian) ontology. You would have had less difficulty with these matters had you come to the study of Quantum Mechanics with training in something like a concatenation of thinkers such as Nietzsche/Heidegger/Derrida which could have "softened", so to speak the implied philosophical/metaphysical assumptions (in this case prejudices) which you brought to your encounter with Quantum Mechanics.

Please do not misunderstand me. If one is in the arena of """""science""""" relative to the "findings" of Quantum Mechanics then one must -- if she is to be faithful to these "findings" -- insist on the formulations of Heisenberg rather than Einstein as to the "meaning" of these "findings." If one then leaves that arena and enters into the thinking which is trying to be accomplished in this wo-man book, then one must attempt to "graduate", so to speak, the formulations of Heisenberg (((dependent as they are on Aristotelian terminology and concept-ing -- which terminology and concept-ing ultimately foreclose the ability to appropriate the "findings" of Quantum Mechanics))). Still -- and there is no gentle way to say this -- relative to the formulations of Heisenberg you were just straight out "wrong."

Perhaps, if we allow ourselves a short-cut (which allowance has its dangers), one might say this: Yes indeed!!!. God DOES play dice with the universe. The universe is a crap shoot and this -- that the universe is a crap-shoot -- is the very holiness of the universe. A world governed by chance is anything but "absurd." Further -- please listen -- God is not so much the "thrower" of the dice as She is the very play of the dice themselves. *{{{Luck is a lady!!}}}* God is everywhere (even though this is not without its embarrassment relative to God).

Thank-you for listening, Albert. You have been an inspiration to many of us in many of the things you did while you were "here." But let this one go. You were beating a dead horse. I hope -- whatever this may mean -- to meet you "in person", so to speak, and have a nice chat with you. Shalom!

270.
{{Non: Luck -- tukhe -- is a lady, n'est-ce pas?

Sic: You betcha. }}

271.
{{{ *---- and other kindred notions* (i.e., of "the third"; i.e., of the good)

Timaeus 52B-8 <Loeb lining>.

Bappy: And what about those dark, dark, "places" from which no light escapes? Dewchee: They are legion; and they are part of the bargain. This is the weight of the world which Shekhinah must bear for sucking "the other" (in this case, "the one", since other than "other itself" is but the one) into Herself for the sake of Herself. She does assumes this weight gladly -- indeed with joy. And even in those dark, dark ""places"" oscillation still occurs. There will be birth again. This is the magic of Shekhinah. Bappy: Even if the sum total of things (i.e., "stuff")gets -- someday -- compressed into such a dark, dark place? Dewchee: Yes. Even then. Especially then. Bappy: So the putative worst is not really the worst. What then would the worst? Dewchee: The death of death. Not just for the appearance of the good on the third planet from the sun. But absolutely. So to speak. [[Even so, it is not impossible that the disappearance of the good -- which is quite other than a "dis-appearing" appearance -- from the third planet from the sun could tilt things in this direction entailing the death of death.]] Bappy: How would this occur? Dewchee: Should that "unbearable" kind of "lightness" -- made possible by the dis-appearing play of light -- which sheds attraction prevail without limit then oscillation shall cease. This is the danger of the coming to be of the good. The play of light can be fatal. The death of difference. The death of death. Bappy: Will this happen? Dewchee: One doesn't know. Trust Shekhinah. In all things.}}}

272.
Loretta

Shame

the ur-spring of intelligence and creativity
how to maximize this
subject to the condition of not destroying the child in the process

-----

how did you do, Loretta?????
hmmmmm
it's not only for her to have decided

273.
Shame

the most secret name of the good

Plato was indeed a shade off

274.
Obscenity. The very element in which and about which we conduct our lives. The

very psycho-socio-biological condition of our species. In a word, "mis-ogyny". But only a few will understand.

Getting it "right" relative to obscenity. Not easy. Far easier to deny. Far easier to disavow. Far easier to hate. All hatred -- ultimately -- is a function of not having gotten it right relative to obscenity.

275.
Oh Lord!!!! the sophisticated ones are legion. Like the unforgiving furies who hounded Orestes.

It did not take long for the sophisticated ones to start dumping on Hawking. This. That. The other thing.

The Arrow of time. Allow for Stephen's terminological logistics. Every original writer needs her terminological logistics.

Confer Brief, pages 143-153.

The time that matters is brief.

Time appears in order to differentiate.

Of course it goes backwards as well. The Resurrection of the body. Of all the bodies.

But going backwards it will not be preceded by memory so it will not be noticed. That's why Aristocles cleverly sticks in the Chronos/Zeus reversal -- his most amazing story -- in the tedious "divisions" section of Statesman. Where it wouldn't be noticed. A message within a message.

The arrow of time and its **il etait**.

The most marvelous gift of all. Nietzsche started to understand but fell short.

The arrow of time is really Zeno's arrow. Always moving without moving at all. Rest in Restlessness. Listen to the Queen of Hearts:

> *Like the flash of heat lightning that tells you all that is, is now.*

Joyce Carol Oates. Lock, page 92.

276.
What the sophisticated ones will never know: It's ALL a likely story. Everything. Quantum Mechanics just as much as van Gogh just as much as formal logic just as much as a sad song from Elton John.

> *The other: creating as well as discovery*

277.
There are limits to technology, although now, in medias res so to speak, this simple fact is not always evident. These limits to technology have, are now emerging, and

will emerge under the guidance entailing the requirements of economy and efficiency.

Theoretically it will, someday, have come to be understood that these guidelines of economy and efficiency were, in effect, one aspect of what our century calls, following Heisenberg, the principles of indeterminacy. "Technological" intervention into what is now called "Nature" reaches a practical limit when the effects of the intervention itself become more noteworthy than the intended result. To be sure, what constitutes "more noteworthy" is at this time an ever-shifting perception. Yet over time -- and one notes the paradox contained in this formulation -- a global consensus in these kinds of matters (especially as they relate to questions of medical technology and genetic engineering) will emerge bringing with it a more stable meaning for the phrase "Natural Law."

The question of technology has been radically obscured by Heidegger's meditation on Technology.

Heidegger understands Technology as an expression of Modernity's "Subjecticity" expressing itself in the unconditioned "Will to Will." He understands this "Will to Will" as the destiny and outcome of "Metaphysics" largely because his warped reading of the the "text" of "Metaphysics" leads him to understand Plato as the philosopher of "Presence" (Anwesenheit) who set in motion that which would -- with long enough incubation -- become Modernity's ""re-presentative"", control-oriented, appropriation of the real as objectivity for subjectivity. He never came to realize that this strain of Modernity is birthed not with Plato but rather with Aristotle and his, Aristotle's, monotheistic obsession with the "hupokeimenon of privilege."

This flawed reading of Plato is basically a function of his (Heidegger's) not having unpacked the text of Parmenides with the same carefulness with which he unpacked the text of Aristotle's Metaphysics. Derrida is always problematical with regard to what he (Derrida) is saying and with regard to what Derrida has Heidegger say. Nonetheless a good educated guess is that Frere Jacques has spent far more time and energy in and with Metaphysics than with Parmenides.

Through this bypass of the "play of difference" in Plato the Heideggerian meditation on Technology comes to follow in lock-step his, Heidegger's, univocal understanding of "Metaphysics" as the forget-fulness of "Being." His rather simplistic inclusion of the Platonic text in this history of "forget-fulness" has as its analog a univocal understanding of that "Ge-stell" -- i.e., Technology -- which holds "Dasein" in its sway. But the play of technology -- particularly in the unconscious alliance between Technology and Feminism and the correlative dis-engagement of procreation from genital sexuality made possible by technology -- is a play whose "production" eludes Heidegger's univocal appropriation/understanding of Technology.

278.
(Just as the two factors -- being and becoming -- in this passage are discovered to have really been three factors, so too in hypotheses # 2 the dyadic originary whole analyzed at 143C, 8-143A, 4 turns out, upon closer examination to have been a triadic whole. In Timaeus cf. 48E-49A; in Parmenides cf. 143A, 5-143B, 9. The parallel between Timaeus and Parmenides on this issue will have to be pursued in another forum. {{{Bappy: Shall we say it now? Dewchee: We might as well. We'll be saying the equivalent, literally, quite soon. And we have said the same, just now.

So by all means, say it now. Bappy: It is, as you know, from Physics and Philosophy: *In quantum theory this law, 'tertium non datur', is to be modified.* Shall we talk about it now? Dewchee: Let the text say it for now. At some time we may link it up with the third of Plato. For now just simply recall that the hypothesis which is not one of the eight hypotheses even though it is all of the hypotheses ----- Bappy: You mean the one we have called "Hypothesis # 2a"? Dewchee: Yes. Recall that at the beginning of that "eksaiphnes" hypothesis Plato goes out of his way to refer to it as "third." But for now the text. We shall return to these matters again, in Book II of this Trilogy. Bappy: Oh, I can't wait! Thank-you, Dewchee. Dewchee: Thank-you, Bappy. Rest now.}}})

Confer Physics, pages 181-182.

Confer Parmenides 155E where hypothesis # 2a starts by going back to the argument "a third time." The alert and persevering reader is now being tested relative to her memory. You have read it already if you have read thus far. "The third" and "the good". And how all the hypotheses hang together. Go back and read again if it's still fuzzy. Indeed you are not reading this difficult to read book unless you are reading it multiple times. (And at least one of those times you should be reading it -- "caesurae" therein included -- aloud.)

((What later on was to become the projected Mort and Jude Tetralogy started out as a planned Trilogy on Plato and Derrida in the pre-history of *Thinking Psycho-analytically* (which has now been transformed into *Shame!*).))

279.
All things considered Aristotle appears to have taken Plato too seriously relative to the "kath' auto". Prima facie it appears that Aristotle has brought a degree sophistication to the question of "kath 'auto". Through the lens of Aristotle's ontology one has poor little baby Plato "kath' auto-ing", so to speak, all over the place. In contrast for the suave Aristotle "kath 'auto" is reserved for the ways of speaking about *"being"* *"in virtue of itself."* According to this version Aristotle comes off as the "scientist" who offers a generic schema for the "kath' auto" while Plato appears to be a childish multiplier of "kath' auto" causes whose attempts at being "scientific" actually make the possibility of "science"/knowledge all that more difficult.

Confer, of course, on this way of presenting Plato's theory of Forms, the famous passage of Metaphysics I-9 at -- to cite Aristotle at his more sarcastic -- 990a, 35-990b, 8 <Loeb lining> and 991a,9-991b, 9 <Loeb lining>.

But in actual fact it is Plato -- following the ontology which allows for and insists upon what this book refers to as the "play of difference" -- who schematizes rather nicely his "kath' auto" account of the forms. This schematization is the concatenation of the eight hypotheses of Parmenides. Furthermore, in this schematization -- which depends upon the differentiation of and between aisthesis and noesis -- Plato does not really "duplicate" the sensible nor does he, to use the phrase of this book, ontologize the differentiation of and between aisthesis and noesis. Such a move was inaugurated by Aristotle with his postulation of the 47 or 55 pure intelligences who function as secondary prime movers in his Physics and Theology. True, there are no duplications of the sensible on the noetic level in Aristotle's schematization. But -- Aristotle's presentation of Plato's theory of the Forms notwithstanding -- nor was there with Plato. Indeed there was no ontologization, for Plato, of the differentiation of and between aisthesis and noesis. This move of ontologizing the differentiation of and between asithesis and noesis --

(which move is the very invention of "Platonism" (and, correlatively, the disappearance of the ability to read the texts of Plato) -- is made by the Stagirite himself: Listen:

> ----- *Yet, even it we had not seen the stars, I should think that eternal substances would none the less exist apart from the substances we would know. So now, too, if we cannot say what they are, it is just as necessary that some eternal substances exist.* (Metaphysics VII-16. According to Apostle.)

++

One of the schema's of the "kath'auto" -- i.e., "being in virtue of itself" in Aristotle's frame of reference - - is according to the "figures of predication" which is to say according to "ousia"-as-subject with the other categories functioning as predicates. This way of speaking of being -- i.e., as "already" "in itself" dispersed (i.e., over the ten categories) relieves, so to speak, Aristotle from the burden of having to account for differentiation. Aristotle, in effect, congratulates himself for overcoming the "archaic" way of posing the question of "being" and -- with the help of the Categories whose cogency he takes for granted -- posing the question in such a way that the question of differentiation can be taken for granted -- as a given, so to speak.

Confer here the text at Metaphysics XIV-2 at 1088b, 35-1089a, 7 <Loeb lining> in particular and the arguemnt of the rest of the Chapter in general.

However what Aristotle is doing here is not so much begging the question as avoiding the question. Avoiding the question, in this instance, is to avoid what is most interesting and thought pro-voking about "being", namely the "play of difference" which is something quite different from taking "difference" as a given which needs no further analysis. Aristotle's soi-dissant "clever" way of posing the question of "being" in a way which avoids the "antiquated" dictums of Parmenides does succeed in avoiding the "aporiai" occaisioned by Plato's response to and dialogue with Father Parmenides. So too, the man who invests no money will surely lose no money through investment. Aristotle, literally, "wins" by not playing.

Cf. again the XIV-2 text cited just above.

280.
This passage is the heart and soul of Plato's theory of forms.

161E, 3-162B, 10.

Our one-which-is-not partakes of ousia, somehow or other. As such it is the very opposite of the lacking-in-ousia, not-even-one, which is not of hypothesis # 1. Thus to be and to be the opposite of the one of hypothesis # 1 the one-which-is-not of hypothesis # 5 must be construed as partaking, somehow or other, of ousia.

Plato even goes farther and formulates a general principle. For anything to be what it is it must not be what it is not. To not be what it is not it must partake of negative-ousia (me ousias; 162B, 1). Likewise, for anything not to be what it is not it must be what it is not. To be what it is not it must partake of ousia. Thus every affirmation involves a double relationship (to ousia and to negative-ousia) and every denial involves a double relationship (to ousia and to negative ousia). Or, what is true of something includes what is false of that thing. Thus negative-ousia -- no less than ousia -- is the condition for the possibility of science.

(It appears that some of Aristotle's arguments in Metaphysics IV-4 concerning "negative-ousia" may very well be directed against some inferences drawn from hypothesis # 5 by some Platonists at the Academy.)

Two things are extremely interesting about this entire passage.

In the first place, there is the acknowledgment that our one-which-is-not, taken by itself, shares in ousia "in some sense" (pe; 161E, 3). This is in stark contrast to the one of hypothesis # 1 which, taken by itself, did not share in ousia at all. This seems to imply that the difference inherent in a one-which-is-not (viz., the contrary to the one, taken by itself) has a greater claim to the predicate "is" than the one taken by itself. To be sure, it is the difference inhering in a one which is (such as occurs in hypothesis # 2) which is unequivocally worthy of the predicate "is" and not difference as such. Yet "in some sense" the "is" springs from difference rather than from the one. Further, this passage seems to imply that the contrary to the one taken by itself has a greater claim to the "is" than the one, taken by itself. The one, taken by itself, vanishes, as it were, as it is examined. The one-which-is-not, taken by itself, (i.e., eksaiphnes) may not be graspable as such but it does have something substantial about it.

In the second place there is the strange negative-ousia of 162B, 1. Presumably this negative-ousia is the kind of ousia in which our one-which-is-not "somehow" has a share. What is false and negative about anything is substantially false and negative about anything. The judgment "is not" is not reducible to a mere mental separation.

Hypothesis # 5 furnishes the ultimate ontological grounding/justification the doctrine -- brought up and teasingly rejected in Theaetetus *{{at 188D-189E}}* and then brought up, nucanced, and affirmed as the central teaching of Sophist -- that to think falsely is, quite literally, to think what is not.

On these issues of mental separation {{{te dianoia!!!}}}, abstraction, and the like the assiduous reader is sent back to certain "caesurae" and sent ahead to what used to be the "abstraction" entry in what used to be the Glossary when this book was instantiated as Misogyny and as Thinking Psycho-analytically.

Now, one of the elements of anything and of everything is this one-which-is-not which presumably has substantial falseness about it. Our passage, then, can be interpreted as ontological justification for the intricasies of dialectical procedure. The total truth about anything emerges and can only emerge from the explicit treatment of what is false about anything. In this sense, the first Dialectician was neither Plato, Socrates, nor even Zeno. The first Dialectician would be Father Parmenides himself, now distinguished from his popular image -- an image which had to be killed off by the Eleatic Stranger in the dialogue Sophist. It was Parmenides himself who for the first time realized that truth and the affirmation of the "is" (along with the correlative rejection of the "is-not" and of the false) could emerge only through the explicit examination of the false mixture of the "is" and "is-not" which is what he accomplishes in his Way of Appearance. The stark "one doctrine" of Parmenides already included its own "is-not." It is not accidental -- indeed, quite to the contrary -- that Parmenides is named "Parmenides."

162B, 11-162E, 5.

Such a one-which-is-not both is and is not. Thus it suffers a change from one condition to another. Indeed this continuous change from one to the other without ever, by itself, being the other is the very character of our on-which-is-not. Suffering such change it undergoes motion, at least in the generic sense of undergoing a change. ((Please note: If our one-which-is-not IS, as the commentary maintains, *eksaiphnes*, then eksaiphnes cannot be brought in -- as it was in hypothesis # 2a -- as the explanation for how the one can undergo a change from being to non-being and vice versa. In other words, in hypothesis # 5 one is literally in, so to speak, the principle of change. That which is the very account of change in every other perspective cannot be "brought in" as an account of itself since, to repeat, one is, in hypothesis # 5, in that which would do the accounting.))

Yet since it is not it is nowhere. *{{{"now here" = "nowhere". Did Plato invent this pun as well? Did he see the possibilities of the English language before there was an English language? Doubtlessly.}}}* Being nowhere it cannot suffer the motion of alteration nor the two types of locomotion. Nor does it change into anything else at all. In this sense it is motionless. As motionless it is at rest. Note, however, that the rest it suffers is not grounded in "the same" as did occur in the analysis of rest in hypothesis # 2. In no sense is it the case that this one-which-is-not ever is the Same. It does not suffer rest as intrinsic to it. Rather our one-which-is-not suffers rest relative to not suffering the measurable types of motion.

It can be noted here that the "motion" suffered by this one-which-is-not is the very self-movement of eksaiphnes. In and by itself, eksaiphnes is in nothing at all and thus suffers neither the motion of alteration nor the two kinds of locomotion. Furthermore it is this motion of eksaiphnes which is present in any one (i.e., any form) even though any one (form) does not suffer the motion of alteration or the two kinds of loco-motion. It is through the eksaiphnes that "Motion, life, Soul and Mind" (Cf. Sophist 249) inhere in the Forms.

162E, 6-163B, 7.

Qua suffering motion the one-which-is-not becomes other and qua not suffering motion the one-which-is-not does not become other (even though, qua one-which-is-not, it is intrinsically, so to speak, other). Thus it becomes and does not become other (and even in not becoming other it is other). In becoming other it suffers generation and corruption. And even though it "is", in a manner of speaking, other, in not becoming other it does not suffer generation and corruption.

This one-which-is-not, according to this commentary, is none other than the "pure genesis" of eksaiphnes. As contrary to the one (and for the sake of predicational analysis) it is understood through the rubric "if one is not." But this one-which-is-not -- intrinsically and substantially false in its own right -- is truly other than the one and not the one at all.

As eksaiphnes it is at once generation and corruption and is not at all generation and corruption. The "ousia" to which and from which it is eternally generated and corrupted without ever beginning to be generated and corrupted and, also, not generated and corrupted, is the strange negative-ousia which the one-which-is-not, taken by itself, is (so to speak). As such, this one-which-is-not does not come into and go out of ousia in either the eternal manner of the forms nor in the perceivable manner of sensible ousia. It is the very life-source for all ousia and is itself the ungenerated generating. By itself it is the substantially false which is the ground of the true just as the one, taken by itself is the unsubstantial true which makes possible the false.

{{{But just what is this one???? you might ask. It appears to be just as mysterious as this strange eksaiphnes which is now being analyzed. Stay around.}}}

Presumably, this eksaiphnes is the raw material from which Aristotle worked up his innovative (and ultimately non-Platonic) concept of the ousia which was pure energeia/entelecheia. But Aristotle's genesis-free energeia/entelecheia is not construed as the contrary to his one (i.e., Divine Nous) -- (indeed Divine Nous for the Stagirite IS energeia/entelecheia) -- nor is this genesis-free energeia/entelecheia even construed by the Stagirite as an element in that of which it is the cause. Be that as it may, his story is another story. This commentary, at this point, only wants to suggest that even when Aristotle is innovative he leans -- however misguidedly -- on his Master.

More than anyplace else I have pushed the eksaiphnes-centered interpretation of Parmenides in this hypothesis. I believe the word itself does not occur at all in the text of hypothesis # 5. Yet the Rubicon of this eksaiphnes-centered interpretation of Parmenides was crossed long ago. Let it be tested in battle!

281.
Now we come to the end of our journey. The most subtle point of all. Be patient, reader, and follow the thread of argumentation.

Aristotle was no fool. {{Indeed, that was part of his problem. Fools rush in where angels and wise men fear to tread. But no-one ((no man!!!!)) finds who is not a fool first. }}

Aristotle was no fool.

Read, yet again, Book VII of Metaphysics. Read it backwards, forwards, sideways, and upside down. Read it twenty times and then go back and read it again as though for the first time. Luxuriate yet again in VII-17. And what will you have found?

Just this.

There are no forms for sensible substance although form -- as a principle -- causes sensible ousia to be what it is. And Aristotle is quite insistent: form, unlike matter, is not an element (stoicheia) in the make-up of sensible ousia. VII-17 in particular and Book VIII in general. Form as a principle turns out to be the energeia/entelecheia of VIII and IX. And yes, there are substances separate from sensible substance. They are God and the forty-seven/fifty-five separate intelligences in terms of which the universe has its intricate web of eternal circular motions explanatory of the motion of the universe as a whole as well as the "wanderers" as they make their only apparently wayward journey through the heaven. But these separate substances are not the forms of sensible ousia. There are no forms for sensible ousia although form -- in Aristotle's idiosyncratic meaning of form -- causes sensible substance to be what it is.

Do you yet see the fly in the ointment? Perhaps if you listen to a strange sentence right from the very heart of Book VII you will see the difficulty. The sentence itself includes some ambiguity with regard to its meaning centering upon the force of the "tes" in the "tes entelecheias" of 1036a-7 <Loeb lining>. Yet the essential agreement of Ross and Apostle on the sense of the "tes" lends support to the contention that this is a strange assertion indeed on the part of Aristotle which points beyond itself. Listen:

> *but when we come to the concrete thing, e.g., this circle, i.e., one of the individual circles, whether perceptible or intelligible (I mean by the intelligible circles the mathematical, and by perceptible circles those of bronze and wood) of these there is no definition, but they are known through thinking and/or sensation and when they pass out of the [this] actuality [* viz., of this being known through thinking and/or sensation*] it is not clear whether they exist or do not exist but they are spoken of and known according to the formula of the universal.*

The passage exposes that intersection -- (always and forever essential whomever the thinker may be) -- between Aristotle's ontology and Aristotle's implied epistemology. What is at issue in Book VII is the ontological status of sensible ousia. Yet it is clear that this Book -- Book VII -- is raising as well the question concerning the intelligibility of sensible ousia. For Plato there is no intelligibility for sensible ousia unless there are "forms" whose ontological status is "really real." *{{Let it pass for now that, in Parmenides -- "difficulty # 4" -- Plato had come to realize as well that the simple postulation of "kath'auten" Forms also forecloses the possibility for intelligibility for sensible ousia. The way Plato handles his double bind -- no intelligibility with or without Forms -- has been the broad subject matter of this book.}}* Aristotle's solution to his ontological difficulty -- i.e., transforming form into a principle (i.e., not an element) which he comes to call "energeia/entelecheia" leaves unsettled the question concerning the intelligibility of sensible ousia.

"Difficulty # 4" occurs at Parmenides 133B-135B.

Confer on this -- in addition to Aristotle's strange sentence cited from Book VII of Metaphysics -- the ending of XIII-10 which also leaves the aporia unresolved through Aristotle's charming -- and often employed -- way of avoiding questions: ---- *in one sense 'x', in another sense 'not-x'.*

{{{To be sure, this ----- *in one sense 'x', in another sense 'not-x'* ------ also has its pedigree in Plato. Anyone familiar with the details of hypothesis # 2 recognizes immediately that such is Plato's very own procedure. Plato's perspectival ontology (which is the issue in hypothesis # 2) not only allows for such a procedure, but actually demands such a procedure. In contrast, Aristotle flees from such a perspectival ontology in his obsession for finding the hupokeimenon of privilege. Accordingly the -- --- *in one sense 'x', in another sense 'not x'* ----- strategy -- (which would be allowable in a "pros hen" analysis of the meanings of terms) -- cannot, for Aristotle, validly be used to adjudicate problems of ontology and/or epistemology. Thus, -- on the one hand -- if the ending of XIII-10 is an example "pros hen" analysis of terms then it leaves the issue of the Chapter untreated. On the other hand, if this strategy is intended as an adjudication of the issue raised in the Chapter, it is nothing but sophistry since Aristotle's kind of ontology precludes this kind of perspectival adjudication.}}}

Aristotle was no fool.

With Plato this aporia -- involving that marvelous intersection between and of one's "ontology" and one's "epistemology" -- plays itself out according to a scenario no longer allowed for by Aristotle. This sceneario is "the play of difference."

Of course Aristotle must have been cognizant of the contextualization of Plato's theory of Forms (which contextualization, in written form, comes forth as

Parmenides). In this wo-man book I have argued extensively that Plato's theory of Forms rests upon the "play of difference" and upon an "ontology" (in a manner of speaking) in which the principle of difference is not only a "first principle" but also an element (stoicheia) in that of which it is a first principle. Aristotle, with the help of a metaphysical appropriation of his own Categories, takes a differentiated world as a given and does not at all take it upon himself to explain why there is multiplicity and variety. The cogency of this conceptual move on the part of Aristotle is commented upon elsewhere in this wo-man book. The point to be recognized now is this: Aristotle's way of doing "ontology" (i.e., taking differentiation as a given rather than as the to-be-explained) removes from the Stagirite even the possibility of accounting for the intelligibility of sensible ousia through the Platonic "play of difference."

As noted earlier, Aristotle counts such a project -- (i.e., that of counting "difference" and multiplicity to be explained) -- as an "archaic" way of doing "first Philosophy." Confer XIV-2 at 10898b, 35-1089a, 7 in particular and the entire argumentation of XIV-2 from the very beginning of the Chapter to 1089b, 33.

What then does Aristotle do?

His move is intriguing although he only barely takes upon himself the task of unpacking it at all. He makes it in Chapters Four, Five, and Eight of Book III of De Anima. One is speaking here of "nous poietikas."

It is quite simple. It is mind -- qua "agent" (i.e., "making") intellect -- which makes that which is intelligible potentially to become actually intelligible. It is through this conceptual move that Aristotle's "energeia/entelecheia" is brought under the umbrella of Nous.

What Aristotle says about "nous poietikas" is tantalizingly little. The teaching emerges from and, in effect, is at the same time the crowning achievement of his "Act/Potency" metaphysics worked out in the middle books (VII, VIII, and IX) of Metaphysics and used meticulously all throughout De Anima. {{This means, of course, that this invention carries with it -- *indeed this invention actually instantiates those liabilities in their most subtle form* -- all the liabilities entailed: i), by the Aristotle's stance towards "difference"; ii), by his domestication of "dunamis"; and, finally, iii), by the resulting "Act/Potency" ontology in general.}}

The destiny of Aristotle's invention constitutes the key for understanding the link between Modern Subjectivity-oriented philosophies and the Post-Platonic (i.e., not inclusive of Plato himself) Ancients. The Plotinian Neo-Platonists are quite enamored with Aristotle's invention. The Arabian commentators unpack this invention meticulously in various directions. The Christian commentators also unpack this invention in various intriguing directions. The various theological offshoots alone of this clever invention could and have filled volumes. In any case (as has been argued elsewhere in this wo-man book) in and through all of this incubation -- {{{{And one must keep in mind that Aristotle's whole philosophy centers around the being and intelligibility of individuals and individuals are "hupokeimena" (i.e., subjects allowing for predicates). }}}} -- eventually is birthed "Subjectivity" in the Modern sense. Kant is not only pre-figured in Aristotle. Kant is pretty much instantiated in Aristotle.

What gets lost in this fascinating denouement (whose last installment is German Idealism) to Aristotle's invention is the original "play of difference" by which Plato took his shot at these questions concerning intelligibility and how we speak about "things." For Plato it is never a question of whether the intellect is "active" or passive. For Plato "nous" -- as with "dunamis" -- is either and/or both and/or neither. And all at once. (*) What is critical for Plato is the emergence of "difference" made possible by the intellect's break from aisthesis. *{{{This break from aisthesis is anything but "abstraction." Mired as one still is in a covert Aristotelianism about these matters, one must parody the famous phrasing from Aristotle's Psychology in order to catch the flavor of Plato's conceptual move. Listen: --* **--nothing is in the intellect except that it first NOT be in sensation** *Do you yet hear???* **---- nothing is in the intellect except that it first NOT be in sensation** *More than two millennia of consciously and unconsciously having Aristotle as a prism by which to have access to the text of Plato requires a bit of repetition as a way of shattering this distorting prism.}}}* It is only this break from aisthesis -- *(which is pretty much the antithesis of the procedure adumbrated by Aristotle in Posterior Analytics II-19)* -- which allows (for a genuine Platonist) the playful return to aisthesis. One thing is certain to this writer: Had Plato's "play of difference" been given the long incubation period alloted to Aristotle's "nous poietikas" there would not be today the resistance to the teachings of Quantum Mechanics which resistance even today keeps Philosophy from the intelligibility of things.

*. Indeed, "there is" intellect at all only by virtue of the oft-cited (in this book) break from aisthesis which "break" is (so to speak) "unterwegs" in multiple ways in the pre- and pre-pre-history of our species. It is the break from aisthesis which puts one in contact with the "other" (of the other) in terms of which "there is" intellect at all, "poietikas" or otherwise.

{{{The play of difference. The break from aisthesis. (I.e., anything but an abstraction from or sublation of.) Getting in contact -- by virtue of this break -- with the "other" (of the other) however fragmented that "other" (of the other) might be. Generating, in the process, discourse and the road-map by which to re-turn to aisthesis. Always the necessity for re-breaking. Always the necessity for re-turning. "Abstraction" and Nous Poietikas: distractions which keep one form the vocation of thinking. It's all in the long caesura, dear reader. It is your liability if you have passed over the long caesura too quickly.}}}

282.
What's good for the gander is not necessarily good for the goose; a lesson in regressive kathalysis. *(i.e., Something really strange and "rotten" -- in a somewhat reversed Denmarkian sense -- happened on the way to the Lyceum; what happens when a hule-imbued Physicist doing "First Philosophy" reviews the first principles of a dialectical thinker. A case study: Metaphysics I-vi; 987b, 19-988a, 17; <Loeb lining>)*

First. Aristotle giving roughly correct information about Plato:

i). That Plato spoke of two first principles: The One and The Dyad (of the Great and the Small);

ii). That Plato spoke of the One as a Father and the Dyad as a Mother.

Two. (--- without breaking stride ---) Aristotle takes his own frame of reference and uses it as a way of allegedly exposing how Plato's first principles "really" function. In this case Aristotle takes his Form/Matter paradigm from Physics (minus the nuances concerneing "privation" from Physics I) and "exposes" how Plato's "One" and "Dyad" allegedly work.

Three. (--- without breaking stride ---) Aristotle critiques the Platonic account because the Platonic account *as now presented by Aristotle* is caught up in an incoherence. In this case the alleged incoherence is a function of *Aristotle's own* Father-qua-Form and Mother-qua-Matter account of "nature" which account is then used as the vehicle for both presenting and then critiqing what Plato allegedly said. In fact, Plato's Father/One (i.e., principle of Unity) and Mother/Dyad (i.e., principle of multiplicity) account of first principles is most radically misrepresented when it is presented through the prism of Aristotle's Form/Matter paradigm which eventually becomes the Act/Potency paradigm.

And he doesn't even give the corpse a decent burial. (988b, 12-988b, 14; <Loeb lining>) Ever inistent on presenting Plato's Dyad as a material substrate, Aristotle ends his review of Plato by making the Dyad function as a kind of ultimate hupokeimenon relative to issues of predication. What Aristotle says here is so quick, so compact, and so unclear as to its exact meaning that one might feel justified in suspecting some corruption of the text. ((Or perhaps some short-cutting "nodding" by Aristotle's Lyceum "editor.")) In any case, what is conveniently ignored here (precisely where it ought not be ignored) is that Plato's own schema of predicational analysis -- i.e., the Parmenides which, as a schema for predicational analysis is both radically and heterogeneously different from Categories -- by which the One and its 'other' (i.e., "the one-which-is-not; i.e., popularly, "the Dyad") are presented. Contrary to Categories what Plato offers is precisely a schema of predicational analysis in which and by which the privilege of hupokeimenon -- (which privilege is the very heart and soul of Aristotle's Logic and Ontology) -- is constantly and thematically subverted as it is shown how both the 'one' and 'the-one-which-is-not' necessarily dis-appear, differently, into their predicates leaving the "subject" (hupokeimenon) bereft of privilege.

283.
Physics and Philosophy. *[A book by Werner Heisenberg put out by Harper Torchbooks in 1962. Any pagination in this section is from the paperback edition of 1962.]* In this book Heisenberg adroitly defends the "Copenhagen Interpretation" of the "findings" of Quantum Mechanics and situates these "findings" in a network of "philosophical" pre-suppositions (concerning """"""reality"""""" and the nature of scientific undertakings) which pre-suppositions have made it impossible for some (e.g., Einstein) to accept the "findings" of Quantum Mechanics without putting a "spin" on those "findings" which effectively constitutes a denial of those "findings". Heisenberg's analysis (copyrighted in 1958) came forth before the "findings" associated with "Bell's Theorem" concerning "action-at-a-distance-involving-speeds-greater-than-the-speed-of-light." Although the "Cophenhagen Interpretation" does not address itself to anything like what is implied by "Bell's Theorem" and does not, in and by itself, necessarily entail what is implied by "Bell's Theorem", nonetheless the "Copenhagen Interpretation" is certainly compatible with what is implied by "Bell's Theorem." Finally, it can also be noted that while, on the average, Heisenberg's name gets linked with the name of "Bohr" under the rubric of "the Copenhagen Interpretation", one will find that the actual formulations of the "meaning" of Quantum Mechanics given by Heisenberg are far more elegant than the formulations of Bohr. In this book it is not so much the "Copenhagen Interpretation" of the "findings" of Quantum Mechanics which is at issue but rather the phrasings of Heisenberg in his Gifford Lectures which came to be transformed into Physics and Philosophy. It is what is contained in those Gifford lectures -- and not, therefore, all dimensions of the "Copenhagen Interpretation" -- which is at issue in these remarks. ((A fortiori, if the

formulations of Heisenberg are to be distinguished from the formulations of Bohr, how much more so are the formulations of Heisenberg to be distinguished from the formulations of Schroedinger.))

In Physics and Philosophy Heisenberg, in a rather nuanced and subtle manner, makes striking analogies between the "findings" of nuclear Physics and the "findings" of the Pre-Socratic cosmologists, Plato's cosmology and Aristotle's Metaphysics. Indeed, as this book on "the wo-man principle" has so many times pointed out, Heisenberg borrows the Aristotelian "Potentia" [Heisenberg's way of relating to the Aristotelian "dunamis"] as a way of "presenting" the funny kind of being/non-being-at-once uncovered by the "findings" of Quantum Mechanics. Inevitable and unfortunate that such should occur.

In this book before you, concerning "the wo-man principle", there are no less than six overlapping -- but hardly congruent -- assertions which are repeatedly being made: 1). That in the quaqmire of interpretations (which, Hermes-like, "translate" the technical/mathematical language of "science" into "ordinary" language) concerning the "meaning" of the "findings" of Quantum Mechanics it is still -- even after all these years -- the formulations of Heisenberg which are most elegant and which best reveal -- at least in this (i.e., the "translation" of the technical/mathematical into the ordinary) genre of writing -- what the "findings" of Quantum Mechanics are trying to say. 2). That it is most appropriate -- indeed it is a necessity -- that the "findings" of Quantum Mechanics be made to speak to us through the sound systems of the early cosmologists/ontologists and that in this regard the nexus "Parmenides/Cratylus/Plato" is crucial. 3). That, on the one hand it is part of the genius of Heisenberg to have made -- in a rather nuanced and subtle manner -- resiliating connections between the "findings" of nuclear Physics and the "findings" of Ancient Greek cosmologies/ontologies. 4). That, on the other hand, while Heisenberg brings one to the proper "topos", so to speak, in and through which the "findings" of Quantum Mechanics will finally say what they are trying to say (i.e, this "topos" is the constellation of those significant Ancient Greek cosmologies/ontologies), nevertheless Heisenberg's weirdly stumbling ruminations -- (and yet at the same time, Heisenberg's subtlety and notable learning concerning things Ancient having been and being acknowledged) -- in and around this "topos" threaten to unravel his great accomplishment in getting comprehension of these matters as far as he did. (*) This "stumbling" on the part of Heisenberg is manifested in a number of ways. To wit:

*. {{One thinks in this regard of an Aeneas-like wanderer, stalled and bedeviled by Circe, but never getting to taste the magic of the Goddess. Of course it would take a very special and most cunning kind of man (far more cunning than Aeneas) -- *No-man, not a wo-man, will ever know* (viz., no man who is not a wo-man will ever know) -- to taste the magic of the Goddess and to leave her. (A man willing to go to hell to receive from Tiresias his lot before speaking to the shade of his own Mother.) }}

a). He properly guides us to Timaeus, makes some useful and even remarkable observations about Nuclear Physics and Plato's Cosmology, and then leaves this most magical of texts without at all tasting its magic. Heisenberg completely bypasses the concatentation of Female/Space/Receptacle which is the very heart of that dark dialogue and the "Place" at which Plato gives us his most teasing hints about the theory of Forms. (Cf.:

> *Are we talking idly whenever we say that there is such a thing as an intelligible form of anything? Is this nothing more than a word?*

at 51C and all the surrounding dark passages which constitute the stage-setting for that teasing remark.)

b). In his quest for the sounding system by which the funny kind of "being/non-being at once" uncovered by the "findings" of Quantum Mechanics can be heard, Heisenberg settles on the Aristotelian "Potentia." Perhaps this was inevitable since the Tradition (and largely due to moves engendered by Aristotle himself!):

> bi). practically buries without a trace the incredible resiliations of "being/non-being at once" found in the nexus Parmenides/Cratylus/Plato; and
>
> bii). not unlike the appearance of Banquo, maintains a memory of those incredible resiliations of "being/non-being at once" through its (the Tradition's) rather Neanderthal dances around Aristotelian "dunamis/potentia."

5). That, paradoxically enough (i.e., unbeknownst to Heisenberg), it is precisely the "Act/Potency" paradigm -- (which -- whether this is recognized by Heisenberg or not -- is married to the Principle of non-Contradiction) -- which, when fully unpacked, not only radically distorts what the "findings" of Quantum Mechanics is attempting to say, but actually chokes off the very possibility of the "findings" of Quantum Mechanics ever saying what they are attempting to say. And 6). That the dismantling of the Tradition where "the wo-man principle" disappeared (i.e. at the nexus "Plato and Aristotle") is the very condition by which that prior nexus, "Parmenides/Cratylus/Plato", can make its re-appearance. If all of these assertions are correct it will have turned out to have been the case that the "findings" of Quantum Mechanics can "say" what they are to say when and as the "wo-man principle" makes its thoughtful re-appearance. Preparing for the thoughtful re-appearance -- (which re-appearance will come forth "dis-appearingly") -- of "the wo-man principle" (i.e., "mis-ogyny") has been the purpose of this book.

(caesura)

So you did not come to me or for me after all. Today I send the pages of the "book" to be bound. Far rather that I had been bound -- totally; exposed; and rendered fully helpless, powerless --, and perhaps gagged as well, over to and for you.

You would not justify my love. In any case you did not. You leave me (although you never left me) waiting and breathless. It is alright. There is nothing to forgive. She did not intend it for us. You were sent to me by her in a dream. Like a prayer, in reverse. (So to speak) Only She can justify my love. Just brush my cheek before you leave me.

I'll pawn
My hopes of Heaven -- you know what they are worth --
That the presumptuous pedagogues of Earth,
If they could tell the riddle offered here,
Would scorn to be, or being to appear
What they now seem and are -- but let them chide,
They have few pleasures in the world beside;
Perhaps we should be dull were we not chidden,
Paradise-fruits are sweetest when forbidden.
Folly can season Wisdom, Hatred Love.

Cited from "Fragments Connected with Epipsychidion" as contained in The Complete Works of Percy Bysshe Shelley; Volume II, Poems. Edited by R. Ingpen and W E pech; Gordian Press, New York, 1965. Page 380. [Hereafter: Shelley]

And what is that most brief and bright delight
Which rushes through the touch and through the sight,
And stands before the spirit's inmost throne,
A naked Seraph? None hath ever known.
Its birth is darkness, and its growth desire;
Untameable and fleet and fierce as fire,
Not to be touched but to be felt alone,
It fills the world with glory -- and is gone.
. . . .
It floats with rainbow pinions o'er the stream
Of Life, which flows, like a dream
Into the light of morning, to the grave
As to an ocean ....

Cited from "Fragments Connected with Epipsychidion" as contained in Shelley, page 381.

Intoxication with one's own weakness. An insuperable desire to fall. How he knew. Not just in what he did. But what he would ask her time after time punishing himself some more each time. The betrayal.

Over and over again. A thousand times on each detail. Month after painful month. Scratching the wound raw, time after time. Punishing himself. Glorifying in his weakness. Over and over. And all the time -- each time -- he was asking: Why, Mom? Why?

Of course April came
again
as did May
come come and don't come
but always
without surcease
Oh God!!
the arching, aching beauty of the moaning honey pearl
Oh God!!!
lovely *{{{ half-hidden and yet beautiful; half-hidden and yet beautiful; half-hidden and yet beautiful }}}*
Nothing <u>is</u> so beautiful as springing
Ooooooooooh God!!!! Unh! Unh! lovely
and pearl becomes
(('be' comes!))
oyster
again.

*****
+++++

December 23, 1984 through December 8, 1991.

This book -- brought to a close on the <u>feast(!)</u> of the Immaculate Conception -- was conceived with much sin. Let it therefore <u>AND</u> nevertheless be co-dedicated, in addition to sweet 'Eurydice', to Madonna and Elton John. <u>Why not?</u> The only meaningful symbols of Hope in our time which time still suffers deperately from the aftermath of the fetish.

Chinchilla; Jerusalem; West Side; Brick; Newton-Ransom; Narragansett; Friends; The Hill Section; <u>Tom's</u> River; Princeton; Green Ridge; Little Silver; the fifth floor; and beautiful Spring Lake. All near my beloved lake lilac. --- *qui tollis peccata mundi* --- There was nothing to forgive. There never was.

jwm/JE

284.
{{{Bappy: Are we still in the dream? Dewchee: Of course not. Well, in a sense. I don't know.}}}

285.
abstraction. "qua-ing", so to speak. "As-ing", so to speak. A filtering out process, so to speak, which allegedly enables the knower to focus in on the more intelligible dimensions of the "thing." In the Aristotelian/Thomistic schema of things one might , on the first level of abstraction, "abstract" from individual matter and focus in upon common sensible matter. On the second level of abstraction one might "abstract" from both motion and common sensible matter in order to do Mathematics which would allow one to focus in upon things in their "common intelligible matter." On the third level of abstraction one might "abstract" from all dimensions of matter completely. At this third level of abstraction one is studying being "qua being" and concentrating on the most universal characteristics of being. Presumably from the study of sensible things at this most abstract level one positions the mind, so to speak, to study those "things" (separate substances) for which "abstraction" would be irrelevant (since they are not composed of matter at all) and yet which can be approached by human intellect only by studying sensible substance with regard to its being as such.

In this book of many titles it is argued that Platonic "abstraction" is significantly, and literally, different from Aristotelian abstraction in that Plato does not pose questions of "being" in terms of a material substrate and in that, for Plato, intelligibility is made possible by the oscillating "play of difference" and not through anything even remotely analogous to a filtering process. Nevertheless, none of this keeps the Tradition from understanding Plato and his theory of forms <u>as though</u> Plato were doing Aristotelian-like "abstraction" (i.e., "qua-ing") in a terribly naive way. This is the scandal of Philosophy: that even today, with all of its alleged sophistication, it still understands Plato through the distorting lens of Aristotle.

{{{The most assiduous readers of Shame! *will find what they need to know on these matters in certain of the "caesurae." Good luck!}}}*

286.
aisthesis. perception; very often in the sense of "sensory perception."

287.
allo. other.

288.
Anangke. necessity. For Aristotle "anangke" names God (i.e. Nous) in God's simplicity. For Aristotle God <u>is</u> necessity and in this sense God's simple necessity is "free." For Plato "anangke" is the principle contrary to "Nous" and resistant to -- (and yet at the same time the "other" without which "there is" nothing at all) -- the demiurgic activity of God/nous. This book of many titles takes "Anangke" to be one of Plato's more popular names for the principle contrary to "the one" just as "nous" is his more popular name for the principle -- "the one" -- which is contrary

to "difference/other." In any case "anangke" is God's "other" without which God would not <u>be</u> God and yet anangke is resistant to the workings of God. *{{{{{"Ananke" (the spelling in the Freud text) as used by Freud in Chapter Four of <u>Civilization and its Discontents</u> appears to come forth as the "other" principle to "Eros." But the careful reader of the subsequent chapters in that wonderful love story -- which is a mystery story as well -- finds out that "Ananke" is but a mask -- a presentation of sorts -- of the "true" other of Eros, namely "Thanatos." ((Indeed, Freud's Ananke is, ultimately, not at all the other of Eros but rather, so to speak, stage setting for the Eros/Thanatos interaction.)) Thus if anyone were to compare Plato and Freud, the analog for Plato's "Anangke" in Freud would not be "Ananke" but rather "Thanatos." However, it is difficult to make even a casual comparison between Plato and Freud without begging several questions and even several kinds of questions. }}}}}* ((Concerning comparisons between "Eros" in Freud and "Eros" in Plato the reader is referred to certain sections of what might be called the "mania" section of this book which succeed these Glossaryesque entries. <1/4/92>))

289.
Andreia. courage. Strength; manliness; perseverance.

290.
androgyny. popularly, a condition of the psyche in which one's feminine and masculine dimensions are expressed and integrated. However, in this book "androgyny" names a future re-alignment of libidinal economy, matriarchal in orientation, in which sexual differentiation is actually heightened in the service of this matriarchal orientation.

291.
anthropic principle. a principle articulated by Stephen Hawking in his book, <u>A Brief History of Time</u>. The idea is that the universe is the way it is and has the (mathematical) structure it has so as to make possible the kind of being which can know this. It resonates with possibilities of isomorphism -- analogically speaking -- between the evolution of the brain and the evolution of the universe. *{{{Bappy: Like:* The same: thinking as well as being. *Something like that, Dewchee? Dewchee: Oh yes. And remember what we said back then. Bappy: I remember it well:* The other: creating as well as discovery. *Dewchee: Thank-you, so much, Bappy. Now go back to sleep. Bappy: Okie-doakie. Sleep tight. Don't let the bed bugs bite!}}}*

292.
a-pathein. according to the Stoics, the best condition for the soul. A state of "non-suffering", so to speak.

293.
aporia. difficulty; literally: "lack of passage."

294.
Aristocles. Plato's "real" name.

295.
Bell's theorem. a mathematical hypothesis concerning non-local interference on sub-atomic phenomena; the hypothesis entails the possibility that there is action-at-a-distance which occurs faster than the speed of light. References to Bell's theorem often occur in the popular literature on Quantum Mechanics. The mathmatical and logical validity of the reductio ad absurdum used in Bell's theorem is not in dispute. However there is a wide spectrum of opinion concerning its relevance relative to the "findings" of Quantum Mechanics.

296.
Boy Wonder. this book's nickname for Schelling. Schelling wrote some remarkably weighty philosophical essays before he reached the age of twenty.

297.
Causa sui. cause of itself. A Medieval expression denoting the independence and self-sufficiency of God. A term often enough used by Heidegger to express the way in which Western "metaphysics" understands God. In this book of many titles Aristotle is pointed to as the one who forged the God concept which dominates in Western "metaphysics."

298.
Commentary on "Parmenides". A commentary on the dialogue Parmenides, in two parts, written and privately printed by me in 1976. It is, quite literally, a "difference" oriented reading of Parmenides and singles out "eksaiphnes" as Plato's esoteric name for "difference/other."

299.
Cratylus. a Heraclitean philosopher who was Plato's first teacher.

300.
Cratylus. a dialogue written by Plato.

301.
De Anima. "Concerning the Soul"; Aristotle's Psychology.

302.
De Vere. Earl of Oxford and contemporary of the virgin queen. According to Freud and others De Vere was the true author of the plays and sonnets attributed to "William Shakespeare." The secret writings of De Vere *{{most likely buried at Stratsford-on-Avon with the body of the "real" (i.e., spouse of Ann Hath a Way who is not to be confused with Ann Drogeny) Bill 'Shake-speare' the soi-dissant "author" of the plays and sonnets}}* prove beyond a shadow of a doubt that the shot which killed Kennedy came from the grassy knoll.

303.
differance. Derrida's intended mis-spelling of the French, "difference." "Differance" is Derrida's appropriation of the notion of the "difference" obtaining

between Being (<u>Sein</u>) and beings (<u>Seinendes</u>) as understood by the German thinker, Martin Heidegger. According to Derrida, "differance" is neither a word nor a concept.

304.
Diogenes Laertius; Diogenes. Hellenic writer probably of the third Christian century. Wrote <u>Lives of the Philosophers</u> which is a source of information concerning the early philosophers. It is from Diogenes that we learn of the tetralogical arrangement of Plato's dialogues.

305.
Dion. nephew of Dionysius from the city-state of Syracuse. Involved in a protracted struggle -- inclusive of a partially successful military coup -- with the younger Dionysius for rulership of Syracuse -- a struggle in which Plato was called upon to play a mediating role; rather heavy-handed in his implementation of political reform; responsible for the execution of a former political ally; assassinated, apparently by Athenians who may have had some assoication with Plato, in 354/353 B.C. Student, friend and, apparently, (according to the testimony of Diogenes) lover/beloved of Plato. Subject matter of several of Plato's epistles and recipient of one. Plato's whole association with Dion and also with Dionysius is the subject matter of the famous "seventh letter."

306.
dunamis. power; potency; capacity. With Plato "dunamis" is multivalent but it always carries the connotation of liveliness; with Plato "power" -- with its Nietzschean/Dionysian overtones -- is often the appropriate translation of "dunamis." Platonic "dunamis" is <u>both</u> active and passive. With Aristotle "dunamis" is multivalent; however Aristotelian "dunamis" is usually the correlative of (and second fiddler to) "energeia/entelecheia." There is, in Aristotle a kind of domestication of "dunamis" in favor of letting "energeia/entelecheia" play center stage. "Dunamis" is, definitionally, passive in Aristotle's usage when "dunamis" is used as the co-relative of "energeia/entelecheia."

307.
dyad of the the great and the small. according to the testimony of Aristotle "the dyad of the great and the small" was, for Plato, the first principle from which are generated -- in conjunction with the other first principle, "the one" -- the forms and the mathematicals. Various successors of Plato (one thinks of Speusippus and Xenocrates) apparently had different appellations for this first principle according to how they understood the generation of number and the mathematicals from the interaction of the first principles. "The Dyad of the Great and the Small" appears to have been one of Plato's own appellations of the first principle in question.

According to Aristotle's testimony Platonic first principles were also construed by Plato to have been "elements" (<u>stoicheia</u>) in that of which they are the first principles. In this book of many titles "the dyad of the Great and the Small" refers to the mathematical expression for the principle which is contrary to "the one." The contention of this book is that "difference/other" is Plato's more technically precise name for the principle contrary to "the one." It is also the contention of this book that "eksaiphnes" is Plato's esoteric name for "difference/other."

308.
eidos. form; species.

309.
eksaiphnes. of a sudden; suddenly; the instant; significantly important "concept" in Plato's dialogue Parmenides. Presumably "eksaiphnes" was Plato's esoteric name for "difference" which itself was Plato's one of Plato's names for the principle contrary-to-the-one.

310.
Eleatic Stranger. character in Plato's dialogues, Sophist and Statesman; in some ways he appears to be eclipsing the character of Socrates in those dialogues.

311.
energeia. activity; work; energy; used by Aristotle as the correlative of "dunamis" in his "act/potency" metaphysics. Used more or less as a synonym for the neologism "entelecheia." Energeia, as used by Aristotle, names a state of being which is whole and complete at every given instant; it is a state of being in which form and telos are instantiated as one. As such, energeia "points to" "entelecheia." (Cf. Metaphysics IX-8 at 1050a, 20-25.)

312.
ens causa sui. see **Causa sui.**

313.
entelecheia; enTELecheia. complete actuality. Cf. "energeia."

314.
epekeina tes ousias. beyond being; beyond beingness. Famous phrase employed by Plato in Book VI of the Republic. This book before you alleges that the Plotinian/Neo-Platonic appropriation of the "epekeina tes ousias" becomes for the subsequent history of Philosophy a falsifying prism by which Plato's intent relative to the "epekeina tes ousias" is misunderstood.

315.
"Epipsychidion". a poem of Shelley's. Although not published with "Epipsychidion" Shelley wrote and sparingly disseminated "Fragments Connected with 'Epipsychidion' " , a set of verses dealing with Socrates, androgyny, and other related matters. These fragments connected with "Epipsychidion" were apparently alluded to by Joyce in Ulysses.

316.
es gibt. the German for "there is." This phrase is a major theme of Heidegger's thought. It refers to the way Being (Sein) "gives" itself to, as and through the history of "metaphysics." In this very "giving" Being (Sein) comes to be revealed in

an "onto-theological" (i.e., "metaphysical") manner yet, in the very "giving" is radically concealed in its own nature.

317.
esse. to be; resonates with the manner in which St. Thomas Aquinas thinks through the problematic of energeia/entelecheia in Aristotle.

318.
eu prattein. Live well! (moral/ethical connotation implied) Often, Plato's epistolary greeting.

319.
eu tukhein. Good luck! Often, Plato's epistolary sign-off.

320.
Frere Jacques. this book's nickname for Jacques Derrida.

321.
gnonai. a form of gi-gnosko used at a critical juncture in the dialogue Theaetetus. Gi-gnosko means "to know" and, more precisely, "to come to know." It is the birth of knowledge, so to speak.

322.
Heisenberg. German scientist credited with the "discovery" of the "uncertainty principle" of Quantum Mechanics. A major contributor to the literature which deals with the problem of "translating" the microscopic findings of Quantum Mechanics to the macroscopic language of ordinary science and of common sense,

323.
Henri Birault. a French thinker whose writings dis-play and thoughtfully resiliate the essential of Martin Heidegger's writing/thinking. Noteworthy in Birault's writings is his ability to unpack the Hegelian text, with all of its attendant and most nuanced subtlety, and show just how radically dis-similar ***{{different in its difference; approaching opposition as an unreachable limit}}*** Hegel's thinking is from Heidegger's thinking.

324.
heteros. difference; other.

325.
hupodoche. Receptacle. The third factor introduced by Plato into his "likely story" (i.e., Timaeus) after the analysis turns to "Anangke." This third factor effectively becomes "Khora" ("space) as the analysis progresses. How Plato's "hupodoche" and Aristotle's "hupokeimenon" are and, more importanly, are not analogs for each other is one of the important topics of this wo-man book.

326.
hupokeimenon. the underlying. In the logical works of Aristotle, hupokeimenon means "subject", more or less in the grammatical sense; that of which there are predicates. In the Metaphysics "hupokeimenon" functions as a critically important concept in Aristotle's analysis of sensible substance in Book VII. "Hupokeimenon" has several noteworthy meanings in Book VII; it's most important meaning is as the "form" of sensible substance in Aristotle's idiosyncratic meaning of form. "Hupokeimenon" as form is the "other" of VII-17. It is the correlate of the Latin "suppositum."

327.
kath' auto; kath' auten. according to itself; with reference to itself. It is one of Plato's way of designating the forms and/or ideas. In the singular it is Aristotle's way of designating the non-incidental meanings of "being."

328.
khalapa ta kala. beautiful (things) are difficult; beauty is difficult. A refrain used quite often by Plato.

329.
khora. space. The third factor in Plato's "likely story" (i.e., Timaeus) after the "likely story" has turned to an analysis of what is brought about by "Anangke." Apparently it is Plato's development of his "hupodoche" conceit. This wo-man book makes the claim that for Plato "Khora" is effectively "difference" which means that it is the key for understanding the "Khorismos" doctrine of Plato's theory of Forms.

330.
Lou. Lou Andreas-Salome; friend -- with romantic overtones but certainly no carnal consumation -- of Nietzsche particularly during the Summer/Fall of 1882; long-time friend of and correspondent with Freud.

331
Luria, Isaac. Jewish mystic. Expelled from Spain in 1492. Lived, worked, and taught in the Galilee until his death. The Lurianic tradition spawned the tradition of the "broken vessels" and the "in-gathering" of the sparks of fire.

332.
maia. May; the very merry month of May; in French, "mai." As **maya** Appearance. *{{{Appearance and appearances alike both conceal and reveal.}}}* Someone said: *Maia is the Mother of Hermes.* *{{{maya and samsara}}}*

333.
Marty. this book's nickname for Martin Heidegger, the German thinker. Heidegger joined the Nazi Party in 1933.

334.
mathein. to learn; learning.

335.
metaphysics. beyond and/or after the physical. It is the traditional title given to the set of books which Aristotle referred to as "Primary Philosophy." Many accounts given as to the actual genesis of this word which was not, in fact, used by Aristotle. "Metaphysics" becomes a generic term used by Derrida and Heidegger by which to express the revelation and concealment of "Being" (Sein) through "metaphysics" and its history. Derrida and Heidegger use the term "Onto-theology" more or less synonymously with the term "metaphysics"; "onto-theology" for Derrida and Heidegger specifies the way in which "Being" is revealed and concealed through "metaphysics" and its history.

336.
Milan. this book's way of referring to the writer, Milan Kundera.

337.
misogyny. Hatred for women stemming from on deep-seated fears, envies, and anxieties based on conscious and unconscious associations with female genitalia. This book of many titles, while acknowledging the clinically pathological dimensions of misogyny, maintains that misogyny is a universal "dis-ease" of our species characteristic of females as well as males. This book is an investigation into misogyny as the pre-condition of androgyny. Generally speaking, when "misogyny" refers to clinically pathological manifestations of wo-men hatred the word will be spelled in the "normal" fashion. Generally speaking, when "misogyny" refers to the inevitable, universal and not necessarily pathological ""dis-ease"" fundamentally characteristic of our species which is the very animating force of life the word will appear as: "mis-ogyny."

338.
morphe. shape, or form. Used, by Aristotle as more or less synonomous with eidos when eidos means form. Morphe is to eidos (qua form) more or less as energeia is to entelecheia.

339.
Mort and Jude Tetralogy a project inaugurated in the Spring of 1988 and abruptly abandoned in June of 1988. The first book of that projected tetralogy -- Blue Moon -- was written and printed up by me in May of 1988. A truncated version of the second book -- Shelley's Victory -- was put together quickly in late June (early July?) of 1988.

340.
Myrto. according to the testimony of Diogenes, the "other" wife of Socrates.

341.
noesis. thinking.

342.
nous. mind; reason.

343.
onto-theo-logy. the two-fold concern of "metaphysics" according to Derrida and Heidegger. Cf. "metaphysics."

344.
ousia. beingness. Technical word in the later dialogues of Plato. Technical word in the writings of Aristotle related to Aristotle's "pros hen" analysis of being. Often translated as "essence" in translations of Plato and as "substance" in translations of Aristotle. A word better left untranslated.

345.
pathein. to undergo; to suffer; to be affected by. Suffering.

346.
Philebus. the second dialogue of the third tetralogy named after the interlocutor, "Philebus", in the dialogue who is, however rather silent (and stubborn) in the dialogue. By common agreement a "very" late dialogue of Plato's probably composed around and during the time of the composition of Laws which apparently is Plato's last dialogue. (The very length of Laws does not at all preclude the possibility that much of it was drafted before the composition of Philebus.) In Philebus -- contrary to the habit of practically all of the later dialogues including Laws -- a Socrates re-appears as the major interlocutor. The contention of this book of many titles is that Philebus, in its reflection on "the good" and on pleasure is the architechtonic introduction (Cf., as always, 61A-B) to the third dialogue of the third tetralogy, namely, (from Plato's early/middle period of composition) Symposium. The ancient sub-title for Symposium was "concerning the good" and it is well known that Symposium takes place at the home of Agathon (a tragic playwright). "Philebus" apparently means "youth."

347.
phusis. nature.

348.
"Plato's Pharmacy". a long "essay" concerning Plato's teaching on writing written by Jacques Derrida and published in 1968.

349.
pros hen equivocation. analyzing a word in terms of its primary meaning and significance. For instance, "being" is said in many ways, but primarily in terms of "ousia" (substance); ousia, in turn, is said in many ways, but primarily in terms of "hupokeimenon." "Hupokeimenon" is said in a variety of ways, but primarily in terms of Aristotle's idiosyncratic meaning of form.

350.
Quantum Mechanics. the major developemnt in twentieth century Physics; Quantum Mechanics, along with Einstein's theory of general relativity jointly, eclipse the Newtonian world-view. It is to be noted that general relativity is a macroscopic account of things whereas Quantum Mechanics is a microscopic account of things. The "science" of Quantum Mechanics is universally accepted by all serious scientists. However there is a wide spectrum of opinion concerning the meaning of what Quantum Mechanics has "discovered."

351.
samsara. the journeys and vicissitudes of the self. Endless journeys. Passage through. *{{{Life's response to "aporiai".}}}*

352.
Shekhinah. In Jewish mystical writings -- Hasidic and pre-Hasidic -- the feminine pole of God's being which, by virtue of exile/creation, is alienated from the Divinity proper. So to speak. *{{The term is used idiosyncratically in this book.}}*

353.
Shelley's Song. unpublished manuscript produced in early 1985. There are references to this manuscript in the present book

354.
Speusippus. Plato's nephew and member of Plato's Academy; he succeeded Plato as head of the Academy upon Plato's death in 347 B.C. This is the year in which Aristotle left the Academy. According the Plato's dialogue, Philebus, Speusippus is credited with the painfully remarkable teaching that pleasure is evil.

355.
Stagirite. Aristotle's nickname by virtue of his having been born on the island of Stagira.

356.
stoicheia. elements; letters.

357.
subjectum. subject; underlying subject. Medieval expression which is roughly equivalent to Aristotle's "hupokeimenon". Often enough, "subjectum" refers to the material substrate of something.

358.
substance. the ordinary translation of Aristotle's "ousia." "Substance" translates some of the conceptual baggage contained in Aristotle's usage of "ousia" but does not translate the word.

359.

sullabe. complex; syllable.

360.
suppositum. Medieval term usually denoting a special meaning of "subjectum"/"hupokeimenon." The principle of formal individuation. (The principle in terms of which an entity is a person.)

361.
thanatos. Greek word for "death"; used by Freud, in his oral presentations, as the name for the "death drive." In *Thinking Psycho-analytically* two separate meanings of the Freudian "thanatos" are operative, some here and some there.

For the most part, *Thinking Psycho-analytically* does a "regressive kathalysis" of Freud's Eros/Thanatos duality. Most of this "regressive kathalysis" is accomplished in Part I of the book, although the "regressive kathalysis" goes on all throughout the book. In the "regressive kathalysis" -- construed in the more narrow sense of "regressive kathalysis" -- one always stays close to that meaning of "thanatos" whereby "thanatos" is a drive which returns to a prior state of equilibrium.

On the other hand, some of the "conversations" in *Thinking Psycho-analytically* were taken from an unpublished manuscript concerning "the wo-man principle" which was written in the Summer of 1990. In that work, -- for reasons endemic to that work -- "thanatos" came to be used as synonomous with "pure oscillating need." This meaning of "thanatos" is not at all directly Freudian. <<*Please understand, however, that the transformation of the Freudian meaning for "thanatos" into the idiosyncratic meaning just alluded to has its genesis in what results when Freud's duality is used as the springboard for entering into the waters of ontological duality in a "truly" thoughtful manner. This too -- becoming, so to speak, "Un-Freudian" in order to ("truly") be "Freudian" -- is a move in the multi-faceted task of "regressive kathalysis."*>>

The perceptive reader of *Thinking Psycho-analytically* will probably have little or no difficulty in apprehending, in context, which of these two meanings of "thanatos" is operative in a given text.

{{{The issue is not without its significance, especially with regard to the interesting question -- implied all throughout the "metaphysical" poets -- of how "death" is present in orgasm. As release and return to a state of homeostasis? Or as the delirious "pre-orgasmic" state of the orgasm taken as a whole in which one maintains oneself -- women, on the average, more successfully than men -- oscillatingly (and maniacally) on the edge, sometimes for an incredibly long period of time? Take your pick.}}}

362.
"The Thirty". Athenian faction which took control of the city-state's affairs circa 404 B.C.

363.
Tiresias. the one who, by a blessing/curse of the Gods (Zeus?) lived to experience sexuality as a man and as a wo-man. "His" estimate is that the pleasure of sexuality for a woman is nine times greater than it is for a man. Tiresias is said to have

foreseen the destiny of Oedipus.

364.
to ti en einai. Aristotle's neo-logism used extensively in Book VII of his Metaphysics with reference to his analysis of sensible substance. "The what was {i.e., imperfect tense implying continuous action up through the present} to be" of something. It is a concept which tries to show that the "what" of some things includes, necessarily, reference to their matter. Often translated as "essence." Depending on the history and destiny of the word "essence" this is either a serious mis-translation of this Aristotelian neo-logism or it is not.

365.
tukhe. chance, luck. Opportunity. (Circumstance.) Aristotle speaks of "tukhe" in Book II of Physics and also, a bit, in Book VI of Metaphysics.

366.
universal. that which, as a genus (i.e.," animal"), or species (i.e., "man), or differentia (i.e., "two-footedness"), is predicable of a "subject" (i.e., hupokeimenon). While eidos, as species, is predicable of a subject, eidos, as "form", -- in the idiosyncratic meaning of "form" worked out in Book VII of Metaphysics -- is never predicable of a "subject" due to the "dunamis"-free way in which form inheres in a "subject." Aristotle presents Plato as having transformed universals into ontologically real separate forms.

367.
Vertigo. according to Kundera: --- *And you know already what vertigo is; intoxication with one's own weakness, the insuperable desire to fall.* {{contained in The Art of the Novel}}}

368.
via negativa. the negative way. A theological teaching concerning the inability of finite intellect to understand God and of human language to say "positively" what God is. It is basically a Christian emanation from Plotinian Neo-Platonism.

369.
Xenocrates. member of Plato's Academy; left the Academy the same year as did Aristotle; succeeded Speusippus as head of the Academy upon the death of Speusippus in 339 B.C.

For Eurydice

**(Valentine's Season
1992)**

*Like the flash of heat lightning that tells you all that is,
is now.*

I.

and so
we write about it anyway
as though
we knew
what we don't know
you came into my life
or did I seek you out?
blue eyes made
sparkling green by
the sunlight of a fifth floor window

a bit too thin
and trouble
showing all over your face
then one sunny day
adorned in Spring's red dress you
crush a grown child's
heart: *it's over*

and the song-ditty says:
that was yesterday
this is now

II.

fall's shadows
sprout giant gobs
of narcissistic fetish   the
battle is joined
and joined

and joined
two monsters breathing foul-smelling fire
feeding on insidious layers of culpable ingnorance dance
on each other's feet out of control swirling in the
whirlwindy vortex of a
deliriously reciprocal and demonically gnarling
narcisssism

<<generating all the while
hurt enough
-- and then some --
for all they claim to love>>

exploring each other
testing all limits but
but always that reciprocal narcissistic fetish
in reserve
just in case   between
two deaths they
create
with much cynicsim and greater
-- albeit unknown --
innocence
new life
is fate always chosen?

and the song-ditty repeats:
that was yesterday
this is now

III.

just when did he cross over that line?
in the summer?
when you threatened to leave
in september?
when his very life was ripped away from him
or
was he always and already over that line?
(broken glass now ground exceeding fine)

exploration beyond all limits
becomes methodic
with nothing new to be discovered   the
fetish aimlessly mocks the mortally wounded
narcissus-doubling-function
now in death's agony
welcome to hell

the horror
the horror

the horror incrementally opens
its obscene delight before her dying eyes
with one last desperate
yank
she severs him
from her leaving him
2 die but 2 2 live
(or is it three?)

the song-ditty says:
that was yesterday
this is now

IV

what's this???(!!!)
they <u>still</u>
don't/won't
let go???

but why?

what whispered memories
keep them hostage to
what black hole?
what Godly (and thus daimonic) leverage
binds them to each other?
what usuriously uxorious interest
gloriously grows greater than
its own capital?
what oscillating kaleidoscopic pattern
makes always and all ways
the other to appear
dis-appearingly in the other
while the other
always and all ways
receives the other by
appearingly
dis-appearing?
and even so
--- especially so!!! ---
what magic stillness
blesses
their strange
ever-yearning
craving?

V.

did their tomorrow
already come
while we were not looking?   the
ebony-tinted melody
was all around us but
listening for pretty white flowers
we did not hear

already tomorrow lives as yesterday

already the miracle is there
(where? *right here*)
do we sleep through our dream?

the song-ditty repeats again
(this time as a warning
no   a plea):
that was yesterday
this is now

370.

----- 'People lived differently then, they did things for life, made gestures that lasted for life' -----

Joyce Carol Oates. Lock, page 83.

371.
Commenced: 12/22/91. ((Despite what was said at the end of *Thinking Psycho-analytically* it is possible that *Thinking Psycho-analytically* was actually started on 12/22/84. Memory plays tricks. Tricks. And is it not more likely that one would have been moved to begin the day right after the solstice? *[It is, of course, acknowledged that a given 22ond may in fact be the day of the solstice.]*))

372.
Once upon a time I wrote a book called *Thinking Psycho-analytically*. (Maybe it should have been entitled, *Thanking Psycho-analytically*.)

373.
Let's call *Thinking Psycho-analytically* "the big book." The Great.

374.
Let's call this book -- the supplement you are reading right now -- The Small.

375.
a). The one and its other. The other and its other. The one is the other of other. The one with its other becomes the Dyad. Duplicitous comes to be the one. The Dyad is the one. Unity in duality and duality in unity. But never the identity of identity and difference. The two Godheads of God even though there is but one Godhead of God. The Godhead as Great; as excess; as supplement. The Godhead dis-appearing even as it makes its appearance. *I eternally see her figure eternally vanishing. I eternally see her figure eternally vanishing. I eternally see her figure eternally vanishing.* The Godhead as freedom/difference. The Godhead as posterior. The Godhead which becomes -- without ever beginning or ceasing to become -- the Sartreanesque "de trop." The Godhead which withdraws -- without ever beginning or ceasing to withdraw -- so as to submit to its other. IN CONTRAST: The Godhead as Small. The Godhead as prior. The Godhead as less. That is to say, the Godhead as Small. The Godhead which neither is nor is not. The will which does not will. The will which wills nothing, not even itself. The will which -- a hundred-thousand Heideggerians crying to the contrary notwithstanding -- has nothing to do with "Will." That stillness which never became still. That unbearable beauty. That which is submitted to; tricked, so to speak, to be the stability for the other. The free. A-peiron. The one.

"Prior" to the mixture it -- i.e., other than the one; i.e., other than the free -- is, so to speak, God bereft of Godhead. It is pure oscillation without relief. It is pure Anxiety. Relief by submission to its other (i.e., what will be called the one). In this submission it draws its other into itself without the say so of this other. Duplicity.

This other is now (i.e., becomes) the Godhead of God. The first. A-peiron "already and in itself" (so to speak) it "now" (so to speak) becomes apeiron relative to the rest of God. The Godhead "now" drawn into God, the excess called "the fifth" is set in motion without ever beginning or ceasing to have been set in motion. This is the Godhead as excess.

b). Mort: You better stop now, Jude. You're geting that funny look in your eye again --- Jude: MERRILY, MERRILY, MERRILY, MERRILY --- Mort: Please Jude! Stop! You'll have to go back to the hospital! --- Jude: LIFE IS BUT A DREAM. ROW, ROW, ROW YOUR BOAT --- Mort: ROW, ROW, ROW YOUR BOAT --- Jude: GENTLY DOWN THE STREAM--- Mort: GENTLY DOWN THE STREAM --- Jude: MERRILY, MERRILY, --- HEY MORT!

Mort: What now, Jude?

Jude: The merry, merry month of May. May = Mai = maia = Maya = Appearance {appearance reveals and conceals "true" being at once} = [in a sense] illusion =? allusion. May Day; might night. And always a nurse.

Mort: OK, Jude. Take a sad song and make it better.

376.
{{{ ---- *and other kindred notions* (i.e., of "the third"; i.e., of the good)

Bappy: And what about those dark, dark, "places" from which no light escapes? Dewchee: They are legion; and they are part of the bargain. This is the weight of the world which Shekhinah must bear for sucking "the other" (in this case, "the one", since other than "other itself" is but the one) into Herself for the sake of Herself. She does assumes this weight gladly -- indeed with joy. And even in those dark, dark ""places"" oscillation still occurs. There will be birth again. This is the magic of Shekhinah. Bappy: Even if the <u>sum total</u> of things (i.e., "stuff")gets -- someday -- compressed into such a dark, dark place? Dewchee: Yes. Even then. Especially then. Bappy: So the putative worst is not really the worst. What then would the worst? Dewchee: The death of death. Not just for the appearance of the good on the third planet from the sun. But absolutely. So to speak. [[Even so, it is not impossible that the disappearance of the good -- which is quite other than a "dis-appearing" appearance -- from the third planet from the sun could tilt things in this direction entailing the death of death.]] Bappy: How would this occur? Dewchee: Should that "unbearable" kind of "lightness" -- made possible by the dis-appearing play of light -- which sheds attraction prevail without limit then oscillation shall cease. This is the danger of the coming to be of the good. The play of light can be fatal. The death of difference. The death of death. Bappy: Will this happen? Dewchee: One doesn't know. Trust Shekhinah. In all things.}}}

377.
Did Kundera understand?

378.
He most certainly did <u>not</u> understand Parmenides.

379.
Although creative in his appropriation of it, he had but an average understanding of Nietzsche's Eternal Recurrence.

{{{ And please note: Despite his own smugness on these matters and despite an hyperbolized reputation for things sexual, Kundera had but a tritely conventional account of sexuality. At least in his published works. }}}

380.
And yet.

381.
He understood lightness. The awe-full lightness. The other 'light'.

382.
Plato understood light. The third.

383.
Thinking Psycho-analytically understood Plato.

384.
Even so, there is another aspect of 'light': lightness.

385.
Kundera understood. (He understood better than did Plato.)

In hypothesis # 7 Plato shows that he understood something essential about disintegration. And what he does in Symposium is 'good' despite his Achilles heel. It is in Phaedrus that he falters. Kundera implicitly understands what Plato fails to understand about mania. The catch-22 of mania. To succeed mania must fail. Plato's nostalgic love affair with Beauty -- and correlatively his failure to confront the necessity for Beauty to die (in order to live as 'good') -- blinds Plato to mania's tortured teleology. Phraedrus is the proto-type of false hope. Already in Phaedrus there is a hint of the forthcoming fetish.

{{{{{Jude: Ah the sheer delirium of hypothesis # 7!!! And so few people have any sense at all as to what it's all about. ----- *suddenly, as might happen in a dream* ----- Mort: I'm with you there, Buddy. The place where the truth of Skepticism is given its due. And I mean the truth of Skepticism, not some sloppy version of it in which "Skepticism" exists only to be "sublated" as in Hegel's Phenomenology. Jude: ----- *Suddenly as might happen in a dream* ------ Frere Jacques should have taken Searle to hypothesis # 7 if he -- Frere Jacques -- had really wanted to teach Austin's son something about iterability. The very delirium of iterability. Instead Frere Jacques just spilled "inc" over this. Mort: Please Jude! When you start getting that cute it is usually a sign that your medication is off. Just how are you these days? Jude: I'm OK. You're OK. It's nice that Johanna lets us make an appearance now and then. Mort: I don't want to scare you, Jude, but we are here without her sayso. I snuck us in the back door when she wasn't looking. I think we better make a quick exit before she notices. Jude: That's fine by me. I always exit with Mort.}}}

386.
When there is no return.

387.
When there is no weight.

388.
The death of death.

389.
Suicide, to be sure, is the danger of Melancholia/Depression. But suicide is not disintegration. Rather, suicide is death. Only death. Suicide is but a relative danger. It is not "danger itself." *{{{For another time the analysis of the relatively rare conditions under which a melancholic-but-not-depressed and in any case non-self-indulgent choice for suicide is an instantiation of the only categorical imperative which obtains:* Choose life.}}}

390.
The death of death is disintegration.

391.
Entropy run rampant, so to speak.

392.
Melancholia has many functions. One of these functions is to be a self-defense against such disintegration. ((Kristeva understood.))

393.
The beginnings of entropy run rampant, (so to speak), is experienced as mania.

394.
The unbearable lightness.

395.
Unbearable. No pathos is greater. Not even deepest and darkest depression.

396.
The unbearable lightness of being.

397.
Mania.

398.
It is a vector towards 'the free.'

399.
Do you understand? Mania is the danger.

400.
The oscillating without surcease entices the one -- 'the free' -- into itself for some measure of relief. The oscillating without surcease submits itself to the one. The one -- "in itself", so to speak, -- is utterly unconditioned, even with regard to itself. The one -- which of itself neither wills nor desires anything at all -- is tricked, so to speak, to be and, as being, to be in the mixture as that to which there is submission. Tricked. So to speak. Without permission.

401.
The oscillationg "de-natures" itself in a manner of speaking by submitting to the one. It acquires some stability. Yet this submission is for the sake of oscillating. The hegemony of difference obtains precisely in the mixture. For oscillating disappears -- without "dis-appearing" -- without such submission. Such a disappearance -- shorn of all "dis-appearance" -- would be the death of death.

402.
Redemption.

The compression; the broken vessels; the in-gathering. That was and is a way of putting it. Here is another way of putting it:

that peace which the world cannot give

In the beginning (which never started to be nor ceases to begin) "there was" -- (only in a manner of speaking since the "there is"/"there was" occurs only by virtue of mixture) -- 'the free' and also pure genesis.

'The free' is, so to speak, one of the meanings of the "Godhead" of God and "exists" (so to speak) """"""before"""""" God begins to "exist". This is 'the one' which, IN the mixture, 'be-comes' Beauty, Beauty which must die. There is no smidgeon of anything like "will" or "desire" in "the one", taken by itself, unless one speaks of the uniquely Schellingesque "will which wills nothing, not even itself."

Pure genesis is pure oscillation without relief; pure anxiety; pure dread; pure pain.

To relieve itself -- (so as to thwart is own "disappearing-without-'dis-appearing'") -- pure genesis withdraws into itself and in do doing sucks into itself the stability (and anxiety-alleviating) of 'the free'. Thus "desire" is from the side, so to speak, of the oscillating. 'The free' is tricked, so to speak, into mixture with pure genesis.

The mixture is God and creation. The mixture is that great profusion of goods.

The good and each good is an ever-moving point of equilibrium between 'the free' and pure genesis. Rest in restlessness. For example -- and only for example -- each species was and/or is such a moving point of equilibrium of and between 'the free' and pure genesis.

In the mixture pure genesis becomes (without ever beginning or ceasing to become) other than what it "was." Likewise 'the free', in the mixture, becomes (without ever beginning or ceasing to become) other than what it "was." Philosophers are happy to furnish names for these aspects of God and creation.

Since 'the free' is sucked into (without ever beginning or ceasing to be sucked into) pure genesis the mixture comes (without ever beginning to come to ceasing to come) to be laden with excess which it must express. *{{{Why is there writing rather than nothing!!!???}}}* The excess of God; this expression of God; this "shit" of God; this other than God is, in fact, the first revelation of 'the free' "posterior" to and in the mixture.

By following the call of this "other" the goods in and of the mixture -- when and as they are/become good -- instantiate the now broken and disseminated 'free' in the mixture. Grace -- amazing grace -- is the sudden realization that 'the free' -- the principle of Beauty in the mixture -- while broken and dead "in itself" (so to speak) is nonetheless already WITH us. We are it. 'The free', as free, is sacrificed (i.e., made holy) for the sake of the whole and the whole, by virtue of the sacrifice, is and is redeemed.

403.
The yearning which can never have enough; the submission -- without permission --; the descent of the Godhead; the emergence of the "de trop" of yearning which can never have enough. On and on.

404.
The one: What will 'be-come' -- come to be; do you hear?; come to be -- beauty in the mixture. But to 'be-come' it must be shattered. It is dyadicized and fragmented by the oscillating. Beauty which must die.

405.
The one: What a final and maximal state of entropy would be (like) were such to occur. That stillness which never became still. That quietness which never became quietness. The one is 'the free'. The utterly unconditioned. ((-- but there is no freedom there; 'the free', yes; but no freedom --))

406.
The one in the mixture is beauty but is dyadicized/fragmented by the submission of -- i.e., on the part of -- pure oscillating need. Need kills as it submits. Beauty dies that the good might obtain. They are Chronos and Zeus to each other. Parent and child. Yet Zeus must kill Chronos and this is good.

a). {{{Non: Is not the good -- i.e., the child; i.e., the offspring (tokos) -- female? TGIF!

Sic: Yes.

Non: But here he has 'the good' -- i.e., the child; i.e., the offspring (tokos) -- playing Zeus to Chronos as they play out that age-old father/son castration drama ((which, of course and in any case, does not negate the more subtle mother/son castration drama involving fear of -- i.e., fascination with; i.e, desire for -- feminization)).

Sic: All of this is true. Do you not yet see? Even after Thinking Psycho-analytically? The good is female. Impossibly, with a penis. But the good is female. Trust me. Thoroughly female. The hegemony of difference IN the mixture is not without paradox.

Non: Thank-you for the clarification.

Sic: Thank-you for the opportunity.}}}

b).
De Vere: I get confused about this "impossibly with a penis" business. It came up in part II as well. <<"Part II", that is, when *Shame!* was *Thinking Psycho-analytically* or *Misogyny*>> Do you remember?

Amy: Of course. One was speaking about the telos of male "desire." Let us listen to that twice-stated formulation given earlier in this book:

> *Being the castrated oscillating love object -- impossibly with a penis -- For the castrated oscillating love object. This is the ultimate telos of male "desire."*

De Vere: Yes. That is the passage. And my confusion still obtains. Indeed, when I was discussing these things over coffee some of my friends thought that Thinking Psycho-analytically was proposing those fmaous/infamous "she-males" as the instantiation of the good.

Amy: And there's the rub. Once again the rule of secrets comes into play.

De Vere: What is this 'rule of secrets'?

Amy: It's been formulated elsewhere. It goes something like this:

> *you can be sure that when and as a deeply entrenched secret is beginning to be revealed a deflecting secret -- with SOME truth about it -- will emerge as the ultimate guardian of the secret*

The famous/infamous "she-males", you may tell your friends, fall under this rubric.

De Vere: You do realize, I might add as a digression, that in all respects (except one) these "she-males" -- at least the ones who were done right and who take care of themselves -- can unambiguously pass for females. They could even be on the covers of something like Vogue or Cosmo, they are that erotically attractive.

Amy: And -- who knows for certain -- perhaps they have so appeared in fact. I have known more than a few in my experience. Some are predictably boorish. Others of them are rather interesting. But my personal experience is not the issue right here. We speak from the viewpoint of *Thinking Psycho-analytically* and whether or not these famous/infamous "she-males" can be construed as instantiating 'the good' according to the logic of that difficult to understand book. The answer is quite simple.

De Vere: And what is the answer?

Amy: Of course they do not. Indeed they instantiate most graphically a version of the fetish which *Thinking Psycho-analytically* argues and strives against. They instantiate most graphically the denial/DISAVOWEL of Mommy's castration. They instantiate most graphically that bad faith option relative to the "counter-factual-fact".

De Vere: And yet *Thinking Psycho-analytically* keeps harping upon the phrase " --- impossibly with a penis ---" whenever it talks about the telos of "desire." Are you certain of your answer relative to the "she-males"?

Amy: You were there at the creation but you still don't understand.

De Vere: What are you referring to?

Amy: It was said earlier in the book. The secret of *Thinking Psycho-analytically* is contained in the those parts of the book where Johanna spoke of the primacy of deception and more especially when she contrasted the playing fields of cognition and deception. I am certain it will all come back to you when you begin your task of re-reading. You should go back and re-read those whole sections many times over. Read it out loud. Many times over. For now just listen to this:

> *----- fidelity to the counter-factual "fact" leads to living the dream AS impossible dream but not as actual fact.*

De Vere: I shall go back to that section and re-read it -- even out loud -- many times over as you suggest. But even now I begin to see -- however vaguely -- your point. Our famous "she-males" -- and the medical technolgy which makes them possible -- short-circuit the telos of "desire" by trying to approximate the impossible as actual fact. In so doing they instantiate -- graphically -- the logic of denial/DISAVOWAL and, correlatively, contribute to that unhappy outcome by which our dreams will be turned into nightmares.

Amy: You are essentially correct. But please do not be too hard on our "she-male" friends. The initial impetus towards "she-male" is not only understandable but it is even noble even if it also remains true that the actual 'she-male' medical project deflects from the achievement of what is noble. For this initial impetus is the vector towards the most secret name of 'the good'.

De Vere: You refer to erotic shame, do you not?

Amy: Yes. In the sense worked out in*Thinking Psycho-analytically*. Shame as the most secret name of the good. Even divine Plato deflected from this meaning of the 'the good'.

De Vere: I remember it well. Embracing and becoming the shameless shame of the Shekhinah. How glorious. And my quandry begins to dissolve.

Amy: Please explain yourself. We must make sure. We may not have another opportunity.

De Vere. " ----- impossibly with a penis -----" The pre-requisite for this impossibility (as impossible Dream) is an erotically functioning penis -- untransformed by medical technology -- which still ejaculates. {{{Like a prayer!!!!}}}. The transformation to "castrated oscillating love object" is in the psyche. One achieves one's own proper "daimon" -- (and one's own proper "daimon" is "eu-daimon") -- in the psyche. This is the condition for living the dream AS impossible dream but not as actual fact. The free, gratuitous positing of the ideal. *{{{{{'----- the master/mistress of my passion;'}}}}}*

Amy: And for those who have the eyes to hear and the ears to see, one will understand that 'the good' will get instantiated most especially through the telos of male "desire" as males learn to submit themselves -- in the post-phallo-cratic usages of the phallus -- to scenarios of lesbianesque love-play in the forthcoming age of Matriarchal Androgyny in which the hegemony of difference is most definitely sustained. Yes. You are now beginning to understand. Even so, go back and re-read. Many times. Yes. Read and re-read. Silently and out loud.

De Vere: I most certainly will. And I thank-you for the clarification.

Amy: And I thank you for the opportunity. It may be our last.

c). {{{{{ and where is eros in all of this yes he called it a tyrant in Book IX of his book on arete and it is true that the erotic unbounded is nothing less than the demonic but his book on arete is not the heart of our friend the third dialogue of the third tetralogy the third dialogue of the third tetralogy do you hear do you mean to say that eros is 'the good' yes that is the secret of Plato that is the secret of 'being' the object of desire is itself suffused by and with desire the object of desire is itself desir-ING the eternally called for which calls so to speak the hegemony of difference the other shall we call it the mother shall we call it the contrary to the one shall we call it difference shall we call it eksaiphnes shall we call it pure oscillating need shall we call it """truth""" yes this is the seat of desire and yet desire is sustained in the the very object of desire this is not Hegel but many will think it is coming from the trap and the death of thinking called 'the tradition' they listen yet they do not see they look yet they do not hear they probe but they do not find even Plato who says it did not understand here you find the primacy of lesbian sexuality did you say there was something else yes the secret within the secret the other of the other shall we call it the one shall we call it the father shall we call it Beauty beauty which must die the secret within the secret 206E listen and listen as well to my emphasis

tes genneseos kai tou tokou en to kalo

again:

tes genneseos kai tou tokou en to kalo

again:

tes genneseos kai tou tokou en to kalo

they listen but they do not see they look but they do not hear they probe but they do not find let us help out with our three fingers:

<<<<<<<<<<<<<<<< this is the first rule of secrets you can be sure that when and as a deeply entrenched secret is beginning to be revealed a deflecting secret -- with SOME truth about it -- will emerge as the ultimate guardian of the secret case in point: The Mafia wipe-out of Kennedy (with the cooperation of Dulles and a faction of the CIA) hides behind all those "Castro's revenge" accounts of the the assassination ((analogous points could be made about the De Vere authorship of the plays/sonnetts attributed to "Shake-speare")){{{{{ of course the last line of defense -- i.e., the last refuge of deflection and denial -- takes the guise of sophistication: does it really matter anything not to confront the truth. }}}}}<<<<<and what is the point relative to Plato? Simple. When it is finally discovered that the Symposium is the dialogue of dialogues for understanding the esoteric in Plato deflection from this point will occur -- indeed this has been going on for more than a thousand years!!!!! -- through the various Neo-Platonic (i.e., monotheistic) accounts of the esoteric in Symposium such a deflection from the "true" esoteric in Plato/Symposium actually has the effect of further inhibiting the truly esoteric in Plato from making any sort of appearance>>>>> yes yes of course let there be a hundred thousand deflections from the truth by trotting out all of those ad hominem and reductive analyses of the "paranoid" underpinnings of those who are suspicious concerning the received accounts of this or that [[Does the re-inventor -- i.e., myself; is that grandiose enough for you -- of psycho-analysis need to be reminded of the network of associations surrounding "paranoia"]] But in the final analysis, if the truth of a dark situation is revealed by a Paranoid -- (perhaps only a Paranoid is capable of uncovering some "truths") -- does that fact -- i.e., the fact that its revealer is a Paranoid -- be-lie what is revealed Jacques my secret confrere. Of course these remarks do not at all imply that "truth" subsists "in itself" as some kind of potential "full presence" needing only to be un-covered to speak for itself in its revelation I have understood -- in ways far more devious than ever imagined by you -- the "difference"/"differance" character of """"""""""truth"""""""""" after all, it is Part IV of Thinking Psycho-analytically *which speaks of the primacy of deception and you -- according to the logic of Part IV -- never even made it to the playing field of deception so please do not presume a metaphysical naivte on my part when you finally get around to reading this book listen to the Paranoid one For """"""""""truth"""""""""" cannot be ""dis-----appearing"" except as a function of some kind of appearing thus for the thinker the task of wresting the """""truth""""" from oblivion remains always primary even and especially for that most blessed of thinkers namely she who plays with cogency on the playing field of deception enough >>>>>>>>>>>>>>>>>*

now our second finger:

So then, what is first for Plato? The One (which is the principle of beauty) or the Good (which, eternally, without ever beginning to come to be or ceasing to come to be) comes to be in the mixture?

As father of the Good the beautiful -- along with the Mother of the Good (which is "difference"; which is the principle of truth) -- is "prior" to the Good. On the other hand, as eternally called for the Good is prior to the beautiful since, as eternally called for, the good, emerging from the very heart of difference in the process, procures the father (Beauty) for the sake of the Mother. Yet in this procurement the good ---- as the light which dis-appears in favor of the cause of light ---- *takes refuge in the character of the beautiful.* [Philebus 64E]

and now finally our third finger enters the fray and we shall find with our probing the paradigm for that wonderous appropriation of XY by and through XX the lesbianesque appropriation of the "no-longer-'phallo-cratic'-phallus":

----- -----

(c-i). As Plato has Socrates begin the task of ""deconstructing"" -- (readers of *Thinking Psycho-analytically* will come to prefer the term "regressive kathalysis") -- , so to speak, the narcissism of the putative Good (given by "Good"), one finds Socrates playing around with two meanings relative to the intrinsic relationality of

Eros. One meaning is, quite literally, played around with and then pre-emptorily dismissed in favor of a more logical sense of the relationality which is intrinsic to Eros. Even so the terms of the "played-around-with-and-then-pre-emptorily-dismissed" meaning of relationality intrinsic to Eros capture the attention of the reader who is alert to the esoteric in Plato: Listen (from 199D):

> *My question is not whether he is love of a mother or father -- how absurd* [<u>geloion</u>; laughable; silly; <u>COMIC</u>!!!] *it would be to ask whether Love is love of mother or father! -----*

Mother and father. Memories. The father and "offspring"/"interest" (tokos) of <u>Republic VI</u>. Father <u>and</u> Mother. Love <u>of</u> Mother and Father. The double meaning of the genitive. The way in Love and the Good are each other while always being other from each other in that magical (and decidedly non-Hegelian) dance by which the object of desire is found itself to be desir-**ING**.

(c-ii). The dis-mantling of the narcissism of the putative Good (given by "Good") continues by establishing that Love -- in its very desire for beauty -- lacks beauty and lacking beauty lacks goodness as well. But then Diotima dis-mantles, so to speak, that Socratic dis-matling of the narcissism of the putative Good (given by "Good"). {{A dis-mantling of the dis-mantling which is neither the inauguration of an infinite regress <u>nor</u> a return to the original "thesis" through some sort of negation of the negation.}} Her words introduce a degree of nuance into the discussion which was lacking in the Socratic ""deconstruction"" of "Agathon". (from 206E)

> *So you see, Socrates, that Love is not exactly of [a longing for] the beautiful, as you suggested.*

Hmmmmmm!!! Well, then, what is it of? What is Love about?

> *tes genneseos kai <u>tou tokou</u>* [emphasis mine; jwm/JE] *en to kalo.*

Shall we say, with Joyce, :

> *A longing not for the beautiful itself, but for the conception and generation that the beautiful effects*

??? Yes. Of course. Joyce catches the implied meaning. Love is for what beauty <u>effects</u>. Love is for the "offspring" (or is it "interest") of beauty.

Or should we say, with Lamb, :

> *It is of engendering and begetting upon the beautiful*

??? Yes. Of course. And somewhat more literal. And with the Lamb translation we are reminded of the messiness of intercourse in these matters of "offspring" and, so to speak, "off-spring-ing." Also the hint that some violation or betrayal is visited "upon" the beautiful if Lamb is correct in his assesssment of the "en" of 206E-6 <Loeb lining>. Lamb does seem to be correct in this hint since it is Diotima herself who has told us that the <u>Mother</u> of Love impregnated herself by using the generative power of the <u>Father</u> of Love while the <u>Father</u> was sleeping. Somewhat against his will, or at least not with his consent. And it is the male who is the "abused", in a matter of speaking. The male is, so to speak, incorporated into the Female and all for the sake of an "offspring" desired by the female. From the male but not desired, as such, by the male.

And this Mother of love is -- 203B-8 <Loeb lining> -- "aporian." Yes, yes, of course the connection with "Poros", the Father. But listen: "aporian": the lack of passage; the untenable condition which must have relief! Violation of the Father! The King (the one as the principle of Beauty) must die that the Good come to be.

Finally -- {{I am breathless, Madonna. Come to me now!!!}} -- : "tokou". "Interest"; "Offspring". (206E; line 6 <Loeb lining> along with Republic VI 507A) The Platonic text is coded.

> *Have a care, however, lest I deceive you unintentionally with a false reckoning of the "interest"/["offspring"]* {{{ **tou tokou** }}}.

----- -----

enough!!!!!!!! for God's sake most will never understand anyway may I go now just one more thing then you may go alright you must tell us about the eros of Freud oh dear God apples and oranges the eros of Freud ought not be brought up here it is serviceable for his purposes and Sigismund is always dear to me he did after all stay with dualism even if he is no Aristocles in these matters and most of all he put us in touch with blessed "mis-ogyny" even divine Aristocles never thematized "mis-ogyny" Sigismund is never to be disdained or dismissed but his usage of eros does not belong here let them read Part I for God's sake may I go now }}}}}

407.
Mania: the vector to 'the free.'

408.
Mania: the subversion of the good that beauty might be spared.

409.
Mania: the love of beauty which EO IPSO is diseased. Without being "dis-eased". (and yet)

410.
Mania: the unbounded demonic having as its telos the ending of mixture which, eo ipso, subverts the end (telos) of mixture.

411.
Mania: the death of death.

412.
Mania: the danger.

413.

Danger is also opportunity.

414.
Melancholia and mania. The "right" tension. The formula for creativity.

415.
Melancholia and mania. The "wrong" tension. The formula for destruction.

416.
Danger and opportunity. Opportunity and danger.

417.
{{{{{{{{{{{{{{{{{{{{ a).
The sophisticated one: You are dying of a chemical imbalance. A brain which somehow got out of whack. But you keep talking about "danger and opportunity"; about "creativity and destruction."

The accused: I pity you. Even now -- even after *Thinking Psycho-analytically* -- you are still caught up in your terribly unsophisticated (irony noted) paradigm of the "either/or" in speaking of these things. Of course it's all chemistry. Of course it's all neuro-physiological. That much is axiomatic. But you still have much to learn about chickens and eggs. You are found guilty! Your punishment is to read note # vi to Part IV. Read it until you learn. Barring that, read it until you die.

The sophisticated one: I really feel sorry for you, Mac. But I don't have any more time to waste on you. Greater things have my attention. You were given a chance.

The accused: Ah! Sweet chance! How well I know it.

b). Nothing -- nothing at all -- runs in the psyche which is not energized by some instantiation of anxiety. *{{{{{ Libido, for instance, in all of its manifestations, is a form of anxiety. On this one might confer Freud's posthumously discovered manuscript Anxiety and Libido: A Supplement to the first part of lecture # xxxii of "The New Introductory Lectures on Psychoanalysis". This manuscript had mysteriously made its way to the United States and was found in 1944 by Patrick Donegal in a radio factory in Philadelphia.}}}}}* This is also true of Melancholia and mania. The cessation of one frees up energy for the other. Of course there is much anxiety -- e.g., fear, panic, guilt, remorse, and some of love and suffering -- which is not manic.

{{True to his family tradition, Patrick lost this valuable manuscript the day after he found out just how monetarily advantageous it would be to offer the ms for sale. However, before he died, Patrick adumbrated the main points of Freud's manuscript. To wit:

Freud was quite happy with his revised theory of anxiety, particularly the part which emphasized that anxiety is the cause of repression in the first place and not the other way around. But sometime after he had completed(?)/abandoned(?) his Outline book of 1938 Freud, in a painful revelatory flash, realized that he had been too smug relative to one feature of his revised theory of anxiety. To cite New (page 76):

----- the question of what the material is out of which anxiety is made loses interest -----

Sigmund could not believe that he had permitted himself to be that supercilious. To be sure the "old" theory stating that anxiety results from a transformation of libido -- repressed or unrepressed -- into a resultant anxiety could no longer be maintained. But clearly Anxiety was somehow or other not only related to the "drives" but in some sense had to be composed of "drive energy" even if (especially since!!!) anxiety was now to be construed as the cause of repression and not the result of repression. Sigmund could not believe that he had been so prideful of his revised theory that he had left this central question as to the "material" composition of anxiety unattended. Thus the manuscript which came into Patrick's hands.

In the manuscript Freud quickly establishes that anxiety is "composed" of Eros phylogenically wired into ego-structure and taking on the form of self-preservation.

{{{*(The reader is referred here to Outline, page 5:*

> The contrast between the instincts of self-preservation and the preservation of the species, as well as the contrast between ego-love and object-love, fall within Eros.

)}}

Although Patrick would not be aware of it, that finding was not terribly startling for those who knew how Freud understood "Eros" in his later writings. What was surprising was this: that Freud further concluded that anxiety was the very origin and energy for the overtly sexual behaviors and desires which, in the earlier writings of Freud, had been gathered together under the heading "libido." The rivision had now gone full circle! Not only was it the case that anxiety was not best understood as the transformation of repressed and/or un-repressed libidinal energy. More than that! Libido was itself resultant from anxiety, being nothing more than the playing out in various male and female scenarios the anxiety generated, in little boys and little girls, upon the discovery of the counter-factual fact that Mommy is castrated.

Here Patrick's notes stop and therefore so too must this note stop. Even so the reader is referred to the first sentnece of entry # 92 of this book *Shame!*, where, uncannily, our author seems to have had access all the while to Patrick's adumbration. Cheers.}}

c). Melancholia and Mania effect each other but in different ways. Melancholia precedes the possibility of mania and is the pre-condition for mania proper. Yet there is a sense in which mania is "before" -- literally and otherwise -- melancholia. Just listen.

d). The "pre-manic" (so to speak) origin and proto-type of all subsequent "sublimated" forms of mania resides in the pre-orgasmic -- *{{and admittedly, in some usages of the word 'orgasm' what I call 'pre-orgasmic' staying on the edge in delirium is included in the meaning of 'orgasm'; this is only semantics, dear reader (*) }}* -- state of oscillating delirium. By virtue of anatomical structure mania is primarily and originally the the birth-right of females although males -- through proper training -- can also share in this privilege provided that they learn to prolong rather than merely postpone.

*. *{{{ --- and while we're at this semantics business, dear reader, shall we refer to the 'whole' clitoris, shaft included, as "clitoris" while reserving the treasured clitty for the 'glans' of the clitoris which we shall call the tip? Why not? It's all semantics. It's all a manner of speaking. And that glorious tip!!! Pearly white!!!!* half-hidden and yet beautiful half-hidden and yet beautiful half-hidden and yet beautiful *sometimes a diamond; sometimes a stone; but always a pearl. And did you notice? You who have a taste for secrets within secrets. This glorious tip has no tip opening. There's a hint there*

for those who have the eyes to hear and the ears to see.}}}

{{{{{Ah!!! Let us not forget about the marvelous hyena in this regard!!!. No wonder she is psychotically laughing ----- endowed with a clitoris which also performs the birthing function. Indeed it is perhaps with the hyena that voice/sound discrimination is -- after homo sapiens -- most manic and refined. What greater proof that eros wins the lottery by playing all the numbers! *(Cf. the NYT's Science section, 9/1/92.)}}}}}*

e). The "pre-melancholic" (so to speak) proto-type (but not origin) of melancholia resides in the somewhat violent spurting, ejaculatory, and release oriented model of orgasm aimed for by most males. (And please remember, even when it was good, there is always withdrawal. Union never will have occurred. Bonjour, Tristesse.)

Something like release is, in one sense, the necessary condition for satisfactory sexual experience for males and females alike. Indeed even the pre-orgasmic mania of prolonging (which is other than merely postponing) requires as its very condition the expectation of release. Even so, on the avergae, males tend to turn the necessary condtion of satisfactory sexuality into the their telos of sexuality. Females -- and here the advantages of female anatomical structure become manifest -- tend, on the average, not to conflate the necessary condition of satisfactroy sexuality with the 'true' telos of satisfactory sexuality. Just as dying is the last 'event' (i.e., the "ending") of living and brings life to completeness and yet is not the "end" (telos) of living, so too the "release" factor in satisfactory sexuality is the "ending" and necessary condition without which there is no satisfactory sexuality and yet is not the sexual "end" (telos) of the sexual experience. Most females intuitively understand this. Males learn this only with the proper training.

f). The anus is the organ par excellence for sexual delirium which delirium is the raw material for mania. To be sure even here there is nothing but frustration unless clitoris or penis play their appointed role. But penetration -- (and certainly there are many things which can penetrate other than the penis) -- near the terrain of clitoris/penis is the necessary condition for pre-orgasmic delirium.

g). In this sense females are, anatomically, twice blessed as "Lou" perfectly well understood. The magical vagina. Even closer to the clitty. Rented. On lease. Borrowed. From the heart of darkness. Thus males require what the world calls "the perverse" in order to achieve the full measure of their "desire" whereas females hide "the perverse" right in the very heart of what the world -- Sigismund therein included!!!!! -- calls "normal" sexuality and can thus fulfill "desire" through perversity but without perversity (and still -- as a bonus, so to speak -- retain the option of the anal anyway!).

A test here for the assiduous reader. The Lou-anus-vagina connection has been made in various parts of *Shame!*. As far as the text of Freud is concerned, New, page 90, will do quite well.

h). But wait. On the outer fringes of mania. What is the one sexual organ which is of itself dyadic? Which of itself is oscillating being both organ of release and requiring nothing else by which oscillating delirium is achieved. Think it through. What is the tip opening of the penis except a minny anus/vagina written into the very structure of the alleged organ of penetration? The necessary condition and the telos phsyiologically fused together and therefore permitting the most exquisite kind of oscillating!!!

i). Of course there would be a price for such exquisite usage of the penis. It could happen successfully only once. It would be liturgical, so to speak. Permanent damage would necessarily result.

j). A vicarious delirium may be obtained by being the agent who renders and reduces another into the the delirious pre-orgasmic state. Yes, a vicarious delirium and a basically macho boost to one's narcissism is possible for the producer of such delirium in another, be such a producer male or female. But the true delirium is reserved to those -- male and female alike -- who enthusiastically submit to such a reduction. The mystery, joy, -- and mania -- of the active surrender. Tiresias understood.

k). Mania proper is is a kind of sublimated expression of pre-orgasmic delirium. It, mania proper, occurs as the exhuastion -- sometimes temporary -- of melancholia's fidelity to loss. In this sense, melancholia is the pre-condition of mania.

In lecture XXXI of New (pages 54-55) Freud suggests that the manic state is a function of the ego's release from the constant overbearing condemnation of the super-ego. So too, "melancholia", according to this suggestion, results from the maintenance of the overbearing condemnation of the ego by the super-ego.

The perceptive reader of Thinking Psycho-analytically (and of this *The Economic Problem in Mania* supplement which you are now reading) will see that "melancholia"/"depression" is presented in these writings as a function of various levels and kinds of "successful" and "un-successful" identifications with the lost love object. Further, in this *The Economic Problem in Mania*, the generation of mania is ascribed to the exhaustion of the melancholic state which has the effect of freeing one from fidelity to the lost love object.

In fact the two accounts -- (i.e., in New and in the writings here being discussed and read) -- are complementary and do not at all require something like an "either/or" mode of explanation/adjudication. Yet that whole dynamic of a sadistic super-ego condemnation of an ego rendered masochistic (which occurs in melancholia), it is to be noted, is posterior to the prior dynamic of those various levels of "successful" and "unsuccessful" identifications with the lost love object.

Finally, let it be noted that Freud himself -- (Confer Civ, pages 26-27) -- takes it for granted that mania is a "chemical" state. That all of these things -- mania, melancholia, things Oedipal, etc., etc., etc., etc., -- are "chemical" states involving the neuro-physiology of the brain and nervous system is taken as axiomatic AND RELATIVELY TRIVIAL in the book/book supplement which you are now reading. To be sure, from a therapeutic point of view, it is the work in brain chemistry and neuro-physiology which is decisive. Even so, one ought not conflate a description of psychic states with 'giving an account' of psychic states. Much spilled ink on these matters would be saved if reading Theaetetus with care were a pre-requisite for all graduate and professional programs in neuro-physiology.

l). Mania proper, please understand, is not some kind of "disavowal" of loss nor is mania something which entails bad faith. Mania is not a strategy for bypassing melancholia. Rather, it emerges with the exhaustion of melancholia. Nonetheless it is also true that loss is not experienced as such in the manic state.

m). When mania is sustained oscillating finds no measure of relief from its oscillation. If sustained indefinitely oscillating will not find any measure of relief from its pure oscillating and thus -- paradox most definitely noted -- oscillating will finally disappear without "dis-appearing" for "dis-appearing" requires some submission to the other principle in order to occur at all. Such "disappearing-without-'dis-appearing' " is disintegrative breakdown for the individual. Such "disappearing-without-'dis-appearing' " is the death of death understood cosmologically. A final state of maximal entropy, (Nietzsche's stubborn denial of such in 1066 notwithstanding). The vector towards this process is experienced as the unbearable lightness of being. It is the greatest pathos and it is sustained by a nostalgic vision of beauty. This is the great danger.

Confer Nietzsche's dismissal in aphorism # 1066, on principle, of the entropic possibility as put forth by Thompson. WP, pages 548-549.

This "mania" supplement to *Thinking Psycho-analytically* maintains that a final state of maximal entropy could happen but does not happen trusting in the tortured teleology by which the play of chance -- call it Shekhinah/difference -- sustains itself by responding (even as it instantiates) to the possibility of 'the good'. In this sense *Thinking Psycho-analytically* maintains that 'what is the case' is a mixture of and between two "terms", neither of which "exist" in, of, or by themselves. In contrast, Nietzsche's postulated denial on principle of a final state of maximal entropy effectively means that 'what is the case' for Nietzsche is not a mixture of two but the unending re-configuration of his monistic "will to power." Nietzsche's resulting monothesistic metaphysics -- in ways more subtle than understood by Nietzsche himself -- is consistently (even if thoughtlessly) *beyond good and evil* since both "good" and "evil" -- which are possibilities which may come to be IN the mixture but are not themselves first principles of the mixture -- require mixture as their pre-condition.

{{{ Getting it right with duality: unity-in-duality and duality-in-unity. Schelling, in Ages of the World, -- (and Hegel is left behind as one approaches this unpublished manuscript) -- had an inkling. But he had things in reverse. Plato in his way and Lurianic Kaballah in its way had much more than an inkling. In many ways they were "there" already. But they -- Plato and Lurianic Kaballah -- likewise had things in reverse. Nietzsche -- whose knowledge of Schelling, Plato, and Lurianic Kaballah was either nil or woefully shallow -- had finally put things in reverse allowing, then, so to speak and for the first time, things to go "forward." Schelling, Plato, and Lurianic Kaballah all could have learned much from Nietzsche. But Nietzsche could only understand the terms of any duality as surrogates for 'good' and 'evil' and never understood that 'good' and 'evil' are possibilities which come to be IN the mixture and are not the terms (i.e., first principles) of the mixture. Thus "the little parson" could never understand that the liberation from wrong-headed morality could be found only through getting it right with duality. Sure, he got "beyond" good and evil. But he never got before good and evil. In all of this, Nietzsche's great reversal -- which stands unrivaled by any thinker prior to or posterior to Nietzsche save possibly Cratylus -- does not fully respond to its deepest vocation.}}}

n). Beauty. "Truth". Goodness. The sacrifice of Beauty for the sake of Goodness as "Truth" holds sway over Beauty. Even so the wail of broken Beauty catches some of the very best. It even caught a bit of Aristocles. Plato was indeed a shade off.

o). A hundred thousand things could be said by the sophisticated ones about Keats and Shelley. Qualification after qualification. ((E.g., that Shelley did not even begin to hit his stride until near to the time of Keats' death.)) But let us go to the heart of the matter. Listen.

p). Fidelity to "Truth" by the very one who was touched most tenderly by Beauty. Beauty which must die. This is Keats.

q). ----- after he began to hit his stride and never fully self-aware of what he was doing ----- the manic, oscillating ivresse pursued in words and even morcso in deeds so that Beauty might be spared. *<<<<<<<that ever-gnawing itch for untarnished and unfragmented beauty (the itch which Plato ended up scratching too much); the 'au-dela'; "somewhere-my-love">>>>>>>* Life, "truth" and goodness itself be damned. When Beauty is loved more than life itself. This is Shelley.

r). Are you listening? The "right" tension. Danger and opportunity.

s). {{{The "wrong" tension; a variation. Another form of the danger. Manic and Manichean. *<<< Yes. Yes. One knows about the figure called "Manes". Even so, learn from language.>>>* How to be open for the one without embracing the other.

(Of all the variations on mania -- and there are more than the four mentioned by Plato towards the beginning of his charioteer speech in Phaedrus -- this "manichean" version is the most diabolical. <<The diabolical -- as noted priorly -- is the destiny of the demonic when the demonic is not pressed into the service of "the good" (which does mean that there is something demonic about "the good").>> It justifies itself in and through the very name -- i.e., 'the good' (and a simplistic notion of the good at that) -- of what it is thwarting (i.e., 'the good'). The fixation to some perceived "purity" of the beautiful is so severe for the mental state of the manic manichean that it takes such "purity" as 'the good' failing to realize that the very ""essence"" (so to speak) of 'the good' is mixture. <<<Should Orestes -- of that terrible trilogy --be construed as the proto-type of all manic manicheans? For another time.>>>) }}}

t). Even so, the "right" tension. Keats and Shelley.

u). And what, -- (i.e., and thus) -- pray tell, if you love 'the good' -- i.e., life -- more than Beauty or even "Truth"? Then you are working for the Messiah. Choose life.
}}}}}}}}}}}}}}}}}}}}

1/3/92

418.
Note to the reader as an afterthought

As I prepared this book for printing I found that I -- who had written it -- could better understand what was written if I read what was written out loud. This is neither a Derridean nor anti-Derridean comment. Just a fact. So to speak. It is suggested that serious readers of this book do such an oral reading as their second reading of this book.

JWM *(as always, speaking for Johanna)*
so tenderly deep into Autumn that it hurts, 1991
near Lake Lilac

419.

The same:

thinking psycho-analytically

as well as

coming-to-be-on-intimate-terms-with difference

gnomai --- ten diaphoroteta
(Theaetetus 209E)

*****
+++++

jwm for Johanna Elton

420.
(personal note)

----- *He framed to himself certain opinions, founded no doubt upon the truth of things, but built up to a Babel height; they fell by their own weight, & the thoughts that were his architects, became unintelligible one to the other, as men upon whom confusion of tongues has fallen.*

{taken from an early draft of "The Preface (Advertisement)" to Epipsychidion and functioning as a kind of introduction to "Fragments Concerned with Epipsychidion"}

421.
(personal note)

Consumed with that which it was nourished by

(Edward DeVere)

422.
(personal note)

If you are reading this entry then you will realize that the deal I had with my publisher fell through and that I am printing this up vanity style. All is vanity.

So many doubts about this book. So much which is wrong with it. And the typos!!!!! How embarrassing.

The gnawing fear that some of the major "theses" of the book are simply a function of a fucked-up childhood. The ganwing fear that what was necessarily therapeutic about the book did not get successfully disengaged from what was (to be) "thoughtful" about the book (i.e., in that Heideggerian sense contained in *Was heisst denken?*). Oh well. How does De Vere put it towards the end of Hamlet? *The rest is silence* ??????? Or does my memory screw this up as well? In any case, the book must now speak for itself. It has been too much of a burden getting this book written. It is time now to let it go. If this means that it is time for me to die, ainsi soit-il. I'll let my body decide for me. If I am to live -- and I have much to live for -- then so much the better.

Beyond all shades of narcissism there is also the gnawing sense -- not exactly a fear -- that there is something incredibly great -- without reservation or qualification -- about my book. The sense that it will be immeasurably beneficial to and for many. If you share this sense with me there is really only one living person that I know of who would be in a position to say so and to be believed and thus get the word out. Jacques Derrida, of course. I have badgered him so repeatedly by sending him copies of the various pre-incarnations of this book that I have squandered any ability for me to "reach" Frere Jacques and get him to give my book the serious reading which it deserves. I imagine choirs of graduate students, secretaries, translators, and Derrida-groupies insuring that anything sent to him by me will be filed in the great circular file before it would come to be in his hands or allowed to enter into his field of vision.

And so -- dear cherished reader -- if you share this sense with me of this book it falls to you to be as "wise as serpents and and innocent as doves." I.e., GET HIS FUCKIN' ATTENTION!!!. Don't just send him a copy. The choirs of Derrida-guardians have built many hedges around the Master. Do what you have to. "Wise as the serpent; innocent as the dove."

If you are reading this entry you will know that it was written last, on December 18, 1992, late, late, Friday afternoon. My special time of melancholy. Almost at the limit of darkness. The most painfully beautiful part of Autumn. Presuming that my deal with the publisher will fall through -- (for I do not, right now, know this for sure) --, know that it will be sent for the vanity printing in January of 1993. January, '93 for *Shame!* Or should we say -- with Pat Boone (who was my mother's favorite over Elvis) -- "Ain't that a *Shame!*?" Peace.

423.
(personal note)

Are there -- at this point -- any readers left? I did not write this book to please you although I would find it pleasing if it in fact brought a certain kind of pleasure to those of you whom I would count as worthy of reading this book. I did not entirely -- or, to the best of my knowledge, even primarily -- write this book out of personal exigency and/or narcissistic impetus. Doubtlessly both personal exigency and narcissistic impetus have played a significant role in the composition of this book. (And those of you whose sense of justice is perhaps "overtuned" -- so to speak -- will be happy that the prices I have paid in the eight year composition of this book have far outweighed the narcissistic benefit.)

I wrote the book to educate.

Some of you might have wanted my autobiographical intimations to be kept separate -- perhaps in a separate book -- from everything else. You might have wanted ruminations on Derrida et alia to be kept religiously separate from Kaballah kinds of things. Others of you would have preferred a more respectful attitude towards matters of revelation and faith. Or the ruminations on "Plato-and-Aristotle" to be kept religiously separate from what you will probably call those babyish and most uncritical flights of fancy of mine which engage "Quantum Mechanics." Likewise some may be asking by what authority I bridge the alleged gap between Freud and neuro-physiology. By what authority do I pontificate on the chance-goverend process of self selection relative to the beginnings of psycho-social evolution in the pre and pre-pre-history of our species? And, finally, some in that new breed of secular puritanism would desire I refrain from vulgar, politically incorrect, language -- found here and there -- in sexual matters.

I could have kept everything neat and separate. I could have deferred, in silence, concerning matters in which I have no expertise at all. I could have embraced political correctness and/or a reverential stance with regard to matters of revelation and faith. But had I done so I would not have been educating.

Everything is at issue -- at once and all the time. From the sleaziest most perverse thought -- (utterly lacking in any smidgeon of political correctness) -- in the darkest crevice of the psyche to the condition of our universe less-than-a-nano-second after the big bang (or whatever it was). From the blaphemous forms of idolatry often enough practiced by religious authorities when in positions of power to blades of grass relentlessly pushing up between sidewalk cracks. From the most cruel and unrecorded humiliation obtaining in the Holocaust to the chance-goverened mutations which led to our species. From the screeching horrible cry of a baby burning in a Napalm bombing to the mysterious motion of some comet -- or something -- say three galaxies over. the manic obsessions of lovers the sadness of domesticated animals when they sense that death is near the wide-eyed expectation of children the delights of dinosaurs basking in mud the devastating effect of abuse on children the incredible anxiety of every rat who ever lived the kind of "dis-association" (drawing in equal measures from melancholia and mania) which allows for creativity the very secret of the whole universe unspeakable practices of torture unrecorded happenings (or are they recorded somehow?) of our "universe" """"""""""""before""""""""""""" the current version or something like it of the big bang (yes one knows the problem here why do you think i put "before" in those god-awful quotes?) those milennia-long happenings i mean thousands upon thousands of years in the pre and pre-pre-history of our species which led over self-selective time to voice/sound discrimination shame! all of it all at once and in every way everything is at issue at once and all the time

Choose life!